Taking SIDES

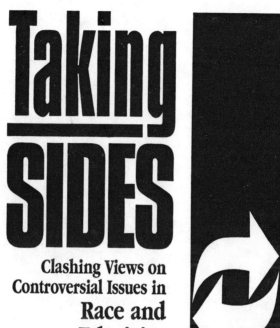

Clashing Views on Controversial Issues in
Race and Ethnicity

Taking SIDES

Clashing Views on
Controversial Issues in
Race and
Ethnicity

Edited, Selected, and with Introductions by

Richard C. Monk
Coppin State College

The Dushkin Publishing Group, Inc.

*To Goober, who in the land of lies and deceit, taught me to love again;
and to her daughter, Midnight, who taught me to laugh again.*

Photo Acknowledgments

Part 1   UN PHOTO 152,990/Christina D. Sagona
Part 2   Michelle Agins/NYT Pictures
Part 3   K. Jewell/Congressional News Photos
Part 4   New York State Department of Commerce

Cover Art Acknowledgment

Charles Vitelli

Library of Congress Cataloging-in-Publication Data

Main entry under title:
   Taking sides: clashing views on controversial issues in race and ethnicity/edited, selected,
and with introductions by Richard C. Monk.—1st ed.
   Includes bibliographical references and index.
   1. United States—Race relations. 2. United States—Ethnic relations. 3 Minorities—
United States. 4. Social classes—United States. I. Monk, Richard C., *comp.*
   EI84.A1T338   305.8'00973—dc20
   ISBN: 1-56134-127-4   93-35780

 Printed on Recycled Paper

*The Dushkin Publishing Group, Inc.
Sluice Dock, Guilford, CT 06437*

PREFACE

Do not at the outset of your career make the all too common error of mistaking names for things. Names are only conventional signs for identifying things.... If a thing is despised, either because of ignorance or because it is despicable, you will not alter matters by changing its name. If men despise Negroes, they will not despise them less if Negroes are called 'colored' or 'Afro-American.'
... Your real work... does not lie with names. It is not a matter of changing them, losing them, or forgetting them.

—W. E. B. Du Bois (1928)

When you control a man's thinking, you do not have to worry about his actions.

—Carter G. Woodson, *The Mis-Education of the Negro* (1933)

I have sworn upon the altar of God, eternal hostility against every form of tyranny over the mind of man.

—Thomas Jefferson (1800)

In part, this work grew out of the prodding of my former student Deputy U.S. Marshal Barrett Gay. As a Black American, he wanted to know where he could find a challenging book on controversial issues on racial and ethnic minorities. He challenged me to edit such a work, and he provided many outstanding suggestions. I was delighted both by his encouragement and the opportunity to work in my favorite area of sociology: ethnic and racial studies.

As a teacher of the social sciences, my goal with this book is to generate student dialogue about racial and ethnic issues. This is so because there is simply so much—especially in sociology and minority relations—that remains problematic. These problems concern not only questions about statistics, such as: How many members of a particular minority group are there? Are minorities' incomes increasing, decreasing, or remaining the same? What is the rate of victimization of minorities? And so on. Questions also concern how scholars ought to conceptualize various groups: Should we refer to minorities using the labels that their leaders currently use, that nonmembers use, or that the "average" group member prefers? This question goes considerably beyond mere "political correctness" or "oversensitivity." There is much more that is controversial, complicated, and utterly fascinating about the study of minorities, including the question of whether or not nonminorities can successfully study minorities (see Issue 1).

i

Plan of the book   This volume contains 17 controversial issues in race and ethnicity, and each issue is debated in a pro and con format. Each issue is expressed as a single question in order to draw the lines of debate more clearly. The authors of the essays—sociologists, political commentators, historians, and others—reflect a broad range of disciplines and perspectives. For each issue I have provided an issue *introduction*, which provides some background information and sets the stage for the debate as it is argued in the YES and NO selections, and a *postscript* that summarizes the debate, considers other views on the issue, and suggests additional readings on the topics raised in the issue. These issues are organized into four sections: Social Theory and Basic Concepts; Cultural Issues: Ideology and Conflict; Ethnic Stratification: Power and Inequality; and Immigration, Demographic Changes, and Pluralism.

Taking Sides: Clashing Views on Controversial Issues in Race and Ethnicity is a tool to encourage critical thinking on important issues concerning racial and ethnic minorities. Although students may find themselves supporting one side of an issue or the other, readers should not feel confined to the views expressed in the articles. Some readers may see important points on both sides of an issue and may construct for themselves a new and creative approach to the issue, which may incorporate the best of both sides or provide an entirely new vantage point for understanding.

I feel that the issues and articles found in *Taking Sides* are representative of what is currently going on in the area of race and ethnic relations. They also allow students to get into this important area of sociology without having old prejudices reinforced or new doctrines internalized. My hope is that students will find these debates stimulating and will use them to clarify their own thinking about issues that are all vital and frequently emotional as well as controversial.

A word to the instructor   An *Instructor's Manual With Test Questions* (multiple-choice and essay) is available through the publisher for the instructor using *Taking Sides* in the classroom. A general guidebook, *Using Taking Sides in the Classroom*, which discusses methods and techniques for using the pro-con approach in any classroom setting, is also available.

Acknowledgments   No book, particularly an edited one, is created in a vacuum free of the influences of significantly supportive and helpful others. As mentioned, Deputy U. S. Marshal Barrett Gay was instrumental in the creation of the book. I would also like to thank my many other students who tested in classes many of the ideas presented here. At Coppin State College these students include: Sharon D. Barnett, Tracy Douglas, Constance Stevenson, Larry Schuyler, and Maxine Shay. I am especially honored to have been the teacher of the writers and researchers of the student journal *Kaleidoscope* at Valdosta State University. Their work remains a beacon illuminating the surrounding land.

Several colleagues, scholars, and administrators provided comments and/or support that were immensely helpful and are greatly appreciated. Thanks are extended to T. J. Bryan, Dean of Arts and Sciences, Elizabeth Gray, Chair of Criminal Justice, Genevieve Knight, Chair of Mathematics, and Judith Willner, Chair of Fine and Communication Arts, all at Coppin State College; Maurice St. Pierre and Stephan Goodwin of Morgan State University; Ed Tiryakian of Duke University; Kurt Finsterbusch of the University of Maryland; Alex Hooke of Villa Julie College; Harv Greisman of West Chester State University; Tom Gitchoff and Joel Henderson of San Diego State University; Daniel B. Monk of Arlington, Virginia; Paul A. Wortman of New York City Public School 252; Rudy Faller of the Inter-American Development Bank; Horst Senger of Simi Valley, California; and Sam Webb of Lake Park, Georgia.

If as you read this book you are reminded of a selection or issue that could be included in a future edition, please write to me in care of The Dushkin Publishing Group with your recommendations.

Richard C. Monk
Baltimore, MD

CONTENTS IN BRIEF

PART 1 SOCIAL THEORY AND BASIC CONCEPTS 1

Issue 1. Are Nonethnic Scholars Able to Successfully Research Minorities? 2

Issue 2. Is the Concept of the Underclass Useful for Studying Race and Ethnic Relations? 26

Issue 3. Are Asian Americans a "Model Minority"? 42

Issue 4. Do Italian Americans Reject Assimilation? 64

PART 2 CULTURAL ISSUES: IDEOLOGY AND CONFLICT 83

Issue 5. Should We Call Ourselves African Americans? 84

Issue 6. Do Cultural Differences Between Home and School Explain the High Dropout Rates for American Indian Students? 102

Issue 7. Should Bilingual Education Programs Be Stopped? 124

Issue 8. Should Black Women Join the Feminist Movement? 146

Issue 9. Are Positive Images of African Americans Increasing in the Media? 160

PART 3 ETHNIC STRATIFICATION: POWER AND INEQUALITY 177

Issue 10. Should Minorities Continue to Demand More Rights? 178

Issue 11. Does "Lower-Class" Culture Perpetuate Poverty Among Urban Minorities? 192

Issue 12. Is Affirmative Action Reverse Discrimination? 208

Issue 13. Are Hispanics Making Significant Progress? 222

Issue 14. Is Systemic Racism in Criminal Justice a Myth? 242

PART 4 IMMIGRATION, DEMOGRAPHIC CHANGES, AND PLURALISM 257

Issue 15. Is Italy Solving Its Immigration Problem? 258

Issue 16. Is There an Ethnic Revolt Against the Melting Pot? 272

CONTENTS

Preface   i

Introduction   xiv

PART 1   *SOCIAL THEORY AND BASIC CONCEPTS*   1

ISSUE 1.   Are Nonethnic Scholars Able to Successfully
Research Minorities?   2

YES: Robert K. Merton, from "Insiders and Outsiders: A
Chapter in the Sociology of Knowledge," *American Journal of
Sociology*   4

NO: Patricia Hill Collins, from "Learning from the Outsider
Within: The Sociological Significance of Black Feminist
Thought," *Social Problems*   15

Columbia University professor emeritus Robert K. Merton politely but point-edly challenges claims that superior insights automatically result from mem-bership in a specific group. In so doing, he generates several useful hy-potheses for researching and understanding ethnic and racial minorities. Sociologist Patricia Hill Collins, while acknowledging the value of Merton and others, discusses the merits of the insider's claim to better understanding. She combines criticism of traditional methods for researching and theorizing about racial minorities, especially Black females, with suggestions for how sociology can be enriched by the insights of Black feminist scholars.

ISSUE 2.   Is the Concept of the Underclass Useful for
Studying Race and Ethnic Relations?   26

YES: William Julius Wilson, from *The Truly Disadvantaged:
The Inner City, the Underclass, and Public Policy*   28

NO: José Hernández, from "Latino Alternatives to the
Underclass Concept," *Latino Studies Journal*   32

University of Chicago sociologist and president of the American Sociological Association William Julius Wilson insists that factors such as the shift of heavy manufacturing industries out of cities, the movement of the middle classes out of the cities, and the segregation and isolation of many of the people who remain have all contributed to the decay of poorer urban areas. This has created a permanent underclass or urban poor, who are often neglected by policymakers and researchers. Hunter College Black and Puerto Rican studies professor José Hernández rejects the term *underclass* as just another example of dominant group efforts to denigrate and humiliate the poor. He feels that when the term is applied to any category of people, and especially to Latinos, it is inaccurate and charged with negative connotations.

ISSUE 3.   Are Asian Americans a "Model Minority"?   42

YES: David A. Bell, from "America's Greatest Success Story:
The Triumph of Asian-Americans," *The New Republic*   44

NO: Ronald Takaki, from *Strangers from a Different Shore: A
History of Asian Americans*   55

Journalist and historian David Bell reflects on the current, frequently expressed enthusiasm for the successes of Asian Americans that appears in the mass media. Although he acknowledges some difficulties and hurdles faced by Asian Americans, Bell nevertheless portrays the road taken by Asian Americans as "America's greatest success story." University of California-Berkeley historian Ronald Takaki faults the mass media and some ethnic studies scholars for misunderstanding the statistics and examples used as "proof" that Asians are a model minority. Takaki argues that within Asian groups there are vast differences in success, and he reviews the prejudice and exploitation experienced by Asian Americans.

ISSUE 4.   Do Italian Americans Reject Assimilation?   64

YES: Kathleen Neils Conzen, David A. Gerber, Ewa
Morawska, George E. Pozzetta, and Rudolph J. Vecoli, from
"The Invention of Ethnicity: A Perspective from the U.S.A.,"
Journal of American Ethnic History   66

NO: Herbert J. Gans, from "Comment: Ethnic Invention and
Acculturation, A Bumpy-Line Approach," *Journal of American
Ethnic History*   73

Historians and sociologists Kathleen Conzen, David Gerber, Ewa Morawska, George Pozzetta, and Rudolph Vecoli reject many standard theories of ethnic acculturation and assimilation. Instead, they attempt to prove, with several cases, including the Italian one presented here, that many ethnic groups elect to remain separate in important ways from the dominant culture. Columbia University sociologist Herbert J. Gans insists that even recent ethnic groups, as well as the Italians, while sometimes following an indirect or uneven path to assimilation, are still far more American than not, and prefer it that way.

PART 2   *CULTURAL ISSUES: IDEOLOGY AND
          CONFLICT*   83

ISSUE 5. **Should We Call Ourselves African Americans?** 84

YES: **John Sibley Butler,** from "Multiple Identities," *Society* 86

NO: **Walter E. Williams,** from "Myth Making and Reality
Testing," *Society* 95

Professor of sociology John Sibley Butler briefly traces the history of the terms that Black Americans have applied to themselves, and he contrasts their ethnic-racial identities with those of other Americans. He argues that it makes sense to be African Americans. Walter E. Williams, professor of economics, acknowledges the baggage contained in the labels that people select for themselves. He dismisses those who opt for African American (or related terms) in order to achieve cultural integrity among Blacks. He says that there are serious problems in the Black community that need to be addressed, none of which will be solved by a new name.

ISSUE 6. **Do Cultural Differences Between Home and
School Explain the High Dropout Rates for
American Indian Students?** 102

YES: **Jon Reyhner,** from "American Indians Out of School: A
Review of School-Based Causes and Solutions," *Journal of
American Indian Education* 104

NO: **Susan Ledlow,** from "Is Cultural Discontinuity an
Adequate Explanation for Dropping Out?" *Journal of American
Indian Education* 113

Professor of curriculum and instruction John Reyhner argues that the school dropout rate for Native Americans is almost double that of other groups. He blames this on schools, teachers, and curricula that ignore the needs and potentials of North American Indian students. Educator Susan Ledlow argues that data on dropout rates for North American Indians is sparse. She questions the meaning and measurement of "cultural discontinuity," and she faults this perspective for ignoring important structural factors, such as employment, in accounting for why Native American students drop out of school.

ISSUE 7. **Should Bilingual Education Programs Be
Stopped?** 124

YES: **Diane Ravitch,** from "Politicization and the Schools:
The Case of Bilingual Education," *Proceedings of the American
Philosophical Society* 126

NO: Donaldo Macedo, from "English Only: The
Tongue-Tying of America," *Journal of Education*   **135**

History of education professor Diane Ravitch analyzes the ways in which
politics has commingled with education in the United States, particularly
in regards to bilingual education programs. She argues that certain cultural,
ideological, and political interest groups are usurping students' educational
needs in order to impose their own agendas. Associate professor of linguistics Donaldo Macedo dismisses Ravitch and other education traditionalists
who attack bilingual education as misguided at best, dishonest at worse. He
insists that learning in public schools is not simply a matter of acquiring a
neutral body of information. Instead, for non-English-speaking minorities,
it frequently entails dehumanization through forced repetition of dominant
group values.

**ISSUE 8.   Should Black Women Join the Feminist
                  Movement?**   **146**

YES: bell hooks, from *Talking Back: Thinking Feminist,
Thinking Black*   **148**

NO: Vivian V. Gordon, from *Black Women, Feminism and
Black Liberation: Which Way?*   **154**

Scholar and writer bell hooks argues that Black and white women have
worked together for generations to solve mutual problems. They have shown
that they are able to transcend racism. Hooks feels that Black activists should
not avoid the feminist movement or maintain separate memberships in Black
movement groups only. The extent of sexism among Blacks and whites necessitates women working together. Activist-scholar Vivan V. Gordon maintains
that she is not a racist but has good reasons to urge Blacks to separate
themselves from a white-dominated feminist movement. She contends that,
historically, white women as a group, no matter how benign some individuals may have been, benefited from and encouraged the exploitation of Blacks.
In spite of the sexism of some Black males, Gordon feels that Black women
would be better off to maintain their own agenda for liberation.

**ISSUE 9.   Are Positive Images of African Americans
                  Increasing in the Media?**   **160**

YES: J. Fred MacDonald, from *Blacks and White TV: African
Americans in Television Since 1948*, 2d ed.   **162**

NO: Ash Corea, from "Racism and the American Way of
Media," in John Downing et al., eds., *Questioning the Media: A
Critical Introduction*   **168**

Professor J. Fred MacDonald sees the need for improvements in images of African Americans presented on television, yet he feels that TV producers, because of their desire to reach Black consumers, have significantly altered, for the better, images of Blacks in the media. Professor Ash Corea insists that Blacks remain underrepresented as actors, directors, and executives in the television media. Some roles for Blacks are demeaning, and Blacks, like other minorities, are disproportionately linked on television with crime.

PART 3   ETHNIC STRATIFICATION: POWER AND
          INEQUALITY   177

ISSUE 10. Should Minorities Continue to Demand More
           Rights?   178

YES: David Hatchett, from "The Future of Civil Rights in
the Twenty-first Century," *Crisis: The Journal of Lay Catholic
Opinion*   180

NO: Glenn Loury, from "The Struggle to Return to
Self-Help," *Issues and Views*   186

Writer and social commentator David Hatchett sees greater internationalization in the future of the civil rights movement. And he completely concurs with several prominent Black leaders that the desperation of many Black communities alone justifies continued demands for more rights. Boston University professor of economics Glenn Loury traces the debate between Black leaders W. E. B. Du Bois and Booker T. Washington that rocked the Black intellectual community 80 years ago. Loury sides with Washington in recommending self-help over government favors, which he says casts Blacks into playing the role of the victim.

ISSUE 11. Does "Lower-Class" Culture Perpetuate Poverty
           Among Urban Minorities?   192

YES: Edward Banfield, from *The Unheavenly City*   194

NO: William Ryan, from *Blaming the Victim*   199

Political scientist Edward Banfield, in a classic debate, argues that it is the life-styles of the poor that keep them impoverished. This so-called culture of poverty thesis examines the values and behaviors of the poor and finds in them the causes of poverty. Social critic and psychologist William Ryan counters that Banfield's thesis is a corruption of science and only functions to blame the victim for society's ills. Economic discrimination, racism, and a history of maltreatment explains poverty among urban minorities, not lifestyles that are often rational efforts to survive in an irrational situation.

ISSUE 12. Is Affirmative Action Reverse Discrimination? 208

YES: **Shelby Steele**, from *The Content of Our Character* 210

NO: **Herman Schwartz**, from "In Defense of Affirmative
Action," *Dissent* 215

Associate professor of English Shelby Steele contends that instead of solving racial inequality problems, affirmative action mandates have generated racial discrimination in reverse. Professor of law Herman Schwartz argues that we must somehow undo the cruel consequences of racism that still plague our society and its victims.

ISSUE 13. Are Hispanics Making Significant Progress? 222

YES: **Linda Chavez**, from *Out of the Barrio: Toward a New Politics of Hispanic Assimilation* 224

NO: **Robert Aponte**, from "Urban Hispanic Poverty: Disaggregations and Explanations," *Social Problems* 233

Scholar and former political candidate Linda Chavez takes great pride in documenting the accomplishments of Hispanics. They are making it in America, she says. Michigan State University social scientist Robert Aponte suggests that social scientists, following an agenda driven by government policy, have concentrated on Black poverty, which has resulted in a lack of accurate data and information on the economic status of Hispanics. Researchers have also tended to treat Hispanics as a whole. Aponte argues that disaggregation of demographic data shows that Hispanics are increasingly poor.

ISSUE 14. Is Systemic Racism in Criminal Justice a Myth? 242

YES: **William Wilbanks**, from "The Myth of a Racist Criminal Justice System," *Criminal Justice Research Bulletin* 244

NO: **Coramae Richey Mann**, from "The Reality of a Racist Criminal Justice System," *Criminal Justice Research Bulletin* 249

Florida International University criminology professor William Wilbanks advances the thesis that the criminal justice system is not now racist, and he says that claims that it is are myths. Indiana University criminologist Coramae Richey Mann generously welcomes Wilbanks's ideas as part of a healthy debate. However, after careful research and thought, she dismisses them as analytically and empirically flawed, and permeated with elitism.

PART 4   IMMIGRATION, DEMOGRAPHIC CHANGES, AND PLURALISM 257

ISSUE 15. Is Italy Solving Its Immigration Problem?   258

YES: Marco Martiniello, from "Italy: Two
Perspectives—Racism in Paradise?" *Race and Class*   260

NO: Paul Kazim, from "Italy: Two Perspectives—Racism Is
No Paradise!" *Race and Class*   265

Marco Martiniello, a professor at the European Institute of Florence University in Italy, admits that the suddenness of Italy's immigration problem caught Italians off-guard, yet he feels that rational steps are being taken to resolve the problem. Film researcher Paul Kazim argues that Italy is far more racist than it cares to admit. To him, the government's responses to the problem of immigration as well as the growing hostility toward immigrants demonstrates this. The government's amnesty program, he feels, sometimes results in little more than "authorized starving."

**ISSUE 16. Is There an Ethnic Revolt Against the Melting
              Pot?**   272

YES: Editors of *Social Justice*, from "Five Hundred Years of
Genocide, Repression, and Resistance," *Social Justice*   274

NO: Arthur M. Schlesinger, Jr., from *The Disuniting of
America: Reflections on a Multicultural Society*   278

The editors of *Social Justice* reject almost all previous formulation of ethnicity and assimilation in the United States. Their aim is to "reclaim the true history" of the continent, which, they say, is one of enslavement, torture, and repression of people of color, who are now in revolt against lies and exploitation. Harvard University historian, and advisor to President Kennedy, Arthur M. Schlesinger, Jr., argues that the genius of the United States lies in its unity—the ability of its citizens to embrace basic, common values while accepting cultural diversity. He bitterly attacks "ethnic ideologues" who are bent on disuniting America, not bringing about positive changes.

Contributors   284

Index   290

INTRODUCTION

Issues in Race and Ethnicity

Richard C. Monk

> Modern man finds himself confronted not only by multiple options of possible courses of action, but also by multiple options of possible ways of thinking about the world.
>
> —Peter Berger, *The Heretical Imperative* (1979)

> The world is a giant lab waiting for your exploration.
>
> —Robert Park

Bienvenidos (Welcome)! Your intellectual voyage into controversial issues in race and ethnicity is bound to be an exciting one. Some ancient ethnic groups would wish their members: "May you live in interesting times." Every person living in the last decade of the twentieth century seems to be a direct recipient of this benediction. This is especially true for students both experiencing and studying the rapidly changing and controversial mosaic of ethnic and racial relations.

Every day it seems we are provided with new facts, raw information, or an innovative interpretation concerning ethnic and racial relations in the United States and around the world. Recent newspaper headlines have proclaimed that over two dozen people were killed in racial violence in Los Angeles, that over 1,000 people were slaughtered in ethnic riots in India, and that Muslim women and children have been wounded by Serbs and Croatians who are perpetrating a modern-day "ethnic cleansing" of Bosnia.

Another topic that seems to be in the news frequently is illegal immigration. A *Los Angeles Times* survey reports that illegal immigration is seen by 86 percent of Californians as a major if not *the* major problem in that state. A *Newsweek* poll shows that 60 percent of all Americans now feel that immigration, even if done legally, is a bad thing. In the 1980s alone, over 10 million known racial and ethnic minorities settled in the United States. The number of *alambrista* (border jumpers, undocumented workers) is probably much higher than that figure, although social scientists do not know for sure how many illegal immigrants stay in the United States, how many return to their native countries, or even what they do while they are here.

In spite of increased awareness of racial and ethnic minority concerns within the political arena, in schools and universities, in communities, and in religious associations, insensitivities remain. Elected state and national offi-cials have reportedly used racial and ethnic slurs to register their opposition to the North American Free Trade Agreement (NAFTA). Analysts indicate that by attacking NAFTA in this way (and its merit per se is not the issue here), officials are actually attacking immigration and Mexico. In many west-ern and southwestern states, in which the majority of people are against immigration, this is a way to win votes.

Another example in which opinions were split over the appropriateness of an event occurred when Wilma Mankiller, chief of the Cherokee Nation of Oklahoma, and Sherman Bold Warrior, spokesperson for the Ponca tribe, bitterly criticized the recent centennial celebration of Oklahoma's land run. "To us, it's analogous to the Germans celebrating the Holocaust," Bold War-rior said. Others staunchly defended the celebration as commemorating an important part of North American history.

In addition to racially and ethnically based oppression and conflict, both physical and symbolic, frequently tragic and devastating, and sometimes trivial, that we see daily in the media, we also hear about (and hopefully experience) positive aspects of minority relations. One example of this that ironically arose from a violent racial conflict is that of a Black family who contacted a white truck driver who was almost killed during the 1992 Los Angeles riots and extended spontaneous, deep sympathy through many acts of kindness to him. Similarly, there was a national outpouring of sympathy and support for a Black tourist in Tampa, Florida, whom some local white criminals attempted to burn alive.

Some examples of positive ethnic relations with which you may more closely identify would be if you were to invite a foreign student home for Thanksgiving or Christmas (extremely lonely times for "outsiders") or if you were to take the time to learn about and appreciate holidays and ceremonies of a culture or religion that is different from yours.

At another level of analysis, the pervasiveness of ethnicity, in spite of as-similation in the United States, remains both bold and subtle. Countless news articles and electronic media reports document the integration of racial and ethnic minorities into the sports and entertainment worlds. Achievements in other sectors such as education, government, medicine, and law are also noted. Thus, it is obvious that we exist in a world of racial and ethnic minority interactions.

It is also obvious from the few examples cited above as well as your own experiences growing up in the modern world that the types, meanings or in-terpretations, and consequences of minority-based actions and the majority's responses are complex. Moreover, as contemporary sociologist Peter Berger notes, you are confronted not only by different ways of responding to your world, including your interactions with minority members and/or majority ones, but you also face "multiple options of possible ways of thinking about the world." This includes how you view ethnic and racial groups and the controversies related to their presence, their actions, and the ways in which other members of society respond to them.

THE STUDY OF RACIAL AND ETHNIC RELATIONS

For generations many social scientists, as trained "people watchers" (a term coined by Berger), have found minority relations to be among the most fascinating aspects of social life. Initially, sociologists and anthropologists tended to have an intellectual monopoly on the formal, systematic study of this area. More recently, historians, economists, and political scientists have increased significantly their studies of minority group relations. Although the work of these people is generally narrower and more focused than that of sociologists (typical subjects for study would be the historical treatment of one region's slave system in a specific time period, attitudes of Italian American voters, or consumption and marketplace behavior of selected Asian groups), their gradual inclusion of minorities in their research is a welcome addition to scholarship.

Sociologists and anthropoligists have energized research methods, theories, and perspectives within minority scholarship, but the process has been painful and the source of acrimonious controversies among sociologists about proper scholarly work *vis-à-vis* ethnic and racial minorities. Two major events sparked this critical examination of the foundations of concepts and studies: (1) the civil rights movement in the 1960s and the rapid changes that resulted from it; and (2) breakthroughs in the philosophy of science that increased understanding of science, theories, and methods.

The civil rights movement in the United States politicized and moved onto the public stage minority groups, especially Blacks. Articulate and militant, they were finally listened to by the majority, including sociologists. Moreover, agents of social control, especially the federal government, assumed a direct role in supporting increasing changes for minorities.

The antiwar protest against the Vietnam War of the same period functioned to undermine both social science characterizations of uniformity and the consensus of American society as well as the government's claims of fairness and veracity in its justification for the war. Both the civil rights movement and the antiwar protest generated a radical cohort of social scientists who were suspicious of both the political-military and the educational-university establishments, including the establishment teachers and their graduate programs.

Two areas within ethnic and racial minority theories and research that were bitterly attacked during this time were the standard minorities relations cyclical model, which was originally formulated in the 1920s by sociologist Robert Park (1864–1944) and his students at the University of Chicago (hereinafter referred to as "Chicago sociologists"), and the studies that were generated in the 1950s and 1960s by structural functionalists such as Talcott Parsons and Robert Merton and their students. The Chicago model consists of a series of stages that ethnic and racial minorities pass through in their contacts with the dominant group. Partially based on models from plant ecology and from Park's newspaper days, as well as on ideas he learned during the time he was a secretary for Booker T. Washington, founder of the Tuskegee Institute, the model identifies several minority-majority relations processes, such as conflict, accommodation, and eventual assimilation. The latter stage reflects the turn-of-the-century emphasis on the American "melting pot." Up through the 1950s, major U.S. institutions simply assumed for the most part that racial and ethnic minorities wanted to and tried to "blend in" with American society. Minorities were encouraged to Anglicize their names, learn and speak English, embrace Anglo middle-class customs and norms, and so on.

Although pluralism (a stage in which a cultural, ethnic, or racial minority group coexisted equally within a nation-state while maintaining harmoniously its own values, attitudes, language, and customs) was identified by the Chicago sociologists, it remained a relatively undeveloped concept until the 1940s and 1950s. Then anthropologists and others (such as F. J. Furnival and M. G. Smith) utilized pluralism, but primarily to depict social processes in the Caribbean and other areas outside of the United States. However, since conflict, oppression, and exploitation were viewed by radical sociologists in the 1960s and 1970s (and currently) as areas ignored by Park and his followers, the Chicago sociologists' model was dismissed.

Many standard, or liberal, sociologists were horrified at what they viewed as the desecration of Park and his memory. They were especially incensed by the charges of racism against Park and the Chicago race relations theory and research. These supporters argued that the Chicago sociologists were very progressive for their time. The Chicago model clearly allowed for conflict, although Park generally viewed conflict in terms of prejudice and discrimination at the interpersonal level. Because it tended to focus on influences of the individual, Chicago sociology was often more like social psychology. Oppressive institutions and structurally induced and maintained inequalities simply were not part of the vocabulary of most sociologists in the United States until the 1960s. Two important exceptions were the turn-of-the-century writings of black intellectual W. E. B. Du Bois and the later writings of Professor Oliver Cox (e.g., *Caste, Class, and Race*, 1948), but their work was largely ignored by both the public and sociology.

Structural functionalist theory, which originated at Harvard and Columbia Universities and generally dominated sociology throughout the 1960s, was also bitterly attacked. Structural functionalist theory basically states that a society acquires the characteristics that it does because they meet the particular needs of that society. This theory stresses cohesion, conformity, and integration among the society's members. Some of the charges against this theory were that it was inherently conservative, it celebrated middle-class values while ignoring the pains of the minority status, it excluded contributions of minority scholars, and it relied unduly on the natural science model, omitting systematic efforts to understand the subjective experiences of human beings—including ethnic and racial minorities.

These criticisms (and I only mentioned selected salient points) resulted in a reexamination of sociological work, including ethnic and racial minorities scholarship. Unfortunately, although some of this investigation was infused with sociology of knowledge concepts—that is, sociologists attempted to systematically trace the origins of ideas to the positions that intellectuals held within groups—much of it was largely reduced to name-calling. Many social scientists would argue that hunting down ideological biases in research and theory does not necessarily advanced understanding, especially if strengths in the existing work are ignored and/or no alternative programs are developed. A few would even claim that the social sciences have not advanced significantly in ethnic and racial minority theories beyond the Chicago sociology of the 1920s and 1930s or some of the essays of the structural functionalists of the 1960s, such as Talcott Parsons's *The Negro American* (1968).

Another factor that stimulated change in minority research and theorizing is less direct but possibly as important: breakthroughs in the philosophy of science that occurred in the 1950s and that continue to occur through the present. The philosophy of science is generally narrower than the sociology of knowledge. It aims to rigorously identify and explicate the criteria that scientists use to develop and evaluate theory, concepts, and methods. The structures of scientific work and the standards used to accept or reject it are carefully delineated by the philosophy of science.

Before the 1960s, the philosophy of science had eschewed "mere" ideology hunting that characterized some variants of the sociology of knowledge. It was considerably more formal and analytic. However, beginning with the works of Thomas Kuhn, especially his *Structure of Scientific Revolutions* (1961), as well as the writings of British philosopher Sir Karl Popper and his student Imre Lakatos, physical and social scientists became sensitized to the importance of both formal analytical aspects of scholarship *and* communal elements.

Links between variants of the philosophy of science and ethnic-racial minorities issues include: analyses of schools of thought within which particular race relations scientific research programs have emerged; the basic terms and their utilizations (e.g., pluralism, and whether or not it is being observed); and conflict, as well as styles of operationalization (how terms are measured). In addition, the kinds of data (information) that are collected—attitudes, consumption patterns, behaviors (observed, implied, elicited from questionnaires, income levels, and so on)—who collects the facts, and how the facts are analyzed (through narrative summaries, tabular presentations, and statistics), have all been subject to scrutiny drawing from the methods of the philosophy of science.

Part of the philosophy of science's influence is expressed directly in some of the more current and influential discussions of theory and theory formation, such as in the writings of sociologists George Ritzer and Edward A. Tiryakian. Ritzer combines the sociology of knowledge and the philosophy of science concerns in studying the underlying structure of sociological theory. Tiryakian, taking a tack somewhat closer to traditional sociology of knowledge, has argued for the importance of systematically examining hegemonic or dominant schools of thought within the social sciences. Such an examination includes social influences on theory development and the methodological agenda. The former is primarily a sociology of knowledge concern, and the latter is a philosophy of science concern.

Thus far, most contemporary ethnic and racial minority researchers and theorists do not directly draw from Ritzer, Tiryakian, and others; at least not in a systematic, comprehensive fashion. However, they do routinely acknowledge these concerns and often attack other researchers and studies on philosophy of science grounds. Moreover, most introductory racial minorities textbooks raise and briefly discuss underlying assumptions of studies they survey, though frequently in a simplistic manner. Most of the issues in this book indirectly touch on these concerns, and some grapple with them directly.

ADDITIONAL BASIC CONCEPTS AND TERMS

Many definitions and typologies (classificatory schemes) of minority groups exist. At the very least, it would seem, a scientifically adequate conceptualization ought to take into account both subjective aspects (attitudes, definitions of the situation, and assignment of meanings) and objective ones (proportion, ratio, and quantity of minority members, their income, amount of education, percentage of specific occupations, and so on).

One definition of minority that seems to have hung on since its inception 50 years ago and remains vital and remarkably serviceable was provided by sociologist Louis Wirth. According to Wirth, a minority is a "group of people who, because of their physical or cultural characteristics, are singled out from the others ... for differential and unequal treatment and who therefore regard themselves as objects of collective discrimination. [This] implies the existence of a corresponding dominant group enjoying social status and greater privileges ... the minority is treated and regards itself as a people apart." This definition clearly includes ethnic and racial minorities. It does not mean *numerical* minority since, as Wirth points out, frequently a sociological minority group could be a numerical majority (e.g., Blacks in South Africa). The point is that minority members are systematically excluded from certain societal privileges and that they have less power than others.

Although ethnic and racial minorities can be included in Wirth's 50-year-old definition, ethnicity and racism are relatively new concepts. Strict biological classifications of groups by race are scientifically untenable. However, the social construction of images and stereotypes of categories of people based upon attributed racial characteristics are quite real. Although individuals of different racial origins may dress like you do, speak like you do, and have the same attitudes as you, if you view them in terms of their race, then they will be so defined. This is true even if there is absolutely no discernable trait or behavioral characteristic that can be accurately traced to race, as opposed to class, nationality, or region, for example. Unfortunately, while sociologically fascinating, the construction of the myth of race and its perpetuation in terms of attitudes and treatment has had frequently devastating consequences. Ironically, such world-taken-for-granted classifications, along with the concomitant attribution of all kinds of behaviors (often perceived as quite different and negative), is relatively unique to recent history and to the West. Among the ancients there was little or no understanding of the differences of peoples based on race. Nor were there objectionable connotations placed upon peoples of different physiological appearances.

Groups arranged in terms of ethnicity, however, have far more empirical accuracy than those arranged by race. Although negative attributes have been inaccurately and unfairly fixed to different ethnic groups, ethnicity does imply common characteristics such as language, religion, custom, and nationality. Wirth would identify ethnic minority groups as those with distinguishable characteristics who have less power than the dominant group and who are singled out for negative differential treatment.

This reader is restricted to selected controversial issues pertaining to ethnic and racial minorities. I acknowledge that other, equally important minorities exist. Indeed, some argue that the original minority groups were women and children! Certainly they were known to be mistreated and discriminated against long before racial, national, ethnic, or religious groups were on the scene. Although I have incorporated into the book specific gender-relevant issues, the controversial issues in this reader emphasize ethnic and racial minority membership.

Another useful term that students of minority relations will draw from frequently is *ethnocentrism*, which was coined by sociologist William Graham Sumner. He introduced the concept of ethnocentrism in his delightful book *Folkways* (1907). To be ethnocentric is to be group-centered, to take the attitudes, values, customs, and standards of one's group and impose them on the members of another group. To the extent that the latter's behavior differs from the behavior or norms of one's own group, negative connotations are attached to the others' actions. The opposite of this is reverse ethnocentrism, which means to deprecate one's own group and embrace the behaviors and norms of the members of another group, possibly with a blind eye to the problems of that group.

The purpose of much of your training in the social sciences, especially in sociology and minority relations, is to liberate you from ethnocentrism as well as reverse ethnocentrism. In the first issue of the *Journal of Negro History* (1916), Carter G. Woodson, a founder of Black history, warned against controversies that, in the treatment of Blacks, either "brands him as a leper of society" or treats him "as a persecuted saint."

Your goal in reading these controversies, writing about them, criticizing them, and perhaps reformulating them or even eventually resolving them is to learn how to think about and understand major ethnic and racial minority issues.

Part 1, Social Theory and Basic Concepts, consists of four controversial issues pertaining to social theory and basic concepts. Before they can think clearly, scholars must first do conceptual work. This includes learning what the key ideas are, what myths and conceptual baggage exist and need to be weeded out before knowledge can grow, and what the core problems of researching minority members are. Part 1 ought to assist you in this endeavor.

Part 2, Cultural Issues: Ideology and Conflict, introduces you to areas often forgotten in minority relations. The symbolic, value, and cultural levels of analysis are often paramount. Although the early Chicago sociologists were frequently intrigued (as are some current scholars) by minorities' esoteric customs and life-styles, few efforts have been made to incorporate these cultural differences and their meanings into theory and understanding.

For some, Part 3, Ethnic Stratification: Power and Inequality, represents the "payoff" in doing social scientific research. That is, for theorists who emphasize power and economic inequalities and other forms of social stratification, these controversial issues are the most important because they emphasize a better understanding of minorities (and the majority that oppresses and exploits them) and the formulation of intelligent policies.

Part 4, Immigration, Demographic Changes, and Pluralism, revisits key concepts, terms, and processes, and it looks at the issue of immigration, how to control it, and how to address the alleged problems resulting from it from the perspective of another country.

You will learn, then, how to look at controversial issues in a new way. Not only will you learn new arguments and facts pertaining to minorities and society's responses to them, but you will learn—to paraphrase Peter Berger—new ways of thinking about these issues and problems.

PART 1

Social Theory and Basic Concepts

What are minority groups? How should research on minority groups be conducted? Are standard sociological theories on ethnicity and race still valid? What are some of the myths that have been created about minorities? The debates in this section explore how to study racial and ethnic relations and some of the basic sociological terminology and concepts.

- Are Nonethnic Scholars Able to Successfully Research Minorities?

- Is the Concept of the Underclass Useful for Studying Race and Ethnic Relations?

- Are Asian Americans a "Model Minority"?

- Do Italian Americans Reject Assimilation?

ISSUE 1

Are Nonethnic Scholars Able to Successfully Research Minorities?

YES: **Robert K. Merton,** from "Insiders and Outsiders: A Chapter in the Sociology of Knowledge," *American Journal of Sociology* (July 1972)

NO: **Patricia Hill Collins,** from "Learning from the Outsider Within: The Sociological Significance of Black Feminist Thought," *Social Problems* (December 1986)

ISSUE SUMMARY

YES: Columbia University professor emeritus and dean of American sociology Robert K. Merton politely but pointedly challenges claims that superior insights automatically result from membership in a specific group. In so doing, he generates several useful hypotheses for researching and understanding ethnic and racial minorities.

NO: Sociologist Patricia Hill Collins, while acknowledging the value of Merton and others, discusses the merits of the insider's claim to better understanding. She combines criticism of traditional methods for researching and theorizing about racial minorities, especially Black females, with suggestions for how sociology can be enriched by the insights of Black feminist scholars.

At the end of his discussion Merton quotes favorably the preeminent Black historian John Hope Franklin, "For there is nothing so irrelevant in telling the truth as the color of a man's skin."

Not so, counters Colins. Indeed, not only is the color of skin sometimes very relevant, but gender and the nature of specific, shared experiences can be equally relevant for truth telling. She questions the validity of traditional sociological studies of racial, ethnic, and gender minorities since they were usually carried out by white Anglo-Saxon males, with detectable patriarchical biases. She also points out the frequency with which minority groups' research programs in the past were ignored or dismissed when they did not conform to dominant white male paradigms, and how members of minority groups found standard social scientific descriptions of themselves to be quite alien.

Her analysis of sociological work on minority-related topics is sophisticated, and her article is not simply a cheap shot at establishment science. Professor Collins does not totally dismiss as inferior research done by outsiders, for she focuses on the scientific competence of any research. Collins has no problem with the scientific way of knowing (embracing explanations of phenomena based upon establishing cause-and-effect relationships, gathering facts in an objective, systematic fashion, including the subjective experiences of people being studied). If anything, Collins both accepts and expands upon the strictly scientific way of knowing by insisting that an understanding of any group of people should include quantitative analyses of patterns of behavior, such as crime, illegitimate births, degrees obtained, income, and so on, as well as qualitative knowledge. Qualitative knowledge would include insights into the meaning of being a particular group member, such as impoverished minority females or a sociology graduate student.

The sociology of knowledge can be traced back to Karl Marx's assertion that "the ruling ideas of any age are the ideas of the ruling class." Unlike philosophy of science, sociology of knowledge pays less attention to the formal substance of the validity of knowledge claims but instead looks at the location of the intellectuals and their schools within society to account for their research problems, their theories and methods, their findings and interpretations, and how their interpretations are used. A fundamental insight of sociology is that a person's location within a social structure influences his or her actions and attitudes. For instance, a lower middle-class Irish Catholic female living in a rural area of New York in the 1920s would think and behave differently as a result of her positions in the social structure than would an upper middle-class suburban Protestant Black male in the 1990s, or an urban Jewish female college student in the 1960s. "Location in social structure" entails occupying several positions based on group memberships that together influence behaviors and attitudes. People occupying the same or similar locations tend to have similar attitudes and actions.

Thus to be consistent, sociological analysis of any group, including scholars and intellectuals, will trace the "causes" of behavior to position in social structure.

Merton is genuinely puzzled by those who argue that a member of a minority group is automatically or intrinsically more knowledgeable than even a fair, curious, and expert outsider researcher. He questions the thesis that not only are outsiders ignorant of insiders' lives, but that they are unable to ever understand or teach about it, nor should they be encouraged to try.

Collins, regardless of ideological motives of researchers and/or their sponsors, takes it for granted that certain social categories, such as exploited Black mothers, can and will "tell their story" and have it understood far more effectively when the recorder of the tale is an "outsider within," that is, a sociologist who is a member or former member of the group.

As you are reading these two important articles, try to formulate examples from your own experiences of the points being made about "outsiders" and "insiders." Note points of agreement between Merton and Collins, points that are ambiguous to you, and points where there is obvious disagreement.

3

YES

Robert K. Merton

INSIDERS AND OUTSIDERS:
A CHAPTER IN THE SOCIOLOGY
OF KNOWLEDGE

The sociology of knowledge has long been regarded as a complex and esoteric subject, remote from the urgent problems of contemporary social life. To
some of us, it seems quite the other way. Especially in times of great social
change, precipitated by acute social conflict and attended by much cultural
disorganization and reorganization, the perspectives provided by the various
sociologies of knowledge bear directly upon problems agitating the society.
It is then that differences in the values, commitments, and intellectual orientations of conflicting groups become deepened into basic cleavages, both
social and cultural. As the society becomes polarized, so do the contending
claims to truth. At the extreme, an active reciprocal distrust between groups
finds expression in intellectual perspectives that are no longer located within
the same universe of discourse. The more deep-seated the mutual distrust,
the more does the argument of the other appear so palpably implausible or
absurd that one no longer inquires into its substance or logical structure to
assess its truth claims. Instead, one confronts the other's argument with an
entirely different sort of question: how does it happen to be advanced at all?
Thought and its products thus become altogether functionalized, interpreted
only in terms of their presumed social or economic or psychological sources
and functions.... In place of the vigorous but intellectually disciplined mutual checking and rechecking that operates to a significant extent, though
never of course totally, within the social institutions of science and scholarship, there develops a strain toward separatism, in the domain of the intellect
as in the domain of society. Partly grounded mutual suspicion increasingly
substitutes for partly grounded mutual trust. There emerge claims to group-
based truth: Insider truths that counter Outsider untruths and Outsider truths
that counter Insider untruths.

In our day, vastly evident social change is being initiated and funneled
through a variety of social movements. These are formally alike in their
objectives of achieving an intensified collective consciousness, a deepened
solidarity and a new or renewed primary or total allegiance of their members

to certain social identities, statuses, groups, or collectivities. Inspecting the familiar list of these movements centered on class, race, ethnicity, age, sex, religion, and sexual disposition, we note two other instructive similarities between them. First, the movements are for the most part formed principally on the basis of ascribed rather than acquired statuses and identities, with eligibility for inclusion being in terms of who you are rather than what you are.... And second, the movements largely involve the public affirmation of pride in statuses and solidarity with collectivities that have long been socially and culturally downgraded, stigmatized, or otherwise victimized in the social system. As with group affiliations generally, these newly reinforced social identities find expression in various affiliative symbols of distinctive speech, bodily appearance, dress, public behavior patterns and, not least, assumptions and foci of thought.

THE INSIDER DOCTRINE

Within this context of social change, we come upon the contemporary relevance of a long-standing problem in the sociology of knowledge: the problem of patterned differentials among social groups and strata in access to certain types of knowledge. In its strong form, the claim is put forward as a matter of epistemological principle that particular groups in each moment of history have *monopolistic access* to particular kinds of knowledge. In the weaker, more empirical form, the claim holds that some groups have *privileged access*, with other groups also being able to acquire that knowledge for themselves but at greater risk and cost.

Claims of this general sort have been periodically introduced.... [T]he Nazi

Gauleiter of science and learning, Ernest Krieck, expressed an entire ideology in contrasting the access to authentic scientific knowledge by men of unimpeachable Aryan ancestry with the corrupt versions of knowledge accessible to non-Aryans. Krieck could refer without hesitation to "Protestant and Catholic science, German and Jewish science." ... Nobel laureate in physics, Johannes Stark, could castigate... his... scientific contemporaries... for accepting what Stark described as "the Jewish physics of Einstein."

... [W]e need not review the array of elitist doctrines which have maintained that certain groups have, on biological or social grounds, monopolistic or privileged access to new knowledge. Differing in detail, the doctrines are alike in distinguishing between Insider access to knowledge and Outsider exclusion from it....

SOCIAL BASES OF INSIDER DOCTRINE

... [W]hite male Insiderism in American sociology during the past generations has largely been of the tacit or de facto rather than doctrinal or principled variety. It has simply taken the form of patterned expectations about the appropriate selection of specialties and of problems for investigation. The handful of Negro sociologists were in large part expected... to study problems of Negro life and relations between the races just as the handful of women sociologists were expected to study problems of women, principally as these related to marriage and the family.

In contrast to this de facto form of Insiderism, an explicitly doctrinal form has in recent years been put forward most clearly and emphatically by some black intellectuals.... The argument holds that, as a matter of social epistemology, *only* black historians can truly understand black history, *only* black ethnologists can understand black culture, *only* black sociologists can understand the social life of blacks, and so on.... [T]he Insider doctrine maintains that there is a body of black history, black psychology, black ethnology, and black sociology which can be significantly advanced only by black scholars and social scientists.

... [T]his represents... the balkanization of social science, with separate baronies kept exclusively in the hands of Insiders bearing their credentials in the shape of one or another ascribed status. Generalizing the specific claim, it would appear to follow that if only black scholars can understand blacks, then only white scholars can understand whites. Generalizing further from race to nation, it would then appear, for example, that only French scholars can understand French society and, of course, that only Americans, not their external critics, can truly understand American society. Once the basic principle is adopted, the list of Insider claims to a monopoly of knowledge becomes indefinitely expansible to all manner of social formations based on ascribed (and, by extension, on some achieved) statuses. It would thus seem to follow that only women can understand women—and men, men. On the same principle, youth alone is capable of understanding youth.... [O]nly Catholics, Catholics; Jews, Jews, and to halt the inventory of socially atomized claims to knowledge with a limiting case that on its face would seem to have some merit, it would then plainly follow that only sociologists are able to understand their fellow sociologists.

In all these applications, the doctrine of extreme Insiderism represents a new credentialism. This is the credentialism of ascribed status, in which understanding becomes accessible only to the fortunate few or many who are to the manner born. In this respect, it contrasts with credentialism of achieved status that is characteristic of meritocratic systems.

Extreme Insiderism moves toward a doctrine of *group* methodological solipsism. [The belief that all one *really* knows is one's subjective experience is sometimes described as the "egocentric predicament."] In this form of solipsism, each group must in the end have a monopoly of knowledge about itself.... The Insider doctrine can be put in the vernacular with no great loss in meaning: you have to be one in order to understand one....

We can quickly pass over the trivial version of that rationale; the argument that the Outsider may be incompetent, given to quick and superficial forays into the group or culture under study and even unschooled in its language. That this kind of incompetence can be found is beyond doubt but it holds no principled interest for us. Foolish men (and women) or badly trained men (and women) are to be found everywhere.... But such cases of special ineptitude do not bear on the Insider *principle*. It is not merely that Insiders also have their share of incompetents. The Insider principle does not refer to stupidly designed and stupidly executed inquiries that happen to be made by stupid Outsiders; it maintains a more fundamental position. According to the doctrine of the Insider, the Outsider, no matter how careful and talented, is excluded in principle from gaining access to the social and cultural truth.

In short, the doctrine holds that the Outsider has a structurally imposed incapacity to comprehend alien groups, statuses, cultures, and societies. Unlike the Insider, the Outsider has neither been socialized in the group nor has engaged in the run of experience that makes up its life, and therefore cannot have the direct, intuitive sensitivity that alone makes empathic understanding possible.... [T]o take a specific expression of this thesis by Ralph W. Conant: "Whites are not and never will be as sensitive to the black community precisely because they are not part of that community."...

A somewhat less stringent version of the doctrine maintains only that Insider and Outsider scholars have significantly different foci of interest.... [T]his weaker version argues only that they will not deal with the same questions and so will simply talk past one another. With the two versions combined, the extended version of the Insider doctrine can also be put in the vernacular: one must not only be one in order to understand one; one must be one in order to understand what is most worth understanding.

Clearly, the social epistemological doctrine of the Insider links up with what Sumner long ago defined as ethnocentrism: "the technical name for [the] view of things in which one's own group is the center of everything, and all others are scaled and rated with reference to it."...

Theodore Caplow... examined 33 different kinds of organizations—ranging from dance studios to Protestant and Catholic churches, from skid row missions to... university departments—and found that members overestimated the prestige of their organization some "eight times as often as they underestimated it" (when compared with judgments by Outsiders).... [W]hile members tended to disagree with Outsiders about the standing of their own organization, they tended to agree with them about the prestige of the other organizations in the same set. These findings can be taken as something of a sociological parable. In these matters at least, the judgments of "Insiders" are best trusted when they assess groups other than their own; that is, when members of groups judge as Outsiders rather than as Insiders.... Ethnocentrism... becomes intensified under specifiable conditions of acute social conflict. When a nation, race, ethnic group, or any other powerful collectivity has long extolled its own admirable qualities and, expressly or by implication, deprecated the qualities of others, it invites and provides the potential for counterethnocentrism. And when a once largely powerless collectivity acquires a socially validated sense of growing power, its members experience an intensified need for self-affirmation. Under such circumstances, collective self-glorification, found in some measure among all groups, becomes a predictable and intensified counterresponse to long-standing belittlement from without.... What is being proposed here is that the epistemological claims of the Insider to monopolistic or privileged access to social truth develop under particular social and historical conditions. Social groups or strata on the way up develop a revolutionary élan. The new thrust to a larger share of power and control over their social and political environment finds various expressions, among them claims to a unique access to knowledge about their history, culture, and social life.

On this interpretation, we can understand why this Insider doctrine does not argue for a Black Physics, Black

Chemistry, Black Biology, or Black Technology. For the new will to control their fate deals with the social environment, not the environment of nature.... [T]he black Insider doctrine adopts an essentially social-environmental rationale, not a biologically genetic one....

With varying degrees of intent, groups in conflict want to make their interpretation the prevailing one of how things were and are and will be. The critical measure of success occurs when the interpretation moves beyond the boundaries of the ingroup to be accepted by Outsiders. At the extreme, it then gives rise, through identifiable processes of reference-group behavior, to the familiar case of the converted Outsider validating himself, in his own eyes and in those of others, by becoming even more zealous than the Insiders in adhering to the doctrine of the group with which he wants to identify himself, if only symbolically. He then becomes more royalist than the king, more papist than the pope. Some white social scientists, for example, vicariously and personally guilt ridden over centuries of white racism, are prepared to outdo the claims of the group they would symbolically join. They are ready even to surrender their hard-won expert knowledge if the Insider doctrine seems to require it....

The black Insider doctrine links up with the historically developing social structure in still another way. The dominant social institutions in this country have long treated the racial identity of individuals as actually if not doctrinally relevant to all manner of situations in every sphere of life. For generations, neither blacks nor whites, though with notably differing consequences, were permitted to forget their race. *This treatment of a social status (or identity) as relevant when intrinsically it is functionally irrelevant constitutes the very core of social discrimination.* As the once firmly rooted systems of discriminatory institutions and prejudicial ideology began to lose their hold, this meant that increasingly many judged the worth of ideas on their merits, not in terms of their racial pedigree.

What the Insider doctrine of the most militant blacks proposes on the level of social structure is to adopt the salience of racial identity in every sort of role and situation, a pattern so long imposed upon the American Negro, and to make that identity a total commitment issuing from within the group rather than one imposed upon it from without. By thus affirming the universal saliency of race and by redefining race as an abiding source of pride rather than stigma, the Insider doctrine in effect models itself after doctrine long maintained by white racists.

Neither this component of the Insider doctrine nor the statement on its implications is at all new. Almost a century ago, Frederick Douglass hinged his observations along these lines on the distinction between collective and individual self-images based on ascribed and achieved status:

One of the few errors to which we are clinging most persistently and, as I think, most mischievously has come into great prominence of late. It is the cultivation and stimulation among us of a sentiment which we are pleased to call race pride. I find it in all our books, papers, and speeches. For my part I see no superiority or inferiority in race or color. Neither the one nor the other is a proper source of pride or complacency. Our race and color are not of our own choosing. We have no volition in the case one way or another. The only excuse for pride in individuals or races is in the fact of their own achievements.... I see no benefit to be derived from this everlasting exhortation of speakers and writers among us to the cultivation of race pride. On the contrary, I see in it a positive evil. It is building on a false foundation....

Just as conditions of war between nations have long produced a strain toward hyperpatriotism among national ethnocentrics, so current intergroup conflicts have produced a strain toward hyperloyalty among racial or sex or age or religious ethnocentrics. Total commitment easily slides from the solidarity doctrine of "our group, right or wrong" to the morally and intellectually preemptive doctrine of "our group, always right, never wrong."...

SOCIAL STRUCTURE OF INSIDERS AND OUTSIDERS

... In structural terms, we are all, of course, both Insiders and Outsiders, members of some groups and, sometimes derivatively, not of others; occupants of certain statuses which thereby exclude us from occupying other cognate statuses. Obvious as this basic fact of social structure is, its implications for Insider and Outsider epistemological doctrines are apparently not nearly as obvious. Else, these doctrines would not presuppose, as they typically do, that human beings in socially differentiated societies can be sufficiently located in terms of a single social status, category, or group affiliation—black or white, men or women, under 30 or older—or of several such categories, taken seriatim [in a series] rather than conjointly. This neglects the crucial fact of social structure that individuals have not a single status but a status set: a complement of variously interrelated statuses which interact to affect both their behavior and perspectives.

The structural fact of status sets, in contrast to statuses taken one at a time, introduces severe theoretical problems for total Insider (and Outsider) doctrines of social epistemology. The array of status sets in a population means that aggregates of individuals share some statuses and not others; or, to put this in context, that they typically confront one another simultaneously as Insiders and Outsiders. Thus, if only whites can understand whites and blacks, blacks, and only men can understand men, and women, women, this gives rise to the paradox which severely limits both premises: for it then turns out, by assumption, that some Insiders are excluded from understanding other Insiders with white women being condemned not to understand white men, and black men, not to understand black women, and so through the various combinations of status subsets....

This symptomatic exercise in status-set analysis may be enough to indicate that the idiomatic expression of total Insider doctrine—one must be one in order to understand one—is deceptively simple and sociologically fallacious (just as ... is the case with the total Outsider doctrine). For, from the sociological perspective of the status set, "one" is not a man *or* a black *or* an adolescent *or* a Protestant, *or* self-defined and socially defined as middle class, and so on. Sociologically, "one" is, of course, all of these and, depending on the size of the status set, much more.... [T]he greater the number and variety of group affiliations and statuses distributed among individuals in a society, the smaller, on the average, the number of individuals having precisely the same social configuration....

[I]t is precisely the individual differences among scientists and scholars that are often central to the development of the discipline. They often involve the differences between good scholarship and bad; between imaginative contributions to science and pedestrian ones; between the consequential ideas and stillborn ones. In arguing for the monopolistic access to knowledge, Insider doctrine can make no provision for individual variability that extends beyond the boundaries of the ingroup which alone can develop sound and fruitful ideas....

Yet sociologically, there is nothing fixed about the boundaries separating Insiders from Outsiders. As situations involving different values arise, different statuses are activated and the lines of separation shift. Thus, for a large number of white Americans, Joe Louis was a member of an outgroup. But when Louis defeated the Nazified Max Schmeling, many of the same white Americans promptly redefined him as a member of the (national) ingroup. National self-esteem took precedence over racial separatism. That this sort of drama in which changing situations activate differing statuses in the status set is played out in the domain of the intellect as well is the point of Einstein's ironic observation in an address at the Sorbonne: "If my theory of relativity is proved successful, Germany will claim me as a German and France will declare that I am a citizen of the world. Should my theory prove untrue, France will say that I am a German and Germany will declare that I am a Jew."...

INSIDERS AS "OUTSIDERS"

... [W]hat some Insiders profess as Insiders they apparently reject as Outsiders.

For example, when advocates of black Insider doctrine engage in analysis of "white society," trying to assay its power structure or to detect its vulnerabilities, they seem to deny in practice what they affirm in doctrine. At any rate, their behavior testifies to the assumption that it is possible for self-described "Outsiders" to diagnose and to understand what they describe as an alien social structure and culture....

The strong version of the Insider doctrine, with its epistemological claim to a monopoly of certain kinds of knowledge, runs counter, of course, to a long history of thought....

[First Georg] Simmel and then... Max Weber... adopted the memorable phrase: "one need not be Caesar in order to understand Caesar." In making this claim, they rejected the extreme Insider thesis which asserts in effect that one *must* be Caesar in order to understand him just as they rejected the extreme Outsider thesis that one must *not* be Caesar in order to understand him.... The Insider argues that the authentic understanding of group life can be achieved only by those who are directly engaged as members in the life of the group. Taken seriously, the doctrine puts in question the validity of just about all historical writing.... If direct engagement in the life of a group is essential to understanding it, then the only authentic history is contemporary history, written in fragments by those most fully involved in making inevitably limited portions of it. Rather than constituting only the raw materials of history, the documents prepared by engaged Insiders become all there is to history. But once the historian elects to write the history of a time other than his own, even the most dedicated Insider, of the national, sex, age, racial, ethnic, or religious variety, becomes the Outsider, condemned to error and misunderstanding.

Writing some 20 years ago in another connection, Claude Lévi-Strauss noted the parallelism between history and ethnography. Both subjects, he observed,

are concerned with societies *other* than the one in which we live. Whether this *otherness* is due to remoteness in time (however slight) or to remoteness in space, or even to cultural heterogeneity, is of secondary importance compared to the basic similarity of perspective. All that the historian or ethnographer can do, and all that we can expect of either of them, is to enlarge a specific experience to the dimensions of a more general one, which thereby becomes accessible as *experience* to men of another country or another epoch. And in order to succeed, both historian and ethnographer, must have the same qualities: skill, precision, a sympathetic approach and objectivity....

Simmel develops the thesis that the stranger, not caught up in commitments to the group, can more readily acquire the strategic role of the relatively objective inquirer. "He is freer, practically and theoretically," notes Simmel, "he surveys conditions with less prejudice; his criteria for them are more general and more objective ideals: he is not tied down in his action by habit, piety, and precedent."... It is the stranger, too, who finds what is familiar to the group significantly unfamiliar and so is prompted to raise questions for inquiry less apt to be raised at all by Insiders.... Outsiders are sought out to observe social institutions and cultures on the premise that they are more apt to do so with detachment. Thus, in the first decade of this century, the Carnegie Foundation for the Advancement of Teaching, in its

search for someone to investigate the condition of medical schools, reached out to appoint Abraham Flexner, after he had admitted never before having been inside a medical school. It was a matter of policy to select a total Outsider who, as it happened, produced the uncompromising Report which did much to transform the state of American medical education at the time.

Later, casting about for a scholar who might do a thoroughgoing study of the Negro in the United States, the Carnegie Corporation searched for an Outsider,... with the quest ending... with the selection of Gunnar Myrdal [a Swedish social scientist]. In the preface to *An American Dilemma*,* Myrdal (1944, pp. xviii–xiv) reflected on his status as an Outsider who, in his words, "had never been subject to the strains involved in living in a black-white society" and who "as a stranger to the problem... has had perhaps a greater awareness of the extent to which human valuations everywhere enter into our scientific discussion of the Negro problem."

Reviews of the book repeatedly alluded to the degree of detachment from entangling loyalties that seemed to come from Myrdal's being an Outsider. J. S. Redding (1944), for one, observed that "as a European, Myrdal had no American sensibilities to protect. He hits hard with fact and interpretation." Robert S. Lynd (1944), for another, saw it as a prime merit of this Outsider that he was free to find out for himself "without any side glances as to what was politically expedient." And for a third, Frank Tannenbaum (1944) noted that Myrdal brought "objectivity in regard to the special foibles and shortcomings in American life. As an

---

* [*An American Dilemma* (1944) was a benchmark study of race relations.—Ed.]

outsider, he showed the kind of objectivity which would seem impossible for one reared within the American scene." Even later criticism of Myrdal's work—for example, the comprehensive critique by Cox (1948, chap. 23)—does not attribute imputed errors in interpretation to his having been an Outsider.

Two observations should be made on the Myrdal episode. First, in the judgment of critical minds, the Outsider, far from being excluded from the understating of an alien society, was able to bring needed perspectives to it. And second, that Myrdal, wanting to have both Insider and Outsider perspectives, expressly drew into his circle of associates in the study such Insiders, engaged in the study of Negro life and culture and of race relations, as E. Franklin Frazier, Arnold Rose, Ralph Bunche, Melville Herskovits, Otto Klineberg, J. G. St. Clair Drake, Guy B. Johnson, and Doxey A. Wilkerson....

The cumulative point of this variety of intellectual and institutional cases is not—and this needs to be repeated with all possible emphasis—is *not* a proposal to replace the extreme Insider doctrine by an extreme and equally vulnerable Outsider doctrine. The intent is, rather, to transform the original question altogether.... Just as with the process of competition generally, so with the competition of ideas. Competing or conflicting groups take over ideas and procedures from one another, thereby denying in practice the rhetoric of total incompatibility. Even in the course of social polarization, conceptions with cognitive value are utilized all apart from their source. Concepts of power structure, co-optation, the dysfunctions of established institutions and findings associated with these concepts have

for some time been utilized by social scientists, irrespective of their social or political identities.... Such diffusion of ideas across the boundaries of groups and statuses has long been noted. In one of his more astute analyses, Mannheim (1952) states the general case for the emergence and spread of knowledge that transcends even profound conflicts between groups:

> Syntheses owe their existence to the same social process that brings about polarization; groups take over the modes of thought and intellectual achievements of their adversaries under the simple law of 'competition on the basis of achievement.'... In the socially-differentiated thought process, even the opponent is ultimately forced to adopt those categories and forms of thought which are most appropriate in a given type of world order. In the economic sphere, one of the possible results of competition is that one competitor is compelled to catch up with the other's technological advances. In just the same way, whenever groups compete for having their interpretation of reality accepted as the correct one, it may happen that one of the groups takes over from the adversary some fruitful hypothesis or category—anything that promises cognitive gain....

FROM SOCIAL CONFLICT TO INTELLECTUAL CONTROVERSY

... Insider and Outsider perspectives can converge, in spite of such differences, through reciprocal adoption of ideas and the developing of complementary and overlapping foci of attention in the formulation of scientific problems. But these intellectual potentials for synthesis are often curbed by social processes that divide scholars and scientists. Internal divisions and polarizations in the society at large often stand in the way of realizing those potentials....

When a transition from social conflict to intellectual controversy is achieved, when the perspectives of each group are taken seriously enough to be carefully examined rather than rejected out of hand, there can develop trade-offs between the distinctive strengths and weaknesses of Insider and Outsider perspectives that enlarge the chances for a sound and relevant understanding of social life....

If indeed we have distinctive contributions to make to social knowledge in our roles as Insiders or Outsiders—and it should be repeated that all of us are both Insiders and Outsiders in various social situations—then those contributions probably link up with a long-standing distinction between two major kinds of knowledge, a basic distinction that is blurred in the often ambiguous use of the word "understanding." In the language of William James (1932, pp. 11–13),... this is the distinction between "acquaintance with" and "knowledge about." The one involves direct familiarity with phenomena that is expressed in depictive representations; the other involves more abstract formulations which do not at all "resemble" what has been directly experienced (Merton 1968, p. 545)....

These distinct and connected kinds of understanding may turn out to be distributed, in varying mix, among Insiders and Outsiders. The introspective meanings of experience within a status or a group may be more readily accessible, for all the seemingly evident reasons, to those who have shared part or all of that experience. But authentic awareness, even in the sense of acquaintance with, is not guaranteed by social affiliation, as the concept of false consciousness is designed to remind us. Determinants of social life—for an obvious example, ecological patterns and processes—are not necessarily evident to those directly engaged in it. In short, sociological understanding involves much more than acquaintance with. It includes an empirically confirmable comprehension of the conditions and often complex processes in which people are caught up without much awareness of what is going on. To analyze and understand these requires a theoretical and technical competence which, as such, transcends one's status as Insider or Outsider. The role of social scientist concerned with achieving knowledge about society requires enough detachment and trained capacity to know how to assemble and assess the evidence without regard for what the analysis seems to imply about the worth of one's group....

The acceptance of criteria of craftsmanship and integrity in science and learning cuts across differences in the social affiliations and loyalties of scientists and scholars. Commitment to the intellectual values dampens group-induced pressures to advance the interests of groups at the expense of these values and of the intellectual product.

The consolidation of group-influenced perspectives and the autonomous values of scholarship is exemplified in observations by John Hope Franklin who, for more than a quarter-century, has been engaged in research on the history of American Negroes from their ancient African beginnings to the present.... Franklin's application of exacting, autonomous and universalistic standards culminates in a formulation that, once again, transcends the statuses of Insiders and Outsiders:

... It takes a person of stout heart, great courage, and uncompromising honesty to look the history of this country squarely in the face and tell it like it is.... And when this approach prevails, the history of the United States and the history of the black man can be written and taught by any person, white, black, or otherwise. For there is nothing so irrelevant in telling the truth as the color of a man's skin.

NO

Patricia Hill Collins

LEARNING FROM THE OUTSIDER WITHIN: THE SOCIOLOGICAL SIGNIFICANCE OF BLACK FEMINIST THOUGHT

Afro-American women have long been privy to some of the most intimate secrets of white society. Countless numbers of Black women have ridden buses to their white "families," where they not only cooked, cleaned, and executed other domestic duties, but where they also nurtured their "other" children, shrewdly offered guidance to their employers, and frequently, became honorary members of their white "families." These women have seen white elites, both actual and aspiring, from perspectives largely obscured from their Black spouses and from these groups themselves.

On one level, this "insider" relationship has been satisfying to all involved. The memoirs of affluent whites often mention their love for their Black "mothers," while accounts of Black domestic workers stress the sense of self-affirmation they experienced at seeing white power demystified—of knowing that it was not the intellect, talent, or humanity of their employers that supported their superior status, but largely just the advantages of racism. But on another level, these same Black women knew they could never belong to their white "families." In spite of their involvement, they remained "outsiders."

This "outsider within" status has provided a special standpoint on self, family, and society for Afro-American women.... [T]he emerging Black feminist literature reveals that many Black intellectuals, especially those in touch with their marginality in academic settings, tap this standpoint in producing distinctive analyses of race, class, and gender. For example, Zora Neal Hurston's 1937 novel, *Their Eyes Were Watching God*, most certainly reflects her skill at using the strengths and transcending the limitations both of her academic training and of her background in traditional Afro-American community life. Black feminist historian E. Frances White (1984) suggests that Black women's ideas have been honed at the juncture between movements for racial and sexual equality, and contends that Afro-American women have

From Patricia Hill Collins, "Learning from the Outsider Within: The Sociological Significance of Black Feminist Thought," *Social Problems*, vol. 33, no. 6 (December 1986), pp. 14–21, 24–30. Copyright © 1986 by The Society for the Study of Social Problems. Reprinted by permission. References and some notes omitted.

been pushed by "their marginalization in both arenas" to create Black feminism. Finally, Black feminist critic bell hooks captures the unique standpoint that the outsider within status can generate. In describing her small-town, Kentucky childhood, she notes, "living as we did—on the edge—we developed a particular way of seeing reality. We looked both from the outside and in from the inside out... we understood both" (1984:vii).

In spite of the obstacles that can confront outsiders within, such individuals can benefit from this status. [Georg] Simmel's essay on the sociological significance of what he called the "stranger" offers a helpful starting point for understanding the largely unexplored area of Black female outsider within status and the usefulness of the standpoint it might produce. Some of the potential benefits of outsider within status include: (1) Simmel's definition of "objectivity" as "a peculiar composition of nearness and remoteness, concern and indifference"; (2) the tendency for people to confide in a "stranger" in ways they never would with each other; and (3) the ability of the "stranger" to see patterns that may be more difficult for those immersed in the situation to see. [Karl] Mannheim labels the "strangers" in academia "marginal intellectuals" and argues that the critical posture such individuals bring to academic endeavors may be essential to the creative development of academic disciplines themselves. [Alfred M.] Lee notes, "for a time this marginality can be a most stimulating, albeit often a painful, experience. For some, it is debilitating... for others, it is an excitement to creativity."[1]

Sociologists might benefit greatly from serious consideration of the emerging, cross-disciplinary literature that I label Black feminist thought, precisely be-cause, for many Afro-American female intellectuals, "marginality" has been an excitement to creativity. As outsiders within, Black feminist scholars may be one of many distinct groups of marginal intellectuals whose standpoints promise to enrich contemporary sociological discourse. Bringing this group—as well as others who share an outsider within status vis-a-vis sociology—into the center of analysis may reveal aspects of reality obscured by more orthodox approaches....

THE SOCIOLOGICAL SIGNIFICANCE OF BLACK FEMINIST THOUGHT

... The sociological significance of Black feminist thought lies in two areas. First, the content of Black women's ideas has been influenced by and contributes to on-going dialogues in a variety of sociological specialties. While this area merits attention, it is not my primary concern in this section. Instead, I investigate a second area of sociological significance: the process by which these specific ideas were produced by this specific group of individuals. In other words, I examine the influence of Black women's outsider within status in academia on the actual thought produced....

Two Elements of Sociological Paradigms

[Thomas S.] Kuhn defines a paradigm as the "entire constellation of beliefs, values, techniques, and so on shared by the members of a given community" (1962:175). As such, a paradigm consists of two fundamental elements: the thought itself and its producers and practitioners. In this sense, the discipline of sociology is itself a paradigm—it consists of a system of knowledge shared by sociologists—

and simultaneously consists of a plurality of paradigms (e.g., functionalism, Marxist sociology, feminist sociology, existential sociology), each produced by its own practitioners.

Two dimensions of thought itself are of special interest to this discussion. First, systems of knowledge are never complete. Rather, they represent guidelines for "thinking as usual." Kuhn refers to these guidelines as "maps," while [Alfred] Schutz (1944) describes them as "recipes." As Schutz points out, while "thinking as usual" is actually only partially organized and partially clear, and may contain contradictions, to its practitioners it provides sufficient coherence, clarity, and consistency. Second, while thought itself contains diverse elements, I will focus mainly on the important fact/theory relationship. As Kuhn suggests, facts or observations become meaningful in the context of theories or interpretations of those observations. Conversely, theories "fit the facts" by transforming previously accessible observations into facts. According to [Michael] Mulkay, "observation is not separate from interpretation; rather these are two facets of a single process" (1979:49).

Several dimensions of the second element of sociological paradigms—the community formed by a paradigm's practitioners—are of special interest to this discussion. First, group insiders have similar worldviews, acquired through similar educational and professional training, that separate them from everyone else. Insider worldviews may be especially alike if group members have similar social class, gender, and racial backgrounds. Schutz describes the insider worldview as the "cultural pattern of group life"—namely, all the values and behaviors which characterize the social group at a given moment in its history. In brief, insiders have undergone similar experiences, possess a common history, and share taken-for-granted knowledge that characterizes "thinking as usual."

A second dimension of the community of practitioners involves the process of becoming an insider. How does one know when an individual is really an insider and not an outsider in disguise? [Robert] Merton suggests that socialization into the life of a group is a lengthy process of being immersed in group life, because only then can "one understand the fine-grained meanings of behavior, feeling, and values... and decipher the unwritten grammar of conduct and nuances of cultural idiom" (1972:15). The process is analogous to immersion in a foreign culture in order to learn its ways and its language (Merton, 1972; Schutz, 1944). One becomes an insider by translating a theory or worldview into one's own language until, one day, the individual converts to thinking and acting according to that worldview.

A final dimension of the community of practitioners concerns the process of remaining an insider. A sociologist typically does this by furthering the discipline in ways described as appropriate by sociology generally, and by areas of specialization particularly. Normal foci for scientific sociological investigation include: (1) determining significant facts; (2) matching facts with existing theoretical interpretations to "test" the paradigm's ability to predict facts; and (3) resolving ambiguities in the paradigm itself by articulating and clarifying theory (Kuhn, 1962).

Black Women and the Outsider Within Status

Black women may encounter much less of a fit between their personal and cultural experiences and both elements of sociological paradigms than that facing other sociologists. On the one hand, Black women who undergo sociology's lengthy socialization process, who immerse themselves in the cultural pattern of sociology's group life, certainly wish to acquire the insider skills of thinking in and acting according to a sociological worldview. But on the other hand, Black women's experienced realities, both prior to contact and after initiation, may provide them with "special perspectives and insights... available to that category of outsiders who have been systematically frustrated by the social system" (Merton, 1972:29). In brief, their outsider allegiances may militate against their choosing full insider status, and they may be more apt to remain outsiders within.[3]

In essence, to become sociological insiders, Black women must assimilate a standpoint that is quite different than their own. White males have long been the dominant group in sociology, and the sociological worldview understandably reflects the concerns of this group of practitioners. As Merton observes, "white male insiderism in American sociology during the past generations has largely been of the tacit or de facto... variety. It has simply taken the form of patterned expectations about the appropriate... problems for investigation" (1972:12). In contrast, a good deal of the Black female experience has been spent coping with, avoiding, subverting, and challenging the workings of this same white male insiderism. It should come as

no surprise that Black women's efforts in dealing with the effects of interlocking systems of oppression might produce a standpoint quite distinct from, and in many ways opposed to, that of white male insiders.

Seen from this perspective, Black women's socialization into sociology represents a more intense case of the normal challenges facing sociology graduate students and junior professionals in the discipline. Black women become, to use Simmel's (1921) and Schutz's terminology, penultimate "strangers."

> The stranger... does not share the basic assumptions of the group. He becomes essentially the man who has to place in question nearly everything that seems to be unquestionable to the members of the approached group.... To him the cultural patterns of the approached group do not have the authority of a tested system of recipes... because he does not partake in the vivid historical tradition by which it has been formed (Schutz, 1944:502).

Like everyone else, Black women may see sociological "thinking as usual" as partially organized, partially clear, and contradictory, and may question these existing recipes. However, for them, this questioning process may be more acute, for the material that they encounter—white male insider-influenced observations and interpretations about human society—places white male subjectivity at the center of analysis and assigns Afro-American womanhood a position on the margins.

In spite of a lengthy socialization process, it may also be more difficult for Afro-American women to experience conversion and begin totally to think in and act according to a sociological worldview. Indeed, since past generations of white male insiderism has shaped a sociological worldview reflecting this group's concerns, it may be self-destructive for Black women to embrace that worldview. For example, Black women would have to accept certain fundamental and self-devaluing assumptions: (1) white males are more worthy of study because they are more fully human than everyone else; and (2) dichotomous oppositional thinking is natural and normal. More importantly, Black women would have to act in accordance with their place in a white male worldview. This involves accepting one's own subordination or regretting the accident of not being born white and male. In short, it may be extremely difficult for Black women to accept a worldview predicated upon Black female inferiority.

Remaining in sociology by doing normal scientific investigation may also be less complicated for traditional sociologists than for Afro-American women. Unlike Black women, learners from backgrounds where the insider information and experiences of sociology are more familiar may be less likely to see the taken-for-granted assumptions of sociology and may be more prone to apply their creativity to "normal science." In other words, the transition from student status to that of a practitioner engaged in finding significant facts that sociological paradigms deem important, matching facts with existing theories, and furthering paradigmatic development itself may proceed more smoothly for white middle-class males than for working-class Black females. The latter group is much more inclined to be struck by the mismatch of its own experiences and the paradigms of sociology itself. Moreover, those Black women with a strong foundation in Black women's culture

(e.g., those that recognize the value of self-definition and self-valuation, and that have a concrete understanding of sisterhood and motherhood) may be more apt to take a critical posture toward the entire sociological enterprise. In brief, where traditional sociologists may see sociology as "normal" and define their role as furthering knowledge about a normal world with taken-for-granted assumptions, outsiders within are liable to see anomalies.

The types of anomalies typically seen by Black female academicians grow directly from Black women's outsider within status and appear central in shaping the direction Black feminist thought has taken thus far. Two types of anomalies are characteristically noted by Black female scholars. First, Black female sociologists typically report the omission of facts or observations about Afro-American women in the sociological paradigms they encounter. As [Patricia B.] Scott points out, "from reading the literature, one might easily develop the impression that Black women have never played any role in this society" (1982:85). Where white males may take it as perfectly normal to generalize findings from studies of white males to other groups, Black women are more likely to see such a practice as problematic, as an anomaly. Similarly, when white feminists produce generalizations about "women," Black feminists routinely ask "which women do you mean?" . . . Afro-American female scholars are repeatedly struck by their own invisibility, both as fully human subjects included in sociological facts and observations, and as practitioners in the discipline itself. It should come as no surprise that much of Black feminist thought aims to counter this invisibility by presenting sociological analyses of Black women as fully human subjects. . . .

A second type of anomaly typically noted by Black female scholars concerns distortions of facts and observations about Black women. Afro-American women in academia are frequently struck by the difference between their own experiences and sociological descriptions of the same phenomena. For example, while Black women have and are themselves mothers, they encounter distorted versions of themselves and their mothers under the mantle of the Black matriarchy thesis. [Here, Professor Collins is referring to Black female stereotypes, which she feels are actually distorted renderings of those aspects of Black female behavior seen as most threatening to white patriarchy. Labeling strong Black mothers "matriarchs" and assertive Black women "Sapphires" (see below) represents an effort to keep Black women "in their place" and to protect the status quo.—Ed.] Similarly, for those Black women who confront racial and sexual discrimination and know that their mothers and grandmothers certainly did, explanations of Black women's poverty that stress low achievement motivation and the lack of Black female "human capital" are less likely to ring true. The response to these perceived distortions has been one of redefining distorted images—for example, debunking the Sapphire and Mammy myths.

Since facts or observations become meaningful in the context of a theory, this emphasis on producing accurate descriptions of Black women's lives has also refocused attention on major omissions and distortions in sociological theories themselves. By drawing on the strengths of sociology's plurality of subdisciplines,

yet taking a critical posture toward them, the work of Black feminist scholars taps some fundamental questions facing all sociologists. One such question concerns the fundamental elements of society that should be studied. Black feminist researchers' response has been to move Black women's voices to the center of the analysis, to study people, and by doing so, to reaffirm human subjectivity and intentionality. They point to the dangers of omission and distortion that can occur if sociological concepts are studied at the expense of human subjectivity. For example, there is a distinct difference between conducting a statistical analysis of Black women's work, where Afro-American women are studied as a reconstituted amalgam of researcher-defined variables (e.g., race, sex, years of education, and father's occupation), and examining Black women's self-definitions and self-valuations of themselves as workers in oppressive jobs. While both approaches can further sociological knowledge about the concept of work, the former runs the risk of objectifying Black women, of reproducing constructs of dichotomous oppositional difference, and of producing distorted findings about the nature of work itself.

A second question facing sociologists concerns the adequacy of current interpretations of key sociological concepts. For example, few sociologists would question that work and family are two fundamental concepts for sociology. However, bringing Black feminist thought into the center of conceptual analysis raises issues of how comprehensive current sociological interpretations of these two concepts really are. For example, labor theories that relegate Afro-American women's work experiences to the fringe of analysis miss the critical theme of the interlocking nature of Black women as female workers (e.g., Black women's unpaid domestic labor) and Black women as racially-oppressed workers (e.g., Black women's unpaid slave labor and exploited wage labor). Examining the extreme case offered by Afro-American women's unpaid and paid work experiences raises questions about the adequacy of generalizations about work itself. For example, Black feminists' emphasis on the simultaneity of oppression redefines the economic system itself as problematic. From this perspective, all generalizations about the normal workings of labor markets, organizational structure, occupational mobility, and income differences that do not explicitly see oppression as problematic become suspect. In short, Black feminists suggest that all generalizations about groups of employed and unemployed workers (e.g., managers, welfare mothers, union members, secretaries, Black teenagers) that do not account for interlocking structures of group placement and oppression in an economy [are] simply less complete than those that do.

Similarly, sociological generalizations about families that do not account for Black women's experience will fail to see how the public/private split shaping household composition varies across social and class groupings, how racial/ethnic family members are differentially integrated into wage labor, and how families alter their household structure in response to changing political economies (e.g., adding more people and becoming extended, fragmenting and becoming female-headed, and migrating to locate better opportunities). Black women's family experiences represent a clear case of the workings of race, gender, and class oppression in shaping family life.

Bringing undistorted observations of Afro-American women's family experiences into the center of analysis again raises the question of how other families are affected by these same forces.

While Black women who stand outside academia may be familiar with omissions and distortions of the black female experience, as outsiders to sociology, they lack legitimated professional authority to challenge the sociological anomalies. Similarly, traditional sociological insiders, whether white males or their nonwhite and/or female disciples, are certainly in no position to notice the specific anomalies apparent to Afro-American women, because these same sociological insiders produced them. In contrast, those Black women who remain rooted in their own experiences as Black women—and who master sociological paradigms yet retain a critical posture toward them—are in a better position to bring a special perspective not only to the study of Black women, but to some of the fundamental issues facing sociology itself.

TOWARD SYNTHESIS: OUTSIDERS WITHIN SOCIOLOGY

Black women are not the only outsiders within sociology. As an extreme case of outsiders moving into a community that historically excluded them, Black women's experiences highlight the tension experienced by any group of less powerful outsiders encountering the paradigmatic thought of a more powerful insider community. In this sense, a variety of individuals can learn from Black women's experiences as outsiders within: Black men, working-class individuals, white women, other people of color, religious and sexual minorities, and all individuals who, while from social strata that provided them with the benefits of white male insiderism, have never felt comfortable with its taken-for-granted assumptions.

Outsider within status is bound to generate tension, for people who become outsiders within are forever changed by their new status. Learning the subject matter of sociology stimulates a reexamination of one's own personal and cultural experiences; and, yet, these same experiences paradoxically help to illuminate sociology's anomalies. Outsiders within occupy a special place—they become different people, and their difference sensitizes them to patterns that may be more difficult for established sociological insiders to see. Some outsiders within try to resolve the tension generated by their new status by leaving sociology and remaining sociological outsiders. Others choose to suppress their difference by striving to become bonafide, "thinking as usual" sociological insiders. Both choices rob sociology of diversity and ultimately weaken the discipline.

A third alternative is to conserve the creative tension of outsider within status by encouraging and institutionalizing outsider within ways of seeing. This alternative has merit not only for actual outsiders within, but also for other sociologists as well. The approach suggested by the experiences of outsiders within is one where intellectuals learn to trust their own personal and cultural biographies as significant sources of knowledge. In contrast to approaches that require submerging these dimensions of self in the process of becoming an allegedly unbiased, objective social scientist, outsiders within bring these ways of knowing back into the research process. At its best, outsider within status

seems to offer its occupants a powerful balance between the strengths of their sociological training and the offerings of their personal and cultural experiences. Neither is subordinated to the other. Rather, experienced reality is used as a valid source of knowledge for critiquing sociological facts and theories, while sociological thought offers new ways of seeing that experienced reality.

What many Black feminists appear to be doing is embracing the creative potential of their outsider within status and using it wisely. In doing so, they move themselves and their disciplines closer to the humanist vision implicit in their work—namely, the freedom both to be different and part of the solidarity of humanity.

NOTES

1. By stressing the potentially positive features of outsider within status, I in no way want to deny the very real problem this social status has for large numbers of Black women. American sociology has long identified marginal status as problematic. However, my sense of the "problems" diverge from those espoused by traditional sociologists. For example, Robert Park states, "the marginal man ... is one whom fate has condemned to live in two societies and in two, not merely different but antagonistic cultures." From Park's perspective, marginality and difference themselves were problems. This perspective quite rationally led to the social policy solution of assimilation, one aimed at eliminating difference, or if that didn't work, pretending it was not important. In contrast, I argue that it is the meaning attached to difference that is the problem.

2. On this point, I diverge somewhat from Berger and Luckmann's definition of specialized thought. They suggest that only a limited group of individuals engages in theorizing and that "pure theory" emerges with the development of specialized legitimating theories and their administration by full-time legitimators. Using this approach, groups denied the material resources to support pure theorists cannot be capable of developing specialized theoretical knowledge. In contrast, I argue that "traditional wisdom" is a system of thought and that it reflects the material positions of its practitioners.

3. [Jacquelyn] Jackson (1974) reports that 21 of the 145 Black sociologists receiving doctoral degrees between 1945 and 1972 were women. Kulis et al. (1986) report that Blacks comprised 5.7 percent of all sociology faculties in 1984. These datasuggest that historically, Black females have not been sociological insiders, and currently, Black women as a group comprise a small portion of sociologists in the United States.

POSTSCRIPT

Are Nonethnic Scholars Able to Successfully Research Minorities?

For generations North American sociologists embraced in their work Max Weber's notion of value free sociology. That is, they contended that their research was completely neutral, objective, unbiased, and free of value contamination. Many in minority relations and other areas of the social sciences were caught off guard in 1944 with the publication of Gunnar Myrdal's *American Dilemma*, arguably the most significant study of its kind in the twentieth century. In this study of U.S. treatment of Blacks, Myrdal, a Swedish economist, simply said it was wrong, it contradicted the creed of the United States, and he personally opposed exploitation and prejudice.

At about the same time or shortly afterward a variety of "radical" sociologists, such as Robert Lynd, C. Wright Mills, Howard Becker, and Alvin Gouldner, partially following Myrdal, elected to take stands on issues. Moreover, they contended that a "value free" science of human beings was impossible. Just the fact that one elected to research the poor instead of the rich, the discriminated against instead of the discriminators, for instance, automatically implied a value position.

Mills and Gouldner insisted that not only did sociological research and theory contain implicit values (generally conservative and in support of the status quo), it was impossible for this not to be the case. Moreover, Mills sharply attacked the dominant perspective in the 1950s in American sociology: structural functionalism (Mills had been a colleague of Merton at Columbia, Gouldner was Merton's student).

To a large extent, Collins and other feminist scholars, and/or those within this race-ethnic relations tradition, are reflecting the ideas of Mills and others. Merton, although even a quick reading of most of his writings would show that he is far more complex, is almost always linked to the dominant figures of structural functionalism (a label he himself has embraced).

In places both Merton and Collins, but especially Merton, hint that the ideal research is one that combines insider and outsider knowledge. While there are problems with this middle way, it would appear to be a minority research goal worth considering.

What situations can you think of, if any, in which "outsiders" may better understand members of your group's problems (e.g., your family)? Do you ever find yourself understanding your friends' families better than they seem to themselves? Describe this. How many new insights into minority relations did Collins and Merton generate for you? Identify some of them. Whose thinking do you find the most useful in your current or future research of ethnic or racial minorities?

For recent discussions of research in ethnic and race relations with helpful bibliographies, see John H. Stanfield II, ed., *Race and Ethnicity in Research Methods* and *A History of Race Relations Research,* both published by Sage (1993). See especially M. Andersen's "Studying Across Difference: Race, Class, and Gender in Qualitative Research," in *Race and Ethnicity in Research Methods.* An excellent dialogue between two prominent new generation Black scholars, which reflects some of Collins's ideas, can be found in *Breaking Bread: Insurgent Black Intellectual Life,* by bell hooks and Cornel West (South End Press, 1990).

For a stiumlating collection of essays predating Collins's ideas and to which Merton's article is a partial response, see *The Death of White Sociology,* edited by Joyce A. Ladner (Vintage Books, 1973). Jack Niemonen provides a relevant critical overview of several major racial and ethnic minorities texts in his "Some Observations on the Problem of Paradigms in Recent Racial and Ethnic Relations Texts," *Teaching Sociology* (July 1993).

ISSUE 2

Is the Concept of the Underclass Useful for Studying Race and Ethnic Relations?

YES: William Julius Wilson, from *The Truly Disadvantaged: The Inner City, the Underclass, and Public Policy* (University of Chicago Press, 1987)

NO: José Hernández, from "Latino Alternatives to the Underclass Concept," *Latino Studies Journal* (January 1990)

ISSUE SUMMARY

YES: University of Chicago sociologist and president of the American Sociological Association William Julius Wilson insists that factors such as the shift of heavy manufacturing industries out of cities, the movement of the middle classes out of the cities, and the segregation and isolation of many of the people who remain have all contributed to the decay of poorer urban areas. This has created a permanent underclass or urban poor, who are often neglected by policymakers and researchers.

NO: Hunter College Black and Puerto Rican studies professor José Hernández rejects the term *underclass* as just another example of dominant group efforts to denigrate and humiliate the poor. He feels that when the term is applied to any category of people, and especially to Latinos, it is inaccurate and charged with negative connotations.

Human beings are unique in having a complicated symbolic system of communication known as language, and throughout this century, the importance of the words we use has been emphasized by philosophers and social scientists. Language can both liberate and imprison people.

Traditionally, almost all Western scholars in the recent past supported the importance of free expression in a democratic society and the right to the free exchange of opinion. But these days, some humanists and social scientists challenge that. They insist that words can cause psychological damage and humiliation. Thus, they argue, it is imperative to be sensitive to terms used, especially if they could function to belittle some category of people.

In theory, scientific writing avoids conceptual confusions and ideological biases. Scientific language is expected to be concise, operationalistic (or measurable), and universal. The baggage of ideological biases, political correctness or incorrectness, emotionality, and so on should be shed the minute a scientist-scholar focuses on an issue. No matter how controversial the topic, the terms used in an analysis of it should not be insulting or laudatory but instead neutral and clarifying.

University of Chicago sociologist and former president of the American Sociological Association William J. Wilson argues that scholars over the past twenty-five years have tiptoed evasively around the realities of the urban poor.

Based on his extensive research, Wilson proposes that these people, through no fault of their own, constitute a permanent underclass. Their poverty, hopelessness, welfare dependency, high rates of teenage pregnancies, lack of education, and exposure to crime and violence are perpetuated from generation to generation.

Wilson wants to know this: If a significant number of the urban poor are a permanent underclass that has readily distinguishable attributes, then why not say so? At the very least, he feels, such knowledge would enable policymakers to better assist them. Why not identify the urban poor as such, then?

Professor José Hernández, of the Department of Black and Puerto Rican Studies at Hunter College, says that such classifications contain empirical inaccuracies and ideological distortions. Furthermore, such designations perpetuate feelings of inferiority among racial and ethnic minorities while propping up feelings of superiority among dominant group members. Pointing out that even the terms used to identify minorities (e.g., American Indians, Hispanics) can have negative connotations, he suggests that a better understanding of minority groups and impoverished people could be gained by using the terms *entitlement* and *empowerment*.

Entitlement simply has to do with the rights that minorities have by virtue of being citizens. The denial of these rights should be the source of investigation, according to Hernández, not an opportunity to negatively label the ethnic or racial victims of oppression. Empowerment has to do with coalition formation and self-help among minorities. "Perhaps the greatest barrier to Latino empowerment today is a popular movement inspired by the underclass concept," Hernández argues.

As you are reading Wilson and Hernández, recall what you've learned about science, objectivity, and what sort of influence a scholar's position in the social structure might have on who he or she studies and on how the study is conducted. Does Wilson feel that liberal scholars have been free of ideological biases in their research of the urban poor? As you read Wilson, consider this: If real problems are ignored or de-emphasized in order to avoid offending people, how might that research be harmful for subjects?

As you read Hernández, note the different issues he is simultaneously addressing (e.g., colonization, slavery, prejudice, and discrimination). Does he seem to treat Latinos as a homogeneous group (does he group Latinos all together), or does he reflect awareness of real differentials in Hispanic accomplishments and poverty?

YES

William Julius Wilson

CYCLES OF DEPRIVATION AND THE GHETTO UNDERCLASS DEBATE

In the mid-1960s, urban analysts began to speak of a new dimension to the urban crisis in the form of a large subpopulation of low-income families and individuals whose behavior contrasted sharply with the behavior of the general population. Despite a high rate of poverty in ghetto neighborhoods throughout the first half of the twentieth century, rates of inner-city joblessness, teenage pregnancies, out-of-wedlock births, female-headed families, welfare dependency, and serious crime were significantly lower than in later years and did not reach catastrophic proportions until the mid-1970s.

... There was crime, to be sure, but it had not reached the point where people were fearful of walking the streets at night, despite the overwhelming poverty in the area. There was joblessness, but it was nowhere near the proportions of unemployment and labor-force nonparticipation that have gripped ghetto communities since 1970. There were single-parent families, but they were a small minority of all black families and tended to be incorporated within extended family networks and to be headed not by unwed teenagers and young adult women but by middle-aged women who usually were widowed, separated, or divorced. There were welfare recipients, but only a very small percentage of the families could be said to be welfare-dependent. In short, unlike the present period, inner-city communities prior to 1960 exhibited the features of social organization—including a sense of community, positive neighborhood identification, and explicit norms and sanctions against aberrant behavior.

... [T]he only study that provided at least an abstract sense of how the problem had changed down through the years was the Moynihan report on the Negro family, which presented decennial census statistics on changing family structure by race.

However, the controversy surrounding the Moynihan report had the effect of curtailing serious research on minority problems in the inner city for over a decade, as liberal scholars shied away from researching behavior construed as unflattering or stigmatizing to particular racial minorities. Thus, when liberal scholars returned to study these problems in the early 1980s, they were dumbfounded by the magnitude of the changes that had taken place and expressed little optimism about finding an adequate explanation. Indeed, it had become quite clear that there was little consensus on the description of the problem, the explanations advanced, or the policy recommendations proposed. There was even little agreement on a definition of the term *underclass.* . . .

[D]espite pious claims about objectivity in social research, it is true that values influence not only our selection of problems for investigation but also our interpretation of empirical data. And although there are no logical rules of discovery that would invalidate an explanation simply because it was influenced by a particular value premise or ideology, it is true that attempts to arrive at a satisfactory explanation may be impeded by ideological blinders or views restricted by value premises. The solution to this problem is not to try to divest social investigators of their values but to encourage a free and open discussion of the issues among people with different value premises in order that new questions can be raised, existing interpretations challenged, and new research stimulated.

I believe that the demise of the liberal perspective on the ghetto underclass has made the intellectual discourse on this topic too one-sided. It has made it more difficult to achieve the above objective and has ultimately made it less likely that our understanding of inner-city social dislocations will be enhanced. . . .

THE DECLINING INFLUENCE OF THE LIBERAL PERSPECTIVE ON THE GHETTO UNDERCLASS

The liberal perspective on the ghetto underclass has become less persuasive and convincing in public discourse principally because many of those who represent traditional liberal views on social issues have been reluctant to discuss openly or, in some instances, even to acknowledge the sharp increase in social pathologies in ghetto communities. . . .

Regardless of which term is used, one cannot deny that there is a heterogeneous grouping of inner-city families and individuals whose behavior contrasts sharply with that of mainstream America. The real challenge is not only to explain why this is so, but also to explain why the behavior patterns in the inner city today differ so markedly from those of only three or four decades ago. To obscure these differences by eschewing the term *underclass,* or some other term that could be helpful in describing changes in ghetto behavior, norms, and aspirations, in favor of more neutral designations such as *lower class* or *working class* is to fail to address one of the most important social transformations in recent United States history.

. . . Today's ghetto neighborhoods are populated almost exclusively by the most disadvantaged segments of the black urban community, that heterogeneous grouping of families and individuals who are outside the mainstream of the American occupational system. Included in this group are individuals who lack training and skills and either experience long-term unemployment or are not members of the labor force, individuals who are engaged in street crime and other forms of aberrant behavior, and families that experience long-term spells of poverty and/or welfare dependence. These are the populations to which I refer when I speak of the *underclass*. I use this term to depict a reality not captured in the more standard designation *lower class*.

In my conception, the term *underclass* suggests that changes have taken place in ghetto neighborhoods, and the groups that have been left behind are collectively different from those that lived in these neighborhoods in earlier years. It is true that long-term welfare families and street criminals are distinct groups, but they live and interact in the same depressed community and they are part of the population that has, with the exodus of the more stable working- and middle-class segments, become increasingly isolated socially from mainstream patterns and norms of behavior. It is also true that certain groups are stigmatized by the label *underclass*, just as some people who live in depressed central-city communities are stigmatized by the term *ghetto* or *inner city*, but it would be far worse to obscure the profound changes in the class structure and social behavior of ghetto neighborhoods by avoiding the use of the term *underclass*. Indeed, the real challenge is to describe and explain these developments accurately so that liberal policymakers can appropriately address them. And it is difficult for me to see how this can be accomplished by rejecting a term that aids in the description of ghetto social transformations....

In sum, the liberal perspective on the ghetto underclass and inner-city social dislocations is less persuasive and influential in public discourse today because many of those who represent the traditional liberal views on social issues have failed to address straightforwardly the rise of social pathologies in the ghetto. As I have attempted to show, some liberals completely avoid any discussion of these problems, some eschew terms such as *underclass*, and others embrace selective evidence that denies the very existence of an underclass and behavior associated with the underclass or rely on the convenient term *racism* to account for the sharp rise in the rates of social dislocation in the inner city....

THE INCREASING INFLUENCE OF THE CONSERVATIVE PERSPECTIVE ON THE UNDERCLASS

If the most forceful and influential arguments on the ghetto underclass in the 1960s were put forth by liberals, conservative arguments have moved to the forefront in the 1980s, even though they have undergone only slight modification since the 1960s. Indeed, many students of social behavior recognize that the conservative thesis represents little more than the application of the late Oscar Lewis's culture-of-poverty arguments to the ghetto underclass. Relying on participant observation and life-history data to analyze Latin American poverty, Lewis described the culture of poverty as "both an adaptation and a reaction of the poor to their marginal position in a class stratified, highly individuated, capitalistic society. However, he also noted that once the culture of poverty comes into existence, "it tends to perpetuate itself from generation to generation because of its effect on the children. By the time slum children are age six or seven," argued Lewis, "they have usually absorbed the basic values and attitudes of their subculture and are not psychologically geared to take full advantage of changing conditions or increased opportunities which may occur in their life-time."

Although Lewis was careful to point out that basic structural changes in society may alter some of the cultural characteristics of the poor, conservative students of inner-city poverty who have built on his thesis have focused almost exclusively on the interconnection between cultural traditions, family history, and individual character. For example, they have argued that a ghetto family that has had a history of welfare dependency will tend to bear offspring who lack ambition, a work ethic, and a sense of self-reliance. Some even suggest that ghetto underclass individuals have to be rehabilitated culturally before they can advance in society....

CONCLUSION: TOWARD A REFOCUSED LIBERAL PERSPECTIVE

If the liberal perspective on the ghetto underclass is to regain the influence it has lost since the 1960s, it will be necessary to do more than simply react to what conservative scholars and policymakers are saying. Liberals will also have to propose thoughtful explanations of the rise in inner-city social dislocations. Such explanations should emphasize the dynamic interplay between ghetto-specific cultural characteristics and social and economic opportunities. This would necessitate taking into account the effects not only of changes in American economic organization but also of demographic changes and changes in the laws and policies of the government as well. In this connection, the relationships between joblessness and family structure, joblessness and other social dislocations (crime, teenage pregnancy, welfare dependency, etc.), and joblessness and

social orientation among different age-groups would receive special attention.

However, thoughtful explanations of the recent rise in the problems of the underclass depend on careful empirical research. It is not sufficient to rely solely on census data and other secondary sources. Liberals will have to augment such information with empirical data on the ghetto underclass experience and on conditions in the broader society that have shaped and continue to shape that experience. This calls for a number of different research strategies ranging from survey to ethnographic to historical.

But first, liberals will have to change the way they have tended to approach this subject in recent years. They can no longer afford to be timid in addressing these problems, to debate whether or not concepts such as the *underclass* should even be used, to look for data to deny the very existence of an underclass, or, finally, to rely heavily on the easy explanation of racism.

These are my suggestions for refocusing the liberal perspective. It will not be easy and there is a lot of work to be done. But such an effort is needed if we are to provide a more balanced public discourse on the problems of the ghetto underclass.... I follow these suggestions in an attempt to describe the growing problems of urban social dislocations in the inner city, explain why these problems sharply increased when they did and in the way that they did, and then use this analysis to suggest a comprehensive policy agenda that moves beyond race-specific issues to confront more fundamental problems associated with changes in advanced industrial society, changes that have had a significant impact on life and experience in the inner city.

NO

José Hernández

LATINO ALTERNATIVES TO THE UNDERCLASS CONCEPT

In recent times an "underclass" concept has been used by some writers for analyzing and explaining the Latino situation in the United States. According to these writers, some Chicanos and most Puerto Ricans are trapped in the economic bottom of American society, either by discrimination and declining opportunities or their lack of ability and motivation, or both. Unlike most of the underclass literature (which is oriented to quantitative evaluations of life conditions and public policy), this essay is concerned with the significance of the concept, especially as an expression of ideologies inspiring its use in regard to Latinos. My first purpose is to uncover the historical roots of the underclass concept in the much broader field of Latino-Anglo relations in America. The considerations presented here began in discussions among Latino Studies scholars who wonder why the underclass concept became so popular in the 1980s, and worry about its use in supporting a negative social construction of the Latino situation. Typically, what is said in particular about Puerto Ricans is projected to all Latinos, either by implication or comparisons aiming to measure the characteristics of Latinos belonging to an underclass in the other nationality groups. These applications of the concept originated in an effort to explain why some Americans of African descent have been successful, while others remain in poverty. Writers developing the underclass concept at least implicitly assert that any group must be labeled with underclass attributes, if it includes a sizable segment of persons not conforming with American majority (or Anglo middle-class) expectations of economic and social behavior. Because this so closely resembles past instances of inequality resulting from negative group concepts, we conclude that the underclass concept manifests a historical trend of subordination, supported by group labels devised by the dominant class. Experience from current use also shows that the underclass concept is used by certain writers, the media, and politicians to justify an intensified discrimination of Latinos.

My second purpose is to call for positive concepts of use in explaining the Latino situation, concepts more validly grounded in our historical and contemporary reality, and more reliable as guides to analysis and interpre-

From José Hernández, "Latino Alternatives to the Underclass Concept," *Latino Studies Journal* (January 1990). Copyright © 1990 by José Hernández. Reprinted by permission of the author.

tation without stigma. I propose entitlement and empowerment as a pair of concepts, the first for our relation to the American "system" or structure of political, economic, and social institutions, the other for our identity, life and organization as a national collectivity.

By entitlement is meant the fulfillment of the rightful expectations of a people admitted to citizenship by a nation, as expressed in laws, treaties and understandings, and as an ongoing reality of well-being and harmonious relations with other citizens. Empowerment is a personal and group process to gain power, or the ability to be self-determining and to influence others. Empowerment is used here in regard to civic reform and actions that bring about entitlement. Both concepts will be further defined and illustrated in application to Latinos.

HISTORICAL ANTECEDENTS

The peoples of Arizona, California, Colorado, New Mexico, and Texas shared the Latin American dream of independence from Spain, along with those of Cuba, Filipinas, Guam, Puerto Rico and Santo Domingo—all colonies for 300 years in the Viceroyalty of New Spain, or Mexico. Most Latinos in the U.S. today descend from these peoples, and in various ways embody the racial and cultural blends that gave rise to Latinismo, a revolutionary sense of peoplehood and an assertion of emancipation from Spanish colonial oppression. In their beginnings, Latinismo resembled American values of freedom, equality and prosperity—national ideals supporting the independence struggle with Great Britain. By the early 1800s, a conservative ideology was gaining power in the

United States. As it developed in that century, this belief system made use of the "manifest destiny" concept. The concept provided a reason for public actions contrary to the values of freedom, equality and prosperity for all human beings within the U.S. geopolitical domain. It assumed that lands west of the Appalachians were to be conquered by white Anglo Americans, a race and culture chosen by God as superior to those of the local residents. For this purpose, deceit, coercion and violence were justified in ways easily understood and supported by ordinary citizens. According to the conservative ideology, the resources gained were divinely destined to enrich the Anglos, and the conquered peoples to serve as cheap labor in development. The U.S. war with Mexico (1845–48) and with Spain (1898) took place at times when this ideology was strong, and were actions inspired by the manifest destiny concept. As a result, Latinos entered the U.S. labeled as destined by God to work for only food, shelter and basic needs, and Latinismo was repressed an an enemy system of thought, contrary to American values.

INSTITUTIONAL SUBORDINATION AND INFERIOR CITIZENSHIP

The conquering Anglo Americans perpetuated the consequences of war by establishing institutions of subordination. A civilian occupation used the manifest destiny concept in laws, organizations and rules which assumed Anglo superiority and Latino inferiority as a basic principle governing everyday behavior. The wishes of the powerful and rich were identified with conservative ideology, converting everything dominant and Anglo into objects of patriotism.

This confused a partisan ideology and the spoils of conquest with the basic values supporting the establishment of the United States. When Latinos refused to talk and act as Anglo Americans, they were further labeled as alien and subversive. The penalties for trying to break out of their conquered and subordinate position made it clear that freedom, equality and prosperity applied to Anglos only, as the "real" or dominant-class citizens. History shows that this caste-like division became more rigid with time, and gave shape to the historical Latino experience of discrimination, deprivation and poverty.

This pattern was sanctioned by Anglo politicians as the "right" way of conducting the nation's affairs. Institutional subordination evolved into inferior citizenship, as the colonial peoples of New Spain became colonial subjects of the U.S. in detrimental ways that closely resembled treatment of the original peoples called "American Indians," and Africans enslaved by the Anglo system. From this background came the pauperization now called "underclass" as a contemporary label.

In Puerto Rico, for example, Americanization meant that public schools obliged children to learn only things about the Anglo United States, in English. It made education a harsh reality of humiliation, distaste, boredom, and failure for most Puerto Ricans, and alienated generations of talent from 1898 to the 1950s. Along with other aspects of American colonial rule, this intensified poverty and produced life conditions that made the world look as if migration to cheap-labor jobs in the United States was the lower classes' only chance for survival.

The rights of young Chicano citizens were flagrantly disregarded in the Pachucho violence of the early 1940s, and the contributions of Chicano servicemen to World War II were largely ignored in the granting of social and economic rewards. The resulting stigma severely reduced Chicano opportunities to participate in the prosperity experienced by most Anglo Americans during the postwar period, and further strengthened their image as undeserving outsiders to the U.S. distribution of recognition and wealth, when the massive Anglo middle class was formed.

LIBERAL IDEOLOGY PRODUCED NEW CONCEPTS AND SOME CHANGES

In the 1960s Puerto Ricans in the U.S. and Chicanos were portrayed as victims of racism and internal colonization by a literature oriented to liberal ideological concepts brought back from the times of the Bill of Rights, Reconstruction and the New Deal. The same concepts inspired institutional changes allowing for a limited exit from subordination and inferior citizenship, to conditions stipulated for "minorities" as an entitled segment of the nation's population. With leadership from the Rev. Martin Luther King, Jr., Cesar Chaves, and many other progressive Americans, we began to experience hope for freedom, a sense of belonging and inclusion on an equality basis, and a determination to improve our life conditions in positive ways.

That period passed much too quickly, however, for Latinos to gain a genuine enfranchisement. Our participation in the political, economic and social life of the nation followed on policy decisions made by others, and our opinions had a very limited influence, if at all. Among the American people, Latinos were not viewed as a national collectivity in need of public consideration on its own terms. Instead, we were the Chicanos in Los Angeles and San Antonio, the Puerto Ricans in New York and Chicago, the Hispanos in New Mexico, the Cubans in Miami, and so on. We were small and scattered Spanish-speaking groups, vaguely alien people, and disadvantaged, yes. But as a remedy, we were told to somehow "fit into" the minority policies, and be quietly integrated by acculturation in someone else's program for a "New Frontier" or a "Great Society."

As a result, our original situations of institutional subordination and inferior citizenship became incidental to the stigma of being different from the mainstream. We were simply redefined according to the "cultural deprivation" concept long instilled as an Anglo explanation for justifying the Latino subordinate and inferior condition, made part of the liberal ideology as an easy response to the challenge in our agenda. Americanization then became a measure of modernization, liberation, and belonging to a society in which acceptance and equality could be found in respect for racial diversity, only. Latino culture, despoiled of its meaning for peoplehood and values, was allowed some legitimate but token expressions: as an aid in learning English through bilingual education, and as another heritage in a panoply of ethnic residues, to be displayed in occasional, symbolic ways. To so many of us disappointed by such a blundering and inadequate solution, the writers, the media and the politicians all promised a better world in the "Decade of the Hispanics," the 1980s.

THE UNDERCLASS CONCEPT SURFACES

A return to the conservative ideology inspiring the manifest destiny concept concurred with a rebirth of American capitalism in the 1980s, when services and consumerism replaced manufacturing as a basis for the nation's economy. Self-righteous and preclusive thinking, domination for economic gain, racial and cultural superiority, all seemed matterof-fact again to those pleased with this transition, and successful in the political, economic and social reforms.

To liberals concerned with the costs of the capitalist revival—an enormous external debt, a devalued currency, a damaged ecosystem, the decline of unionism, structural unemployment— the times resembled previous conservative periods. To the homeless, the destitute and working poor, those displaced by factory closings—in sum, the groups and persons rejected, the 1980s were an era of economic subordination as an "underclass."

Once again, the popular rationale called for the refurbishing of military strength, patriotism, and religious moralism. Instead of conquering more territory, however, the manifest destiny aimed at displaying power in competition with the Soviet Union, and in control of nations considered part of the American geopolitical domain. In "el patio del Tío Sam" (the U.S. backyard in Central America and the Caribbean) the agenda resembled that of Presidents Polk and McKinley in the wars with Mexico and Spain.

This time, the manifest destiny was fortified by the American outreach in telecommunication, tourism and cheap-labor manufacturing. An advanced civilization—doing God's will—would enlighten the natives with values superior to their quaint and primitive cultures, by television programs. It would acquaint them with Americans as customers at vacation facilities that re-create the Anglo culture in the tropics, and the U.S. would be assured of their loyalty in factories assembling items formerly produced in the United States at much higher labor costs. As in Puerto Rico with Operation Bootstrap, people left out of progress were encouraged (in this case by the new immigration) to join the United States population, many destined to an underclass status.

Within the United States, white Anglo elitism showed renewed strengthened conformity with the styles and ideas of the educated and affluent, making acculturation to the majority a universal value. In the public eye, the opposite was often identified with Latinos, whose appearance and language contradicted the norm and indicated lower school and economic standing.

Rapid growth in numbers, physical mobility, the continual arrival of immigrants, and a diversity of nationalities sharpened the contrast with Anglos and changed the Latino public image from a localized minority to a national aggregate, somehow "new," and very different. "Hispanic" became conventional in government and media, with a dictionary meaning of Americans of Spanish colonial origin, and many worthy applications according to the meaning. But in common use it often remained "hiSPanIC," a euphemism of the acronym "SPIC" (SPanish + Indian + Colored): a long-ago label in Anglo street language for a racial mix so inferior and at odds with the dominant culture, as to deserve an underclass treatment in everyday life. This became the ultimate impact of the group label and the concept so often used to explain our situation.

LATINO ENTITLEMENT

Although many changes in concepts have obscured our history, most Latinos remain U.S. citizens in descent from peoples conquered by American and made citizens as a result of war, treaties and legislation. We have an understanding of how we became part of a nation established to support freedom, equality and prosperity—regardless of race and culture, and regardless of conservative and liberal ideologies. Latinos aware of this heritage believe that our entitlement implies a public commitment to compensate for damages of conquest, institutional subordination, inferior citizenship, cultural deprivation, and most lately, an underclass status.

The basic compensation of entitlement is embodied in support for cultural (in addition to racial) diversity, and in respect for ourselves and our values as equally constituent of America. Secondly, civic reform and action mean replacing the underclass tradition and the bad life conditions it has inspired with improvement through institutional change—not "band-aid" programs that make America look good, but do little to really heal the wounds and make Latinos a genuine part of the nation.

In other words, entitlement means to find out how freedom, equality and prosperity can happen for Latinos, and to make this an effective part of our daily life. Immigrants who have joined our communities generally share our wishes to attain the benefits of the peace and happiness promised to all U.S. citizens on an equality basis, making entitlement a fundamental goal of our collectivity, regardless of nationality or citizenship origin.

Until the 1980s our efforts to gain entitlement relied mainly on proving "how bad conditions are," in hopes that Anglo America would have pity on us and provide a remedy for inequality. Many things were gained, especially as the public conscience was stirred to take action in civil rights legislation, policies and programs that gave us an initial but limited participation in the means of reaching success in the American system. These remain an important way in which Latinos find opportunity in America, our only foothold on entitlement having some kind of public legitimacy.

Such changes have benefited only a small number of people, however. In general, the culture and living conditions of Latinos remain in the underclass situation of our conquered peoples in the United States, such as American Indians and native Hawaiians. Whatever the multivariate analyses may show, we know this to be the product of nationwide patterns of massive ignorance, neglect and discrimination. Our daily experience of unfair practices in schools and at work tell us that American institutions are still geared to firmly keep the underclass down and out. One does not have to read and write in English to be convinced by what happens in everyday life that the Anglo American willingness to change is hardly enough to make entitlement real for all Latinos.

LATINO EMPOWERMENT

An ancient concept now called empowerment relies on our own strength, instead, as the principal agent of change. It assumes that along with discrimination and exclusion in education, jobs, and money, an obstacle to equality is a negative self-vision.

Institutional subordination included the learning of stereotypes produced and supported by Anglo Americans as a routine way of thinking. People, events and the ordering of life consistently told us that we were inferior, ugly and unwanted. In time, we were persuaded to believe these stereotypes and act according to the conservative ideology underlying the manifest destiny concept—*nos tragamos el cuento* (we swallowed the fairy tale), although if asked about it, we tend to deny the influence. Eventually, we took our inferior citizenship, our cultural deprivation and our underclass status for granted.

A negative self-image blocks our use of power, defined as the ability to be self-determining and to influence others. It tends to make us Anglo-determined and preserves our underclass bondage. It deprives us of the chance to turn adversity into advantage, by wasting our potential to change the environment. It defeats us at home, by keeping us from defining our needs and desires in positive ways, and from convincing other Americans to change their ideologies and concepts, so as to make our entitlement goals attainable in everyday life.

Empowerment is a personal and group process to gain freedom from mental and practical forms of repression in being labeled as subordinate, inferior, culturally deprived and underclass. As persons move from a negative to a positive self-vision, they gain strength to solve their own problems and help others in the same stigmatized situation.

As a group gains strength, unity comes about and enables an originally conquered people to influence the dominant in society, replace negative images with favorable attitudes, improve life conditions, and eventually, reach equality. *Un pueblo unido jamas sera vencido* (an united people will never be defeated)—in unity we will find the power for entitlement.

All of this can be developed in political, economic and social ways that benefit the entire population. The many groups that exist among Latinos can increase their empowerment by networking their efforts, forming coalitions and seeking entitlement as a national collectivity. As Latino entitlement is gained, the basic values of freedom, equality and prosperity in American society will be revitalized, for all citizens. These are the founding United States values, and not a necessity to sustain poverty and alienation for the benefit of the Anglo middle class.

OBSTACLES TO EMPOWERMENT AND ENTITLEMENT

Perhaps the greatest barrier to Latino empowerment today is a popular movement inspired by the underclass concept as a master policy idea. It assumes white, Anglo images as normative and positive, and treats brown, Latino images as alien and negative, by default. We are vulnerable to accept this social construction of identity because our principal weakness is ignorance of our self-worth, first as citizens entitled to freedom, equality, and prosperity, and secondly as a people with a great inborn potential and a wealth of values from European, American Indian and African sources, useful in giving shape and guidance to our empowerment and entitlement.

Many follow the Anglo concepts and ignore empowerment, thinking that to be Hispanic means to like certain types of food, popular music, and external symbols—and, of course, to keep our place in society. We are often unwilling to seek the inner meaning of identity and empower ourselves, because everywhere the mentality instilled by the underclass concept tells us that to be Hispanic is a status of shame.

To assuage the anxiety over the Anglo demand for drugs, we are targeted as the primary agent of supply, and the "cause of the problem." We are further stereotyped as vandals, thieves, rapists, and "illegal aliens" who have escalated American's law enforcement problems. Our families are said to menace public well-being with the prospect of population growth. A national drive aims to amend the Constitution to make English America's only language, getting rid of Spanish, by official intention. Our youth are singled out as the least successful in a school system far from adequate in meeting their needs, but still safely on top in political power. In sum, we have become the scapegoat for the negative feelings of the new conservative era.

The governmental, philanthropic and academic elite have contributed wealth and work to validate the underclass concept in supposedly objective ways that serve to justify its consequences. This has provided a rationale for shame, and a denial of the public recognition and support we need for entitlement, just as religious beliefs once supported the manifest destiny.

Much effort has been made to study the underclass, how many of us belong, certain predefined life features recorded in a quick questionnaire, and volumes of secondary data—all thought to explain why we remain in poverty and cause trouble. But no one bothers to examine the Anglo institutions that we must deal with on an everyday basis. Few social scientists make an effort to listen and learn what is really happening in our communities, how we feel about life in America. Instead of directing minds to figure out how entitlement can be made a living reality, how Latino people can succeed in adversity, and how our culture can serve us to get out of the underclass, the Anglo establishment produces negative information that generally serves to further stigmatize us.

These "facts" receive final approval in statements supported by either functionalist or marxist theories still in vogue. Of course, the conclusions differ. But regardless of functionalist or marxist orientation, all assume that Latinos are an inevitable underclass in American society. Packaged in buzzwords for Anglo telecommunication, the functionalist or marxist conclusions then become the gist of conservative or liberal ideology, rationales for policies that leave us where we always have been, a stigmatized group of (originally conquered and now underclass) citizens, with no real entitlement.

A LATINO STUDIES RESPONSE

Our mission is to provide an alternative vision: an indigenous and original discipline that answers the universal questions posed by the humanities and social sciences, with positive concepts and valid knowledge of what it means to be a Latino. We need to build on what Chicano, Puerto Rican and other Latino Studies have accomplished in setting forth an intellectual basis for a very different future. Although much has been done already, the work is still in its infancy, depending on the few scholars willing to risk their careers in being critical or proposing new ideas, and in joining an effort (which like our people)

has been stigmatized in the historical trends described.

The now 20 million Latinos want a positive, progressive and motivating rationale for their success and recognition in American society. Our most critical need is for research and writing about Latino values and their usefulness to enable people to gain a positive self-image and achieve rewarding goals. This means that Latino Studies and similar efforts must serve empowerment and entitlement purposes as agents for redressing the negative effects of the stigma, and for developing effective means of resolving the cultural lag presently visible in our exclusion from the American system.

For many years we have known that many Latinos are poor. Let's find out how we can gain a decent life-style with dignity! The underground economy exists, for sure. Why not learn how Latino business skills can develop legitimate ways to earn a living and employ other Latinos? Anyone who is idle in the *barrio* will tell you that factory work is declining. But who can tell a "discouraged" worker how to find a good job? These questions must be answered, if we want out of the underclass in which many intellectuals, the media and politicians would like to keep us.

New policy directions must include the strength of Latino culture: the familism and humanism of the Indian and African traditions, the importance of team work and cooperation for group success, and the virtues of patience, courage and vitality. From the Spanish tradition, we must stress self-reliance, dedication, politeness, and respect for our own and other authority.

Such are the qualities that describe many successful Latinos, those seldom studied in Anglo social science, or written about by literary authors and journalists inspired by the underclass concept. Our task must be to enable most Latinos to discover these positive values in their lives through knowledge and appreciation of their history, culture, literature and expressive arts.

In addition, we have a uniquely vital role in developing a collective representation of our contributions to American society. Latino culture can provide an enormous gain for the United States in such values as respect and compassion for others, idealism and optimism. It can give "heart" to a society strongly oriented toward values of individualism, competition and winning at the expense of others. Latino culture can offer humanism to an economy in which "never is enough" for monetary wealth, material comfort and practicality—except, of course, for the underclass losers. It can correct for Anglo American political messianism, the belief that English and white are not just superior to all else, but the sources of solutions to all of the world's problems.

By growing to maturity and in appeal to Anglos, Latino Studies will show that an eventual state of genuine equality in the United States will have emerged from an Anglo acculturation to Latino culture.

POSTSCRIPT

Is the Concept of the Underclass Useful for Studying Race and Ethnic Relations?

The more you formally study ethnic and racial minority controversial issues, the more you begin to realize the multiple levels of reality that exist. Not only must you be able to specifically identify a group, count or measure them (how many, how old, how educated, how impoverished), and determine the consequences of the problem in order to know what policies to recommend, you must also be able to explain and defend the terms you use in studying a group.

Sociologists Douglas Massey and Nancy Denton, in their book *American Apartheid: Segregation and the Making of the Underclass* (Harvard University Press, 1993), present several pages of statistics that they conclude largely refute Wilson: "Residential segregation is the principal structural feature of American society responsible for the perpetuation of urban poverty."

Still others provide a very different kind of argument, which is that, since World War II, and in spite of setbacks in the 1980s, minority peoples have experienced important gains. Sociologist and political scientist Seymour Lipset thinks that this is so. See his "Two Americas, Two Value Systems: Blacks and Whites," in *Social Theory and Social Policy*, edited by A. Sørensen and S. Spilerman (Praeger, 1993).

As editor Bill E. Lawson observed, there is virtually a cottage industry devoted to churning out books and articles on every side of this controversy on the underclass. Among the earlier works, see Ken Auletta, *The Underclass* (Vintage, 1982) and D. Glasgow, *The Black Underclass* (Random House, 1981). More recent studies include *The Urban Underclass*, edited by C. Jencks and P. Peterson (Brookings Institute, 1991) and B. Lawson, ed., *The Underclass Question* (Temple University Press, 1992). For another review of the terms used in this debate, see G. Rolison's "An Exploration of the Term *Underclass* as It Relates to African Americans," *Journal of Black Studies* (March 1991). Another University of Chicago sociologist, but one who sides with Hernández, is Herbert Gans. In *The Chronicle of Education*, "Fighting the Biases Embedded in Social Concepts of the Poor" (January 8, 1992), he dismisses the term *underclass* as "nasty."

41

ISSUE 3

Are Asian Americans a "Model Minority"?

YES: David A. Bell, from "America's Greatest Success Story: The Triumph of Asian-Americans," *The New Republic* (July 15 and 22, 1985)

NO: Ronald Takaki, from *Strangers from a Different Shore: A History of Asian Americans* (Little, Brown, 1989)

ISSUE SUMMARY

YES: Journalist and historian David Bell reflects on the current, frequently expressed enthusiasm for the successes of Asian Americans that appears in the mass media. Although he acknowledges some difficulties and hurdles faced by Asian Americans, Bell nevertheless portrays the road taken by Asian Americans as "America's greatest success story."

NO: University of California-Berkeley historian Ronald Takaki faults the mass media and some ethnic studies scholars for misunderstanding the statistics and examples used as "proof" that Asians are a model minority. Takaki argues that within Asian groups there are vast differences in success, and he reviews the prejudice and exploitation experienced by Asian Americans.

In the study of ethnic and racial minorities, myths play a fantastically important role. They enter society in many ways and forms. Frequently, oppressed peoples develop myths about a distant past when they were in a better situation and/or were the dominant group. Members of dominant or oppressor groups also create myths. These range from myths that extoll their own so-called superiority (and hence justify the exploitation of others) to mythical images of subordinate peoples. The latter are almost inevitably negative and sometimes form the basis of stereotypes.

In this century, science has been frequently used to create and/or maintain negative myths about people. For example, Nazi biology imputed superiority to Aryans and inferiority to others (e.g., Gypsies, Jews) based on genes and race. The terrible ways in which the physiological and biological sciences were used to generate mythical theories of ethnic and/or racial superiorities and inferiorities is well known. However, the possible use of the social sciences for allegedly the same purposes is considerably more complicated and controversial.

In this issue, the problems associated with mythmaking and minority status assume a new and more abstract twist. Citing abundant sources and studies, including professional scholarship and the mass media, David Bell argues that Asian Americans are a model minority. He is not the creator of this label (or mythical stereotype, if we believe Takaki). But he does summarize it, present facts to support it, and, in his enthusiasm, clearly adds to it.

By contrast, historian Ronald Takaki, frequently citing the same sources as Bell, insists that the public as well as social scientists have created the myth of Asian Americans as a "model minority" or an American success story. He sees continuing prejudice, often backed by violence, against Asian Americans. He is also disturbed by the indiscriminate grouping of Asian Americans. Southeast Asians as well as Hindus and others have had very different experiences, often less happy, than the Chinese and Japanese (in spite of the horrible treatment of the Chinese in the 1800s and the fact that Japanese Americans were interned as enemy aliens during World War II).

As you read Bell, carefully note the many examples he cites to prove that Asian Americans are a model minority. As you read Takaki, note the many examples he gives to show that it is a myth to label them a model minority. Who is correct? If both social scientists and the public, particularly the mass media, have created a myth, why do you think this is so? What might be its functions, in your opinion?

Be aware that within the United States ethnic and racial relations have been linked with immigration to a considerable degree. In recent years, this has become as important in many other countries as well (Part 4 in this book deals with these controversies in greater depth).

Essential to the manufacturing of stereotypes, myths, and prejudices about others is the language that is used to label them. (See also Issue 5.) The mass media contributes mightily to such labelling (see Issue 9). What negative labels are mentioned in these two articles? What terms have you heard? What information in these two articles, in spite of their disagreements, might you use in order to point out to those who use derogatory terms just how terrible and unfair and empirically inaccurate they are?

Both Bell and Takaki mention films that each one thinks has been grossly unfair to Asian Americans. Which have you seen? What were your reactions? What current films pertaining to Asian minorities are being shown? Exactly how do they portray Asians?

YES
David A. Bell

AMERICA'S GREATEST SUCCESS STORY:
THE TRIUMPH OF ASIAN-AMERICANS

It is the year 2019. In the heart of downtown Los Angeles, massive electronic billboards feature a model in a kimono hawking products labeled in Japanese. In the streets below, figures clad in traditional East Asian peasant garb hurry by, speaking to each other in an English made unrecognizable by the addition of hundreds of Spanish and Asian words. A rough-mannered policeman leaves an incongruously graceful calling card on a doorstep: a delicate origami paper sculpture.

This is, of course, a scene from a science-fiction movie, Ridley Scott's 1982 *Blade Runner.* It is also a vision that Asian-Americans dislike intensely. Hysterical warnings of an imminent Asian "takeover" of the United States stained a whole century of their 140-year history in this country, providing the backdrop for racial violence, legal segregation, and the internment of 110,000 Japanese-Americans in concentration camps during World War II. Today integration into American society, not transformation of American society, is the goal of an overwhelming majority. So why did the critics praise *Blade Runner* for its "realism"? The answer is easy to see.

The Asian-American population is exploding. According to the Census Bureau, it grew an astounding 125 percent between 1970 and 1980, and now stands at 4.1 million, or 1.8 percent of all Americans. Most of the increase is the result of immigration, which accounted for 1.8 million people between 1973 and 1983, the last year for which the Immigration and Naturalization Service has accurate figures (710,000 of these arrived as refugees from Southeast Asia). And the wave shows little sign of subsiding. Ever since the Immigration Act of 1965 permitted large-scale immigration by Asians, they have made up over 40 percent of all newcomers to the United States. Indeed, the arbitrary quota of 20,000 immigrants per country per year established by the act has produced huge backlogs of future Asian-Americans in several countries, including 120,000 in South Korea and 336,000 in the Philippines, some of whom, according to the State Department, have been waiting for their visas since 1970.

The numbers are astonishing. But even more astonishing is the extent to which Asian-Americans have become prominent out of all proportion to their share of the population. It now seems likely that their influx will have as important an effect on American society as the migration from Europe of 100 years ago. Most remarkable of all, it is taking place with relatively little trouble.

The new immigration from Asia is a radical development in several ways. First, it has not simply enlarged an existing Asian-American community, but created an entirely new one. Before 1965, and the passage of the Immigration Act, the term "Oriental-American" (which was then the vogue) generally denoted people living on the West Coast, in Hawaii, or in the Chinatowns of a few large cities. Generally they traced their ancestry either to one small part of China, the Toishan district of Kwantung province, or to a small number of communities in Japan (one of the largest of which, ironically, was Hiroshima). Today more than a third of all Asian-Americans live outside Chinatowns in the East, South, and Midwest, and their origins are as diverse as those of "European-Americans." The term "Asian-American" now refers to over 900,000 Chinese from all parts of China and also Vietnam, 800,000 Filipinos, 700,000 Japanese, 500,000 Koreans, 400,000 East Indians, and a huge assortment of everything else from Moslem Cambodians to Catholic Hawaiians. It can mean an illiterate Hmong tribesman or a fully assimilated graduate of the Harvard Business School.

Asian-Americans have also attracted attention by their new prominence in several professions and trades. In New York City, for example, where the Asian-American population jumped from 94,500 in 1970 to 231,500 in 1980, Korean-Americans run an estimated 900 of the city's 1,600 corner grocery stores. Filipino doctors—who outnumber black doctors—have become general practitioners in thousands of rural communities that previously lacked physicians. East Indian-Americans own 800 of California's 6,000 motels. And in parts of Texas, Vietnamese-Americans now control 85 percent of the shrimp-fishing industry, though they only reached this position after considerable strife (now the subject of a film, *Alamo Bay*).

Individual Asian-Americans have become quite prominent as well. I. M. Pei and Minoru Yamasaki have helped transform American architecture. Seiji Ozawa and Yo Yo Ma are giant figures in American music. An Wang created one of the nation's largest computer firms, and Rocky Aoki founded one of its largest restaurant chains (Benihana). Samuel C. C. Ting won a Nobel prize in physics.

* * *

Most spectacular of all, and most significant for the future, is the entry of Asian-Americans into the universities. At Harvard, for example, Asian-Americans ten years ago made up barely three percent of the freshman class. The figure is now ten percent—five times their share of the population. At Brown, Asian-American applications more than tripled over the same period, and at Berkeley they increased from 3,408 in 1982 to 4,235 only three years later. The Berkeley student body is now 22 percent Asian-American, UCLA's is 21 percent, and MIT's 19 percent. The Julliard School of Music in New York is currently 30 percent Asian and Asian-American. American medical schools had only 571 Asian-American students in 1970, but in 1980 they had 1,924, and last year 3,763, or 5.6 percent of total enrollment. What is more, nearly all of these figures are certain to increase. In the current, largely foreign-born Asian-American community, 32.9 percent of people over 25 graduated from college (as opposed to 16.2 percent in the general population). For third-generation Japanese-Americans, the figure is 88 percent.

By any measure these Asian-American students are outstanding. In California only the top 12.5 percent of high school students qualify for admission to the uppermost tier of the state university system, but 39 percent of Asian-American high school students do. On the SATs, Asian-Americans score an average of 519 in math, surpassing whites, the next highest group, by 32 points. Among Japanese-Americans, the most heavily native-born Asian-American group, 68 percent of those taking the math SAT scored above 600—high enough to qualify for admission to almost any university in the country. The Westinghouse Science Talent search, which each year identified 40 top high school science students, picked 12 Asian-Americans in 1983, nine last year, and seven this year. And at Harvard the Phi Beta Kappa chapter last April named as its elite "Junior Twelve" students five Asian-Americans and seven Jews.

* * *

Faced with these statistics, the understandable reflex of many non-Asian-Americans is adulation. President Reagan has called Asian-Americans "our exemplars of hope and inspiration." *Parade* magazine recently featured an article on Asian-Americans titled "The Promise of America," and *Time* and *Newsweek*

stories have boasted headlines like "A Formula for Success," "The Drive to Excel," and "A 'Model Minority.'" However, not all of these stories come to grips with the fact that Asian-Americans, like all immigrants, have to deal with a great many problems of adjustment, ranging from the absurd to the deadly serious.

Who would think, for example, that there is a connection between Asian-American immigration and the decimation of California's black bear population? But Los Angeles, whose Korean population grew by 100,000 in the past decade, now has more than 300 licensed herbal-acupuncture shops. And a key ingredient in traditional Korean herbal medicine is *ungdam*, bear gallbladder. The result is widespread illegal hunting and what *Audubon* magazine soberly called "a booming trade in bear parts."

As Mark R. Thompson recently pointed out in *The Wall Street Journal*, the clash of cultures produced by Asian immigration can also have vexing legal results. Take the case of Fumiko Kimura, a Japanese-American woman who tried to drown herself and her two children in the Pacific. She survived but the children did not, and she is now on trial for their murder. As a defense, her lawyers are arguing that parent-child suicide is a common occurrence in Japan. In Fresno, California, meanwhile, 30,000 newly arrived Hmong cause a different problem. "Anthropologists call the custom 'marriage by capture,'" Mr. Thompson writes. "Fresno police and prosecutors call it 'rape.'"

A much more serious problem for Asian-Americans is racial violence. In 1982 two unemployed whites in Detroit beat to death a Chinese-American named Vincent Chin, claiming that they wanted

(continued on p. 48)

ASIANS AND JEWS

Comparing the social success of Asian-Americans with that of the Jews is irresistible. Jews and Asians rank number one and number two, respectively, in median family income. In the Ivy League they are the two groups most heavily "over-represented" in comparison to their shares of the population. And observers are quick to point out all sorts of cultural parallels. As Arthur Rosen, the chairman of (appropriately) the National Committee on United States–China Relations, recently told *The New York Times*, "There are the same kind of strong family ties and the same sacrificial drive on the part of immigrant parents who couldn't get a college education to see that their children do."

In historical terms, the parallels can often be striking. For example, when Russian and Polish Jews came to this country in the late 19th and early 20th centuries, 60 percent of those who went into industry worked in the garment trade. Today thousands of Chinese-American women fill sweatshops in New York City doing the same work of stitching and sewing. In Los Angeles, when the Jews began to arrive in large numbers in the 1880s, 43 percent of them became retail or wholesale proprietors, according to Ivan Light's essay in *Clamor at the Gates*. One hundred years later, 40 percent of Koreans in Los Angeles are also wholesale and retail proprietors. The current controversy over Asian-American admission in Ivy League colleges eerily recalls the Jews' struggle to end quotas in the 1940s and 1950s.

In cultural terms, however, it is easy to take the comparison too far. American Jews remain a relatively homogeneous group, with a common religion and history. Asian-Americans, especially after the post-1965 flood of immigrants, are exactly the opposite. They seem homogeneous largely because they share some racial characteristics. And even those vary widely. The label "Chinese-American" itself covers a range of cultural and linguistic differences that makes those between German and East European Jews, or between Reform and Orthodox Jews, seem trivial in comparison.

The most important parallels between Jews and the various Asian groups are not cultural. They lie rather in the sociological profile of Jewish and Asian immigration. The Jewish newcomers of a hundred years ago never completely fit into the category of "huddled masses." They had an astonishing high literacy rate (nearly 100 percent for German Jews, and over 50 percent for East European Jews), a long tradition of scholarship even in the smallest shtetls, and useful skills. More than two-thirds of male Jewish immigrants were considered skilled workers in America. Less than three percent of

Box continued on next page.

Jewish immigrants had worked on the land. Similarly, the Japanese, Korean, Filipino, and Vietnamese immigrants of the 20th century have come almost exclusively from the middle class. Seventy percent of Korean male immigrants, for example, are college graduates. Like middle-class native-born Americans, Asian and Jewish immigrants alike have fully understood the importance of the universities, and have pushed their children to enter them from the very start.

Thomas Sowell offers another parallel between the successes of Asians and Jews. Both communities have benefited paradoxically, he argues, from their small size and from past discrimination against them. These disadvantages long kept both groups out of politics. And, as Sowell writes in *Race and Economics:* "those American ethnic groups that have succeeded best politically have not usually been the same as those who succeeded best economically . . . those minorities that have pinned their greatest hopes on political action—the Irish and the Negroes, for example—have made some of the slower economic advances." Rather than searching for a solution to their problems through the political process, Jewish, Chinese, and Japanese immigrants developed self-sufficiency by relying on community organizations. The combination of their skills, their desire for education, and the gradual disappearance of discrimination led inexorably to economic success.

—D.A.B.

revenge on the Japanese for hurting the automobile industry. After pleading guilty to manslaughter, they paid a $3,000 fine and were released. More recently, groups of Cambodians and Vietnamese in Boston were beaten by white youths, and there have been incidents in New York and Los Angles as well.

Is this violence an aberration, or does it reflect the persistence of anti-Asian prejudice in America? By at least one indicator, it seems hard to believe that Asian-Americans suffer greatly from discrimination. Their median family income, according to the 1980 census, was $22,713, compared to only $19,917 for whites. True, Asians live almost exclusively in urban areas (where incomes are higher), and generally have more people working in each family. They are also better educated than whites. Irene Natividad, a Filipino-American active in the Democratic Party's Asian Caucus, states bluntly that "we are underpaid for the high level of education we have achieved." However, because of language difficulties and differing professional standards in the United States, many new Asian immigrants initially work in jobs for which they are greatly overqualified.

Ironically, charges of discrimination today arise most frequently in the universities, the setting generally cited as the best evidence of Asian-American achievement. For several years Asian student associations at Ivy League universities have cited figures showing that a smaller percentage of Asian-American students than others are accepted. At Harvard this year, 12.5 percent of Asian-American applicants were admitted, as opposed to 16 percent of all applicants; at Princeton, the figures were 14 to 17 percent. Recently a Princeton professor, Uwe Reinhardt, told a *New York Times* reporter that Princeton has an unofficial quota for Asian-American applicants.

The question of university discrimination is a subtle one. For one thing, it only arises at the most prestigious schools, where admissions are the most subjective. At universities like UCLA, where applicants are judged largely by their grades and SAT scores, Asian-Americans have a higher admission rate than other students (80 percent versus 70 percent for all applicants). And at schools that emphasize science, like MIT, the general excellence of Asian-Americans in the field also produces a higher admission rate.

Why are things different at the Ivy League schools? One reason, according to a recent study done at Princeton, is that very few Asian-Americans are alumni children. The children of alumni are accepted at a rate of about 50 percent, and so raise the overall admissions figure. Athletes have a better chance of admission as well, and few Asian-Americans play varsity sports. These arguments, however, leave out another admissions factor: affirmative action. The fact is that if alumni children have a special advantage, at least some Asians do too, because of their race. At Harvard, for instance, partly in response to complaints from the Asian student organization, the admissions office in the late 1970s began to recruit vigorously among two categories of Asian-Americans: the poor, often living in Chinatowns; and recent immigrants. Today, according to the dean of admissions, L. Fred Jewett, roughly a third of Harvard's Asian-American applicants come from these groups, and are included in the university's "affirmative action" efforts. Like black students, who have a 27 percent admission rate, they find it easier to get in. And this means that the *other* Asian-Americans, the ones with no language problem or economic disadvantage, find things correspondingly tougher. Harvard has no statistics on the two groups. But if we assume the first group has an admissions rate of only 20 percent (very low for affirmative action candidates), the second one still slips down to slightly less than nine percent, or roughly half the overall admissions rate.

Dean Jewett offers two explanations for this phenomenon. First, he says, "family pressure makes more marginal students apply." In other words, many Asian students apply regardless of their qualifications, because of the university's prestige. And second, "a terribly high proportion of the Asian students are heading toward the sciences." In the interests of diversity, then, more of them must be left out.

* * *

It is true that more Asian-Americans go into the sciences. In Harvard's class of 1985, 57 percent of them did (as opposed to 29 percent of all students) and 71 percent went into either the sciences or economics. It is also true that a great many of Harvard's Asian-American applicants have little on their records except scientific excellence. But there are good reasons for this. In the sciences, complete mastery of English is less important than in other fields, an important fact for immigrants and children of immigrants. And scientific careers allow Asian-Americans to avoid the sort of large, hierarchical organization where their unfamiliarity with America, and management's resistance to putting them into highly visible positions, could hinder their advancement. And so the admissions problem comes down to a problem of clashing cultural standards. Since the values of Asian-American applicants differ from the universities' own, many of those applicants appear narrowly focused and dull. As Linda Matthews, an alumni recruiter for Harvard in Los Angeles, says with regret, "We hold them to the standards of white suburban kids. We want them to be cheerleaders and class presidents and all the rest."

The universities, however, consider their idea of the academic community to be liberal and sound. They are understandably hesitant to change it because of a demographic shift in the admissions pool. So how can they resolve this difficult problem? It is hard to say, except to suggest humility, and to recall that this sort of thing has come up before. At Harvard, the admissions office might do well to remember a memorandum Walter Lippmann prepared for the university in 1922. "I am fully prepared to accept the judgment of the Harvard authorities that a concentration of Jews in excess of fifteen per cent will produce a segregation of cultures rather than a fusion," wrote Lippmann, himself a Jew and a Harvard graduate. "They hand on unconsciously and uncritically from one generation to another many distressing personal and social habits...."

* * *

The debate over admissions is abstruse. But for Asian-Americans, it has become an extremely sensitive issue. The universities, after all, represent their route to complete integration in American society, and to an equal chance at the advantages that enticed them and their parents to immigrate in the first place. At the same time, discrimination, even very slight discrimination, recalls the bitter prejudice and discrimination that Asian-Americans suffered for their first hundred years in this country.

Few white Americans today realize just how pervasive legal anti-Asian discrimination was before 1945. The tens of thousand of Chinese laborers who arrived in California in the 1850s and 1860s to work in the goldfields and build the Central Pacific Railroad often lived in virtual slavery (the words ku-li, now part of the English language, mean "bitter labor"). Far from having the chance to organize, they were seized on as scapegoats by labor unions, particularly Samuel Gompers's AFL, and often ended up working as strikebreakers instead, thus inviting violent attacks. In 1870 Congress barred Asian immigrants from citizenship, and in 1882 it passed the Chinese Exclusion Act, which summarily prohibited more Chinese from entering the country. Since it did this at a time when 100,600 male Chinese-Americans had the company of only 4,800 females, it effectively sentenced the Chinese community to rapid decline. From 1854 to 1874, California had in effect a law preventing Asian-Americans from testifying in court, leaving them without the protection of the law.

Little changed in the late 19th and early 20th centuries, as large numbers of Japanese and smaller contingents from Korea and the Philippines began to arrive on the West Coast. In 1906 San Francisco made a brief attempt to segregate its school system. In 1910 a California law went so far as to prohibit marriage between Caucasians and "Mongolians," in flagrant defiance of the Fourteenth Amendment. Two Alien Land Acts in 1913 and 1920 prevented noncitizens in California (in other words, all alien immigrants) from owning or leasing land. These laws, and the Chinese Exclusion Act, remained in effect until the 1940s. And of course during the Second World War, President Franklin Roosevelt signed an Executive Order sending 110,000 ethnic Japanese on the West Coast, 64 percent of whom were American citizens, to internment camps. Estimates of the monetary damage to the Japanese-American community from this action range as high as $400,000,000, and Japanese-American political activists have made reparations one of their most important goals. Only in Hawaii, where Japanese-Americans already outnumbered whites 61,000 to 29,000 at the turn of the century, was discrimination relatively less important. (Indeed, 157,000 Japanese-Americans in Hawaii at the start of the war were *not* interned, although they posed a greater possible threat to the war effort than their cousins in California.)

* * *

In light of this history, the current problems of the Asian-American community seem relatively minor, and its success appears even more remarkable. Social scientists wonder just how this success was possible, and how Asian-Americans have managed to avoid the "second-class citizenship" that has trapped so many blacks and Hispanics. There is no single answer, but all the various explanations of the Asian-Americans' success do tend to fall into one category: self-sufficiency.

The first element of this self-sufficiency is family. Conservative sociologist Thomas Sowell writes that "strong, stable families have been characteristic of... successful minorities," and calls Chinese-Americans and Japanese-Americans the most stable he has encountered. This quality contributes to success in at least three ways. First and most obviously, it provides a secure environment for children. Second, it pushes those children to do better than their parents. As former Ohio state demographer William Petersen, author of *Japanese-Americans* (1971), says, "They're like the Jews in that they have the whole family and the whole community pushing them to make the best of themselves." And finally, it is a significant financial advantage. Traditionally, Asian-Americans have headed into family businesses, with all the family members pitching in long hours to make them a success. For the Chinese, it was restaurants and laundries (as late as 1940, half of the Chinese-American labor force worked in one or the other), for the Japanese, groceries and truck farming, and for the Koreans, groceries. Today the proportion of Koreans working without pay in family businesses is nearly three times as high as any other group. A recent *New York* magazine profile of one typical Korean grocery in New York showed that several of the family members running it consistently worked 15 to 18 hours a day. Thomas Sowell points out that in 1970, although Chinese median family income already exceeded white median family income by a third, their median personal income was only ten percent higher, indicating much greater participation per family.

Also contributing to Asian-American self-sufficiency are powerful community organizations. From the beginning of

Chinese-American settlement in California, clan organizations, mutual aid societies, and rotating credit associations gave many Japanese-Americans a start in business, at a time when most banks would only lend to whites. Throughout the first half of this century, the strength of community organizations was an important reason why Asian-Americans tended to live in small, closed communities rather than spreading out among the general population. And during the Depression years, they proved vital. In the early 1930s, when nine percent of the population of New York City subsisted on public relief, only one percent of Chinese-Americans did so. The community structure has also helped keep Asian-American crime rates the lowest in the nation, despite recently increasing gang violence among new Chinese and Vietnamese immigrants. According to the 1980 census, the proportion of Asian-Americans in prison is one-fourth that of the general population.

The more recent immigrants have also developed close communities. In the Washington, D.C., suburb of Arlington, Virginia, there is now a "Little Saigon." Koreans also take advantage of the "ethnic resources" provided by a small community. As Ivan Light writes in an essay in Nathan Glazer's new book, *Clamor at the Gates*, "They help one another with business skills, information, and purchase of ethnic commodities; cluster in particular industries; combine easily in restraint of trade; or utilize rotation credit associations." Light cites a study showing that 34 percent of Korean grocery store owners in Chicago had received financial help from within the Korean community. The immigrants in these communities are self-sufficient in another way as well. Unlike the immi-

grants of the 19th century, most new Asian-Americans come to the United States with professional skills. Or they come to obtain those skills, and then stay on. Of 16,000 Taiwanese who came to the U.S. as students in the 1960s, only three percent returned to Taiwan.

* * *

So what does the future hold for Asian-Americans? With the removal of most discrimination, and with the massive Asian-American influx in the universities, the importance of tightly knit communities is sure to wane. Indeed, among the older Asian-American groups it already has: since the war, fewer and fewer native-born Chinese-Americans have come to live in Chinatowns. But will complete assimilation follow? One study, at least, seems to indicate that it will, if one can look to the well-established Japanese-Americans for hints as to the future of other Asian groups. According to Professor Harry Kitano of UCLA, 63 percent of Japanese now intermarry.

But can all Asian-Americans follow the prosperous, assimilationist Japanese example? For some, it may not be easy. Hmong tribesmen, for instance, arrived in the United States with little money, few valuable skills, and extreme cultural disorientation. After five years here, they are still heavily dependent on welfare. (When the state of Oregon cut its assistance to refugees, 90 percent of the Hmong there moved to California.) Filipinos, although now the second-largest Asian-American group, make up less than ten percent of the Asian-American population at Harvard, and are the only Asian-Americans to benefit from affirmative action programs at the University of California. Do figures like these point to the emergence of a disadvantaged

Asian-American underclass? It is still too early to tell, but the question is not receiving much attention either. As Nathan Glazer says of Asian-Americans, "When they're already above average, it's very hard to pay much attention to those who fall below." Ross Harano, a Chicago businessman active in the Democratic Party's Asian Caucus, argues that the label of "model minority" earned by the most conspicuous Asian-Americans hurt less successful groups. "We need money to help people who can't assimilate as fast as the superstars," he says.

Harano also points out that the stragglers find little help in traditional minority politics. "When blacks talk about a minority agenda, they don't include us," he says. "Most Asians are viewed by blacks as whites." Indeed, in cities with large numbers of Asians and blacks, relations between the communities are tense. In September 1984, for example, *The Los Angeles Sentinel*, a prominent black newspaper, ran a four-part series condemning Koreans for their "takeover" of black businesses, provoking a strong reaction from Asian-American groups. In Harlem some blacks have organized a boycott of Asian-American stores.

Another barrier to complete integration lies in the tendency of many Asian-American students to crowd into a small number of careers, mainly in the sciences. Professor Ronn Takaki of Berkeley is a strong critic of this "maldistribution," and says that universities should make efforts to correct it. The extent of these efforts, he told *The Boston Globe* last December, "will determine whether we have our poets, sociologists, historians, and journalists. If we are all tracked into becoming computer technicians and scientists, this need will not be fulfilled."

Yet it is not clear that the "maldistribution" problem will extend to the next generation. The children of the current immigrants will not share their parents' language difficulties. Nor will they worry as much about joining large institutions where subtle racism might once have barred them from advancement. William Petersen argues, "As the discrimination disappears, as it mostly has already, the self-selection will disappear as well.... There's nothing in Chinese or Japanese culture pushing them toward these fields." Professor Kitano of UCLA is not so sure. "The submerging of the individual to the group is another basic Japanese tradition," he wrote in an article for *The Harvard Encyclopedia of American Ethnic Groups*. It is a tradition that causes problems for Japanese-Americans who wish to avoid current career patterns: "It may only be a matter of time before some break out of these middleman jobs, but the structural and cultural restraints may prove difficult to overcome."

* * *

In short, Asian-Americans face undeniable problems of integration. Still, it takes a very narrow mind not to realize that these problems are the envy of every other American racial minority, and of a good number of white ethnic groups as well. Like the Jews, who experienced a similar pattern of discrimination and quotas, and who first crowded into a small range of professions, Asian-Americans have shown an ability to overcome large obstacles in spectacular fashion. In particular, they have done so by taking full advantage of America's greatest civic resource, its schools and universities, just as the Jews did 50 years ago. Now they seem poised to burst out upon American society.

* * *

The clearest indication of this course is in politics, a sphere that Asian-Americans traditionally avoided. Now this is changing. And importantly, it is *not* changing just because Asian-Americans want government to solve their particular problems. Yes, there are "Asian" issues: the loosening of immigration restrictions, reparations for the wartime internment, equal opportunity for the Asian disadvantaged. Asian-American Democrats are at present incensed over the way the Democratic National Committee has stripped their caucus of "official" status. But even the most vehement activists on these points still insist that the most important thing for Asian-Americans is not any particular combination of issues, but simply "being part of the process." Unlike blacks or Hispanics, Asian-American politicians have the luxury of not having to devote the bulk of their time to an "Asian-American agenda," and thus escape becoming prisoners of such an agenda. Who thinks of Senator Daniel Inouye or former senator S. I. Hayakawa primarily in terms of his race? In June a young Chinese-American named Michael Woo won a seat on the Los Angeles City Council, running in a district that is only five percent Asian. According to *The Washington Post*, he attributed his victory to his "links to his fellow young American professionals." This is not typical minority-group politics.

Since Asian-Americans have the luxury of not having to behave like other minority groups, it seems only a matter of time before they, like the Jews, lose their "minority" status altogether, both legally and in the public's perception. And when this occurs, Asian-Americans will have to face the danger not of discrimination but of losing their cultural identity. It is a problem that every immigrant group must eventually come to terms with.

For Americans in general, however, the success of Asian-Americans poses no problems at all. On the contrary, their triumph has done nothing but enrich the United States. Asian-Americans improve every field they enter, for the simple reason that in a free society, a group succeeds by doing something better than it had been done before: Korean grocery stores provide fresher vegetables; Filipino doctors provide better rural health care; Asian science students raise the quality of science in the universities, and go on to provide better medicine, engineering, computer technology, and so on. And by a peculiarly American miracle, the Asian-Americans' success has not been balanced by anyone else's failure. Indeed, as successive waves of immigrants have shown, each new ethnic and racial group adds far more to American society than it takes away. This Fourth of July, that is cause for hope and celebration.

NO   Ronald Takaki

THE MYTH OF THE "MODEL MINORITY"

Today Asian Americans are celebrated as America's "model minority." In 1986, NBC *Nightly News* and the *McNeil/Lehrer Report* aired special news segments on Asian Americans and their success, and a year later, CBS's *60 Minutes* presented a glowing report on their stunning achievements in the academy. "Why are Asian Americans doing so exceptionally well in school?" Mike Wallace asked, and quickly added, "They must be doing something right. Let's bottle it." Meanwhile, *U.S. News & World Report* featured Asian-American advances in a cover story, and *Time* devoted an entire section on this meteoric minority in its special immigrants issue, "The Changing Face of America." Not to be outdone by its competitors, *Newsweek* titled the cover story of its college-campus magazine "Asian-Americans: The Drive to Excel" and a lead article of its weekly edition "Asian Americans: A 'Model Minority.' " *Fortune* went even further, applauding them as "America's Super Minority," and the *New Republic* extolled "The Triumph of Asian-Americans" as "America's greatest success story."

The celebration of Asian-American achievements in the press has been echoed in the political realm. Congratulations have come even from the White House. In a speech presented to Asian and Pacific Americans in the chief executive's mansion in 1984, President Ronald Reagan explained the significance of their success. America has a rich and diverse heritage, Reagan declared, and Americans are all descendants of immigrants in search of the "American Dream." He praised Asian and Pacific Americans for helping to "preserve that dream by living up to the bedrock values" of America—the principles of "the sacred worth of human life, religious faith, community spirit and the responsibility of parents and schools to be teachers of tolerance, hard work, fiscal responsibility, cooperation, and love." "It's no wonder," Reagan emphatically noted, "that the median incomes of Asian and Pacific-American families are much higher than the total American average." Hailing Asian and Pacific Americans as an example for all Americans, Reagan conveyed his gratitude to them: we need "your values, your hard work" expressed within "our political system."

But in their celebration of this "model minority," the pundits and the politicians have exaggerated Asian-American "success" and have created a new

From Ronald Takaki, *Strangers from a Different Shore: A History of Asian Americans* (Little, Brown, 1989). Copyright © 1989 by Ronald Takaki. Reprinted by permission of Little, Brown and Company. Notes omitted.

myth. Their comparisons of incomes between Asians and whites fail to recognize the regional location of the Asian-American population. Concentrated in California, Hawaii, and New York, Asian Americans reside largely in states with higher incomes but also higher costs of living than the national average: 59 percent of all Asian Americans lived in these three states in 1980, compared to only 19 percent of the general population. The use of "family incomes" by Reagan and others has been very misleading, for Asian-American families have more persons working per family than white families. In 1980, white nuclear families in California had only 1.6 workers per family, compared to 2.1 for Japanese, 2.0 for immigrant Chinese, 2.2 for immigrant Filipino, and 1.8 for immigrant Korean (this last figure is actually higher, for many Korean women are unpaid family workers). Thus the family incomes of Asian Americans indicate the presence of more workers in each family, rather than higher incomes.

Actually, in terms of personal incomes, Asian Americans have not reached equality. In 1980 the mean personal income for white men in California was $23,400. While Japanese men earned a comparable income, they did so only by acquiring more education (17.7 years compared to 16.8 years for white men twenty-five to forty-four years old) and by working more hours (2,160 hours compared to 2,120 hours for white men in the same age category). In reality, then, Japanese men were still behind Caucasian men. Income inequalities for other men were more evident: Korean men earned only $19,200, or 82 percent of the income of white men, Chinese men only $15,900 or 68 percent, and Filipino men only $14,500 or 62 percent. In New York the

mean personal income for white men was $21,600, compared to only $18,900 or 88 percent for Korean men, $16,500 or 76 percent for Filipino men, and only $11,200 or 52 percent for Chinese men. In the San Francisco Bay Area, Chinese-immigrant men earned only 72 percent of what their white counterparts earned, Filipino-immigrant men 68 percent, Korean-immigrant men 69 percent, and Vietnamese-immigrant men 52 percent. The incomes of Asian-American men were close to and sometimes even below those of black men (68 percent) and Mexican-American men (71 percent).

The patterns of income inequality for Asian men reflect a structural problem: Asians tend to be located in the labor market's secondary sector, where wages are low and promotional prospects minimal. Asian men are clustered as janitors, machinists, postal clerks, technicians, waiters, cooks, gardeners, and computer programmers; they can also be found in the primary sector, but here they are found mostly in the lower-tier levels as architects, engineers, computer-systems analysts, pharmacists, and schoolteachers, rather than in the upper-tier levels of management and decision making. "Labor market segmentation and restricted mobility between sectors," observed social scientists Amado Cabezas and Gary Kawaguchi, "help promote the economic interest and privilege of those with capital or those in the primary sector, who mostly are white men."

This pattern of Asian absence from the higher levels of administration is characterized as "a glass ceiling"—a barrier through which top management positions can only be seen, but not reached, by Asian Americans. While they are increasing in numbers on university campuses as students, they are virtually nonexistent as administrators: at Berkeley's University of California campus where 25 percent of the students were Asian in 1987, only one out of 102 top-level administrators was an Asian. In the United States as a whole, only 8 percent of Asian Americans in 1988 were "officials" and "managers," as compared to 12 percent for all groups. Asian Americans are even more scarce in the upper strata of the corporate hierarchy: they constituted less than half of one percent of the 29,000 officers and directors of the nation's thousand largest companies. Though they are highly educated, Asian Americans are generally not present in positions of executive leadership and decision making. "Many Asian Americans hoping to climb the corporate ladder face an arduous ascent," the *Wall Street Journal* observed. "Ironically, the same companies that pursue them for technical jobs often shun them when filling managerial and executive positions."

Asian Americans complain that they are often stereotyped as passive and told they lack the aggressiveness required in administration. The problem is not whether their culture encourages a reserved manner, they argue, but whether they have opportunities for social activities that have traditionally been the exclusive preserve of elite white men. "How do you get invited to the cocktail party and talk to the chairman?" asked Landy Eng, a former assistant vice president of Citibank. "It's a lot easier if your father or your uncle or his friend puts his arm around you at the party and says, 'Landy, let me introduce you to Walt.'" Excluded from the "old boy" network, Asian Americans are also told they are inarticulate and have an accent. Edwin Wong, a junior manager at Acurex, said: "I was given the equivalent of an ultima-

tum: Either you improve your accent or your future in getting promoted to senior management is in jeopardy.'" The accent was a perceived problem at work. "I felt that just because I had an accent a lot of Caucasians thought I was stupid." But whites with German, French, or English accents do not seem to be similarly handicapped. Asian Americans are frequently viewed as technicians rather than administrators. Thomas Campbell, a general manager at Westinghouse Electric Corp., said that Asian Americans would be happier staying in technical fields and that few of them are adept at sorting through the complexities of large-scale business. This very image can produce a reinforcing pattern: Asian-American professionals often find they "top out," reaching a promotional ceiling early in their careers. "The only jobs we could get were based on merit," explained Kumar Patel, head of the material science division at AT&T. "That is why you find most [Asian-Indian] professionals in technical rather than administrative or managerial positions." ...

Asian-American "success" has emerged as the new stereotype for this ethnic minority. While this image has led many teachers and employers to view Asians as intelligent and hardworking and has opened some opportunities, it has also been harmful. Asian Americans find their diversity as individuals denied: many feel forced to conform to the "model minority" mold and want more freedom to be their individual selves, to be "extravagant." Asian university students are concentrated in the sciences and technical fields, but many of them wish they had greater opportunities to major in the social sciences and humanities. "We are educating a generation of Asian technicians," observed an Asian-American professor at Berkeley, "but the communities also need their historians and poets." Asian Americans find themselves all lumped together and their diversity as groups overlooked. Groups that are not doing well, such as the unemployed Hmong, the Downtown Chinese, the elderly Japanese, the old Filipino farm laborers, and others, have been rendered invisible. To be out of sight is also to be without social services. Thinking Asian Americans have succeeded, government officials have sometimes denied funding for social service programs designed to help Asian Americans learn English and find employment. Failing to realize that there are poor Asian families, college administrators have sometimes excluded Asian-American students from Educational Opportunity Programs (EOP), which are intended for *all* students from low-income families. Asian Americans also find themselves pitted against and resented by other racial minorities and even whites. If Asian Americans can make it on their own, pundits are asking, why can't poor blacks and whites on welfare? Even middle-class whites, who are experiencing economic difficulties because of plant closures in a deindustrializing America and the expansion of low-wage service employment, have been urged to emulate the Asian-American "model minority" and to work harder.

Indeed, the story of the Asian-American triumph offers ideological affirmation of the American Dream in an era anxiously witnessing the decline of the United States in the international economy (due to its trade imbalance and its transformation from a creditor to a debtor nation), the emergence of a new black underclass (the percentage of black female-headed families having almost doubled from 22 percent in 1960 to 40 percent in 1980), and a collapsing white middle class (the percentage of households earning a "middle-class" income falling from 28.7 percent in 1967 to 23.2 percent in 1983). Intellectually, it has been used to explain "losing ground"—why the situation of the poor has deteriorated during the last two decades of expanded government social services. According to this view, advanced by pundits like Charles Murray, the interventionist federal state, operating on the "misguided wisdom" of the 1960s, made matters worse: it created a web of welfare dependency. But his analysis has overlooked the structural problems in society and our economy, and it has led to easy cultural explanations and quick-fix prescriptions. Our difficulties, we are sternly told, stem from our waywardness: Americans have strayed from the Puritan "errand into the wilderness." They have abandoned the old American "habits of the heart." Praise for Asian-American success is America's most recent jeremiad—a renewed commitment to make America number one again and a call for a rededication to the bedrock values of hard work, thrift, and industry. Like many congratulations, this one may veil a spirit of competition, even jealousy.

Significantly, Asian-American "success" has been accompanied by the rise of a new wave of anti-Asian sentiment. On college campuses, racial slurs have surfaced in conversations on the quad: "Look out for the Asian Invasion." "M.I.T. means Made in Taiwan." "U.C.L.A. stands for University of Caucasians Living among Asians." Nasty anti-Asian graffiti have suddenly appeared on the walls of college dormitories and in the elevators of classroom buildings: "Chink, chink, cheating chink!" "Stop the Yellow Hordes." "Stop the Chinese before they flunk you out." Ugly racial incidents have broken out on college campuses. At the University of Connecticut, for example, eight Asian-American students experienced a nightmare of abuse in 1987. Four couples had boarded a college bus to attend a dance. "The dance was a formal and so we were wearing gowns," said Marta Ho, recalling the horrible evening with tears. "The bus was packed, and there was a rowdy bunch of white guys in the back of the bus. Suddenly I felt this warm sticky stuff on my hair. They were spitting at us! My friend was sitting sidewise and got hit on her face and she started screaming. Our boy friends turned around, and one of the white guys, a football player, shouted: 'You want to make something out of this, you Oriental faggots!'"

Asian-American students at the University of Connecticut and other colleges are angry, arguing that there should be no place for racism on campus and that they have as much right as anyone else to be in the university. Many of them are children of recent immigrants who had been college-educated professionals in Asia. They see how their parents had to become greengrocers, restaurant operators, and storekeepers in America, and they want to have greater career choices for themselves. Hopeful a college education can help them overcome racial obstacles, they realize the need to be serious about their studies. But white college students complain: "Asian students are nerds." This very stereotype betrays nervousness—fears that Asian-American students are raising class grade curves. White parents, especially alumni, express concern about how Asian-American students are taking away "their" slots—admission places

that should have gone to their children. "Legacy" admission slots reserved for children of alumni have come to function as a kind of invisible affirmative-action program for whites. A college education has always represented a valuable economic resource, credentialing individuals for high income and status employment, and the university has recently become a contested terrain of competition between whites and Asians. In paneled offices, university administrators meet to discuss the "problem" of Asian-American "over-representation" in enrollments.

Paralleling the complaint about the rising numbers of Asian-American students in the university is a growing worry that there are also "too many" immigrants coming from Asia. Recent efforts to "reform" the 1965 Immigration Act seem reminiscent of the nativism prevalent in the 1880s and the 1920s. Senator Alan K. Simpson of Wyoming, for example, noted how the great majority of the new immigrants were from Latin America and Asia, and how "a substantial portion" of them did not "integrate fully" into American society. "If language and cultural separatism rise above a certain level," he warned, "the unity and political stability of the Nation will—in time—be seriously eroded. Pluralism within a united American nation has been our greatest strength. The unity comes from a common language and a core public culture of certain shared values, beliefs, and customs, which make us distinctly 'Americans.'" In the view of many supporters of immigration reform, the post-1965 immigration from Asia and Latin America threatens the traditional unity and identity of the American people. "The immigration from the turn of the century was largely a continuation of immigration from previous years in that the European stock of Americans was being maintained," explained Steve Rosen, a member of an organization lobbying for changes in the current law. "Now, we are having a large influx of third-world people, which could be potentially disruptive of our whole Judeo-Christian heritage." Significantly, in March 1988, the Senate passed a bill that would limit the entry of family members and that would provide 55,000 new visas to be awarded to "independent immigrants" on the basis of education, work experience, occupations, and "English language skills."

Political concerns usually have cultural representations. The entertainment media have begun marketing Asian stereotypes again: where Hollywood had earlier portrayed Asians as Charlie Chan displaying his wit and wisdom in his fortune cookie Confucian quotes and as the evil Fu Manchu threatening white women, the film industry has recently been presenting images of comic Asians (in *Sixteen Candles*) and criminal Asian aliens (in *Year of the Dragon*). Hollywood has entered the realm of foreign affairs. *The Deer Hunter* explained why the United States lost the war in Vietnam. In this story, young American men are sent to fight in Vietnam, but they are not psychologically prepared for the utter cruelty of physically disfigured Viet Cong clad in black pajamas. Shocked and disoriented, they collapse morally into a world of corruption, drugs, gambling, and Russian roulette. There seems to be something sinister in Asia and the people there that is beyond the capability of civilized Americans to comprehend. Upset after seeing this movie, refugee Thu-Thuy Truong exclaimed: "We didn't play Russian roulette games in Saigon!

The whole thing was made up." Similarly *Apocalypse Now* portrayed lost innocence: Americans enter the heart of darkness in Vietnam and become possessed by madness (in the persona played by Marlon Brando) but are saved in the end by their own technology and violence (represented by Martin Sheen). Finally, in movies celebrating the exploits of Rambo, Hollywood has allowed Americans to win in fantasy the Vietnam War they had lost in reality. "Do we get to win this time?" snarls Rambo, our modern Natty Bumppo, a hero of limited conversation and immense patriotic rage.

Meanwhile, anti-Asian feelings and misunderstandings have been exploding violently in communities across the country, from Philadelphia, Boston, and New York to Denver and Galveston, Seattle, Portland, Monterey, and San Francisco. In Jersey City, the home of 15,000 Asian Indians, a hate letter published in a local newspaper warned: "We will go to any extreme to get Indians to move out of Jersey City. If I'm walking down the street and I see a Hindu and the setting is right, I will just hit him or her. We plan some of our more extreme attacks such as breaking windows, breaking car windows and crashing family parties. We use the phone book and look up the name Patel. Have you seen how many there are?" The letter was reportedly written by the "Dotbusters," a cruel reference to the *bindi* some Indian women wear as a sign of sanctity. Actual attacks have taken place, ranging from verbal harassments and egg throwing to serious beatings. Outside a Hoboken restaurant on September 27, 1987, a gang of youths chanting "Hindu, Hindu" beat Navroz Mody to death. A grand jury has indicted four teenagers for the murder.

Five years earlier a similarly brutal incident occurred in Detroit. There, in July, Vincent Chin, a young Chinese American, and two friends went to a bar in the late afternoon to celebrate his upcoming wedding. Two white autoworkers, Ronald Ebens and Michael Nitz, called Chin a "Jap" and cursed: "It's because of you... that we're out of work." A fistfight broke out, and Chin then quickly left the bar. But Ebens and Nitz took out a baseball bat from the trunk of their car and chased Chin through the streets. They finally cornered him in front of a McDonald's restaurant. Nitz held Chin while Ebens swung the bat across the victim's shins and then bludgeoned Chin to death by shattering his skull. Allowed to plead guilty to manslaughter, Ebens and Nitz were sentenced to three years' probation and fined $3,780 each. But they have not spent a single night in jail for their bloody deed. "Three thousand dollars can't even buy a good used car these days," snapped a Chinese American, "and this was the price of a life." "What kind of law is this? What kind of justice?" cried Mrs. Lily Chin, the slain man's mother. "This happened because my son is Chinese. If two Chinese killed a white person, they must go to jail, maybe for their whole lives.... Something is wrong with this country."...

The murder of Vincent Chin has aroused the anger and concern of Asian Americans across the country. They know he was killed because of his racial membership. Ebens and Nitz perceived Chin as a "stranger," a foreigner, for he did not look like an American. But why was Chin viewed as an alien? Asian Americans blame the educational system for not including their history in the curricula and for not teaching about U.S. society in all of its racial and cultural diversity. Why are the courses and books on American history so Eurocentric? they have asked teachers and scholars accusingly.

POSTSCRIPT

Are Asian Americans a "Model Minority"?

So which point of view do you support? An increasing number of social scientists are beginning to question the model minority label if not reject it as inaccurate, as Takaki does. Yet there are a number of achievements by Asian Americans that on the surface would appear to set them apart from other ethnic minorities.

A serious problem for many Asian Americans, especially newcomers, which neither Bell or Takaki address here, is their experiences as so-called middleman minorities.

That is, like Chinese in parts of Asia outside of China, many first generation Asian Americans, and especially Koreans, provide food and other services for the inner city poor through the small businesses they run. This is an important function. The poor need these services desperately. Rents are cheap. Initial capital for stock is relatively small. The need is there. Required skills are minimal (counting, shelving). Thus a disproportionately high number of immigrants have seized the advantage and opened stores in ghetto areas. Many poorer and/or less skilled Eastern European Jews, Italians, and others have followed this pattern.

These merchants are middlemen since they are not fully members of the poor neighborhoods in which they locate their businesses, but neither are they yet accepted into the dominant society. In order to keep expenses down, many such middleman merchants staff their stores with members of their own families. They rarely live in the area, and they close their stores at night to return home, often to an equally poor area but in another neighborhood.

There is enormous stress between lower class, frequently first generation, Asian Americans and poorer urban Blacks and, to a lesser extent, Hispanics. If a merchant has limited mastery of English, customers can sometimes experience this as rudeness or disrespect. The close scrutiny and matter-of-fact efficiency of middleman minorities can be seen by customers as suspicious and unfriendly behavior. Charging higher prices for items because of the high cost of insurance for inner city businesses is viewed as "ripping off" poor neighborhood people. Hiring of only family is "proof" that they do not like the locals, that and living in other areas.

At another level of analysis, if the model minority notion of Asian Americans is a myth, what do you think its functions might be? How might claiming that one group is a model minority tie into blaming other groups for their particular problems (e.g., unemployment, poverty)? Neither Bell nor

Takaki consider this, but use your own sociological imagination and review Hernández's discussion in Issue 2. How might the term *underclass* be seen as the opposite side of model minority? Drawing from Takaki and your own thinking, what might be some of the unanticipated negative consequences of a positive myth, such as Asian Americans being a model minority?

A thorough discussion of Asian Americans can be found in H. Kitano and R. Daniels, *Asian Americans: Emerging Minorities* (Prentice Hall, 1988). "America's Super Minority," in *Fortune* (November 24, 1986) reflects general sentiments of the model minority view. For an excellent historical discussion of one aspect of the experiences of Asian Americans in the nineteenth century, see D. Liestman's "To Win Redeemed Souls from Heathen Darkness: Protestant Response to the Chinese," *Western Historical Quarterly* (May 1993). A clarification of Korean ethnicity is provided in P. Min's "Cultural and Economic Boundaries of Korean Ethnicity: A Comparative Analysis," *Ethnic and Racial Studies* (April 1991). For information on the Japanese experience in Hawaii see G. Okihiro, *Cane Fires: The Anti-Japanese Movement in Hawaii, 1865–1945* (Temple University Press, 1991). For an outstanding though somewhat more general discussion of middleman minorities, see Edna Bonacich, "A Theory of Middleman Minorities," *American Sociological Review* (Vol. 38, 1983), and also E. Bonacich and J. Modell, *The Economic Basis of Ethnic Solidarity: Small Business in the Japanese American Community* (University of California Press, 1980).

ISSUE 4

Do Italian Americans Reject Assimilation?

YES: Kathleen Neils Conzen, David A. Gerber, Ewa Morawska, George E. Pozzetta, and Rudolph J. Vecoli, from "The Invention of Ethnicity: A Perspective from the U.S.A.," *Journal of American Ethnic History* (Fall 1992)

NO: Herbert J. Gans, from "Comment: Ethnic Invention and Acculturation, A Bumpy-Line Approach," *Journal of American Ethnic History* (Fall 1992)

ISSUE SUMMARY

YES: Historians and sociologists Kathleen Conzen, David Gerber, Ewa Morawska, George Pozzetta, and Rudolph Vecoli reject many standard theories of ethnic acculturation and assimilation. Instead, they attempt to prove, with several cases, including the Italian one presented here, that many ethnic groups elect to remain separate in important ways from the dominant culture.

NO: Columbia University sociologist Herbert J. Gans insists that even recent ethnic groups, as well as the Italians, while sometimes following an indirect or uneven path to assimilation, are still far more American than not, and prefer it that way.

As has been discussed in other issues in this book, understanding myths and mythmaking is important to any study of racial and ethnic relations. For much of this century, a popularly accepted myth was that all ethnic groups, regardless of race or national origin, wanted to succeed as measured by American standards of success. And not only did they want to succeed, this particular myth or assumption went, they could succeed if only they were honest, persevered in the face of adversity, and met all challenges and rejections with resolute cheerfulness. While undoubtedly many did "make it" in America, many others did not, frequently because of structural reasons. These include shifting labor needs, economic depressions or recessions, discrimination, and so on. But this myth put great emphasis on the individual, and any kind of economic failure or reversal was attributed to individual inadequacies.

This myth applied to any ethnic group (e.g., earlier immigrants from southern Europe to more recent Hispanic/Latino immigrants), and it assumed that a significant number would achieve at least middle-class economic status. The end result of economic success would be represented in assimilation.

Former ethnic ties—names, language spoken in the home, customs, values—would more or less fall away with each succeeding generation (usually three or four). In the process of melting into the American pot, a "new person," a "new country" would be created and strengthened. This thinking even found its way into standard sociological theories. Moreover, to a certain extent, sociologists, especially those in the 1920s and 1930s, when public awareness and acceptance of the myth was quite powerful, had a vested interest in adding to the myth.

The 1960s brought a revolution to minority relations studies. Reflecting the broader political shifts in society (and contributing to them), some social scientists began to question some of the prevailing ideas regarding racial and ethnic minorities. They argued that because of economic dislocations as well as the continued force of racism, some minorities were becoming worse off over generations. In addition, insightful sociologists of the period quite accurately questioned why assimilation was even considered a desirable goal. Could not pluralism be a virtue?

Conzen et al. point out that, since the 1960s, ethnicity has had an "unexpected persistence and vitality... as a source of group identity and solidarity." They identify several new models of ethnicity, including those that emphasize its "primordial character," those that emphasize its "symbolic character," and those that consider ethnicity to be sometimes a "collective fiction." They also review the political aspects of ethnic groups.

In their argument that Italians and others reject assimilation, Conzen et al. develop the idea that ethnicity is "a process of construction... which incorporates, adapts, and amplifies preexisting communal solidarities." Conzen et al. suggest that many changes, especially among Italian Americans, are done to maintain and extend ethnic solidarity. Italian Americans are viewed as being agents of change (controlling the direction of change and their own identities), and as such reinvent holidays, ceremonies, customs, festivals, and religious practices in order to consciously and deliberately prevent, or at least minimize, assimilation.

Gans concedes that ethnic groups do reinvent themselves and that ethnicity has ties in group solidarities and traditions. Gans also challenges traditional views of "straight line" assimilation (i.e., minorities immigrate to the United States, then within two or three generations are assimilated). Gans suggests that earlier minorities studies simply did not have the vantage point of the 1990s by which to gauge the diversity of ethnic and racial processes. He develops a rudimentary theory of minority inclusion, which he labels the "bumpy line" theory. But Gans disagrees with Conzen et al. in a fundamental way. To Gans, ethnic processes do take many sidestreams, but these are *not* away from assimilation but instead are toward it, however "bumpy" the road may be.

As you read about Italian Americans and ethnicity, think about how you would invent an ethnic group. What would it consist of? Who would it be like? Who might discriminate against it? On what basis? What would its gender roles most likely be?

YES   Kathleen Neils Conzen, David A. Gerber, Ewa Morawska, George E. Pozzetta, and Rudolph J. Vecoli

THE INVENTION OF ETHNICITY:
A PERSPECTIVE FROM THE U.S.A.

Since the United States has received recurring waves of mass immigration, a persistent theme of American history has been that of the incorporation of the foreign born into the body politic and social fabric of the country. The dominant interpretation both in American historiography and nationalist ideology had been one of rapid and easy assimilation. Various theories which predicted this outcome, i.e., Anglo-conformity and the Melting Pot, shaped the underlying assumptions of several generations of historians and social scientists.

Historical studies in the United States over the past two decades have called these assumptions into question. Scholars have increasingly emphasized the determined resistance with which immigrants often opposed Americanization and their strenuous efforts at language and cultural maintenance. They no longer portray immigrants as moving in a straight-line manner from old-world cultures to becoming Americans. At the same time recent studies agree that the immigrants' "traditional" cultures did not remain unchanged. Rather immigration historians have become increasingly interested in the processes of cultural and social change whereby immigrants ceased to be "foreigners" and yet did not become "One Hundred Per Cent Americans." From immigrants they are said to have become *ethnic Americans* of one kind or another.

Ethnicity has therefore become a key concept in the analysis of this process of immigrant adaptation. Classical social theories as applied to the study of immigrant populations as well as indigenous peoples had predicted the inevitable crumbling of "traditional" communities and cultures before the forces of modernization. However, from the 1960s on, the rise of ethnic movements in the United States and throughout the world have demonstrated an unexpected persistence and vitality of ethnicity as a source of group identity and solidarity. These phenomena stimulated an enormous amount of research and writing on the nature of ethnicity as a form of human collectivity.

From Kathleen Neils Conzen, David A. Gerber, Ewa Morawska, George E. Pozzetta, and Rudolph J. Vecoli, "The Invention of Ethnicity: A Perspective from the U.S.A.," *Journal of American Ethnic History* (Fall 1992). Copyright © 1992 by Transaction Publishers. Reprinted by permission. Notes omitted.

Although there are many definitions of ethnicity, several have dominated discussions of immigrant adaptation. One, stemming from the writings of anthropologists Clifford Geertz and Harold Isaacs, has emphasized its primordial character, originating in the "basic group identity" of human beings. In this view, persons have an essential need for "belonging" which is satisfied by groups based on shared ancestry and culture. For some commentators, like Michael Novak, such primordial ethnicity continued to influence powerfully the descendants of the immigrants even unto the third and fourth generations. Others, like sociologist Herbert Gans, have dismissed the vestiges of immigrant cultures as "symbolic ethnicity," doomed to fade away before the irresistible forces of assimilation.

A different conception of ethnicity, initially proposed by Nathan Glazer and Daniel Moynihan, deemphasizes the cultural component and defines ethnic groups as interest groups. In this view, ethnicity serves as a means of mobilizing a certain population behind issues relating to its socioeconomic position in the larger society. Given the uneven distribution of power, prestige, and wealth among the constituent groups in polyethnic societies and the ensuing competition for scarce goods, people, so the argument goes, can be organized more effectively on the basis of ethnicity than of social class. Leadership and ideologies play important roles in this scenario of "emergent ethnicity." While "primordial ethnicity" both generates its own dynamic and is an end in itself, "interest group ethnicity" is instrumental and situational.

The authors of this essay propose to explore a recently formulated conceptualization: "the invention of ethnicity." With Werner Sollors, we do not view ethnicity as primordial (ancient, unchanging, inherent in a group's blood, soul, or misty past), but we differ from him in our understanding of ethnicity as a cultural construction accomplished over historical time. In our view, ethnicity is not a "collective fiction," but rather a process of construction or invention which incorporates, adapts, and amplifies preexisting communal solidarities, cultural attributes, and historical memories. That is, it is grounded in real life context and social experience.

Ethnic groups in modern settings are constantly recreating themselves, and ethnicity is continuously being reinvented in response to changing realities both within the group and the host society. Ethnic group boundaries, for example, must be repeatedly renegotiated, while expressive symbols of ethnicity (ethnic traditions) must be repeatedly reinterpreted....

The invention of ethnicity furthermore suggests an active participation by the immigrants in defining their group identities and solidarities. The renegotiation of its "traditions" by the immigrant group presumes a collective awareness and active decision-making as opposed to the passive, unconscious individualism of the assimilation model....

The concept of the invention of ethnicity also helps us to understand how immigration transformed the larger American society, engendering a new pluralistic social order. Once ethnicity had been established as a category in American social thought, each contingent of newcomers had to negotiate its particular place within that social order. Anglo Americans had to assimilate these distinctive groups into their conception of the history and future of "their" country, and to prescribe appropriate social and cultural arrangements. Inevitably all Americans, native born and immigrant, were involved in a continual renegotiation of identities. . . .

Americans themselves were engaged in a self-conscious project of inventing a national identity, and in the process found themselves also inventing the category of ethnicity—"nationality" was the term they actually used—to account for the culturally distinctive groups in their midst. These two inventions were closely intertwined. . . .

Ethnicization was not necessarily characterized by an easily negotiated unanimity about the identity of the immigrant group. More often the process was fraught with internal conflicts and dissension over the nature, history, and destiny of its peoplehood. . . . As John Higham has observed, the strategies of ethnic leaders ranged from accommodation to protest, yet all had to address in some fashion the place of the immigrant group within the larger American society.

The invention of ethnicity allows for the revitalization of ethnic consciousness following periods of apparent dormancy. The precondition is a crisis which challenges the core values of either mainstream or sidestream ethnocultures, mobilizing the latent ethnic constituency. . . .

ITALIAN AMERICANS: THE ONGOING NEGOTIATION OF AN ETHNIC IDENTITY

Whether as artisans and peasants in Europe or as immigrants in the United States, Italian workers at the turn-of-the-century confronted a range of competing ideologies and movements seeking to shape their identities and loyalties. Given the *mentalità* [mentality] of the typical Italian immigrant, the spirit of *campanilismo* [parochialism] initially defined their dominant sense of peoplehood. Their feelings of solidarity and identity were largely circumscribed within the boundaries of the *paese* [country]. Once in America, they maintained this spirit of *campanilismo* principally through the cult of the saints, the veneration of the patrons of the particular villages, embodied in elaborate feast day celebrations. The first mutual aid societies, usually named after the local deities, San Rocco, San Gennaro, San Antonio, etc., devoted great effort and expense to ensure the authenticity of the *festa* [holiday]. Immigrants brought statues of the saints and madonnas, exact replicas of those in the *paese*, to America, and attempted to reenact the processions and acts of piety and veneration that were parts of the traditional *festa*. However, changes began to creep into the observances from the beginning. The pinning of money, of American dollars, on the robes of saints, for example, was an innovation. Moreover, the *festa* in the streets of Chicago or Boston did not have the unquestioned claim to public space it did back in the *paese*. Non-*paesani* [noncompatriots] and even non-Italians attended the *feste*, sometimes to mock and jeer. The outcome was that despite every strenuous effort, the *festa* could not be celebrated strictly in the traditional manner. Inevitably the campanilistic basis of the celebration became diluted, elements from the new-world setting were incorporated, and it became over time itself an expression of an emerging Italian-American ethnicity.

Challenging the campanilistic-religious culture of the *paese* was a new military-patriotic form of Italian nationalism. Many mutual aid societies took on this character under the tutelage of *prominenti* who used them as a means of controlling their worker-clients. Those societies espoused the invented symbols and slogans of the recently unified Kingdom of Italy. Named after members of the royal family (*Principe Umberto*) or heroes of the Risorgimento [Renaissance] (Garibaldi was the favorite), these societies sponsored rounds of banquets, balls, and picnics which celebrated national holidays (Constitution Day, *XX settembre*, etc.). When they marched in parades, society members donned elaborate uniforms, of *carabinieri* [Italian military police], for example, with rows of impressive medals. A colonial elite of businessmen and professionals abetted by the Catholic clergy promoted this nationalist version of ethnicity as a means of securing hegemony over the laboring immigrants.

Both of these definitions of Italian immigrant identity were vehemently opposed by the *sovversivi*, the socialists and anarchists. Espousing oppositional ideologies which were anti-religious, anti-nationalist, and anti-capitalist, they sought to inculcate class consciousness as members of the international proletariat among Italian workers. The radicals utilized newspapers, songs, drama, clubs, and their own holidays to evangelize their gospel. Rather than celebrating saints' days or national holidays, they marked the fall of the Bastille, the Paris Commune, and, of course, May Day. On *Primo Maggio* they held balls, picnics, and parades, at which they sang the revolutionary hymns, recited poetry, and held presentations of Pietro Gori's play, *Primo Maggio*.

Each of these forms of ethnicization sought to define the essential character of the immigrants in terms of a collectivity: the *paese*; the nation; the proletariat. Each used a constellation of symbols, rituals, and rhetoric to imbue a sense of identity and solidarity among its followers. In succeeding decades other versions of peoplehood offered the immigrants alternative self-concepts and collective representations. As Italian immigrants became more rooted in America, and the immigrant generation itself began to wane, the necessity of creating an Italian-American identity assumed primacy. The formation of the Sons of Italy in America in 1905, for example, was one effort to reconcile, with appropriate language and symbolism, the duality of being Italian American. Similarly Columbus Day served as the symbolic expression of this dual identity *par excellence*. By placing the Italians at the very beginnings of American history through their surrogate ancestor, the anniversary of the "discovery" of the New World served to legitimize their claims to Americanness at the same time that it allowed them to take pride in their Italianness.

In the 1920s Benito Mussolini's Fascist regime added to the contestation present within Italian America by attempting to win over immigrants and their progeny to its cause. A new cluster of festivals, heroes, and slogans emerged to this end. Fascist elements sought to dominate distinctly Italian-American celebrations, such as Columbus Day; lay claim to the symbols of Italian patriotism and nationalism; and insert their own holy days (e.g., the anniversary of the March on Rome), into the calendar. Oath taking to *il Duce* and the King, playing *Giovinezza* (the Fascist official hymn) and the *Marcia Reale*, singing Fascist battle songs, unfurling banners with Mussolini's commands ("Work and Arms"), and wearing black shirts provided the necessary iconography and pageantry. Sensitive to the generational transition, the Fascists also supplied English-language publications, as well as films and radio programs, for the children of immigrants who could not understand Italian.

Anti-fascist Italians contested these initiatives with counter demonstrations and contrasting values and symbols. Composed of an unlikely mix of Italian-American labor activists, leftist radicals, liberal progressives, and educated Italian exiles, anti-fascists found it difficult to agree upon a united front. Despite these internal divisions, their demonstrations typically attempted to link Italian Americans with the republican legacy of Italy and its champions of freedom, such as Garibaldi and Mazzini. Memorials to Giacomo Matteotti, the martyred socialist deputy, accompanied by renditions of *Bandiera Rossa* and *Inno di Garibaldi*, became fixtures of anti-fascist festivities. After the Italian invasion of Ethiopia in 1935, opponents of Mussolini added anti-imperialism to their cause.

World War II resolved the question of Fascism by making the maintenance of dual loyalties impossible, and the ensuing Cold War further eroded the position of radicals in the Italian-American community. The war crisis and subsequent anti-communist crusade placed a high premium on conformity, loyalty, and patriotism to the United States. To many observers in the 1940s and 1950s it appeared that Italian Americans were comfortably melding into the melting pot as particularly the second generation realized increased social mobility, adopted middle-class values and joined in the rush to mass consumerism.

By the 1960s, however, third and fourth generation Italian Americans unexpectedly began to assert their distinctiveness as part of a wider ethnic revival sweeping America. Italian Americans joined with other ethnics to renegotiate their ethnicities in the midst of a national political crisis during which dominant societal values and identities came under increasing assault. Once again, the self-conscious crafting of symbols, rituals, and images became heightened as Italian Americans attempted to generate as much internal unity as possible, lay claim to being fully American, and inscribe a more dignified place for themselves in the dominant narrative of American history.

Since the Italian-American population was increasingly segmented by generation, class, occupation, education, and residence, there was substantial disagreement over the proper rhetoric and cultural forms to use in expressing Italian-American ethnicity. This diversity of opinion was further sharpened by the proliferation of Italian-American organizations of all kinds during the sixties and seventies. Upwardly mobile and social climbing individuals, for example, attempted to fashion a more positive image by focusing on the glories of Old-Country high culture, seeking to connect Italian Americans with the accomplishments of Dante, DaVinci, and other renowned Italians. In a variant of this strategy, other Italian Americans sought to cash in on the cachet of contemporary Italian design and style by consuming Gucci, Pucci, Ferrari, etc.

Status anxieties engendered by negative stereotypes inherited from the era of peasant immigration generated intensified efforts to highlight the "contributions" of Italians to the development of America. Seeking to compensate for insecurities, filiopietists [people who excessively venerate their ancestors] campaigned for the issuance of commemorative stamps to Filippo Mazzei and Francesco Vigo; recognition of exceptional immigrants such as Constantino Brumidi, Father Eusebio Kino, and Lorenzo da Ponte; and erection of monuments to other overlooked notables. Perhaps the most vigorously fought struggle was the successful effort to have Columbus Day declared a federal holiday. Such a strategy, common to all ethnic groups, challenged the standard rendition of American history—indeed, often stood it on its head—by showing how the group's values and heroes were instrumental in shaping national development.

These filiopietistic initiatives have frequently clashed with the recent work of academics, often themselves Italian Americans, who have portrayed the common experiences of millions of peasant immigrants as representing the key elements of the Italian-American saga. Such historical studies have also questioned the assimilationist interpretation of the Italian-American past, by stressing the ability of ordinary people to preserve aspects of their cultures and to change the dominant society by their presence. This opening up of Italian-American history in all its dimensions for public discussion, including such unpalatable aspects as crime, radicalism, and peasant culture, has led to friction with those interested in concentrating solely on the achievements and contributions of Italian Americans.

Meanwhile, the mass of working and lower-middle class Italian Americans continued to draw upon their "heritage" of peasant and proletarian values and traditions to shape their ethnicity. The ethnic revival by sanctioning cultural difference brought a renewed vitality to street festivals, parades, and celebrations in Italian-American settlements across the nation. Whether refurbished feast days of saints or newly created rituals, these events often highlighted the virtues of close family networks, intimate neighborhoods offering stability and security, and smaller value structures. A recurrent theme emerging from the rhetoric and ritual of these occasions was a "bootstraps" interpretation of the past, focusing on the immigrant work ethic, sacrifice, family, and loyalty. A nostalgia for the "Little Italies" of the past which allegedly embodied these values offered a psychological defense against the perceived materialism, faceless anonymity, and moral chaos of America.

The new Italian-American ethnic activism also took the form of an aggressive anti-defamation campaign designed to counter prejudices and negative stereotypes through pressure group tactics. A major target of this campaign was the pervasive characterizations of Italian criminality in the mass media. Various Italian–American organizations brought intense public pressure against the U.S. Department of Justice, the *New York Times*, and other media to discontinue references to the Cosa Nostra and the Mafia. Similar motivations underlay attempts to halt derogatory "Italian jokes" as well as commercials and media representations which depicted Italian Americans as coarse, uneducated boors. After submitting passively for decades to stereotyping and defamation, Italian Americans had mobilized to renegotiate their ethnicity with mainstream institutions. Their considerable success in doing so demonstrated that they had attained a level of economic and political power which enabled them to bargain from a position of strength. Curiously at a stage of their history which has been characterized as "the twilight of ethnicity," the Italian Americans have demonstrated a greater volubility, creativity and effectiveness in defining their position in the larger society than ever before.

This selective refashioning of Italian-American ethnicity no doubt will continue as individuals dip into their cultural reservoirs and choose aspects that suit their needs at particular moments in time. What emerges as important in this process is not how much of the "traditional" culture has survived, but rather the changing uses to which people put cultural symbols and rituals. The problems inherent in arbitrating complex ethnic identities ensure that there will also be ongoing internal group conflict over which aspects should be selected and used. The patterns of accommodation and resistance that have characterized the invention of Italian-American identity speak to the tensions and contradictions that form a critical component in the American ethnic group experience.

CONCLUSION

The concept of invention offers an optic of power and subtlety for the analysis of ethnicity, this social phenomenon which has demonstrated such unanticipated resilience in the modern world. Since in this conception ethnicity is not a biological or cultural "given," it is restored to the province of history. For the study of immigrant adaptation, this approach, we believe, has significant advantages over preceding theories. It shifts the focus of analysis from the hackneyed concern with individual assimilation to a host society to the sphere of collective, interactive behavior in which negotiations between immigrant groups and the dominant ethnoculture are open-ended

and ambivalent. It further calls into question the assumption that the host society unilaterally dictates the terms of assimilation and that change is a linear progression from "foreignness" to Americanization. Rather it envisions a dynamic process of ethnicization, driven by multiple relationships, among various sidestream ethnicities as well as between them and the mainstream ethnicity, and resulting in multidirectional change. Everyone is changed in this dialectical process. Since such relationships are often competitive and conflictual, contestation is a central feature of ethnicization. Thus power and politics, in the broadest sense, both internal to the groups and in the external relations with "others," are basic to the formation and preservation of ethnicities.

The invention of ethnicity, therefore, offers promising alternatives to the single-group approach which threatened to bog down immigration studies in a sterile parochialism. It further facilitates, we believe, a fresh strategy for addressing the question, "What is American?" Rather than positing a hegemonic Anglo-American core culture, this conceptualization entertains the notion that what is distinctively American has been itself a product of this synergistic encounter of multiple peoples and cultures. A new scholarship on the invention of American identity and traditions as well as on the categories of class, race, and gender, provides a necessary, if still relatively underdeveloped, context which will undergird studies of the invention of particular ethnicities by immigrant groups and the process of ethnicization itself. On such an agenda of research, certainly among the most promising and exciting topics for study are the intersections of class, race, and gender with ethnicity.

NO

Herbert J. Gans

ETHNIC INVENTION AND ACCULTURATION, A BUMPY-LINE APPROACH

Historians and sociologists tend to see the social process quite differently, for the former look at it over the long sweep of time and from the available archives, while the latter look closely at the present, because they can, among other things, observe and interview the participants in the process.

"The Invention of Ethnicity" by Kathleen Conzen and her coauthors is interesting, among other reasons because it is a cooperative venture of historians and sociologists. Nevertheless, I think the article underplays one theme which has long been central to the sociological analysis of ethnicity: the acculturation and continuing Americanization of the immigrants, be they the descendants of the European immigrants who arrived here between 1880 and 1925, or of the latest newcomers to America.

To be sure, I share the authors' disavowal of the primordial notion of ethnicity, which does not even describe the European nationality groups who are at this writing (Summer 1992) once more spilling each other's blood over issues of land, boundaries and political as well as economic dominance. Fortunately, American ethnic groups are not nationality groups; they are not involved in decades or centuries-old struggles over land and national political equality or dominance. Their fights, which are almost never violent, are usually about local political power and public jobs, and respect, i.e., the freedom from discrimination and hostile stereotypes. In addition, they compete for occupational niches in the economy—especially the newest immigrants who are just in the process of becoming ethnic groups.

I also sympathize with the authors' doubts about invention as fiction, although they take Werner Sollors' metaphoric phrase too literally. For reasons to be explained below, I am not fully comfortable with the idea of ethnicity as invention either, but I agree with their statement that "ethnicity is a process... which incorporates, adapts and amplifies pre-existing communal solidarities, cultural attributes and historical memories."

From Herbert J. Gans, "Comment: Ethnic Invention and Acculturation, A Bumpy-Line Approach," *Journal of American Ethnic History* (Fall 1992). Copyright © 1992 by Transaction Publishers. Reprinted by permission. Notes omitted.

Actually, I would emphasize adaptation in this definition (and exclude amplification), for most of what they call ethnicity is people's adaptation of the pre-existing to meet new situations in, as well as opportunities and constraints from, non-ethnic society. (I prefer this term to "the dominant ethnoculture," because no single one dominates more than a few sectors of American life these days,and the still powerful WASPs now feel like a minority, and thus an ethnic group themselves.)

One of these constraints, which the authors do not discuss sufficiently, is the involuntary ethnicity which is generated when people define others in ethnic terms, thus sometimes forcing the latter to be and feel more ethnic than they might otherwise be. All ethnic groups which still suffer from discrimination or cultural stereotyping are occasionally so forced, and might in fact be less ethnic if this did not happen.

Adaptation is always to some extent innovative, but to focus too much on the new strikes me as unnecessarily ahistorical, especially since what is adapted virtually always draws on past cultural resources. Even the "invented traditions," which the authors include as a form of adaptation, are after all invented *as traditions*, which construct an imagined or empirical past. For example, the African-American Kwanzaa holiday, which was invented by Maulana Karenga in 1966, celebrates various elements of an African past.

While it is impossible to predict how innovative future ethnic behavior will be and how many new traditions will be invented, I see no evidence for the authors' belief that the continuing acculturation of immigrant and later ethnic culture will ever be reversed, except perhaps in a now unimaginably severe economic and political national crisis. (More likely, blacks, other poor people, and to a lesser extent Jews, will be scapegoats in future crises as they have been in past ones, joined perhaps by some of the recent immigrants. Like scapegoats everywhere, they will then be forced to define themselves as ethnic and may even draw in their ethnic wagons to defend themselves. However, the ethnic groups Conzen et al. write about are more apt to be the scapegoaters than the scapegoated in such a crisis, and will therefore not need to find new strengths in adaptations of old cultures.)

In short, the basic insights of W. Lloyd Warner and Leo Srole... published in 1945 as *The Social Systems of American Ethnic Groups* remain accurate. Warner and Srole were wrong about a number of things, notably the then prevalent belief that acculturation and assimilation followed a downward straight line trend that would inevitably end with the eventual total disappearance of all traces of ethnicity after several native-born generations.

However, Warner and Srole had only two generations available for study and were probably extrapolating the great changes they saw between the immigrant and second generation. Nonetheless, further and not very different changes have taken place among later generations, for whatever the indicator of ethnicity under study, the numbers continue to decline—be it in language use, endogamy, religious attendance, organizational activity, donations to charity, knowledge of invented or real traditions etc. Those researchers who emphasize the fluid and innovative elements in ethnicity often ignore these data as if they did not exist, but the decision to study only the latest adaptations and the occasional innovations cannot make them disappear.

Still, looking at American ethnicity with the hindsight of forty-five years after Warner and Srole wrote their book, I would replace what has often been described as their straight line theory with *bumpy line* theory, the bumps representing various kinds of adaptations to changing circumstances—and with the line having no predictable end. This is particularly true since acculturating generations are once more being partly replaced by new immigrants from many of the countries that fed the 1880–1925 influx who then have an impact on the overall ethnic culture. Warner and Srole, who were working in the 1930s and early 1940s when no significant immigration took place, could not predict this new population movement. Nor could they predict the findings of the recent and very careful research by Richard Alba and by Mary Waters among third to fifth generation descendants of the European immigrants, which indicates that many still hold to a mild form of ethnic identity, or can at least name an ethnic origin when asked by an interviewer.

Alba and Waters also supplied a good deal of supporting evidence for my hypothesis that for third and later generations, ethnicity is often *symbolic*, free from affiliation with ethnic groups and ethnic cultures, and instead dominated by the consumption of symbols, for example at ethnic restaurants, festivals, in stores that sell ethnic foods and ancestral collectibles, and through vacation trips to the Old Country. Unfortunately, Conzen and her coauthors misread me, for I neither dismiss this latest bump in the bumpy line theory nor do I think it is "doomed to fade away before the irresistible forces of assimilation." Symbolic ethnicity might fade away if people chose to forget everything about the ethnic origins of any of their ancestors, but it could also become a permanent source of extra identity, an occasion for nostalgia, a pleasant leisure time activity—and even an opportunity for conspicuous consumption—what the *New York Times* reporter Maureen Dowd once described as "designer ethnicity." Consequently, symbolic ethnicity could have a long lifespan.

In addition, the authors underemphasize the Glazer-Moynihan conception of ethnic groups as political interest groups, for even if big-city politics has moved beyond the old balanced ticket troika consisting of an Irish, Italian or Polish, and Jewish candidate at the top of the ticket, race and ethnicity still affect the selection of candidates and appointed officials. Moreover, employers, workers, homeowners and other citizens often have political or economic interests, and they will still play an ethnic card if that is useful for advancing these interests. In a number of older American cities, working and lower-middle class people from a variety of European ethnic origins have periodically coalesced to oppose what they see as the excessive power of a growing black or Hispanic community— a political reaction which has also been encouraged in various ways by Republican presidents since Richard Nixon who were seeking to attract an imaginary or real "white ethnic vote" into their party.

Conzen and her colleagues, like others before them, have mistaken these political developments—and some others shortly to be described—as evidence of a major ethnic revival which began during the late 1960s and the 1970s. While these developments were hardly devoid of ethnic features and symbols, they are better described as a class-based social movement clad in ethnic clothes, following the American tradition of using ethnicity as a surrogate for class. Not only did the revivals lack significant and long-lasting ethnic cultural content, but they were in fact coalitions of white ethnic groups which previously had little to do with each other, or had been in conflict.

Now they came together in large part to stop what they saw as the incursions of poor blacks into their jobs and their neighborhoods, and to protest a War on Poverty they perceived to support these incursions but also to erase the class and status differences between poor blacks and themselves. The coalition continued through the 1960s and early 1970s as national Democratic politics seemed to be increasingly dominated by liberal and pro-black upper middle-class professionals, but it began to end as a number of white ethnics moved into a Republican party that had theretofore shunned them as ethnics and Catholics.

The little ethnic content inside these coalitions had two sources, and again class was a hidden factor. One source reflected the acceptance by the major universities of the first generation of ethnic academics other than Jews. They developed ethnic studies programs which frequently emphasized romanticized views of their ethnic traditions, partly in order to strengthen the ethnic identity of students who, as campus newcomers, were made to suffer from status inferiority. The other source came from the grandchildren of immigrants who, upon entering the professional and technical middle classes in increasing numbers, sought respect from the mass media and other parts of mainstream America. In the process, they fought against Polish jokes, Italian Mafia stereotypes and other demeaning ethnic images and symbols.

This fight did not last very long, however. Polish and other ethnic jokes may have been ended, or driven underground, but the Italian Mafia stereotype continued, especially in the movies, even if Mafia movies are now usually set in the past. Still, Italian-American defense organizations have not been very effective, perhaps because not enough third generation Italian-Americans took offense at the depiction of Sicilian immigrants and their criminal children who have been the major characters in these films, or did not suffer sufficiently from anti-Italian discrimination.

From the long perspective of history, and from a historical method that focusses on highly publicized events such as festivals, it is easy to miss what goes on in everyday life, but the authors' account of contemporary Italian Americans flies in the face of what sociologists have learned by talking to third and fourth generation Italian Americans. For example, James Crispino found a steady decline in Italian and Italian-American identity and activities across the generations, while Richard Alba discovered that although his respondents of Italian ancestry were somewhat more likely to emphasize their ethnic identity than those from other ethnic groups, 85 percent of his Italian-American sample was married to spouses with no Italian ancestry whatsoever. From the available sociological (and anthropological) research, Alba's subtitle for his book about Italian Americans: "Into the Twilight of Ethnicity" is apt.

True, all of the events which Conzen et al. report have taken place, but the authors exaggerate the ethnic significance of that data. For one thing, the authors look at ethnicity with a curiously selective historical time-frame. Most of their modern descriptions emphasize the middle of the twentieth century and end with the 1970s, when there was still a sizeable second-generation population. Conversely, the late 1970s and 1980s, when the third generation, which has meager interest in ethnic affairs, became the majority in many of the European-origin groups, get only passing mention.

Also, the events and other anecdotes the authors report deal with a *very* broad sample of Italian Americans, including people from all over Italy and of all classes, thus "undersampling" the vast majority of Italian Americans, who are the descendants of poor Southern Italians and Sicilians, and who still have little to do with "Gucci, Pucci, Ferrari, etc."

In other cases, the authors impute major cultural significance to events which were organized by a handful of loyal ethnics, ambitious ethnic politicians, or eager merchants, but which did not receive much attention from the rest of the ethnic group. The media, which features an event or incident-centered version of the social process and also likes exotic ethnicity events, turned these into what the authors call the "bootstraps" interpretation of the past.

Saints' days and ethnic festivals may have been revived or even invented in some places, but many did not last long. The venerable San Gennaro festival in New York's Little Italy, which they also cite, is no longer an ethnic ceremonial, just as Little Italy is no longer an Italian-American neighborhood. That festival has become a large street fair, with an attendance of over a million people, in which the food is energetically multi-ethnic and the booths are run by professional operators. Even the organization which runs this event, once an exclusive neighborhood group, has long ago had to let in others, including non-Italians, to help in organizing the "festa." As for the neighborhood itself, it is Little Italy only on the street level, which is still occupied by Italian restaurants, foodstores and tourist shops, but the remainder of the area's four and five story tenements and lofts is now a part of Chinatown.

The authors are also correct to point out that some Italian-American politicians—as well as Greeks, Jews, Poles and other Slavs—have finally been able to make their way onto the national political scene after decades in which it was dominated by WASP and Irish politicians. However, the newcomers have often been careful about their ethnic origins for fear that these, and the pejorative stereotypes they still evoke in parts of the "hinterland," would be held against them. Geraldine Ferraro, who is running for the United States Senate from New York at this writing suffered grievously from her husband's alleged Mafia ties the previous time she ran; and Governor Mario Cuomo was often reported as worried about anti-Italian prejudice if he had thrown his hat into the presidential ring in 1991.

Some politicians do run on an actual or invented ethnic past, but their image is more pastoral working class than ethnic, and thus not altogether different from that of Anglo politicians claiming to have been born in log cabins. Conversely, as far as I can recall, no ethnic candidate has bragged about being born in a European palace—or an Anglo one in a Yankee mansion, indicating once again how much ethnicity remains a codeword for class in a society which still likes to see itself as classless. I wish Conzen et al.

had paid more attention to the ways in which the people they write about have used ethnicity as a surrogate for class because it is so important for understanding America.

THE SHORTCOMINGS OF STRAIGHT LINE THEORY

Sociology and history march to their drummers at a different pace, for ideas like the invention—or what sociologists call the social construction—of ethnicity have been around at least since the 1970s. By now these ideas so dominate ethnic writing that discussing concepts like acculturation, assimilation, generation and straight line theory is judged as being old fashioned, if not antipluralistic or even imperialistic.

Part of the fault lies with straight line theory itself, for it is what sociologists call a macrosociological theory which postulates impersonal or structural forces, and thus leaves out "agency" (in current jargon), i.e., the opportunity for people who have choices to make them.

Invention theorizing has corrected this bias, but it has gone too far in the opposite direction, for structural (or bumpy line) theory remains an often accurate and useful approach—and there is no reason to look at social phenomena from only one angle. Admittedly, impersonal forces are themselves composed of myriads of human decisions, but the question of why these decisions move in the same direction needs to be asked, and the larger, even impersonal, economic, political, demographic and other forces—including nation-states, huge bureaucracies, and large industries—that affect, or take away, choice need to be described.

The approach is useful because the new immigrants who have come to America since World War II and 1965 are following in many of the footsteps of their European predecessors, exhibiting similar patterns of acculturation, and becoming more "Americanized" with each generation. Of course, America has changed considerably, but Cuban teenagers struggle with their parents for the freedom they see among their American peers as did Italian and Jewish youngsters after the previous immigration, and the children of poor Jamaican and Haitian immigrants try to shed their Old-Country culture as quickly as possible as poor European children did before them. Even illegal Irish immigrants coming briefly as sojourners soon develop a taste for American popular culture, including its appliances, and then discover that when they visit or return to Ireland, it no longer looks quite as attractive as they remember it.

One of the other faults of straight line theory is its frame; it looks at the American life of the immigrants and their children from the perspective of the Old-Country culture, and measures the way, extent, and speed with which they give up that culture. Conversely, invention theory looks at the process from the other end, focussing on what ethnics do now. Thus, the former underemphasizes the present, and the latter, the past. Ironically enough, straight line theory may thus have distorted the adaptation process, particularly by overestimating the allegiance of the immigrant generation to the Old-Country culture, and exaggerating the speed of its decline and fall in later generations.

This perspective developed in part because of the national consensus about Americanizing the immigrants, but I think also because of the inability of the early sociologists to study the European immigrants. The interest of empirical sociology in the European newcomers did not really manifest itself until the 1920s, at which time a second generation was already on the scene; moreover, the early sociologists spoke only English and thus could not even interview most immigrants.

Now, for a variety of reasons, a marvelous opportunity has developed to study today's immigrants themselves and from all I can tell, many are not as enamored of their Old-Country culture as the straight line theorists believed. Either they were oppressed in the Old Country and thus have little love for its culture to begin with, or they try to leave the old culture behind them and learn to become good Americans as fast as possible. This does not mean they are rejecting their immigrant relatives, neighbors or friends; and, as in the past, assimilation into American society proceeds more slowly than acculturation into American culture.

Today, we can study how and how quickly the new immigrants—and then those of the next generation—are choosing or being asked, or both, to Americanize, as well as to remain loyal to a version of the old culture—and whether and when they can or want to compromise. In effect, it will be possible to look at the immigrants and their descendants both as they deviate from their ethnic past and as they construct their ethnic present; and by analyzing their choices and their absence of choice, the roles structure and agency play in their ethnic lives. Ultimately, I think the researches will show that both acculturation and invention theories are accurate, for immigrants and their descendants will be moving away from the Old Country culture but concurrently inventing the bumps in bumpy line theory.

Historians would benefit from such analyses too, because they must look at the past from both structural and agency perspectives. Concepts like invention may empower people as actors in control of their fate and contribute to ethnic pride, but such concepts may also overdo agency by ignoring the contexts within which, and the reasons for which, people do what they have to do. If Jews invent the "chanukah-bush," they do so not to be ethnically innovative but to discourage their children from demanding the Christmas trees and other aspects of Christianity they see among their non-Jewish friends. And if middle-class Caribbean immigrants press their children to hold on to their West Indian dialects and accents, they do so not just to preserve a language but to make sure that whites will not mistake their children for, and treat them as, poor American blacks.

ETHNICITY AS INTELLECTUAL INVENTION

Ethnicity has become so much part of the general discourse that it is easy to forget that the term was coined less than half a century ago and that it was first used by sociologists and anthropologists to describe the people they studied. We still do not know how much the people whom we describe as ethnics think and talk about themselves with the same terminology. Indeed, we do not even know when, how and for what reasons they view their identity as being a matter of national origin. They can supply an ethnic identity when asked by social scientists or the Census, but we do not know how many would do so if asked a general and open-ended question about the sources of their personal identity. Judging by the amount of coaxing interview respondents need to discuss their ethnic identity, many might talk about that identity in completely different, and non-ethnic, language.

This does not necessarily mean they would stop acting in ways social scientists describe as ethnic; rather, people maintain these ways because they enjoy them, to give the family an excuse to meet, to please older relatives, to preserve the family as a source of emotional support or because it is necessary for economic survival. After all, ethnic traditions are sometimes maintained or altered to help hold the family together, and profitable economic niches continued to be occupied by ethnic groups whose members do not much act like, or identify as, ethnics.

Consequently, as the turn-of-the-century European immigration turns into fourth and fifth generations of multi-hyphenated Americans, those of us who write about ethnicity should begin to think about the role *we* play in contemporary ethnicity.

POSTSCRIPT

Do Italian Americans Reject Assimilation?

Since the 1960s, ethnic and racial minorities have not only been "inventing" themselves, they have also been rediscovered by both the public and scholars.

Gans says that no single group now dominates others. The traditional hegemonic group, white Anglo-Saxon Protestants, "feel like minority groups themselves." Moreover, the Republican Party, the former bastion of WASPs, has been busy incorporating minorities into the party, observes Gans.

To these assertions, radical sociologists would counter that while the symbolic aspects of such assimilation may be there, in essential ways, such as control of wealth, occupancy of important government positions, and behind-the-scenes political power, racial and ethnic minorities (as well as women) are disproportionately underrepresented.

You might note two subtle but important distinctions in intellectual style between Gans and Conzen et al. Some would attribute this to disciplinary differences, but others could argue that it represents a generational gap. Gans's position reflects the kind of emphasis early symbolic interactionists placed on the role of dress, food, words, and other external codes denoting interesting but relatively superficial group differences. These things are important. However, Conzen et al. reflect a different, more novel and abstract level of cultural analysis. To them, and many other younger analysts, there exist deeper structures of racial and ethnic cultural solidarities. These are rooted in a constellation of attitudes and values, a shared world view. These, they suggest, persist even through superficial metamorphoses. They continue to function to maintain the ethnic-racial group's boundaries.

In addition to most standard minority relations textbooks as well as those mentioned earlier, there are several important works that you should consult. Two recent books by Richard Alba are essential. See his *Ethnic Identity: The Transformation of White America* (Yale University Press, 1990), and *Italian Americans: Into the Twilight of Ethnicity* (Prentice Hall, 1985). For a somewhat technical discussion that links occupations, class, and ethnicity, and is on the cutting edge of research, see M. Hechter's *Principles of Group Solidarity* (University of California Press, 1987). Relating ethnicity to broader political and community values is L. Fuchs's *The American Kaleidoscope* (Wesleyan University Press, 1990). Two works devoted to Italian Americans are *Italian Americans Celebrate Life*, edited by P. Giordano and S. Isolani (1992), and *From the Margins: Writings in Italian Americana*, edited by A. Tamburi et al. (1991).

PART 2

Cultural Issues: Ideology and Conflict

Defining and identifying minority groups and the myths pertaining to them, and scientifically analyzing minority groups, is only the beginning. A vital task is to determine how minorities identify themselves. What aspects of the broader culture do they accept or reject? How and why do convenient, sometimes romantic, myths harden into ideologies that result in conflict, both functional and dysfunctional?

- Should We Call Ourselves African Americans?

- Do Cultural Differences Between Home and School Explain the High Dropout Rates for American Indian Students?

- Should Bilingual Education Programs Be Stopped?

- Should Black Women Join the Feminist Movement?

- Are Positive Images of African Americans Increasing in the Media?

ISSUE 5

Should We Call Ourselves African Americans?

YES: John Sibley Butler, from "Multiple Identities," *Society* (May/June 1990)

NO: Walter E. Williams, from "Myth Making and Reality Testing," *Society* (May/June 1990)

ISSUE SUMMARY

YES: Professor of sociology John Sibley Butler briefly traces the history of the terms that Black Americans have applied to themselves, and he contrasts their ethnic-racial identities with those of other Americans. He argues that it makes sense to be African Americans.

NO: Walter E. Williams, professor of economics, acknowledges the baggage contained in the labels that people select for themselves. He dismisses those who opt for African American (or related terms) in order to achieve cultural integrity among Blacks. He says that there are serious problems in the Black community that need to be addressed, none of which will be solved by a new name.

For over two hundred years (1620 through the early 1800s), the ancestors of most Black Americans were brought to this continent as slaves. They were first hunted, captured, and packaged, often by West Africans, who were engaged in dividing and conquering peoples and their territories. Thus members of captured tribes were mixed together indiscriminately. Sometimes a slave was sold several times over to other slave dealers, with each transaction netting new profits and removing the captured victim one step further from his or her tribe of origin.

Many, but certainly not all, were eventually sold to European slave dealers and then later to American slave dealers, primarily New England Yankee seafarers and merchants. The slave dealers quickly learned how to handle their human chattel: they separated as much as possible members of a tribe or language group from each other and mixed slaves together in an attempt to isolate those with a common background. This obviously minimized coalition formation. They also isolated women and children so that many male slaves would comply with their new owners in the hopes of being reunited with their families. During transport across the Atlantic, 50 percent or more of all slaves would die or commit suicide, resulting in even more fragmentation. Upon arrival, separate members of tribes and families would be sold to different slave owners, although this was not always the case for family members. Over time, a significant portion of a plantation's slaves, or their descendants, would be returned to the slave auction block to be sold yet again, sometimes to new owners residing hundreds of miles away. All of this functioned to increase the separation from tribes of origin and Africa itself.

This obliteration of identity and culture for Black Americans was unlike the experiences of other racial and ethnic groups, who could draw a certain amount of psychic support and relief from the artifacts, the myths, the oral traditions, and the ancestry of their places of origin.

The situation for Blacks in the United States, especially when the many years of slavery are factored in, goes beyond Frantz Fanon's description in *The Wretched of the Earth*: "Colonialism is not satisfied merely with holding a people in its grip and emptying the native's brain of all form and content. By a kind of perverted logic, it turns to the past of the oppressed people, and distorts, disfigures, and destroys it."

To many in the United States whose ancestors suffered these horrors, and who themselves cannot claim with any comfort specific ethnic or tribal heritage, the symbolic stakes in this debate are high. Although not particularly militant on the issue, Professor Butler clearly concurs with Jesse Jackson that, "To be called black is baseless. To be called African American has cultural integrity."

Butler acknowledges that even before the Revolutionary War Blacks disagreed among themselves about what name to use. During the Civil War period (shortly before and after 1861–1865), prominent Blacks such as Frederick Douglas and Martin R. Delany bitterly disagreed on the proper term for Black Americans (Douglas favored Negro).

Prominent economist Williams agrees that people may call themselves anything they wish. However, he has a problem with the term *African American*.

Williams points out that there is no single African culture; Blacks generally have no knowledge of what part of Africa and what tribes they may be from; Black Americans share little or nothing of significance with any groups in Africa, either in the present or past; Black Americans have little to gain by discovering (or inventing) myths about affinities with the continent of Africa.

It is interesting to note that, with important exceptions (e.g., Marcus Garvey, W. E. B. Du Bois in his latter years), most Black leaders until recently wanted to distance themselves from Africa. America was seen as their home and where their destinies were.

As you read these articles, decide if creating a myth is necessarily bad. How might such a "myth" be functional, even if history is somewhat distorted? On the other hand, could playing fast and loose with facts have possible unanticipated negative consequences? What customs would you like to be part of your life if you could pick them?

YES

John Sibley Butler

MULTIPLE IDENTITIES

During the aftermath of the 1989 Presidential election, the Rev. Jesse Jackson announced that *gens de couleur* (people of color) with an African flavor should redefine themselves. Instead of referring to themselves as Black Americans or Afro-Americans (the most frequently used names for the group in recent times), they should use exclusively the term African-Americans. Because the country, and especially Mr. Jackson, was just winding down from discussions of serious campaign issues such as poverty, jobs, the homeless, inflation, and the arms race, the sudden emergence of name identification issue seemed out of place. But the distribution of his comments about name identification for blacks by the national news media prompted a series of debates and general discussions throughout the land. This Pope-like proclamation was made, Jackson said, in order to create among Black-Americans more of an identity with the original homeland of Africa. The Rev. Jackson's comments raise old issues and give us an opportunity to explore the relationship among origin of country, identification with that country, and the American experience.

THE ISSUE IN COMPARATIVE PERSPECTIVE

There have been few, if any, countries in the history of the world that developed as America has in terms of the diversity of racial and ethnic groups. Bringing diverse cultures from all parts of the world, these groups have influenced the nature of everything "American." Although some Africans came as indentured servants and later gained their "freedom," the great majority of the group was forced to leave their homeland and they worked in America as slaves and made "cotton King." Other racial and ethnic groups came to find employment in the developing country while others created entrepreneurial niches to create group economic stability. From this ethnic and racial mixture, the country developed military manpower in order to engage in war and conflict, elected U.S. Senators and Congressmen and women, developed professional sports teams, and sent people to the moon. Over the years, although the country's history contains a record of racial and ethnic conflict, members of the racial and ethnic mixtures have come to refer to themselves as Americans.

Although this is true, under certain conditions groups have hyphenated themselves so as to reflect an identification with their original homeland, thus making name identification conditional on certain historical circumstances. The identification as strictly American is very strong during times of international conflict. During the World Wars all ethnic groups were quick to assert their identification exclusively with America, despite the amount of time that they had been in the country. Italian-Americans, German-Americans, and Japanese-Americans simply identified themselves as Americans. During World War II, German-Americans were not celebrating Wurstfest and Japanese-Americans were not celebrating the greatest of the Japanese Empire. More recently, international events (*e.g.*, the bombing of a plane or restaurant, or the plight of hostages) have generated the same kind of identification with the term American that was present during the World Wars.

Groups that become hyphenated Americans usually have a history of racial or ethnic conflict and inequality. For groups that trace their origins to Europe, it is plausible to say that the more hostility they received when first adjusting to America, the more likely they are to be hyphenated Americans. This can be seen in the cases of Italian-Americans and Irish-Americans, two groups that faced systematic hostility when first entering the country. On the other hand, the terms English-American and Scandinavian-American are seldom if ever used to identify a common history of discrimination in America. In some cases, religious identity, which is usually associated with historical oppression, appears before the hyphen-

ation. Although Jews were historically found in many countries in Europe, in America they refer to themselves mainly as Jewish-Americans rather than German-Americans, English-Americans, or Polish-Americans. Although ethnic groups of European origin get along rather well in America, and see themselves as white Americans, events within the country that divide the issue along ethnic lines (such as elections) have the effect of resurrecting the importance of the hyphenation. It should also be pointed out that at one time in America ethnic conflict was the result of internal competition over jobs and other resources that helped to develop economic stability. At this point in history, conflict among ethnic groups in America can be the result of tension or war in the international market. What goes on in Europe and the Middle-East can cause ethnic groups from those regions to rally around their hyphenation. Throughout the years, ethnic identification among Europeans has been conditional and is influenced by their ethnic history in America and conflicts outside of America.

Racial groups of non-European origin carry with them an almost built-in hyphenation which relates to a continent rather than to a specific country on a continent. The issue before us does not raise the question of which country on the continent of Africa should be the source of identification for black Americans. The debate is not whether they should be called Nigerian-Americans, Zaire-Americans, or Gabon-Americans, but simply African-Americans. Unlike Europeans, who identify with a specific country on the European continent, it is impossible for Americans who are black to identify with their specific country (we can say that most slaves came from West

Africa) of origin because of the slave experience, which included the stripping of national identification and thus the inability to pass down one's country of identification through the years. With all due respect given to an argument which specifies that this question is exactly like the question for European ethnic groups, we must recognize that the issue is not exactly the same. If it were the same, whites would refer to themselves as Euro-Americans rather than Irish-Americans, Italian-Americans, Polish-Americans, etc. Identifying the hyphenation with a continent can also be seen in the case of Japanese-Americans, Mexican-Americans, and Cuban-Americans. As we explore the issue of identification and the Afro-American experience, we will draw on the ethnic experience for comparative purposes.

THE AFRO-AMERICAN EXPERIENCE

Before the Revolutionary War period, free blacks engaged in a general debate about what to call themselves. In the middle of this debate was James Forten, a self-made millionaire from Philadelphia who made his fortune producing sails for vessels on the high seas. After much debate, officially they agreed to call themselves Negro-Americans rather than African-Americans or Afro-Americans. They made this decision because they wished to identify with the New World rather than with the Old World. Although this decision was made, historical records indicate that not all people of African descent agreed with the term Negro-Americans; this can be seen by examining the names of some of their most cherished institutions which carried, and continue to carry, the desig-

nation "Africa." The African Episcopal Church was founded after the Revolutionary War, and the African Blood Brothers was organized after World War II.

As years progressed from the Revolutionary War period, for the most part blacks called themselves names that were not directly identifiable with the African continent, the most frequent being Negroes and "Colored People." Early black scholars argued that this was the result of the almost total annihilation of the African culture in America. Consider the following quotation taken from *Race, Radicalism, and Reform*, by Abram Harris, a noted economist of his day. It is interesting that he argues that in no way can "African Negroes" in America (another name identification) be considered African:

It is not infrequent that the economic and social subjugation of one race or class of another has led the subordinated group to adopt the culture of the dominant. This has happened to the Negro in the United States. If the first African Negroes who came to America brought with them concepts of social institutions or culture typically African they could not practice them in America. Moreover, we have no attempts by Negroes to establish African culture in the United States. Nor can the American Negro be considered in any logical way African. The assimilation of the Negro to American culture has been so complete that one [white] observer remarked: with most marvelous certainty, the Negro in the South could be trusted to perpetuate our political ideas and institutions if our republic fell, as surely as the Gaul did his adopted institutions.

Although Harris acknowledged the growing research at that time that attempted to link elements of African culture with the culture of black Americans (Harris noted the work of George Schuyler, "The Negro Art Hokum," in *The Nation* and the reply by Langston Hughes; and Milton Sampson's "Race Consciousness and Race Relations" in *Opportunity*), he concluded that blacks in America cannot be considered in any logical way African. It is plausible that many analyses of the black American situation squared with the ideas of Harris during this time period.

SOCIAL MOVEMENTS

The development of name identification that links blacks to the Motherland Africa has historically been associated with social movements. Although there were many movements before the emergence of Marcus Garvey (*e.g.*, Martin R. Delany in 1852 proclaimed "Africa for Africans" and Daniel Coker, the first bishop of the African Methodist Episcopal Church, sailed for the American Colonization Society with 90 free blacks in 1820), he was instrumental in raising the consciousness of black Americans about the continent of Africa. Although some of his many publications had the word Negro in their titles (*Negro History Bulletin, The New Negro Voice, The New Negro World*), some also stressed the importance of blackness (*The Black May* and *The Black Violet*). Throughout these publications the identification with Africa is stressed and the term African-American is used consistently. More importantly, the Garvey movement incorporated a strong ideology of race pride and praise of African physical characteristics, which were viewed as superior to those of Europeans. He and his followers praised black skin, black hair texture, the shapely image of men and women (e.g., protruding buttocks),

and the alleged slow aging process of the race. His organization, the United Negro Improvement Association, was geared towards developing the group along spiritual, economic, and social lines. During the Garvey years, for those who followed him, there was a convergence of behavior, acceptance of black physical characteristics, and the ideology of identification with the African homeland. Although Garvey's movement used a variety of terms to identify blacks (Negro, Black, African, African-American), it is clear that the emphasis was on blacks as African-Americans. Despite the many criticisms and the outcome of this movement, Garvey was successful in getting blacks to like themselves and above all, to like their physical characteristics.

Unlike during the Garvey years, the term Negro was used throughout the modern civil rights movement. This is reflected in the papers of the period, including those of the NAACP and Southern Christian Leadership Association. This much-needed movement did not stress the importance of African characteristics, nor did it emphasize identification with the continent of Africa. It took the activities of the SNCC (Student Non-Violent Coordinating Committee), the student arm of the NAACP, to reinstate the importance of the African heritage for name identification. In *Black Power: The Politics of Liberation*, Stokely Carmichael and Charles Hamilton noted that an identification change was necessary for black Americans. Unlike Jesse Jackson's comments, which insist on the term African-American, Carmichael and Hamilton equated the terms African-Americans and Afro-Americans with the term black. They also reintroduced the theme of an appreciation of African characteristics that had been so much a part of the Garvey movement:

> There is a growing resentment of the word "negro"... because this term is the invention of our oppressor. Many blacks are now calling themselves Afro-Americans or black people because that is our image of ourselves.... From now on we shall view ourselves as African-Americans and as black people who are in fact energetic, determined, intelligent, beautiful, and peace-loving.

There was also a behavioral component to this movement. Throughout the land blacks began to show an appreciation for their African characteristics as natural hairstyles and an appreciation for the black skin became commonplace among all age groups. There also developed a sense of "color and hair texture democracy." This is a group that ranges in physical characteristics from fair European to the blackest of African ebony. Black publications proudly displayed men and women of all the different colors of the group, with perhaps those displaying the most African characteristics enjoying the most prestige. It was not culturally acceptable within the group to use concepts such as "good hair" and "bad hair" or "black but pretty." Like the Garvey movement at the turn of the century, and indeed like the movements during earlier times when race consciousness was raised, the behavior of the group reflected an identification with Africa (or blackness) not only through name but also through an appreciation of the biological characteristics that they share with Africans. It is important to understand also that the emphasis was on the appreciation of biological characteristics rather than on the type of dress. Although African dress styles played a part in both the Garvey movement and the movement of the 1960s, they never really became the dominant mode of dress.

JACKSON'S CALL: AN ANACHRONISM

The call by Jesse Jackson for blacks to refer to themselves as African-Americans during this historical juncture is not at all associated with any kind of systematic movement, especially one that stresses the importance of racial consciousness of Africans and black Americans. More importantly, it comes at a time when there is a general rejection of African biological characteristics and the decline of any kind of consciousness about color democracy. This is reflected in the everyday styles of black Americans and in major publications where blacks with European characteristics (hair, facial features, etc.) are significantly more likely to be featured. If it is true that the generation of the 1960s reintroduced the importance of presenting oneself in a natural style (natural hairstyles, an appreciation for African art and music), it is also true that the present generation shows no appreciation for African characteristics. Even the people who grew up in the 1960s have rejected natural presentations of self and have reverted to European aesthetics. Perhaps Abram Harris was correct when he observed, in 1927, that blacks in America were simply too acculturated aesthetically to ever accept, even during periods of race-conscious movements, their own physical characteristics over long periods of time:

> [The] cultural accommodation and above all, the physical contact which preceded and paralleled it, could have but one

effect upon the Negro, the annihilation of a Negro national physiognomy—and, in consequence, the Negro's repudiation of African aesthetic standards. The ready market which sellers of bleaching and hair straightening compounds find among Negroes indicates the extent of this repudiation. But a surging race consciousness among Negroes which has expressed itself in art and other forms may seem to belie the repudiation of African aesthetic standards, or it may be mistaken as the Negro's attempt to establish a Negro culture within the United States. Considerable controversy has centered about the question of Negro culture as a product distinct from United States culture. But close examination of the social facts underlying the Negro's position in the United States shows his race consciousness to be merely a device which he has contrived in order to compensate his thwarted ambition for full participation in American society.

Harris' observations are interesting and point to the obvious effect of European aesthetic standards on black Americans, and his observations about the 1920s can be applied to the group today. It is interesting to listen to and watch blacks argue for the use of the term African-American rather than other terms to identify the group. At a recent gathering, as the debate grew hot, all of the females had relaxed hair, high-powered faces, and some even had on blue contact lenses. Many of the males were "sporting" curls in their hair and other forms of "processed" hair. If some native Africans were to have shown up at such a gathering, they may have wondered in amusement and asked, "What race are these people?" Put simply, this is a strange time in black Americans' aesthetic history to issue a message asking people to call themselves African-Americans.

The behavior vis-à-vis aesthetics of black Americans today are in direct contrast to Jesse Jackson's comments when he called for the name African-American. He said, "To be called black is baseless... To be called African-American has cultural integrity." While it may be true that people want to identify themselves as descendants of Africa, it is also true presently that it is chic to look as European as possible. This fact gives new meaning to W.E.B. DuBois' concept of "two-ness," wherein he stressed the psychological state of living in two American worlds, one white and one black. In this case the emphasis would be placed on aesthetic identification rather than psychological identification. One would certainly think that pride in Africa would be accomplished by at least the acceptance of physical characteristics of Africans in America. Yet the cultural renaissance in America for blackness at this time is dead and shows no sign of reviving itself. It should be stressed that this is an issue that goes well beyond changes in fashion since we are speaking of the actual change of biological characteristics to fit those of Europeans. Those black Americans who have naturally European characteristics do not have to work as hard on changing their biological characteristics as their more African sisters and brothers. Like white Americans who seem to worship and praise those of the group with fair skin and blond hair, black Americans show a gravitation toward those in the group who possess European characteristics. While one cannot change the reality of skin color and hair color variation within black America, a call for the term African-American to identify the group should at least have a behavioral component that shows an aesthetic appreciation for the entire rainbow of the group. While there is certainly nothing wrong with being black and possessing European characteristics (which is also a natural biological state), it is problematic when African biological characteristics are not appreciated in the same manner. Throughout history, black Americans have had to work very hard in order to get their African characteristics accepted (even by themselves) as being "beautiful" on the human landscape of aesthetics.

IDENTIFICATION WITH A HOMELAND

There are, of course, other reasons given as to why black Americans should identify themselves as African-Americans, even if for the most part members of the group reject African aesthetics. One of the major reasons is that it allows the group to identify with a homeland, much like other ethnic groups. This reason is expressed in the following comment published in *Ebony* last year:

Using African-American is of value in that it has some authenticity. The idea of saying "African-American" links us to a foundation.... We don't originally come from Georgia or South Carolina or Mississippi. African-American takes people back to the motherland, a place of origin. It gives us what the Jews have, a homeland. This designation gives us some credibility. We can now claim a land because a landless people are people without clout and without substance. Inasmuch as there is an Africa and that is our ultimate homeland, then to authenticate it we should identify with the homeland itself.

Contained in this quotation are the oldest and most convincing arguments as to why black Americans should call themselves African-Americans, for they are indeed of African descent. It gives the group a continent to identify with, and like other groups in America, this identification is important; this is true even if blacks in America cannot identify with a specific country in Africa. This is also important from an historical point of view, since, as noted earlier, there is no place called Negro, Afro, or blackland in the world.

But how do different ethnic groups relate to their homeland? Is there a difference between how black Americans relate to Africa as compared to their ethnic hyphenated counterparts?

One way that ethnic groups relate to their original homeland is through a celebration of their roots during festivals and other kinds of festive activities. On St. Patrick's Day, Irish-Americans wear green, have parades, and make everyone else Irish for a day. German-Americans celebrate Wurstfest, inviting everyone to enjoy the food and customs of Germany for a day. Throughout America celebrations of this type occur for different ethnic groups.

Ethnic groups in America also identify with their homeland by giving military support so that people in the old country can hold on to, capture, or recapture important historical territory from foreign invaders. Because of the richness of the economic stability of ethnic members in the United States, and the strong military presence that this country has in the world, groups occupying what Americans call "the Old Country" look for military help from their American counterparts. A growing literature reveals the fact that ethnic groups in America are giving military support to their counterparts in other parts of the world. This can be seen in the activities of some Greek American organizations that support arms for Greece so that it can maintain a degree of independence in its historical conflict with the Turks; Irish-Americans supply funds so that the Irish of Southern Ireland can continue their liberation efforts from the British. In a work entitled *The Lobby*, Edward Tivnan examines the importance of Jewish-Americans' lobbying efforts and their commitment to Israel. In an article entitled "The Arab Lobby: Problems and Prospects," Nabeel A. Khoury shows how Arab-Americans are trying to organize in order to influence important aspects of U.S. foreign policy in the Middle East. One can be assured that the purchase of weapons for Arab states will be of great importance to that developing lobby.

Although black Americans celebrate holidays, there is not a single established national holiday which brings out the connection between themselves and the African continent. Instead, important holidays are grounded more in the American experience and some have lost their significance over the years. Emancipation Day, celebrated on January 1, is traditionally a national holiday for black Americans but is not celebrated nationally as it was some 30 years ago (in Texas this is called Juneteenth and is celebrated in June because news of the emancipation of the slaves was late in arriving in the state of Texas). Martin Luther King's Birthday and Negro History Week are also American-specific. Unlike some ethnic groups, there is not a specific national day of celebration that ties the African continent and its food and traditions, to the black American experience of continent identification.

Like other ethnic groups, there has been a concentrated effort by black Americans to support Africans on the continent. Although black Americans have not lobbied Congress to sell weapons to black South Africans so that they can fight for their freedom, they have shown their concern by supporting international boycotts against the South African Government. This stands in sharp contrast to other ethnic groups in America who support the selling of arms to members of their "Old Country" so that they can maintain themselves and their traditions. It remains to be seen if black South Africans can pray and boycott their way to national independence or full political participation in South African society. Certainly they do not have the military clout to recapture their historical homeland from foreign invaders. Black Americans have also shown an interest in other problems on the African continent, such as hunger and education. Since the 1800s, for example, the African Methodist Episcopal Church has supported education in Africa. Black Americans do have a history of supporting, albeit in different ways from other ethnic groups, people of African descent who are on the African continent.

Another important issue is whether or not there is a relationship between what black Americans call themselves and their economic and social progress in the United States. After all, Jesse Jackson declared that to be called black is baseless. Historical evidence suggests that black Americans made the most progress in changing legal codes of discrimination when they referred to themselves as Negroes and that they also made significant economic progress when they called themselves blacks or Negroes. There is no evidence to suggest that calling oneself exclusively African-American translates into economic or any other kind of progress, whether it be spiritual or educational. There is no ethnic data to suggest that there is a relationship between ethnic identification (at the level of what a group called itself vis-à-vis the Old Country) and economic progress.

The issue of what blacks call themselves will continue, as it has in the past, to emerge as an issue during certain historical periods. What makes this period so different is that the call to refer to oneself as African-American by Jesse Jackson was not grounded in any kind of consciousness-raising movement. It comes at a time when, aesthetically, black Americans are as far from Africa as they have ever been. But there is no doubt that black Americans know who they are and that they are descendants of Africans. If one were to do a national survey, it is plausible that the data would show that what group members prefer to call themselves (black Americans, African-Americans, Afro-Americans, people of African descent) will be related to variables such as age, participation in community organizations, and economic status. And although members of this group may argue over what they want to be called, *they certainly know what they do not want to be called.* One can rest assured that African-American, as a name-identification label, will be placed on the census and other questionnaires developed by social scientists as they try to collect data on the diversity of the American experience. Although the issue of name identification will evolve during certain periods in the future, it should not overshadow the continued effort of the group to gain economic stability and political participation in America.

NO

Walter E. Williams

MYTH MAKING AND
REALITY TESTING

Whether blacks should now call themselves African-American surfaces as a result of Reverend Jesse Jackson's declaration: "To be called Black is baseless... To be called African-American has cultural integrity." Little that is meaningful, in the way of agreement or disagreement, can be said about the proposal of a new name. After all, people can call themselves anything they wish and blacks have exercised this option having called themselves: colored, Negro, black, and Afro-American.

But suppose we concede there is a benefit to a name change that has "cultural integrity." It is not clear that African-American is the correct choice. Africa(n) refers neither to a civilization, a culture, or even a specific country. Instead, Africa is a continent consisting of many countries, cultures, ethnic groups, and races. Referring to Africa as a culture reflects near inexcusable ignorance. Africa is a continent with significant cultural distinctions. These distinctions often manifest themselves in unspeakable slaughter such as that between the Tutsi and Hutu in Burundi where 200,000 Hutus lost their lives in the space of two months in 1972 and at least 20,000 in August in 1988. Between 600,000 and a million Lango and Acholi tribesmen perished at the hands of Idi Amin and Milton Obote in Uganda. Similar strife raged between the Ibos and Hausa in Nigeria during the late 1960s, as well as between the Shona and Ndebele in Zimbabwe. The horrors of ethnic conflict continue to this day in many African countries.

Many people who trace their roots to the African continent are not even black. Americans of Egyptian, Libyan, or Algerian descent find their ancestral home on the African continent. Would it be appropriate to call these Americans African-Americans? Would we call a person African-American who is an American citizen of Afrikaner descent, who traces his ancestry back to 1620 when the Dutch settled Cape Town? If one says that these people do not qualify as African-Americans, what meaning can we make from Jesse Jackson's "cultural integrity" argument? In other words, what cultural characteristics do black Americans, Egyptians, Libyans, Algerians, and Afrikaners share in common even though each can trace his roots to Africa?

From Walter E. Williams, "Myth Making and Reality Testing," *Society*, vol. 27, no. 4 (May/June 1990). Copyright © 1990 by Transaction Publishers. Reprinted by permission.

America's ethnic mosaic consists of many hyphenated groups like Polish-Americans, Chinese-Americans, Italian-Americans, Japanese-Americans, and West-Indian Americans. In most cases, the prefix to the hyphenation refers to people of a particular country who may or may not share the same continent. Spanish-Americans, German-Americans, and Italian-Americans designate particular countries. Their ethnic identity would be lost if someone would consolidate them into European-Americans. It would be similar to calling anyone who can trace his or her ancestry to Africa, African-Americans.

If those who seek "cultural integrity" are to be more serious in their efforts, we would expect the new name(s) for blacks to have a country affiliation like: Nigerian-Americans, Ugandan-Americans, Ivory-Coast Americans, or at least south-of-the-Sahara-African-Americans—the latter since, to give a meaningful affiliation for blacks is nearly a hopeless task because of the extensive cross mixture, among blacks, which has occurred over the past 400 years in America.

FOCUS ON NON-ISSUES

American blacks share little or no cultural tie, which is not to deny an ancestral tie, with any of the many black ethnic groups in Africa. There is no shared language, religion, or culture. There are no holidays, ceremonies, or other outward linkages associated with the "motherland." In this sense, blacks are probably culturally more distinctly American than any of the other groups in America.

There is room for considerable legitimate disagreement and debate over what blacks should call themselves, and how much of a cultural tie exists with the many black groups in Africa. But given the deteriorating state of affairs faced by large and increasing numbers within the black community, what blacks should now begin to call themselves is a non-issue and can only serve to divert attention from larger issues without contributing anything to their solution.

Assertions about the benefits of changing the name of blacks to African-Americans puts one in mind of the alleged benefits of "role model" argument fashionable during the 1960s and thereafter. According to this theory, blacks were deficient in role models and thus increasing the number of blacks in responsible positions such as teachers, school superintendents, police chiefs, politicians, and professors would contribute to upward mobility.

Enough time and changes have been made to allow us to tentatively evaluate the benefits of the role model theory. In many urban cities such as Detroit, Philadelphia, Chicago, Los Angeles, Washington, DC, Newark, East St. Louis, and others, blacks have risen to the ranks of mayors, chiefs of police, and firemen, superintendent of schools, school principals, and have wide representation among city councilmen. Yet, in these very cities, blacks are the least safe, live in some of the worst slums, receive the poorest education, and face the greatest breakdown of institutions and living conditions most of the country takes for granted.

Some blacks are now pushing for statehood for the District of Columbia. Whether DC statehood is desirable or not need not concern us here. Whether DC statehood and the promise of two black senators as role models, will mean any more to poor blacks than what black political strength has come to mean at the state and local levels of government seems highly unlikely. That being the case means that black political and economic resources devoted to DC statehood will have been expended, once again, for the benefit of the few.

The point is not to question the dramatic political gains made over the last two decades. They are spectacular and praiseworthy. The point is that the role model theory has not delivered on its promise to provide the kind of incentives envisioned by its advocates. Those who advocate the role model theory of socioeconomic progress have never bothered to explain how they made their own achievements without role models.

THE REAL PROBLEMS

In many black communities, the rate of day-to-day murder, rape, robbery, assault, and property destruction stand at unprecedented levels. Criminal activity is not only a threat to life, limb, and property, it is a heavy tax and, as such, a near guarantee that there will be little or no economic development.

Crime is a tax in the sense that it raises all costs and lowers all values. Crime is a regressive tax borne mostly by society's poorest. High crime means people must bear the expense of heavy doors and window bars. Crime drives away businesses that would otherwise flourish. Poor people must bear higher transportation costs in order to do routine shopping in downtown areas and distant suburban malls, or else pay the high prices at Mom & Pop stores. The wanton destruction and vandalism of public facilities like pay telephones, swimming pools, and parks imposes additional costs on people not likely to have access to private phones,

private swimming facilities, and national parks.

To the extent that crime drives out businesses, it means residents have fewer local employment opportunities. Crime lowers the value of all property held by the residents. Often property that could not fetch as much as $20,000 all of a sudden sells for multiples of $100,000 when "gentrification" occurs in former slum areas.

EDUCATION

By every measure, black education is in shambles. High school dropout rates in some cities exceed fifty percent. Even those who do graduate are often ill-equipped for the demands of jobs or higher education. Evidence of poor education is seen in black performance on standardized achievement tests.

In 1983, across the nation, 66 out of 71,137 black college-bound seniors (less than a tenth of 1 percent) achieved 699, out of a possible 800, on the verbal portion of the SAT (Scholastic Achievement Test), and fewer than 1,000 scored over 600. On the mathematics portion of the SAT, only 205 blacks scored over 699 and fewer than 1,700 scored 600 or higher.

By comparison, of the roughly 35,200 Asians taking the test, 496 scored over 699 (1.4 percent) on the verbal portion, and 3,015 scored over 699 on the mathematics. Of the roughly 963,000 whites taking the test, 9,028 scored over 699 on the mathematics. In 1983, there were 570 blacks who had a combined score on the verbal and mathematics portions of the test above 1,200 (less than one tenth of 1 percent) compared to 60,400 whites who did so (6 percent).

While there is considerable controversy over what academic achievement tests measure and how reliably they do so, the undebatable conclusion is that black students have not achieved the necessary background for the standard college curriculum. This in turn has led to high numbers of black students dropping out of college. Added to the lack of preparedness for colleges, the fact that companies and government agencies must lower entry level position requirements to meet affirmative action hiring guidelines is further testament to poor academic preparation.

There is little that is surprising about these academic outcomes. Given the conditions in many predominantly black schools, where assault, property destruction, high absenteeism rates (of students and teachers), and low academic standards (again, of students and teachers) are a part of the daily routine, one would be surprised by any other outcome.

The standard excuses for poor black academic performance are segregated schools and insufficient financial resources. Yet there are an increasing number of black independent schools whose student performance seems to challenge these standard excuses. Philadelphia's Ivy Leaf School has an entirely black population, in which students come from families earning low and moderate incomes. The cost per student is $1,750, yet 85 percent of the student body tests at, or above, grade level. By contrast, Philadelphia's public school per-student cost of education is nearly $5,000 a year, and less than 35 percent of the student population tests at, or above, grade level.

Other examples of black academic achievement can be found at Chicago's Westside Preparatory School, Los Angeles' Marcus Garvey School, and New York's A. Philip Randolph School. In each of these cases, and others including parochial and black Muslim schools, a higher quality education is achieved at fraction of public school cost and without racial integration.

IMPORTANCE OF FAMILY AND OTHER INSTITUTIONS

In the face of these facts, we can draw several conclusions: racial integration is not a necessary condition for black educational excellence and massive per-pupil expenditures are not a necessary condition either. What seems to be more important are caring and responsible parents, dedicated and qualified teachers, behaving students, and above all, the freedom of the school administrator from micro-management, regulatory burdens of politically motivated central authorities, and the freedom of parents to make choices. To promote academic excellence among black youth, what is needed is turning our focus away from black educational pathology to educational successes and finding out ways of duplicating it.

Very few people who "make it" can attribute their success solely as a result of their own efforts. Most of us need others. The most significant others for most people are parents and family members. Over the past several decades, there has been a virtual collapse of the black family. In 1950, 88 percent of white families and 78 percent of black families consisted of two-parent households. By the end of 1980, black two-parent families had slipped to 59 percent while white family structure remained virtually unchanged. In 1950, the black illegitimacy rate was 17 percent; today it is 55 percent, and black teenagers are a large part of the illegitimacy crisis.

Aside from whatever moral issues are involved in the high rate of illegitimacy, there are several others that spell disaster. There are always problems associated with female-headed households, but they are exacerbated when the female head is herself a child lacking the maturity and resources to assume the responsibility of another individual. High illegitimacy means high rates of dependency and the high probability that the process will be duplicated in the next generation. High rates of illegitimacy also mean that there is not so much a breakdown in the black family as much as the black family not forming in the first place.

In addition to changes in the black family, institutions like black churches and social and civic organizations no longer have the influence on the community that they once did in the past. Part of the answer for this is that government welfare programs have poorly replaced their functions. This has been very harmful in the sense that community-based and related organizations are far better at assessing the need and monitoring the provision of services—be they assisting a family fallen on hard times or the provision of scholarship assistance. Now this assistance is rendered by remote bureaucracies with little knowledge about individual need and perhaps little interest in the overall effects of welfare programs.

With generalized availability of public welfare, along with an erosion in values, behaviors once held as irresponsible and reprehensible have been made less costly for the individual and have become the behavioral norm rather than the exception. Any black over the age of 50 remembers there was once a time when pregnancy without the benefit of marriage was a disgrace to both the young lady and her family. Often she was shipped to live with a relative out of town. Today, there is no such social stigma; and with some high schools setting up day-care centers to accommodate infants of students, the appearance of sanction is given to teen sex and illegitimacy. There is a lower cost attached to behavior which risks pregnancy out of wedlock. Basic economic theory and empirical evidence suggest that whenever the cost of something decreases, one can expect more people to be engaged in that activity.

There is considerable room for debate as to the specific causal connections between crime, poor education, and institutional breakdown, on the one hand, and poverty, dependency, and discrimination, on the other. But the bottom line is that despite the gains made by most blacks, there is a large segment of the black community for whom there appears to be little hope. What we have been doing, as a part of the Great Society welfare programs, appears to have little effect in making a dent in the situation.

Part of the solution to the problems of the black underclass will come from reflection of yesteryear when there was far greater poverty among blacks and much more discrimination. During that period, businesses thrived in black communities, people felt far safer, children did not assault teachers or use foul language in front of adults, adults did not fear children, and there was not the level of property destruction we see today. The black community was one with far more civility than today.

When people ask what are we going to do about helping those for whom there appears to be little hope, a good question to ask first is how did the situation get this way in the first place? Why are some black communities far less civil today than in the past? This important question is swept under the carpet when people blame the problems of the black underclass on poverty and discrimination, failing to recognize that poverty and discrimination existed in the 1920s, 1930s, and 1940s, but they did not generate the level of pathology that we witness today. Answers to this question will go a long way toward generating meaningful solutions.

Advocates of changing the name of blacks to African-Americans bear the burden of showing how resources placed in this effort will do anything to make upward mobility a reality for blacks stuck in the daily nightmare of our major urban areas. It would seem that pride, self-respect, and cultural identity—which the name-change advocates seek—are more likely to come from accomplishment rather than title.

POSTSCRIPT

Should We Call Ourselves African Americans?

"I do not think my people should be ashamed of their history, nor of any name that people choose in good faith to give them."

—Booker T. Washington (1906)

The issue as debated by Butler and Williams and others boils down to these questions: What term is free of negative connotations? Will generate pride among those so named? Does not necessarily do violence to historical realities? Does not deflect from real social problems? Is a term that the majority of Black Americans will use and feel comfortable with? Does not offend the sensitivities of others? Can and will be used consistently?

This debate goes back for generations and appears to be ongoing. It is now fashionable, for example, to use the term *people of color*. This term can be inclusive of African Americans or all nonwhite peoples. For a sophisticated approach to how labels are used to imprison minorities, see T. A. Van Dijk, *Elite Discourse and Racism* (Sage, 1993). For a continuation of the Williams-Butler debate, see Doris Wilkinson, "Americans of African Identity," *Society* (May/June 1990).

A useful overview of negative labels per se is I. L. Allen, *Unkind Words: Ethnic Labeling from Redskin to WASP* (Bergin and Garvey, 1990). A much older work is A. A. Roback's *A Dictionary of International Slurs* (Maledicta Press, 1979, originally published in 1944).

Among the classic statements, see the clear perspective of W. E. B. Du Bois's "The Name 'Negro' " in *The Thought and Writings of W. E. B. Du Bois*, Vol. II (Random House, 1971) and "Proper Name for Black Men in America," by Gilbert T. Stephenson in his book *Race Distinctions in American Law* (Negro Universities Press, 1910).

A work that tries to transcend the debate is George Borden's *Cultural Orientation: An Approach to Understanding Intercultural Communication* (Prentice Hall, 1991). James C. Scott sensitizes us to the "hidden scripts" in oppressed people's verbal utterances; see, for instance, *Domination and the Arts of Resistance: Hidden Transcripts* (Yale University Press, 1990). For an example of Latinos wrestling with this problem, see Joan Moore's "Hispanic Latino: Imposed Label or Real Identity?" *Latino Studies Journal* (May 1990). Native American concerns are expressed by Tim Giago (Nanwica Keiji) in "Team Mascots Are a Mask for Racism: Notes from Indian Country," *Lakota Times* (1989).

ISSUE 6

Do Cultural Differences Between Home and School Explain the High Dropout Rates for American Indian Students?

YES: Jon Reyhner, from "American Indians Out of School: A Review of School-Based Causes and Solutions," *Journal of American Indian Education* (May 1992)

NO: Susan Ledlow, from "Is Cultural Discontinuity an Adequate Explanation for Dropping Out?" *Journal of American Indian Education* (May 1992)

ISSUE SUMMARY

YES: Professor of curriculum and instruction Jon Reyhner argues that the school dropout rate for Native Americans is 35 percent, almost double that of other groups. He blames this on schools, teachers, and curricula that ignore the needs and potentials of North American Indian students.

NO: Educator Susan Ledlow argues that data on dropout rates for North American Indians, especially at the national level, is sparse. She questions the meaning and measurement of "cultural discontinuity," and she faults this perspective for ignoring important structural factors, such as employment, in accounting for why Native American students drop out of school.

One of the things that is striking about this debate between Reyhner and Ledlow is the immense difference in what might be called the skeptical factor. Reyhner without doubt or hesitation embraces and cites the highest available statistic on North American Indian school dropout rates: 35 percent. Ledlow, by contrast, begins by noting that reliable statistics simply do not exist.

Reyhner is highly skeptical of most schools and teachers. He doubts if many, if not most, really have Native American students' interests at heart. He blames the problem on the discontinuity between the backgrounds of the students and those of their white teachers. He seriously doubts that non-North American Indians, especially those whose training has been primarily or exclusively in subject content and not in Indian ways, can be effective teachers of Native Americans.

Formal education for Native American children has long been problematic and controversial, in part because much of it has been directed by the federal government as part of the management of reservation life. There were many efforts in the past to replace Native American children's heritage with the skills and attitudes of the larger, white society, and the earliest formal schooling efforts placed great emphasis on Anglo conformity. Reyhner takes a detailed look at the schools today and the ways in which they are run, and he argues that the continuing discontinuity between the life experiences of Native American school children and the schools and the curricula they teach explains the high dropout rate.

While admitting that some schools and some teachers may be inadequate, Ledlow seriously doubts if the cultural discontinuity theory is sound. She suggests that we must look elsewhere for a more plausible and empirically correct explanation of high dropout rates. She even questions if the rate is indeed as high as the accepted wisdom says it is. She asks, are those high rates derived from misinformation, or misinterpretation of the data, repeated by the mass media and Native American lobbying groups? She points out that, in some cases, the rate may be greatly inflated and/or a statistical anomaly.

Ledlow is also concerned with the assumption of Reyhner and others that a "culturally relevant" curriculum is superior to alternative ones. What is such a curriculum to begin with, she wonders? Even more important, where is the research that demonstrates that it is superior?

After providing an interesting critique of cultural discontinuity theorists, Ledlow advances an alternative theory. Her explanation is largely derived from the neglected (at least within sociology circles) Marxist anthropologist J. U. Ogbu. Hers is basically a structural explanation. She emphasizes the importance of the political and economic structures, especially the latter, in accounting for Native American dropout rates.

As you read these two articles, think back to when you were in high school. Were your "best" teachers necessarily warm and supportive? Were good teachers ever from radically different backgrounds than your own? Was your education geared to any specific minority group's needs? Would it have been more effective if it had been?

Extrapolate from Ogbu's typology as presented by Ledlow. Which minorities that you have studied so far, that you are familiar with, would fit into which part of his classification? Does it appear to be a sound one?

YES

Jon Reyhner

AMERICAN INDIANS OUT OF SCHOOL: A REVIEW OF SCHOOL-BASED CAUSES AND SOLUTIONS

During the summer of 1991, I taught a dropout prevention seminar at Eastern Montana College. In initial class discussions, the students, mostly members of Montana Indian tribes, blamed dysfunctional families and alcohol abuse for the high dropout rate among Indian students. If this allegation is correct, and Indian families and the abuse of alcohol are to be held responsible, then the implication exists that teachers and schools are satisfactory and not in need of change. However, the testimony given at the Indian Nations at Risk (INAR) Task Force hearings, held throughout the United States in 1990 and 1991, and other research reviewed, indicate that, both on and off the reservation, schools and teachers are to be held accountable as well. Academically capable American Indian students often drop out of school because their needs are not being met. Others are pushed out because they protest, in a variety of ways, how they are being treated. This article examines various explanations for the high dropout rate which oppose the dysfunctional Indian family and alcohol abuse resolution so popularly accepted.

American schools are not providing an appropriate education for Indian students who are put in large, factory-like schools. Indian students are denied teachers with special training in Indian education, denied a curriculum that includes their heritage, and denied culturally appropriate assessment. Their parents are also denied a voice in the education of their children....

EXTENT AND BACKGROUND OF THE PROBLEM

The National Center for Education Statistics (1989) reported that American Indian and Alaska Native students have a dropout rate of 35.5%, about twice the national average and the highest dropout rate of any United States ethnic or racial group [cited].... Regional and local studies gave similar rates (see for example Deyhle, 1989; Eberhard, 1989; Platero, Brandt, Witherspoon, & Wong, 1986; Ward & Wilson, 1989). This overall Indian dropout rate (35%) is not much higher than the 27.1% of Indians between the ages of 16 and 19 living on reservations who were found by the 1980 Census to be neither enrolled in

From Jon Reyhner, "American Indians Out of School: A Review of School-Based Causes and Solutions," *Journal of American Indian Education*, vol. 1, no. 3 (May 1992). Copyright © 1992 by The Center for Indian Education, College of Education, Arizona State University, Tempe, AZ 85287-1311. Reprinted by permission. Notes and references omitted.

school nor high school graduates. However, the Census figures also showed wide variation among reservations as to how many Indian teenagers between 16 and 19 were not in school. One New Mexico Pueblo had only 5.2% of those teenagers not getting a high school education whereas several small Nevada, Arizona, Washington, and California sites had no students completing a high school education (Bureau, 1985).

A recent compelling explanation as to why Indian students do poorly in school in the United States involves the cultural differences between Indian cultures and the dominant Euro-American culture [see Jacob and Jordan (1987) for an interesting discussion of explanations for the school performance of minority students]. As Estelle Fuchs and Robert J. Havighurst reported from the National Study of American Indian Education in the late 1960s, "many Indian children live in homes and communities where the cultural expectations are different and discontinuous from the expectations held by school teachers and school authorities" (1972, p. 299). In the INAR Task Force hearings several educators and community members testified on the need for Indian teachers and Indian curriculum to reduce the cultural conflict between home and school (Indian Nations at Risk Task Force, 1991).

Positive identity formation, as the psychiatrist Erik Erikson (1963) pointed out, is an ongoing, cumulative process that starts in the home with a trusting relationship established between mother and child and develops through the child's interaction with other children and adults. To build a strong positive identity, educators that the child interacts with in school need to reinforce and build on the cultural training and messages

that the child has previously received. If educators give Indian children messages that conflict with what Indian parents and communities show and tell their children, the conflicting messages can confuse the children and create resistance to school (Bowers & Flinders, 1990; Jacob & Jordan, 1987; Spindler, 1987). In the words of John Goodlad, ethnic minority children are "caught and often savaged between the language and expectations of the school and those of the home" (1990, pp. 6–7).

Too often, well-meaning remedial programs focus on finding the reason for failure in students and their homes thus, "blaming the victims." The idea that Indian students are "culturally disadvantaged" or "culturally deprived" reflects ethnocentrism rather than the results of educational research. When schools do not recognize, value, and build on what Indian students learn at home, the students are given a watered-down curriculum (meant to guarantee student learning) which often results in a tedious education, and their being "bored out" of school....

Students do not have to assimilate into the dominant Euro-American culture to succeed in school. Two studies (Deyhle, 1989; Platero et al., 1986) of Indian dropouts found that a traditional Indian orientation is not a handicap in regard to school success. The Navajo Student at Risk study reported that "the most successful students were for the most part fluent Navajo/English bilinguals" (Platero, 1986, p. 6). Lin (1990) found that Indian college students with traditional orientations outperformed students with modern orientations. Tradition oriented students are able to learn in school, in spite of negative characteristics of the schools, because of the strong sense of personal and group identity their native cultures give them.

WHY STUDENTS LEAVE SCHOOL

Research indicates a number of factors associated with higher student dropout rates. Particularly critical factors for Indian students include large schools, uncaring and untrained teachers, passive teaching methods, inappropriate curriculum, inappropriate testing/student retention, tracked classes, and lack of parent involvement....

1. LARGE SCHOOLS

The increasing size of American schools, especially the large comprehensive high schools with more than one thousand students, creates conditions conducive to dropping out. Goodlad (1984) criticized large schools for creating factory-like environments that prevent educators from forming personal relationships with students. He recommended that high schools maintain no more than 600 students....

Smaller schools can allow a greater percentage of students to participate in extra-curricular activities. Students participating in these activities, especially sports when excessive travel is not required, drop out less frequently (Platero, et al., 1986). However, many reservation schools do not have drama clubs, debate teams, and other non-sport extra-curricular activities which would help develop Indian student leadership and language skills.

The Navajo Students at Risk study (Platero, et al., 1986) reported that students who travel long distances to get to school are more likely to drop out. Large consolidated high schools in rural areas, in contrast to smaller more dispersed high schools, increase the distance some students must travel, and thus increase their risk of dropping out. Students who miss the school bus often cannot find alternative transportation, and many high schools today maintain strict attendance policies causing students who miss 10 days of school or more to lose their credit for the semester.

2. UNCARING AND UNTRAINED TEACHERS AND COUNSELORS

In an ethnographic study of Navajo and Ute dropouts that included both interviews with students and classroom observations, Deyhle (1989) reported that students "complained bitterly that their teachers did not care about them or help them in school" (1989, p. 39). Students who "experienced minimal ꞏ individual attention or personal contact with their teachers" interpreted this neglect as "teacher dislike and rejection" (p. 39).

In comparison to other racial or ethnic groups, few Indian students report that "discipline is fair," that "the teaching is good," that "teachers are interested in students," and that "teachers really listen to me" (National, 1990, p. 43)....

It can be argued that in an attempt to improve the quality of teaching in the United States, changes have been made in teacher preparation programs and certification standards that aggravate rather than solve the problem of recruiting well-qualified caring teachers for Indian children. Increased certification standards are preventing Indian students from entering the teaching profession because [of] the National Teachers Examination (NTE) and similar tests that neither measure teacher commitment to educating Indian children nor their knowledge of Indian cultures, languages, and teaching practices.

Indian students can successfully complete four or more years of college and receive a Bachelors Degree in education at an accredited college or university and be denied a license to teach Indian students on the basis of one timed standardized examination, usually the NTE, that does not reflect Indian education at all. At the same time, a non-Native who has never seen an Indian student, never studied native history, language, or culture, and whose three credit class in multicultural education emphasized Blacks and Hispanics, can legally teach the Indian students that the Indian graduate cannot.

The Winter 1989 issue of the *Fair Test Examiner* reported how teacher competency tests barred nearly 38,000 Black, Latino, Indian, and other minority teacher candidates from the classroom. In addition, teacher preparation and certification programs are culturally and linguistically "one size fits all," and the size that is measured is a middle-class, Western-European cultural orientation. Recent research (see for example, Reyhner, 1992) identifies a wide body of knowledge about bilingual education, Indian learning styles, and English-as-a-Second-Language (ESL) teaching techniques that teachers of Indian students need to know. In addition, teachers of Indian students should have an Indian cultural literacy specific to the tribal background of their students. But teachers often get just one generic multicultural course in accredited teacher education programs.

This lack of job-specific training is a factor in the high turnover rates among teachers of Indian children. Bureau of Indian Affairs (BIA) professional staff have a 50% turnover rate every two years (Of-

fice, 1988). When teaching, those instructors who are not trained to educate Indian children, as most teachers are not with our present teacher training system, tend to experience failure from the beginning. As these teachers often become discouraged and find other jobs, the students are left to suffer from continued educational malpractice.

Proper training and screening of teachers could solve this problem, especially the training of Indian teachers. However, today's commonly used screening devices of test scores and grade point averages do not measure teacher personality. The Kenney Report (Special, 1969) found that one-fourth of the elementary and secondary teachers of Indian children admitted not wanting to teach them.

These teachers also need to use interactive teaching strategies... to develop positive relationships with their students, because related to the high turnover is the fact that Indian students think worse of their teachers than any other group (Office, 1988). Studies (Coburn & Nelson, 1989; Deyhle, 1989; Kleinfeld, 1979; Platero et al., 1986) clearly show the Indian student's need for warm, supportive teachers....

3. PASSIVE TEACHING METHODS

Too often educators of Indian students use passive teaching methods to instruct Indian children. Cummins (1989) argued that most teachers in the United States use a passive "transmission" method of instruction in which knowledge is given to students in the form of facts and concepts. These teachers, according to Bowers and Flinders (1990), view language simplistically as a conduit for the transmitting of information rather than as a metaphorical medium through which the teacher and students mutually build meaning through shared experiences and understandings. They expect students to sit passively, to listen to lectures, or to read and memorize the information they receive so that they can answer worksheet, chapter, or test questions (Deyhle, 1989). Students who refuse to sit quietly for long periods of time are considered discipline problems who, over time, are gradually encouraged in a variety of ways to drop out of school.

Although it is popularly assumed that students who drop out are academic failures, the Navajo Students at Risk study (Platero et al., 1986) showed that the academic performance of dropouts is not that different from students who remain in school. Forty-five percent of the Navajo dropouts are B or better students (Platero et al., 1986). Navajo students most frequently give boredom with school, not academic failure or problems with drugs and alcohol, as their reason for dropping out or planning to drop out.

Indian and other minority students are most likely to be the recipients of passive teaching strategies, and they are commonly placed in low track classes.... In a study of Alaskan education (Senate, 1989), seniors included the following reasons for their classmates dropping out of school: not being good at memorizing facts, boredom, larger class sizes, and unsupportive teachers.

4. INAPPROPRIATE CURRICULUM

In addition to inappropriate teaching methods, Indian schools are characterized by an inappropriate curriculum that does not reflect the Indian child's unique cultural background (Coladarci,

1983; Reyhner, 1992). Textbooks are not written for Indian students, and thus they enlarge the cultural gap between home and school. In the INAR Task Force hearings, many Indian educators pointed out the need for teaching materials specially designed for Indian students. Despite vast improvement in the past two decades, there are still reports that "too many textbooks are demeaning to minorities" (Senate, 1989, p. 28)....

Related to the lack of Indian-specific curriculum and multicultural curriculum, which increases the cultural distance between the Indian student and school, is the use of standardized tests to measure how well students learn that inappropriate curriculum. The use of these tests, which do not reflect either Indian subject matter or ways of learning, is discussed below.

5. INAPPROPRIATE TESTING/STUDENT RETENTION

The way tests are designed in this country, with an emphasis on standardized testing, a built-in failure is produced (Oakes, 1985; Bloom, 1981). In addition to the built-in sorting function of standardized tests, they have a cultural bias that has yet to be overcome (Rhodes, 1989). Some of the changes made to improve education in American schools recommended in *A Nation at Risk* (National, 1983) and other studies have hurt rather than helped Indian students.

The use of standardized tests to measure school success leads to more Indian students being retained in a grade, and retention leads to over-age students who drop out of high school. The National Education Longitudinal Study of 1988 (NELS:88) reported that 28.8% of Indian students have repeated at least one grade, the highest percentage of any racial or ethnic group reported (National, 1990, p. 9). The research on failing students (retaining them in grade for another year) indicates that it only creates more failure and more dropouts (Weis, et al., 1989). Even retention in kindergarten does not help students who are having academic problems (Shepard & Smith, 1989). With current practices, schools can make themselves look better by pushing out Indian students since they are evaluated on their average test scores. The more "at risk" students educators push out, the higher the schools' average test scores (Bearden, Spencer, & Moracco, 1989).

Without realizing they are comparing bilingual students' test scores with monolingual English student norms, school administrators and teachers use the California Test of Basic Skills (CTBS) and other standardized test scores to show that their present curriculum is not working. It is also common sense that achievement tests given to Indian students be aligned with what they are being taught in their schools. Testimony given at the INAR/NACIE joint issue sessions in San Diego gave instances of the inappropriate use of tests in schools. For example, tests designed for state mandated curricula were used on students who were not taught using those curricula in BIA schools....

The result of this misuse of tests is that educators keep changing the curriculum in a futile attempt to get Native language speaking students in the early grades to have English language test scores that match the test scores of students of the same age who have spoken English all their lives. Research indicates that it takes about five to seven years for non-English speaking students to acquire an aca-demic proficiency in English which will give them a chance to match the English language test scores of students whose native language is English (Collier, 1989; Cummins, 1989).

6. TRACKED CLASSES

Teachers often have low expectations for Indian students and put them in a non-college-bound vocationally-oriented curriculum. This "tracking" of students is a common practice in secondary schools. The study body is divided into high achievers, average achievers, and low achievers, and each group is put in separate classes. Oakes (1985) described the negative effects of tracking in our nation's high schools and how ethnic minority students are disproportionately represented in the lower tracks where they receive a substandard education. She documented how, in tracked classrooms, "lower-class students are expected to assume lower-class jobs and social positions as adults" (p. 117) and that "students, especially lower-class students, often actively resist what schools try to teach them" (p. 120). Data from the NEL:88 show that less than 10% of Indian students are in the upper quartile of achievement test scores in history, mathematics, reading, and science whereas over 40% are in the lowest quartile (National, 1989). The low expectations of teachers for low track students, already unsuccessful in school, make a serious problem worse....

7. LACK OF PARENT INVOLVEMENT

The last factor to discuss is parent involvement. Greater Indian parent involvement can reduce the cultural distance between home and school. Often school staff say they want parent involvement, but what they really want is parents to get after their children to attend school and study....

Although getting parents to get their children to school is important, parent involvement also means educating parents about the function of the school and allowing parents real decision making power about what and how their children learn. Cummins (1989) noted that "although lip service is paid to community participation through Parent Advisory Committees (PAC) in many school programs, these committees are frequently manipulated through misinformation and intimidation" (p. 62). He goes on to list a number of studies supporting the need for minority parent involvement in schools.

PROMISING REMEDIES

Both educational literature and testimony at INAR hearings recommend solutions to the problems that result in Indian student failure. The following suggestions for improving Indian schools are targeted at the seven factors described above and involve restructuring schools, promoting caring teachers, using active teaching strategies, having culturally-relevant curriculum, testing to help students rather than to fail them, having high expectations of all students, and promoting community involvement....

Time and again in the INAR Task Force hearings Indian parents testified about the need for more Indian teachers who will stand as role models for their children. These instructors would offer students a unique cultural knowledge and would maintain the ability to identify with the problems their students face.

ACTIVE TEACHING METHODS

Obviously, just caring is not enough. Teachers also need to learn culturally appropriate teaching strategies in their teacher training and inservice programs and use these instructional methodologies in their classrooms.... Other studies of Indian students show the need for teachers to know more about the home culture of their students....

* * *

Beyond using active and culturally-appropriate teaching strategies, research (see for example Reyhner, 1992) showed the need for a culturally-appropriate curriculum. Extensive material exists to produce elementary and secondary culturally appropriate curriculum for Indian students, however, there is little incentive for publishers to produce material for the relatively small market that Indian education represents. Books such as Jack Weatherford's (1988) *Indian givers: How the Indians of the Americas transformed the world* indicate the wealth of information that could positively affect Indian students' understanding and self-concept. This information, however, does not seem to be reaching Indian students at the elementary and secondary level....

The best way to get schools to reflect parent and community values and to reduce cultural discontinuity between home and school is to have real parent involvement in Indian education. At many successful Indian schools, the school board, administrators, and teachers are Indian people. The extensive parent involvement at Rock Point Community

School in Arizona is one example of how parents can come to feel ownership in their children's school and to translate that feeling into supporting their children's attendance and academic performance. Parent involvement at Rock Point includes quarterly parent-teacher conferences, a yearly general public meeting, and an eight-member elected parent advisory committee that formally observes the school several times a year (Reyhner, 1990). In addition, the Indian school board conducts its meetings in the Navajo language and each classroom has special chairs reserved for parents.

Parents need to have effective input as to how and what their children are taught. This is best achieved through Indian control of schools. However, curriculum restrictions placed by states on public schools, and even the BIA on BIA-funded schools, limit the effectiveness of Indian parent involvement. State and BIA regulations force Indian schools to use curriculum and textbooks not specifically designed for Indian children and to employ teachers who, though certified, have no special training in Indian education.

CONCLUSIONS

Supplemental, add-on programs such as Indian Education Act, Johnson-O'Malley (JOM), Bilingual Education, Special Education, and other federal programs have had limited success in improving the education of Indian children. However, add-on programs are only a first step in making schooling appropriate for Indian children....

If educators continue to get inadequate or inappropriate training in colleges of education, then local teacher-training programs need to provide school staff with information on what works in In-dian education and information about the language, history, and culture of the Indian students. Tribal colleges are beginning to develop teacher training programs to fill this need. Parents and local school boards also need on-going training about what works in Indian education and what schools can accomplish. Head Start, elementary, and secondary schools need the support of tribal education departments and tribal colleges to design and implement effective educational programs that support rather than ignore Indian cultures.

Much testimony was given in the INAR Task Force hearings on the importance of self-esteem for Indian students. It is sometimes unclear that self-esteem is not an independent variable but is a reflection of how competent an Indian child feels. Having students memorize material to show success on standardized tests, a common element of the transmission model of teaching previously described, is a poor way to develop self-esteem. However, if students interact with caring, supportive adults, if students are allowed to explore and learn about the world they live in, including learning about their rich Indian heritage, if they are allowed to develop problem solving skills, if they are given frequent opportunities to read and write and to do mathematics and science in meaningful situations, and if they are encouraged to help improve the world they live in through community service, it is likely that Indian students will feel good about themselves and will be successful in life....

Teachers of Indian students need to have special training in instructional methodologies that have proven effective with Indian students and in using curriculum materials that reflect American Indian history and cultures. They also need to build on the cultural values that Indian parents give their children if teachers want to produce a strong positive sense of identity in their students.

Attempts to replace Indian identity with a dominant cultural identity can confuse and repel Indian students and force them to make a choice between their Indian values or their school's values. Neither choice is desirable or necessary. Students can be academically successful and learn about the larger non-Native world while at the same time retaining and developing their Indian identity. Indian students need to attend schools that reinforce rather than ignore or depreciate Indian cultural values.

NO

IS CULTURAL DISCONTINUITY AN ADEQUATE EXPLANATION FOR DROPPING OUT?

AMERICAN INDIAN DROPOUT RESEARCH

On the national level, there is little information about overall rates for American Indian dropouts. Most national level educational research does not differentiate American Indian students as a separate cohort as with Blacks, Whites, or Hispanics....

There are a number of sources in the educational literature which discuss the issue of American Indian dropouts either directly or indirectly. A comprehensive review of the educational literature regarding American Indian dropout rates disclosed, literally, hundreds of reports; evaluation or annual reports; local, state, or national government reports; senate hearings; task force proceedings; or descriptions of dropout intervention programs. Some reports provided actual dropout rates for local areas or states. These reports suffer from the same weaknesses as many national studies: they define and count dropouts variously and, often, inaccurately (see Rumberger 1987 for a discussion of the problems with dropout research). What is most noteworthy is that there is very little research which specifically address the causes of American Indian students dropping out.

In spite of this dearth of knowledge about the causes for so many Indian students' decision to leave school, many of the reports commonly cite the need for making the school curriculum more "culturally relevant" or adding some type of Indian studies component to the regular curriculum in order to solve the problem. Cultural relevance is rarely defined and almost always assumed to be significant. With no evidence to support the claim and no definition of what a culturally relevant curriculum is, many of the school district and special program reports recommend that a culturally relevant curriculum will ameliorate Indian students' difficulties in school. How and

From Susan Ledlow, "Is Cultural Discontinuity an Adequate Explanation for Dropping Out?" *Journal of American Indian Education*, vol. 1, no. 3 (May 1992). Copyright © 1992 by The Center for Indian Education, College of Education, Arizona State University, Tempe, AZ 85287-1311. Reprinted by permission. Notes and references omitted.

why a relevant curriculum will solve the problems is rarely addressed; one assumes that the proponents of such solutions believe them to be based on some body of empirical knowledge, most probably the cultural discontinuity hypothesis, which originated in the ideas of anthropologists such as Dell Hymes (1974).

THE CULTURAL DISCONTINUITY HYPOTHESIS

The cultural discontinuity hypothesis assumes that culturally based differences in the communication styles of the minority students' home and the Anglo culture of the school lead to conflicts, misunderstandings, and, ultimately, failure for those students. The research focuses on the process, rather than the structure of education and concludes that making the classroom more culturally appropriate will mean a higher rate of achievement. Erickson offered three reasons for this. He stated that cultural adaptation may reduce culture shock for students, it may make them feel that the school and teacher hold a positive regard for them, and it simplifies learning tasks, in that students do not have to master a culturally unfamiliar way of behavior at the same time that they are expected to master academic content.

Susan Philips' research on children at the Warm Springs Reservation in Oregon is the premier example of this type of research. She focused on the differences in communication and interaction patterns in the school and in the Warm Springs community. Her argument is that

the children of the Warm Springs Indian Reservation are enculturated in their preschool years into modes of organizing the transmission of verbal messages that are culturally different from those of Anglo middle-class children. I argue that this difference makes it more difficult for them to then comprehend verbal messages conveyed through the school's Anglo middle-class modes of organizing classroom interaction. (1982, p. 4).

Philips indicated that the hierarchical structure of the classroom, with the teacher as the focus of all communication is fundamentally at odds with the Warm Springs children's understanding of appropriate communication patterns. For example, teachers often assumed that Indian children were not paying attention because they did not look directly at the teacher or provide behavioral feedback that indicated they were listening (p. 101). These behaviors, however, are appropriate in their own community. She also noted that of four possible participant structures—whole class, small group, individual work, and one-to-one with the teacher—Indian students, when allowed to control their own interaction, most actively participated in one-to-one with the teacher and in small group work. Warm Springs students showed little enthusiasm for teacher-directed whole class or small group encounters or for individual desk work, which are the most commonly employed participant structures. The implication of her research is that more Indian teachers, culturally relevant materials, and teaching methods which emphasize appropriate participant structures will allow Indian students to experience greater success and achievement in school.

The Kamehameha Elementary Education Project (KEEP) is another well known example of research supporting the cultural discontinuity hypothesis. KEEP originated in response to the relative lack of success experienced by Native Hawaiian children compared with Japanese, Chinese, and haole (of northern European ancestry) children. The project used research on socialization practices in Hawaiian homes, and how these differed from the patterns of interaction in the school, to develop a "K-3 language arts program that is culturally compatible for Hawaiian children, and that, both in the lab school and public schools, produced significant gains in reading achievement levels for educationally at-risk Hawaiian children" (Vogt, Jordan, and Tharp, 1987, p. 278).

Anticipating that the gains experienced by KEEP children might be interpreted as the result of better teaching methods, rather than culturally specific methods, the Rough Rock Community School on the Navajo reservation in Arizona replicated the KEEP project. Many of the strategies developed for use with Hawaiian children were found to be ineffective or actually counterproductive with Navajo students (Vogt, Jordan, and Tharp, 1987, pp. 282–285). Vogt, Jordan, and Tharp concluded that the KEEP research strongly supports the argument that cultural compatibility between home and school can enhance the likelihood of students' success, and conversely, cultural discontinuity is a valid explanation for school failure (1987, p. 286).

These two research projects are often cited in the field of Indian education and do seem to provide strong evidence that cultural discontinuity plays a role in some minority students' lack of success in school. Unfortunately, however, this hypothesis is now accepted as fact by many researchers and has become an underlying assumption rather than a research question in Indian education. I argue that the unquestioning acceptance of the cultural discontinuity hypothesis by many educators, as a cause for dropping out of school, is misguided for two reasons. First, the body of research on the causes of American Indian students' dropping out does not specifically support the hypothesis, and, second, the focus on cultural discontinuity precludes examination of macrostructural variables which may, in fact, be far more significant.

WHY AMERICAN INDIAN STUDENTS DROP OUT

There are relatively few specific research studies which seek to identify the reasons why American Indian students drop out (Giles, 1985; Coladarci, 1983; Eberhard, 1989; Chan and Osthimer, 1983; Platero, Brandt, Witherspoon, and Wong, 1986; Milone, 1983; Deyhle, 1989), and those few certainly do not explicitly support the cultural discontinuity hypothesis. In fact, few directly address the issue as a research question, although they do contain both explicit and implicit assumptions about the importance of cultural relevance in curriculum.

Giles' (1985) study of urban Indian dropouts in Milwaukee is the only study which explicitly employed (but did not critically examine) the cultural discontinuity hypothesis. She stated that,

Considering the disproportionately high Native American dropout rate, one can reasonably assume that certain culturally-based Indian characteristics exist that clash with the urban public school environment (p. 2).

Based upon this assumption, Giles assigned the eight students she interviewed a place on a continuum between a "Native American value orientation" and an "American middle class value orientation." She reported that "it was evident that the more assimilated an Indian student is into the American middle class value orientation, the more likely that person is to complete high school" (p. 14). She goes on to discuss the implications of this finding with extensive reference to Susan Philips' (1982) work in a Warm Springs, Oregon reservation elementary school. She concluded by recommending that school counselors target those "traditional" students for dropout prevention programs, that Indian cultural values (such as a preference for cooperation) be incorporated into curricula, that Indian cultural activities be provided at the schools, and that teachers be trained to more effectively serve Indian students (pp. 26–27).

Giles' research, although undoubtedly inspired by the best of intentions, typifies the problem with assuming that cultural discontinuity between Indian students' culture and the culture of the school causes their academic difficulties (in this case dropping out), and that creating a congruence between the two cultures will solve the problems. There is no critical examination of this premise; the report attempted to show **how** this is true, rather than **if** this is true. In addition, Giles assumed that there is such a thing as a "Native American value orientation" and an "American middle class value orientation." She further assumed that the findings of Philips' ethnographic research into the communication styles of elementary school students on the Warm Springs reservation in Oregon is directly applicable to the situation of urban high school students in Wisconsin.

Several studies reported interviews with students specifically about the importance of cultural relevance or sensitivity. Coladarci (1983) supervised interviews of American Indian students who dropped out of a Montana school district. Student interviews indicated five factors which significantly influenced their leaving school: 1) the lack of relevance of the school curriculum both in terms of future employment and native culture; 2) the perceived insensitivity of teachers; 3) the peer pressure to leave school; 4) having to remain in school for the full senior year when needing only a few classes to graduate; and 5) the problems at home (pp. 18–19). Coladarci recommended that the district critically examine the curriculum in terms of its relevance to both future job opportunities and sensitivity to American Indian culture (pp. 19–21). There is no independent verification of the student self reports, and Coladarci noted that the results should be considered cautiously and should be supported by ethnographic research.

Eberhard (1989) followed and interviewed four cohorts of urban American Indian students. Low test scores and GPAs were found to be significant to students' dropping out. Family constellation was not statistically significant, but more stay-ins came from two parent homes. Little gender difference was found, but family mobility was very significant (p. 37). Interviews indicated that both parents and students found the schools "culturally insensitive" (p. 38). Students also reported that they need more support from their parents. Again, there is no explicit research into cultural relevance and no supporting evidence which defines culturally insensitive.

Some researchers also related students' participation in or ties to traditional culture to their propensity to drop out. In a case study of Navajo students from public schools, Chan and Osthimer (1983) hired Navajo community researchers to interview nine college bound students, nine graduates with no immediate plans for continuing their education, and six dropouts. In addition, the project used school and community documents, interviews with "experts" on Navajo students, and student records.

Chan and Osthimer found that the student's first language was not as important a determinant to their success in school as the successful transition into English. Students who were English dominant or bilingual were less likely to drop out, regardless of their first language. Bilinguals were most likely to be college bound (pp. 24–27). Of particular interest is their finding that students from less traditional homes dropped out at higher rates. Students who reported their families as "moderate," meaning they observed Navajo traditions while having adopted certain Anglo conveniences, were most likely to be college bound (pp. 27–30). Achievement and attendance were not clear critical markers (perhaps due to the fact that these data were often incomplete), whereas high absenteeism was significant in predicting dropping out (pp. 30–36). Students who travelled long distances to school dropped out more (pp. 36–40), and students who had specific career goals/ambitions tended to persist (p. 42).

In a study commissioned by the Navajo tribal government, Platero, Brandt, Witherspoon, and Wong (1986) calculated the Navajo Nation's dropout rate to be 31%. They used a combination of school records and student questionnaires. They examined student demographic variables, socioeconomic variables, cultural variables, home support for education, transportation factors, academic

expectations and performance, future orientation, extracurricular activities, school support programs, and behavioral problems (pp. 23–43). In addition, they included dropouts' own reports of why they left school. One of their most significant findings was that many students who were assumed to have dropped out had transferred to other schools (p. 63). There was little difference in grades or retention rates between dropouts and persisters (p. 66). Living a long distance from school was a significant factor in dropping out but "absenteeism was likely to be more of a symptom of dropping out, rather than a cause" (pp. 70–72). Having reliable backup transportation was important to students who missed the bus. Stayers were more likely to live within walking distance of their schools or to be driven to school (p. 81). Students themselves reported boredom, social problems, retention, and pregnancy or marriage as the most significant factors in their dropping out (p. 73). Although many of the problems experienced by the students in Platero et al. (1986) seemed to be economic or social, the authors nonetheless noted that,

> There is ample evidence from the student and dropout survey that dropouts have not acquired the cultural drives and behavioral molds the school systems wish to develop in their students.... This is obviously in part due to the variance these cultural values and social codes have with those of traditional Navajo culture and society (p. 74)....

The report makes a number of recommendations to the Navajo tribal government (pp. 182–186) including the development of a system for tracking dropouts in a more systematic manner, the development of prevention programs, and an improvement in transportation systems for students in remote areas. They also recommended that schools incorporate more Navajo cultural values into the school curriculum and daily operations....

Deyhle's 1989 study of Navajo and Ute school leavers represents a welcome departure from the current state of the art in educational research.... [S]ignificant numbers of students she interviewed mentioned the economic necessity of finding a job, long distance commutes to school, pregnancy, and academic problems as contributing to their decisions to leave school.

Particularly interesting in Deyhle's work is her discussion of the curricular issues which dominate other studies. She found that those students who came from the most traditional Navajo homes, spoke their native language, and participated in traditional religious and social activities (who, according to the prevailing assumptions, would experience the greatest cultural discontinuity) did not feel that the school curriculum was inappropriate to them as Indians (p. 42). Ute students who came from the least traditional homes felt that the curriculum was not important to them as Indians. These students experienced the highest dropout rates and most problems academically and socially in school. Deyhle concluded, "A culturally nonresponsive curriculum is a greater threat to those whose own cultural 'identity' is insecure." (p. 42).

Deyhle noted, however, that the relevance of the school curriculum to the economic reality of the community is an important issue. There are few jobs in the community and fewer that require a high school diploma. There is no tangible economic benefit to students to remain in school.

Deyhle also reported specifically the issues of racism and cultural maintenance as important factors influencing students to leave school. She noted that there is considerable conflict between a number of factions in the school: between Anglos and Indians, Utes and Navajos, traditional Navajos and more acculturated Navajos, and Mormons and non-Mormons. These conflicts create an atmosphere of social unease in the school which, when coupled with academic difficulties, leave students with few positive experiences to encourage them to stay in school. In addition, many Indian students who were successful were berated by their peers for trying to act like Whites or for being perceived as looking down on their friends and families (pp. 48–49). Deyhle noted that there is some basis for this attitude; given the lack of jobs on the reservation, those who get more education and training frequently must move away to find jobs for which their training prepares them.

DISCUSSION OF DATA

It is difficult to draw any firm conclusions from the data available on American Indian dropouts. Dropping out is a serious problem for American Indian students, but there is little consensus as to the cause. Virtually all research indicate that Indian students drop out of school at very high rates—invariably at higher rates than Anglos and Asians, and often at higher rates than all other minorities. These rates vary from school to school, year to year, tribe to tribe, male to female, BIA to public school or, in other words, from study to study.

I argue that there is simply not enough evidence to conclude that cultural discontinuity plays a significant role, but there is overwhelming evidence that economic and social issues which are not culturally specific to being Indian (although they may be specific to being a minority) are very significant in causing students to drop out of school. Milone (9183) noted that

> many of the reasons given by Indian students for dropping out of school—such as pregnancy, drugs, wanting to be with friends, and boredom in school—are the same as those of non-Indians (p. 56).

Long commuting distances and the lack of relevance of school to reservation students' economic future may be the only differences between Indian and non-Indian students' reasons for dropping out. In the case of urban Indian students, are the problems they encounter which lead to their dropping out of school any different than the problems encountered by African-American or Hispanic students? Chances are, they are not. If there is a cultural discontinuity, it is not unique to their situation. If there is institutional racism, it is also not unique to them (although the lack of general awareness about American Indians is probably greater than for other groups). Poverty, discrimination, poor health care, and other problems may be more a result of the general status of being a minority in this country than the type of minority that you are. Reservation students may be in an economically and socially different situation. High unemployment rates and menial work opportunities in a community must certainly influence a student's perception of the value of school.

Most research has yet to look beyond the classroom and home to the wider influences of the economic and political environment of the community as a whole. How do the attitudes that teachers from the dominant culture have about Indian students' abilities contribute to their treatment of the students and the students' perceptions of their school experience? How does the curriculum prepare students for the political and economic opportunity structure that they experience when they graduate, especially on the reservation? Do some Indian students consciously avoid academic achievement because it means peer opposition for "acting White?" If so, how can schools hope to separate the two ideas? These questions have rarely been addressed and may point to more profitable areas of inquiry. A promising avenue of inquiry into the dropout problem among Indian students is the macrostructural or Marxist perspective.

MACROSTRUCTURAL EXPLANATIONS OF MINORITY SCHOOLING

Marxist anthropological theorists, principally John Ogbu (1974, 1978, 1981, 1982, 1983, 1985, 1987), found the "structured inequality" of American society to be the cause of minority student failure. Because of racism and discrimination, minority students have a lower "job ceiling" than do Anglo, middle-class students. The idea that hard work and achievement in school lead to economic success is contradicted by the circumstances of poverty in which the members of their communities live, leaving them with "disillusionment and lack of effort, optimism, and perseverance" (1982, p. 21). Ogbu believed that "children's school learning problems are ultimately caused by historical and structural forces beyond their control" (1985, p. 868).

Ogbu recognized that not all minority groups in the United States experience difficulty in school. He makes a distinction between autonomous, immigrant, and castelike (originally labeled subordinate) minorities (1974, 1978, 1982, 1983). Autonomous minorities are groups such as the Jews or the Amish in the United States who are "not totally subordinated by the dominant group politically or economically" (1983, p. 169), whereas immigrant minorities

are people who have moved more or less voluntarily to their host societies.... As strangers they can operate psychologically outside established definitions of social status and relations. They may be subject to pillory and discrimination, but have not usually had time to internalize the effects of discrimination or have those effects become an ingrained part of their culture (1983, pp. 169–170).

The home country is the frame of reference for immigrant minorities who, although experiencing discrimination, may still feel themselves to be better off in the United States than in the political or economic situations they left behind.

Ogbu noted that, as a group, autonomous and immigrant minorities do not experience failure in schools; his concern is the experience of the castelike minorities:

Castelike minorities are distinguished from immigrant and other types of minorities in that (1) they have been incorporated into the society involuntarily and permanently, (2) they face a job and status ceiling, and (3) they tend to formulate their economic and social problems

in terms of collective institutional discrimination, which they perceive as more than temporary. Examples of castelike minorities in the United States include blacks, Indians, Chicanos, and Puerto Ricans (1982, p. 299)....

Castelike minorities... experience secondary cultural discontinuities which "develop *after* members of two populations have been in contact or *after* members of a given population have begun to participate in an institution, such as the school system, controlled by another group" (1982, p. 298). Castelike minority cultures may define themselves in opposition to Anglo culture and include "coping behaviors" which develop in response to systematic oppression. Coping behaviors, although effective in the social and economic context, may actually work against student achievement in school. In addition, defining oneself in opposition to Anglo culture may mean that the student will actively resist the attempts of the school to impart knowledge and values which are seen to be important to Anglo culture. In other words, to say that minority students experience failure merely due to cultural differences between their homes and the school is to deny the historical and structural context in which those differences are embedded.

Ogbu saw the shortcomings of the cultural discontinuity explanation as inherent to the microethnographic approach used so often to study minority student failure. He noted that many of these studies are poorly done in that they are not true ethnographies. The researcher may spend little time, if any, outside of the classroom, and the period of study is often inadequate. Ogbu also criticized the sociolinguistic bias in much of the research which sees schooling as a transmission of culture with little regard for the larger societal context in which it takes place....

CONCLUSIONS

Much more research is needed to understand the complex problem of American Indian dropouts. The cultural discontinuity hypothesis has played the strongest role in influencing the direction of research, or is, at least, used as an underlying assumption guiding the research questions, though it has not been convincingly demonstrated to be true. This exclusive focus on culture and curricular innovation draws attention from the very real possibility that economics and social structure may be more important. According to Ogbu, the castelike status of Indians and Mexican Americans are far more significant factors than their languages and cultures. He stated that

This does not mean that cultural and language differences are not relevant; what it does mean is that their castelike status makes it more difficult for them to overcome any problems created by cultural and language differences than it is for immigrant minorities (1978, p. 237).

Although "culture" itself may truly be a significant factor in student success in school, it may be that the culture in the student's background, not in the school curriculum, is significant. There is some evidence from the research, especially in Deyhle (1989) but also in Chan and Osthimer (1983), that a strong sense of traditional cultural identity (as defined by speaking the native language fluently and engaging in traditional religious and social activities) provides a student with an advantage in school. The idea that traditional Indian students may have an academic advantage over more "acculturated" students is an important issue. This would seem to contradict the idea that the more different the culture of the home and school, the more problems students will experience. Traditional American Indian students might then be seen as more like Ogbu's immigrant minorities in that they have strongly developed identities and do not need to "resist" White culture to have an identity. They, therefore, do better in school. That traditional students do better in school does not necessarily mean that providing non-traditional students with traditional cultural information will make them achieve (even if it could be done). American Indian students from homes with little participation in traditional social or religious activities or little use of the native language may fit more closely into Ogbu's classification of castelike minorities. Those students' resistance to school seems to be a far more significant factor.

The assumption that schools have control over the critical variables affecting any student's success is yet unproven. This is not to say that many schools could not do a much better job, or that some schools are not now doing an excellent job in educating American Indian students. This is merely to note that the relationship between the microlevel and macrolevel variables in schooling remain largely unexplored. I would not argue that research into cultural discontinuities is inappropriate or irrelevant, but that it is surely insufficient to fully explain the problems that American Indian students experience in school. An understanding of minority school failure cannot be captured by focusing on children's "home environment," on their unique cultural background, or on their genetic makeup or idiosyncratic personal attributes (Ogbu, 1981, p. 23).... Further research into the problem of American Indian dropouts must test implicit notions about the importance of culture and devote equal attention to variables outside the boundaries of the school itself.

POSTSCRIPT

Do Cultural Differences Between Home and School Explain the High Dropout Rates for American Indian Students?

This debate deals with a relatively recent concern within minority studies, that of having sensitivity toward ethnic cultural needs, even if it means maintaining separation. Historically, both social scientists and the general public simply assumed that assimilation was the proper goal for everyone. And assimilation demanded that minorities not only conform to the dominant cultural values and practices but also subordinate their own ideas of desirable conduct. This was most pronounced in public schools (see Issues 7 and 17), which were clearly supposed to function to socialize ethnic groups into the American mainstream.

In the past, the primary concerns for public schools were that a teacher should know his or her subject matter, know how to teach it—that is, be organized and present the concepts and assignments clearly in English—and be fair in grading. To many scholars socialized in the more recent generation of minority group theory, or those such as Reyhner who have been teaching for several years and who have embraced the newer perspective, the idea of the above description of "good teaching" is barbaric. It easily equals putting dunce caps on students or even corporal punishment. To them, the idea of a teacher not worrying about students' cultural values but instead being concerned primarily or even exclusively about course content is outmoded.

For an interesting series of debates on Native Americans see *Marxism and Native Americans*, edited by W. Churchill (South End Press, 1983). For a discussion of how scholars have treated North American Indians, see "Still Native..." by D. Lewis, in *Western Historical Quarterly* (May 1993). For an extremely critical point of view on the treatment of Native Americans, see R. Takaki, *A Different Mirror* (Little, Brown, 1993). For an original comparison of two minority groups, see J. Forbes, *African and Native Americans* (University of Illinois Press, 1993). For perspectives dealing with different racial-ethnic "learning styles," see "Western Mathematics: The Secret Weapon of Cultural Imperialism," by A. Bishop, in *Race and Class* (December 1990) and R. Cocking and J. Mestre, eds., *Linguistic and Cultural Influences on Learning Mathematics* (Lawrence Erlbaum Associates, 1988).

ISSUE 7

Should Bilingual Education Programs Be Stopped?

YES: Diane Ravitch, from "Politicization and the Schools: The Case of Bilingual Education," *Proceedings of the American Philosophical Society* (June 1985)

NO: Donaldo Macedo, from "English Only: The Tongue-Tying of America," *Journal of Education* (Spring 1991)

ISSUE SUMMARY

YES: History of education professor Diane Ravitch analyzes the ways in which politics has commingled with education in the United States, particularly in regards to bilingual education programs. She argues that certain cultural, ideological, and political interest groups are usurping students' educational needs in order to impose their own agendas. For Ravitch, bilingual education programs have not met with much success.

NO: Associate professor of linguistics Donaldo Macedo dismisses Ravitch and other education traditionalists who attack bilingual education as misguided at best, dishonest at worse. He insists that learning in public schools is not simply a matter of acquiring a neutral body of information. Instead, for non-English-speaking minorities, it frequently entails dehumanization through forced repetition of dominant group values.

For generations, some social critics have argued, the public school system in the United States has mostly functioned to acculturate foreigners and the poor into mainstream middle-class values. This was allegedly done to enable graduates to have the necessary skills to contribute to an industrial capitalist society. The harms resulting from the standardization of education were not usually considered.

Ravitch and Macedo's disagreements are taking place at a level removed from the classroom trenches occupied each day by millions of children and their teachers. From the point of view of typical girls and boys in the classroom and their teachers, especially in the inner city, this debate may seem irrelevant. Yet, for educators, politicians, many social scientists, and the mass media, the fight between Ravitch and Macedo is important. The stakes are high even if they appear at first to be far removed from the everyday realities of public school education.

Ravitch cites many examples of how interest groups in the past impacted school operations, programs, and policies. Many of these actions directly related to discrimination against minorities, such as the racial segregation of public schools (which was most famously outlawed in 1954 with the Supreme Court's ruling in *Brown v. Board of Education of Topeka*) or the banning of German from school during and immediately after World War I. In spite of the Supreme Court's 1954 ruling on desegregation, the Court was never directly involved with school curricula and other pedagogical matters until 1968. That year, Congress passed the Education Act and provided funds for bilingual education programs.

Ravitch points out that there are many variants of the latter. To her, the best bilingual program is one that would assist youngsters who are not English speakers by providing them with someone to teach them English and other immediately useful skills in their own language. This would prepare them to quickly enter regular classes.

Macedo completely rejects this form of bilingualism. He argues for a multicultural curriculum that would provide all courses of language minorities in their own languages and also offer courses structured around their own cultures, histories, literature, and so on. Such a curriculum, he feels, will empower language minorities with a sense of self-worth. It will also prevent such students from feeling that North American culture and values are superior to their own group's traditions.

Ravitch argues that the current educational debates are politically quite different from those of the past. She identifies reasons why schools have been selected to fight the present ideological and cultural war. Look closely at Ravitch's distinctions between politics in the past and current forms of politicization. The former was supposedly done with the students' best interests at heart, while the latter is a matter of self-aggrandizement for certain ideological groups. Does this distinction hold up in your opinion?

Note the very different styles as well as premises contained in the two selections. Macedo assumes, for instance, that education is merely another institution in the United States that functions to dominate and oppress others. Therefore, since this is so, nothing is lost if at least some students are able to escape this oppression by being placed in totally separate programs based on their being language minorities. Could there be a downside to this approach?

YES
Diane Ravitch

POLITICIZATION AND THE SCHOOLS: THE CASE OF BILINGUAL EDUCATION

There has always been a politics of schools, and no doubt there always will be. Like any other organization populated by human beings, schools have their internal politics; for as long as there have been public schools, there have been political battles over their budget, their personnel policies, their curricula, and their purposes. Anyone who believes that there was once a time in which schools were untouched by political controversy is uninformed about the history of education. The decision-making processes that determine who will be chosen as principal or how the school board will be selected or whether to pass a school bond issue are simply political facts of life that are part and parcel of the administration, financing, and governance of schools. There is also a politics of the curriculum and of the profession, in which contending forces argue about programs and policies. It is hard to imagine a school, a school system, a university, a state board of education, or a national department of education in which these kinds of political conflicts do not exist. They are an intrinsic aspect of complex organizations in which people disagree about how to achieve their goals and about which goals to pursue; to the extent that we operate in a democratic manner, conflict over important and even unimportant issues is inevitable.

There is another kind of politics, however, in which educational institutions become entangled in crusades marked by passionate advocacy, intolerance of criticism, and unyielding dogmatism, and in which the education of children is a secondary rather than a primary consideration. Such crusades go beyond politics-as-usual; they represent the politicization of education. Schools and universities become targets for politicization for several reasons: First, they offer a large captive audience of presumably impressionable minds; second, they are expected to shape the opinions, knowledge, and values of the rising generation, which makes them attractive to those who want to influence the future; and third, since Americans have no strong educational philosophy or educational tradition, almost any claim—properly clothed in rhetorical

From Diane Ravitch, "Politicization and the Schools: The Case of Bilingual Education," *Proceedings of the American Philosophical Society*, vol. 129, no. 2 (June 1985). Copyright © 1985 by The American Philosophical Society. Reprinted by permission.

appeals about the needs of children or of American society—can make its way into the course catalogue or the educational agenda.

Ever since Americans created public schools, financed by tax dollars and controlled by boards of laymen, the schools have been at the center of intermittent struggles over the values that they represent. The founders of the common school, and in particular Horace Mann, believed that the schools could be kept aloof from the religious and political controversies beyond their door, but it has not been easy to keep the crusaders outside the schoolhouse. In the nineteenth century, heated battles were fought over such issues as which Bible would be read in the classroom and whether public dollars might be used to subsidize religious schools. After the onset of World War I, anti-German hostility caused the German language to be routed from American schools, even though nearly a quarter of the high school population studied the language in 1915. Some of this same fervor, strengthened by zeal to hasten the process of assimilation, caused several states to outlaw parochial and private schools and to prohibit the teaching of foreign language in the first eight years of school. Such laws, obviously products of nationalism and xenophobia, were struck down as unconstitutional by the United States Supreme Court in the 1920s. The legislative efforts to abolish nonpublic schools and to bar the teaching of foreign languages were examples of politicization; their purpose was not to improve the education of any child, but to achieve certain social and political goals that the sponsors of these laws believed were of overwhelming importance.

Another example of politicization in education was the crusade to cleanse the schools of teachers and other employees who were suspected of being disloyal, subversive, or controversial. This crusade began in the years after World War I, gathered momentum during the 1930s, and came to full fruition during the loyalty investigations by state and national legislative committees in the 1950s. Fears for national security led to intrusive surveillance of the beliefs, friends, past associations, and political activities of teachers and professors. These inquiries did not improve anyone's education; they used the educational institutions as vehicles toward political goals that were extraneous to education.

A more recent example of politicization occurred on the campuses during the war in Vietnam. Those who had fought political intrusions into educational institutions during the McCarthy era did so on the ground of academic freedom. Academic freedom, they argued, protected the right of students and teachers to express their views, regardless of their content; because of academic freedom, the university served as a sanctuary for dissidents, heretics, and skeptics of all persuasions. During the war in Vietnam, those who tried to maintain the university as a privileged haven for conflicting views, an open marketplace of ideas, found themselves the object of attack by student radicals. Student (and sometimes faculty) radicals believed that opposition to the war was so important that those who did not agree with them should be harassed and even silenced.

Faced with a moral issue, the activist argued, the university could not stand above the battle, nor could it tolerate the expression of "immoral" views. In this spirit, young radicals tried to prevent those with whom they disagreed from speaking and teaching; towards this end, they heckled speakers, disrupted classes, and even planted bombs on campus. These actions were intended to politicize schools and campuses and, in some instances, they succeeded. They were advocated by sincere and zealous individuals who earnestly believed that education could not take place within a context of political neutrality. Their efforts at politicization stemmed not from any desire to improve education as such, but from the pursuit of political goals.

As significant as the student movement and the McCarthy era were as examples of the dangers of politicization, they were short-lived in comparison to the policy of racial segregation. Segregation of public school children by their race and ancestry was established by law in seventeen states and by custom in many communities beyond those states. The practice of assigning public school children and teachers on the basis of their race had no educational justification; it was not intended to improve anyone's education. It was premised on the belief in the innate inferiority of people whose skin was of dark color. Racial segregation as policy and practice politicized the schools; it used them to buttress a racist social and political order. It limited the educational opportunities available to blacks. Racial segregation was socially and politically so effective in isolating blacks from opportunity or economic advancement and educationally so devastating in retarding their learning that our society continues to pay a heavy price to redress the cumulative deficits of generations of poor education.

The United States Supreme Court's 1954 decision, *Brown v. Board of Education*, started the process of ending state-imposed racial segregation. In those southern states where segregation was the cornerstone of a way of life, white resistance to desegregation was prolonged and intense. The drive to disestablish racial segregation and to uproot every last vestige of its effects was unquestionably necessary. The practice of assigning children to school by their race and of segregating other public facilities by race was a national disgrace. However, the process through which desegregation came about dramatically altered the politics of schools; courts and regulatory agencies at the federal and state level became accustomed to intervening in the internal affairs of educational institutions, and the potential for politicization of the schools was significantly enlarged.

The slow pace of desegregation in the decade after the *Brown* decision, concurrent with a period of rising expectations, contributed to a dramatic buildup of frustration and rage among blacks, culminating in the protests, civil disorders, and riots of the mid-1960s. In response, Congress enacted major civil rights laws in 1964 and 1965, and the federal courts became aggressive in telling school boards what to do to remedy their constitutional violations. Initially, these orders consisted of commands to produce racially mixed schools. However, some courts went beyond questions of racial mix. In Washington, D.C., a federal district judge in 1967 directed the school administration to abandon ability grouping, which he believed discriminated against black children. This was the first time that a federal court found a common pedagogical practice to be unconstitutional.[1]

In the nearly two decades since that decision, the active intervention of the federal judiciary into school affairs has ceased to be unusual. In Ann Arbor, Michigan, a federal judge ordered the school board to train teachers in "black English," a program subsequently found to be ineffectual in improving the education of black students. In California, a federal judge barred the use of intelligence tests for placement of students in special education classes, even though reputable psychologists defend their validity. In Boston, where the school board was found guilty of intentionally segregating children by race, the federal judge assumed full control over the school system for more than a decade; even reform superintendents who were committed to carrying out the judge's program for desegregation complained of the hundreds of court orders regulating every aspect of schooling, hiring, promotion, curriculum, and financing. In 1982, in a case unrelated to desegregation, a state judge in West Virginia ordered the state education department to do "no less than completely reconstruct the entire system of education in West Virginia," and the judge started the process of reconstruction by setting down his own standards for facilities, administration, and curriculum, including what was to be taught and for how many minutes each week.[2]

Perhaps this is as good a way of bringing about school reform as any other. No doubt school officials are delighted when a judge orders the state legislature to raise taxes on behalf of the schools. But it does seem to be a repudiation of our democratic political structure when judges go beyond issues of constitutional rights, don the mantle of school superintendent, and use their authority to change promotional standards, to reconstruct the curriculum, or to impose their own pedagogical prescriptions.

Now, by the definition of politicization that I earlier offered—that is, when educational institutions become the focus of dogmatic crusaders whose purposes are primarily political and only incidentally related to children's education—these examples may not qualify as politicization, although they do suggest how thin is the line between politics and politicization. After all, the judges were doing what they thought would produce better education. The court decisions in places like Ann Arbor, Boston, California, and West Virginia may be thought of as a shift in the politics of schools, a shift that has brought the judiciary into the decision-making process as a full-fledged partner in shaping educational disputes, even those involving questions of pedagogy and curriculum.

The long struggle to desegregate American schools put them at the center of political battles for more than a generation and virtually destroyed the belief that schools could remain above politics. Having lost their apolitical shield, the schools also lost their capacity to resist efforts to politicize them. In the absence of resistance, demands by interest groups of varying ideologies escalated, each trying to impose its own agenda on the curriculum, the textbooks, the school library, or the teachers. Based on the activities of single-issue groups, any number of contemporary educational policies would serve equally well as examples of politicization. The example that I have chosen as illustrative of politicization is bilingual education. The history of this program exemplifies a campaign on behalf of social and political goals that are only tangentially related to education. I would like to sketch briefly the bilingual controversy, which provides an overview of the new politics of education and demonstrates the tendency within this new politics to use educational programs for noneducational ends.

Demands for bilingual education arose as an outgrowth of the civil rights movement. As it evolved, that movement contained complex, and occasionally contradictory, elements. One facet of the movement appealed for racial integration and assimilation, which led to court orders for busing and racial balance; but the dynamics of the movement also inspired appeals to racial solidarity, which led to demands for black studies, black control of black schools, and other race-conscious policies. Whether the plea was for integration or for separatism, advocates could always point to a body of social science as evidence for their goals.

Race consciousness became a necessary part of the remedies that courts fashioned, but its presence legitimized ethnocentrism as a force in American politics. In the late 1960s, the courts, Congress, and policymakers—having been told for years by spokesmen for the civil rights movement that all children should be treated equally without regard to their race or ancestry—frequently heard compelling testimony by political activists and social scientists about the value of ethnic particularism in the curriculum.

Congress first endorsed funding for bilingual education in 1968, at a time when ethnocentrism had become a powerful political current. In hearings on this legislation, proponents of bilingual education argued that non-English-speaking children did poorly in school because they had low self-esteem, and that this low self-esteem was caused by the absence of their native language from the classroom. They claimed that if the children were taught in their native tongue and about their native culture, they would have higher self-esteem, better attitudes toward school, and higher educational achievement. Bilingual educators also insisted that children would learn English more readily if they already knew another language.

In the congressional hearings, both advocates and congressmen seemed to agree that the purpose of bilingual education was to help non-English speakers succeed in school and in society. But the differences between them were not then obvious. The congressmen believed that bilingual education would serve as a temporary transition into the regular English language program. But the bilingual educators saw the program as an opportunity to maintain the language and culture of the non-English-speaking student, while he was learning English.[3]

What was extraordinary about the Bilingual Education Act of 1968, which has since been renewed several times, is that it was the first time that the Congress had ever legislated a given pedagogical method. In practice, bilingual education means a program in which children study the major school subjects in a language other than English. Funding of the program, although small within the context of the federal education budget, created strong constituencies for its continuation, both within the federal government and among recipient agencies. No different from other interest groups, these constituencies pressed for expansion and strengthening of their program. Just as lifelong vocational educators are unlikely to ask whether their program works, so career bilingual educators are committed to their method as a philosophy, not as a technique for language instruction. The difference is this: techniques are subject to evaluation, which may cause them to be revised or discarded; philosophies are not.

In 1974, the Supreme Court's *Lau v. Nichols* decision reinforced demands for bilingual education. The Court ruled against the San Francisco public schools for their failure to provide English language instruction for 1,800 non-English-speaking Chinese students. The Court's decision was reasonable and appropriate. The Court said, "There is no equality of treatment merely by providing students with the same facilities, textbooks, teachers, and curriculum; for students who do not understand English are effectively foreclosed from any meaningful education." The decision did not endorse any particular remedy. It said "Teaching English to the students of Chinese ancestry who do not speak the language is one choice. Giving instruction to the group in Chinese is another. There may be others."[4]

Despite the Court's prudent refusal to endorse any particular method of instruction, the bilingual educators interpreted the *Lau* decision as a mandate for bilingual programs. In the year after the decision, the United States Office of Education established a task force to fashion guidelines for the implementation of the *Lau* decision; the task force was composed of bilingual educators and representatives of language minority groups. The task force fashioned regulations that prescribed in exhaustive detail how school districts should prepare and carry out bilingual programs for non-English-speaking students. The districts were directed to identify the student's primary language, not by his proficiency in English, but by determining which language was most often spoken in the student's home, which language he had learned first, and which language he used most often. Thus a student would be eligible for a bilingual program even if he was entirely fluent in English.[5]

Furthermore, while the Supreme Court refused to endorse any given method, the task force directed that non-English-speaking students should receive bilingual education that emphasized instruction in their native language and culture. Districts were discouraged from using the "English as a Second Language" approach, which consists of intensive, supplemental English-only instruction, or immersion techniques, in which students are instructed in English within an English-only context.

Since the establishment of the bilingual education program, many millions of dollars have been spent to support bilingual programs in more than sixty different languages. Among those receiving funding to administer and staff such programs, bilingual education is obviously popular, but there are critics who think that it is educationally unsound. Proponents of desegregation have complained that bilingual education needlessly segregates non-English speakers from others of their age. At a congressional hearing in 1977, one desegregation specialist complained that bilingual programs had been funded "without any significant proof that they would work.... There is nothing in the research to suggest that children can effectively learn English without continuous interaction with other children who are native English speakers."[6]

The research on bilingual education has been contradictory, and studies that favor or criticize the bilingual approach have been attacked as biased. Researchers connected to bilingual institutes claim that their programs resulted in significant gains for non-English-speaking children. But a four-year study commissioned by the United States Office of Education concluded that students who learned bilingually did not achieve at a higher level than those in regular classes, nor were their attitudes toward school significantly different. What they seemed to learn best, the study found, was the language in which they were instructed.[7]

One of the few evidently unbiased, nonpolitical assessments of bilingual research was published in 1982 in the *Harvard Educational Review*. A survey of international findings, it concluded that "bilingual programs are neither better nor worse than other instructional methods." The author found that in the absence of compelling experimental support for this method, there was "no legal necessity or research basis for the federal government to advocate or require a specific educational approach."[8]

If the research is in fact inconclusive, then there is no justification for mandating the use of bilingual education or any other single pedagogy. The bilingual method may or may not be the best way to learn English. Language instruction programs that are generally regarded as outstanding, such as those provided for Foreign Service officers or by the nationally acclaimed center at Middlebury College, are immersion programs, in which students embark on a systematic program of intensive language learning without depending on their native tongue. Immersion programs may not be appropriate for all children, but then neither is any single pedagogical method. The method to be used should be determined by the school authorities and the professional staff, based on their resources and competence.

Despite the fact that the Supreme Court did not endorse bilingual education, the lower federal courts have tended to treat this pedagogy as a civil right, and more than a dozen states have mandated its use in their public schools. The path by which bilingual education came to be viewed as a civil right, rather than as one method of teaching language, demonstrates the politicization of the language issue in American education. The United States Commission on Civil Rights endorsed bilingual education as a civil right nearly a decade ago. Public interest lawyers and civil rights lawyers have also regarded bilingual education as a basic civil right. An article in 1983 in the *Columbia Journal of Law and Social Problems* contended that bilingual education "may be the most effective method of compensatory language instruction currently used to educate language-minority students."[9] It based this conclusion not on a review of educational research but on statements made by various political agencies.

The article states, for example, as a matter of fact rather than opinion: " ... by offering subject matter instruction in a language understood by language-minority students, the bilingual-bicultural method maximizes achievement, and thus minimizes feelings of inferiority that might accompany a poor academic performance. By ridding the school environment of those features which may damage a language-minority child's self-image and thereby interfere with the educative process, bilingual-bicultural education creates the atmosphere most conducive to successful learning."[10]

If there were indeed conclusive evidence for these statements, then bilingual-bicultural education *should* be imposed on school districts throughout the country. However, the picture is complicated; there are good bilingual programs, and there are ineffective bilingual programs. In and of itself, bilingualism is one pedagogical method, as subject to variation and misuse as any other single method. To date, no school district has claimed that the bilingual method succeeded in sharply decreasing the dropout rate of Hispanic children or markedly raising their achievement scores in English and other subjects. The bilingual method is not necessarily inferior to other methods; its use should not be barred. There simply is no conclusive evidence that bilingualism should be preferred to all other ways of instructing non-English-speaking students. This being the case, there are no valid reasons for courts or federal agencies to impose this method on school districts for all non-English speakers, to the exclusion of other methods of language instruction.

Bilingual education exemplifies politicization because its advocates press its adoption regardless of its educational effectiveness, and they insist that it must be made mandatory regardless of the wishes of the parents and children who are its presumed beneficiaries. It is a political program whose goals are implicit in the term "biculturalism." The aim is to use the public schools to promote the maintenance of distinct ethnic communities, each with its own cultural heritage and language. This in itself is a valid goal for a democratic nation as diverse and pluralistic as ours, but it is questionable whether this goal is appropriately pursued by the public schools, rather than by the freely chosen activities of individuals and groups.

Then there is the larger question of whether bilingual education actually promotes equality of educational opportunity. Unless it enables non-English-speaking children to learn English and to enter into the mainstream of American society, it may hinder equality of educational opportunity. The child who spends most of his instructional time learning in Croatian or Greek or Spanish is likely to learn Croatian, Greek, or Spanish. Fluency in these languages will be of little help to those who want to apply to American colleges, universities, graduate schools, or employers, unless they are also fluent in English.

Of course, our nation needs much more foreign language instruction. But we should not confuse our desire to promote foreign languages in general with the special educational needs of children who do not know how to speak and read English in an English-language society.

Will our educational institutions ever be insulated from the extremes of politicization? It seems highly unlikely, in view of the fact that our schools and colleges are deeply embedded in the social and political mainstream. What is notably different today is the vastly increased power of the federal government and the courts to intervene in educational institutions, because of the expansion of the laws and the dependence of almost all educational institutions on public funding. To avoid unwise and dangerous politicization, government agencies should strive to distinguish between their proper role as protectors of fundamental constitutional rights and inappropriate intrusion into complex issues of curriculum and pedagogy.

This kind of institutional restraint would be strongly abetted if judges and policymakers exercised caution and skepticism in their use of social science testimony. Before making social research the basis for constitutional edicts, judges and policymakers should understand that social science findings are usually divergent, limited, tentative, and partial.

We need the courts as vigilant guardians of our rights; we need federal agencies that respond promptly to any violations of those rights. But we also need educational institutions that are free to exercise their responsibilities without fear of pressure groups and political lobbies. Decisions about which textbooks to use, which theories to teach, which books to place in the school library, how to teach, and what to teach are educational issues. They should be made by appropriate lay and professional authorities on educational grounds. In a democratic society, all of us share the responsibility to protect schools, colleges, and universities against unwarranted political intrusion into educational affairs.

REFERENCES

1. *Hobson v. Hansen*, 269 F. Supp. 401 (D.D.C., 1967); Alexander Bickel, "Skelly Wright's Sweeping Decision," *New Republic*, July 8, 1967, pp. 11–12.

2. Nathan Glazer, "Black English and Reluctant Judges," *Public Interest*, vol. 62, Winter 1980, pp. 40–54; *Larry P. v. Wilson Riles*, 495 F. Supp. 1926 (N.D. Calif., 1979); Nathan Glazer, "IQ on Trial," *Commentary*, June 1981, pp. 51–59; *Morgan v. Hennigan*, 379 F. Supp. 410 (D. Mass., 1974); Robert Wood, "The Disassembling of American Education," *Daedalus*, vol. 109, no. 3, Summer 1980, pp. 99–113; *Education Week*, May 12, 1982, p. 5.

3. U.S. Congress, Senate, Committee on Labor and Public Welfare, Special Subcommittee on Bilingual Education, 90th Cong., 1st sess., 1967.

4. *Lau v. Nichols*, 414 U.S. 563 (1974).

5. U.S. Department of Health, Education, and Welfare, "Task Force Findings Specifying Remedies Available for Eliminating Past Educational Practices Ruled Unlawful under *Lau v. Nichols*" (Washington, D.C., Summer 1975).

6. U.S. Congress, House, Subcommittee on Elementary, Secondary, and Vocational Education of the Committee on Education and Labor, Bilingual Education, 95th Cong., 1st sess., 1977, pp. 335–336. The speaker was Gary Orfield.

7. Malcolm N. Danoff, "Evaluation of the Impact of ESEA Title VII Spanish/English Bilingual Education Programs" (Palo Alto, Calif.: American Institutes for Research, 1978).

8. Iris Rotberg, "Some Legal and Research Considerations in Establishing Federal Policy in Bilingual Education," *Harvard Educational Review*, vol. 52, May 1982, pp. 148–168.

9. Jonathan D. Haft, "Assuring Equal Educational Opportunity for Language-Minority Students: Bilingual Education and the Equal Educational Opportunity Act of 1974." *Columbia Journal of Law and Social Problems*, vol. 18, no. 2, 1983, pp. 209–293.

10. Ibid., p. 253.

NO

Donaldo Macedo

ENGLISH ONLY: THE
TONGUE-TYING OF AMERICA

During the past decade conservative educators such as ex-secretary of education William Bennett and Diane Ravitch have mounted an unrelenting attack on bilingual and multicultural education. These conservative educators tend to recycle old assumptions about the "melting pot theory" and our "common culture," assumptions designed primarily to maintain the status quo. Maintained is a status quo that functions as a cultural reproduction mechanism which systematically does not allow other cultural subjects, who are considered outside of the mainstream, to be present in history. These cultural subjects who are profiled as the "other" are but palely represented in history within our purportedly democratic society in the form of Black History Month, Puerto Rican Day, and so forth. This historical constriction was elegantly captured by an 11th-grade Vietnamese student in California:

> I was so excited when my history teacher talked about the Vietnam War. Now at last, I thought, now we will study about my country. We didn't really study it. Just for one day, though, my country was real again. (Olsen, 1988, p. 68)

The incessant attack on bilingual education which claims that it serves to tongue-tie students in their native language not only negates the multilingual and multicultural nature of U.S. society, but blindly ignores the empirical evidence that has been amply documented in support of bilingual education.... [T]he present overdose of monolingualism and Anglocentrism that dominates the current educational debate not only contributes to a type of mind-tied America, but also is incapable of producing educators and leaders who can rethink what it means to prepare students to enter the ever-changing, multilingual, and multicultural world of the 21st century.

It is both academically dishonest and misleading to simply point to some failures of bilingual education without examining the lack of success of linguistic minority students within a larger context of a general failure of public education in major urban centers. Furthermore, the English Only position points to a pedagogy of exclusion that views the learning of English as education itself. English Only advocates fail to question under what conditions English will be taught and by whom. For example, immersing non-English-

From Donaldo Macedo, "English Only: The Tongue-Tying of America," *Journal of Education*, vol. 173, no. 2 (Spring 1991). Copyright © 1991 by the Trustees of Boston University. Reprinted by permission.

speaking students in English as a Second Language [ESL] programs taught by untrained music, art and social science teachers (as is the case in Massachusetts with the grandfather clause in ESL Certification) will hardly accomplish the avowed goals of the English Only Movement. The proponents of English Only also fail to raise two other fundamental questions. First, if English is the most effective educational language, how can we explain that over 60 million Americans are illiterate or functionally illiterate (Kozol, 1985, p. 4)? Second, if education solely in English can guarantee linguistic minorities a better future, as educators like William Bennett promise, why do the majority of Black Americans, whose ancestors have been speaking English for over 200 years, find themselves still relegated to ghettos?

I want to argue in this paper that the answer lies not in technical questions of whether English is a more viable language of instruction or the repetitive promise that it offers non-English-speaking students "full participation first in their school and later in American society" (Silber, 1991, p. 7). This position assumes that English is in fact a superior language and that we live in a classless, race-blind society. I want to propose that decisions about how to educate non-English-speaking students cannot be reduced to issues of language, but rest in a full understanding of the ideological elements that generate and sustain linguistic, racial, and sex discrimination. That is, educators need to develop, as Henry Giroux has suggested, "a politics and pedagogy around a new language capable of acknowledging the multiple, contradictory, and complex subject positions people occupy within different social, cultural, and economic locations"

(1992, p. 27). By shifting the linguistic issue to an ideological terrain we will challenge conservative educators to confront the Berlin Wall of racism, classism, and economic deprivation which characterizes the lived experiences of minorities in U.S. public schools. For example, J. Anthony Lukas succinctly captures the ideological elements that promote racism and segregation in schools in his analysis of desegregation in the Boston Public Schools. Lukas cites a trip to Charlestown High School, where a group of Black parents experienced firsthand the stark reality their children were destined to endure. Although the headmaster assured them that "violence, intimidation, or racial slurs would not be tolerated," they could not avoid the racial epithets on the walls: "Welcome Niggers," "Niggers Suck," "White Power," "KKK," "Bus is for Zulu," and "Be illiterate, fight busing." As those parents were boarding the bus, "they were met with jeers and catcalls 'go home niggers. Keep going all the way to Africa!'" This racial intolerance led one parent to reflect, "My god, what kind of hell am I sending my children into?" (Lukas, 1985, p. 282). What could her children learn at a school like that except to hate? Even though forced integration of schools in Boston exacerbated the racial tensions in the Boston Public Schools, one should not overlook the deep-seated racism that permeates all levels of the school structure....

Against this landscape of violent racism perpetrated against racial minorities, and also against linguistic minorities, one can understand the reasons for the high dropout rate in the Boston public schools (approximately 50%). Perhaps racism and other ideological elements are part of a school reality which forces a high percentage of students to leave school, only later to be profiled by the very system as dropouts or "poor and unmotivated students." One could argue that the above incidents occurred during a tumultuous time of racial division in Boston's history, but I do not believe that we have learned a great deal from historically dangerous memories to the degree that our leaders continue to invite racial tensions as evidenced in the Willie Horton presidential campaign issue and the present quota for jobs as an invitation once again to racial divisiveness.

It is very curious that this new-found concern of English Only advocates for limited English proficiency students does not interrogate those very ideological elements that psychologically and emotionally harm these students far more than the mere fact that English may present itself as a temporary barrier to an effective education. It would be more socially constructive and beneficial if the zeal that propels the English Only movement were diverted toward social struggles designed to end violent racism and structures of poverty, homelessness, and family breakdown, among other social ills that characterize the lived experiences of minorities in the United States. If these social issues are not dealt with appropriately, it is naive to think that the acquisition of the English language alone will, somehow, magically eclipse the raw and cruel injustices and oppression perpetrated against the dispossessed class of minorities in the United States. According to Peter McLaren, these dispossessed minority students who

> populate urban settings in places such as Howard Beach, Ozone Park, El Barrio, are more likely to be forced to learn

about Eastern Europe in ways set forth by neo-conservative multiculturists than they are to learn about the Harlem Renaissance, Mexico, Africa, the Caribbean, or Aztec or Zulu culture. (McLaren, 1991, p. 7)

While arguing for the use of the students' native language in their educational development, I would like to make it very clear that the bilingual education goal should never be to restrict students to their own vernacular. This linguistic constriction inevitably leads to a linguistic ghetto. Educators must understand fully the broader meaning of the use of students' language as a requisite for their empowerment. That is, empowerment should never be limited to what Stanley Aronowitz describes as "the process of appreciating and loving oneself" (1985). In addition to this process, empowerment should also be a means that enables students "to interrogate and selectively appropriate those aspects of the dominant culture that will provide them with the basis for defining and transforming, rather than merely serving, the wider social order" (Giroux & McLaren, 1986, p. 17). This means that educators should understand the value of mastering the standard English language of the wider society. It is through the full appropriation of the standard English language that linguistic minority students find themselves linguistically empowered to engage in dialogue with various sectors of the wider society. What I must reiterate is that educators should never allow the limited proficient students' native language to be silenced by a distorted legitimation of the standard English language. Linguistic minority students' language should never be sacrificed, since it is the only means through which they make sense of their own experience in the world.

Given the importance of the standard English language in the education of linguistic minority students, I must agree with the members of the Institute for Research in English Acquisition and Development when they quote Antonio Gramsci in their brochure:

> Without the mastery of the common standard version of the national language, one is inevitably destined to function only at the periphery of national life and, especially, outside the national and political mainstream. (READ, 1990)

But these English Only advocates fail to tell the other side of Antonio Gramsci's argument, which warns us:

> Each time that in one way or another, the question of language comes to the fore, that signifies that a series of other problems is about to emerge, the formation and enlarging of the ruling class, the necessity to establish more "intimate" and sure relations between the ruling groups and the popular masses, that is, the reorganization of cultural hegemony. (Gramsci, 1971, p. 16)

This selective selection of Gramsci's position on language points to the hidden curriculum with which the English Only movement seeks to promote a monolithic ideology. It is also part and parcel of an ongoing attempt at "reorganization of cultural hegemony" as evidenced by the unrelenting attack by conservative educators on multicultural education and curriculum diversity....

In contrast to the zeal for a common culture and English only, these conservative educators have remained ominously silent about forms of racism, inequality, subjugation, and exploitation that daily serve to wage symbolic and real violence against those children who by virtue of their language, race, ethnicity, class, or gender are not treated in schools with the dignity and respect all children warrant in a democracy. Instead of reconstituting education around an urban and cultural studies approach which takes the social, cultural, political, and economic divisions of education and everyday life as the primary categories for understanding contemporary schooling, conservative educators have recoiled in an attempt to salvage the status quo. That is, they try to keep the present unchanged even though, as Renato Constantino points out:

> Within the living present there are imperceptible changes which make the status quo a moving reality.... Thus a new policy based on the present as past and not on the present as future is backward for it is premised not on evolving conditions but on conditions that are already dying away. (1978, p. 201)

One such not so imperceptible change is the rapid growth of minority representation in the labor force. As such, the conservative leaders and educators are digging this country's economic grave by their continued failure to educate minorities. As Lew Ferlerger and Jay Mandle convincingly argue, "Unless the educational attainment of minority populations in the United States improves, the country's hopes for resuming high rates of growth and an increasing standard of living look increasingly dubious" (1991, p. 12).

In addition to the real threat to the economic fabric of the United States, the persistent call for English language only in education smacks of backwardness in the present conjuncture of our ever-changing multicultural and multilingual society. Furthermore, these conservative educators base their language policy argument on the premise that English education in this country is highly effective. On the contrary. As Patrick Courts clearly argues in his book *Literacy for Empowerment* (1991), English education is failing even middle-class and upper-class students. He argues that English reading and writing classes are mostly based on workbooks and grammar lessons, lessons which force students to "bark at print" or fill in the blanks. Students engage in grudgingly banal exercises such as practicing correct punctuation and writing sample business letters. Books used in their classes are, Courts points out, too often in the service of commercially prepared ditto sheets and workbooks. Courts's account suggests that most school programs do not take advantage of the language experiences that the majority of students have had before they reach school. These teachers become the victims of their own professional ideology when they delegitimize the language experiences that students bring with them into the classroom.

Courts's study is basically concerned with middle-class and upper-middle-class students unburdened by racial discrimination and poverty, students who have done well in elementary and high school settings and are now populating the university lecture halls and seminar rooms. If schools are failing these students, the situation does not bode well for those students less economically, socially, and politically advantaged. It is toward the linguistic minority students that I would like to turn my discussion now.

THE ROLE OF LANGUAGE IN THE EDUCATION OF LINGUISTIC MINORITY STUDENTS

Within the last two decades, the issue of bilingual education has taken on a heated importance among educators. Unfortunately, the debate that has emerged tends to recycle old assumptions and values regarding the meaning and usefulness of the students' native language in education. The notion that education of linguistic minority students is a matter of learning the standard English language still informs the vast majority of bilingual programs and manifests its logic in the renewed emphasis on technical reading and writing skills.

I want to reiterate in this paper that the education of linguistic minority students cannot be viewed as simply the development of skills aimed at acquiring the standard English language. English Only proponents seldom discuss the pedagogical structures that will enable these students to access other bodies of knowledge. Nor do they interrogate the quality of ESL instruction provided to the linguistic minority students and the adverse material conditions under which these students learn English. The view that teaching English constitutes education sustains a notion of ideology that systematically negates rather than makes meaningful the cultural experiences of the subordinate linguistic groups who are, by and large, the objects of its policies. For the education of linguistic minority students to become meaningful it has to be situated within a theory of cultural production and viewed as an integral part of the way in which people produce, transform, and reproduce meaning. Bilingual education, in this sense, must be seen as a medium that constitutes and affirms the historical and existential moments of lived culture. Hence, it is an eminently political phenomenon, and it must be analyzed within the context of a theory of power relations and an understanding of social and cultural reproduction and production. By "cultural reproduction" I refer to collective experiences that function in the interest of the dominant groups rather than in the interest of the oppressed groups that are objects of its policies. Bilingual education programs in the United States have been developed and implemented under the cultural reproduction model leading to a de facto neocolonial educational model. I use "cultural production" to refer to specific groups of people producing, mediating, and confirming the mutual ideological elements that merge from and reaffirm their daily lived experiences. In this case, such experiences are rooted in the interest of individual and collective self-determination. It is only through a cultural production model that we can achieve a truly democratic and liberatory educational experience. I will return to this issue later.

While the various debates in the past two decades may differ in their basic assumptions about the education of linguistic minority students, they all share one common feature: they all ignore the role of language as a major force in the construction of human subjectivities. That is, they ignore the way language may either confirm or deny the life histories and experiences of the people who use it.

The pedagogical and political implications in education programs for linguistic minority students are far-reaching and yet largely ignored. These programs, for example, often contradict a fundamental principle of reading, namely that students learn to read faster and with better comprehension when taught in their native tongue. The immediate recognition of familiar words and experiences enhances the development of a positive self-concept in children who are somewhat insecure about the status of their language and culture. For this reason, and to be consistent with the plan to construct a democratic society free from vestiges of oppression, a minority literacy program must be rooted in the cultural capital of subordinate groups and have as its point of departure their own language.

Educators must develop radical pedagogical structures which provide students with the opportunity to use their own reality as a basis of literacy. This includes, obviously, the language they bring to the classroom. To do otherwise is to deny minority students the rights that lie at the core of a democratic education. The failure to base a literacy program on the minority students' language means that oppositional forces can neutralize the efforts of educators and political leaders to achieve decolonization of schooling. It is of tantamount importance that the incorporation of the minority language as the primary language of instruction in education of linguistic minority students be given top priority. It is through their own language that linguistic minority students will be able to reconstruct their history and their culture.

I want to argue that the minority language has to be understood within the theoretical framework that generates it. Put another way, the ultimate meaning and value of the minority language is not to be found by determining how systematic and rule-governed it is. We know that already. Its real meaning has to be understood through the assumptions that govern it, and it has to be understood via the social, political, and ideological relations to which it points. Generally speaking, this issue of effectiveness and validity often hides the true role of language in the maintenance of the values and interests of the dominant class. In other words, the issue of effectiveness and validity becomes a mask that obfuscates questions about the social, political, and ideological order within which the minority language exists.

If an emancipatory and critical education program is to be developed in the United States for linguistic minority students in which they become "subjects" rather than "objects," educators must understand the productive quality of language. James Donald puts it this way:

> I take language to be productive rather than reflective of social reality. This means calling into question the assumption that we, as speaking subjects, simply use language to organize and express our ideas and experiences. On the contrary, language is one of the most important social practices through which we come to experience ourselves as subjects.... My point here is that once we get beyond the idea of language as no more than a medium of communication, as a tool equally and neutrally available to all parties in cultural exchanges, then we can begin to examine language both as a practice of signification and also as a site for culture struggle and as a mechanism which produces antagonistic relations between different social groups. (Donald, 1982, p. 44)

It is to the antagonistic relationship between the minority and dominant speakers that I want to turn now. The antagonistic nature of the minority language has never been fully explored. In order to more clearly discuss this issue of antagonism, I will use Donald's distinction between oppressed language and repressed language. Using Donald's categories, the "negative" way of posing the minority language question is to view it in terms of oppression—that is, seeing the minority language as "lacking" the dominant standard features which usually serve as a point of reference for the minority language. By far the most common questions concerning the minority language in the United States are posed from the oppression perspective. The alternative view of the minority language is that it is repressed in the standard dominant language. In this view, minority language as a repressed language could, if spoken, challenge the privileged standard linguistic dominance. Educators have failed to recognize the "positive" promise and antagonistic nature of the minority language. It is precisely on these dimensions that educators must demystify the standard dominant language and the old assumptions about its inherent superiority. Educators must develop liberatory and critical bilingual programs informed by a radical pedagogy so that the minority language will cease to provide its speakers the experience of subordination and, moreover, may be brandished as a weapon of resistance to the dominance of the dominant standard language of the curriculum.

In this sense, the students' language is the only means by which they can develop their own voice, a prerequisite to the development of a positive sense of self-worth. As Giroux elegantly states, the students' voice "is the discursive means to make themselves 'heard' and to define themselves as active authors of their worlds" (Giroux & McLaren, 1986, p. 235). The authorship of one's own world also implies the use of one's own language, and relates to what Mikhail

Bakhtin describes as "retelling a story in one's own words" (Giroux & McLaren, 1986, p. 235).

A DEMOCRATIC AND LIBERATORY EDUCATION FOR LINGUISTIC MINORITY STUDENTS

In maintaining a certain coherence with the educational plan to reconstruct new and more democratic educational programs for linguistic minority students, educators and political leaders need to create a new school grounded in a new educational praxis, expressing different concepts of education consonant with the principles of a democratic, multicultural, and multilingual society. In order for this to happen, the first step is to identify the objectives of the inherent colonial education that informs the majority of bilingual programs in the United States. Next, it is necessary to analyze how colonialist methods used by the dominant schools function, legitimize the Anglocentric values and meaning, and at the same time negate the history, culture, and language practices of the majority of linguistic minority students. The new school, so it is argued, must also be informed by a radical bilingual pedagogy, which would make concrete such values as solidarity, social responsibility, and creativity. In the democratic development of bilingual programs rooted in a liberatory ideology, linguistic minority students become "subjects" rather than mere "objects" to be assimilated blindly into an often hostile dominant "common" culture. A democratic and liberatory education needs to move away from traditional approaches, which emphasize the acquisition of mechanical basic skills while divorcing education from its ideological and historical contexts. In attempting to meet this goal, it purposely must reject the conservative principles embedded in the English Only movement I have discussed earlier. Unfortunately, many bilingual programs sometimes unknowingly reproduce one common feature of the traditional approaches to education by ignoring the important relationship between language and the cultural capital of the students at whom bilingual education is aimed. The result is the development of bilingual programs whose basic assumptions are at odds with the democratic spirit that launched them.

Bilingual program development must be largely based on the notion of a democratic and liberatory education, in which education is viewed "as one of the major vehicles by which 'oppressed' people are able to participate in the sociohistorical transformation of their society" (Walmsley, 1981, p. 74). Bilingual education, in this sense, is grounded in a critical reflection of the cultural capital of the oppressed. It becomes a vehicle by which linguistic minority students are equipped with the necessary tools to reappropriate their history, culture, and language practices. It is, thus, a way to enable the linguistic minority students to reclaim "those historical and existential experiences that are devalued in everyday life by the dominant culture in order to be both validated and critically understood" (Giroux, 1983, p. 226). To do otherwise is to deny these students their very democratic rights. In fact, the criticism that bilingual and multicultural education unwisely question the traditions and values of our so-called "common culture" as suggested by Kenneth T. Jackson (1991) is both antidemocratic and academically dishonest. Multicultural education and curriculum diversity did not create the S & L scandal, the Iran-Contra debacle, or the extortion of minority properties by banks, the stewards of the "common culture," who charged minorities exorbitant loan-sharking interest rates. Multicultural education and curriculum diversity did not force Joachim Maitre, dean of the College of Communication at Boston University, to choose the hypocritical moral high ground to excoriate the popular culture's "bleak moral content," all the while plagiarizing 15 paragraphs of a conservative comrade's text.

The learning of English language skills alone will not enable linguistic minority students to acquire the critical tools "to awaken and liberate them from their mystified and distorted views of themselves and their world" (Giroux, 1983, p. 226). For example, speaking English has not enabled African-Americans to change this society's practice of jailing more Blacks than even South Africa, and this society spending over 7 billion dollars to keep African-American men in jail while spending only 1 billion dollars educating Black males (Black, 1991).

Educators must understand the all-encompassing role the dominant ideology has played in this mystification and distortion of our so-called "common culture" and our "common language." They must also recognize the antagonistic relationship between the "common culture" and those who, by virtue of their race, language, ethnicity, and gender, have been relegated to the margins. Finally, educators must develop bilingual programs based on the theory of cultural production. In other words, linguistic minority students must be provided the opportunity to become actors in the reconstruction of a more democratic and just society. In short, education conducted in English only is alienating to linguistic minority students, since it denies them the fundamental tools for reflection, critical thinking, and social interaction. Without the cultivation of their native language, and robbed of the opportunity for reflection and critical thinking, linguistic minority students find themselves unable to re-create their culture and history. Without the reappropriation of their culture, the valorization of their lived experiences, English Only supporters' vacuous promise that the English language will guarantee students "full participation first in their school and later in American society" (Silber, 1991, p. 7) can hardly be a reality.

REFERENCES

Aronowitz, S. (1985, May). "Why should Johnny read." *Village Voice Literary Supplement*, p. 13.

Black, C. (1991, January 13). Paying the high price for being the world's no. 1 jailor. *Boston Sunday Globe*, p. 67.

Constantino, R. (1928). *Neocolonial identity and counter consciousness*. London: Merlin Press.

Courts, P. (1991). *Literacy for empowerment*. South Hadley, MA: Bergin & Garvey.

Donald, J. (1982). Language, literacy, and schooling. In *The state and popular culture*. Milton Keynes: Open University Culture Unit.

Ferlerger, L., & Mandle, J. (1991). *African-Americans and the future of the U.S. economy*. Unpublished manuscript.

Giroux, H. A. (1983). *Theory and resistance: A pedagogy for the opposition*. South Hadley, MA: Bergin & Garvey.

Giroux, H. (1991). *Border crossings: Cultural workers and the politics of education*. New York: Routledge.

Giroux, H. A., & McLaren, P. (1986). Teacher education and the politics of engagement: The case for democratic schooling. *Harvard Educational Review, 56*(3), 213–238.

Gramsci, A. (1971). *Selections from Prison Notebooks*, (Ed. and Trans. Quinten Hoare & Geoffrey Smith). New York: International Publishers.

Jackson, D. (1991, December 8). The end of the second Reconstruction. *Boston Globe*, p. 27.

Jackson, K. T. (1991, July 7). Cited in a *Boston Sunday Globe* editorial.

Kozol, J. (1985). *Illiterate America*. New York: Doubleday Anchor.

Lukas, J. A. (1985). *Common ground*. New York: Alfred A. Knopf.

McLaren, P. (1991). Critical pedagogy: Constructing an arch of social dreaming and a doorway to hope. *Journal of Education, 173*(1), 9–34.

Olsen, L. (1988). *Crossing the schoolhouse border: Immigrant students and the California public schools.* San Francisco: California Tomorrow.

Silber, J. (1991, May). *Boston University Commencement Catalogue.*

Walmsley, S. (1981). On the purpose and content of secondary reading programs: Educational and ideological perspectives. *Curriculum Inquiry, 11*, 73–79.

POSTSCRIPT

Should Bilingual Education Programs Be Stopped?

The controversy over bilingual education programs and whether or not they are effective is ongoing. Part of the controversy involves how to classify and set up bilingual programs, since there are now many variants. How can the needs of students and the role of native language best be addressed in the schools? Who should be making those decisions? Does the research supply any answers?

For examples of current articles that generally concur with Ravitch, see R. McGarvey, "Double Talk: The Bilingual Education Controversy," in *The Social Contract* (Fall 1992); Rosalie P. Porter, *Forked Tongue: The Politics of Bilingual Education* (1990); Thomas Sowell, "Multicultural Instruction," *American Spectator* (April 1993); Linda Chavez, "The Bilingual Background, in which is a chapter in her *Out of the Barrio* (Basic Books, 1991). For readings that reflect Macedo's position (in favor of bilingual and multicultural education as immersion), see Charles V. Willie, "Multiculturalism Bashing: A Review of Magazine Coverage," *Change: The Magazine of Higher Learning* (January/February 1992); Anthony M. Platt, "Defenders of the Canon: What's Behind the Attack on Multiculturalism" *Social Justice* (Summer 1992); and A. Platt, "Beyond the Canon, With Great Difficulty," *Social Justice* (Spring 1993); M. T. Gardia, "Multiculturalism and American Studies," *Radical History Review* (Fall 1992). For an effort at a balanced view, see M. Fox and D. Ward's "Multiculturalism, Liberalism, and Science," *Inquiry* (December 1992). Among the many special issues of journals dealing with the debate see *Change* (January/February 1992 and March/April 1993). Two books attacking multiculturalism that have been widely debated are: D. D'Souza, *Illiberal Education* (Free Press, 1991) and C. Sykes, *A Nation of Victims* (1992). An outstanding new journal that raises important questions about education and culture is *Linguafranca*.

An interesting recent study of education and Americanization is "The Educational Alliance: An Institutional Study in Americanization and Acculturation," by J. Dorinson, in *Immigration and Ethnicity*, by M. D'Innocenzo and J. Sierefman (Greenwood Press, 1992). Two books that provide practical guidelines for improving intercultural interactions are D. Locke's *Increasing Multicultural Understanding* (Sage, 1992) and *Improving Intercultural Interactions*, edited by R. Brislin and T. Yoshida (Sage, 1993).

ISSUE 8

Should Black Women Join the Feminist Movement?

YES: bell hooks, from *Talking Back: Thinking Feminist, Thinking Black* (South End Press, 1989)

NO: Vivian V. Gordon, from *Black Women, Feminism and Black Liberation: Which Way?* (Third World Press, 1987)

ISSUE SUMMARY

YES: Scholar and writer bell hooks argues that Black and white women have worked together for generations to solve mutual problems. They have shown that they are able to transcend racism. Hooks feels that Black activists should not avoid the feminist movement or maintain separate memberships in Black movement groups only. The extent of sexism among Blacks and whites necessitates women working together.

NO: Activist-scholar Vivan V. Gordon maintains that she is not a racist but has good reasons to urge Blacks to separate themselves from a white-dominated feminist movement. She contends that, historically, white women as a group, no matter how benign some individuals may have been, benefited from and encouraged the exploitation of Blacks. In spite of the sexism of some Black males, Gordon feels that Black women would be better off to maintain their own agenda for liberation.

Prior to the Civil War, the movement for women's rights had ties to and was influenced by abolitionists' efforts to end slavery, and, throughout the twentieth century, various waves of the feminist movement and the civil rights movement have commingled and have been mutually reinforcing. However, the women's or feminist movement, despite its frequent linkage with other progressive causes, was primarily a white woman's movement. Segregation laws and social customs as well as class differences functioned to create and maintain a barrier between Black and white women. But in the 1960s through the present, genuine efforts were made, and pressure exerted, to expand the movement so that it was truly a universal women's movement, including all women in the United States and in other countries.

The heart of the issue debated in these two selections in part comes down to this: Can the contemporary women's movement serve the interests of all women, or do the experiences and concerns of Black women argue for a separate agenda? Jordon argues that the oppression of all Blacks during and after slavery in the United States qualitatively distinguishes their experiences from all other groups. Also, this argument continues, white women vicariously participated in the exploitation of Blacks, or at the least enjoyed the many conveniences and rewards for whites that were reaped from the oppression of Blacks.

But notice how bell hooks addresses this issue. One of her arguments is that Black and white women behind the scenes of history and politics have frequently worked together for mutual goals.

Black women were more likely as a consequence of racial discrimination to be poorer and less formally educated than other members of society, including Anglo females. One of the many negative consequences that accompanies poverty among all groups everywhere is a forced foreclosure of life's options. That is, the capacity to travel, to join political movements, to organize, to take educational courses, to join recreational associations, and other activities that are taken for granted by middle-class citizens. This is even more true of poor females, especially those of racial and ethnic minority status.

In the past, another source of strain between white women and Black women was the issue of violence perpetrated against Black males, particularly in the form of lynchings. According to the National Association for the Advancement of Colored People (NAACP), between 1882 and 1968 there were 3,446 known lynchings of Blacks (the vast majority were males). It is difficult for students in the 1990s, either Black or white, to comprehend the horror that many Black women lived with day in and day out—the fear that their brothers, sons, or fathers could be attacked and murdered by a white mob.

So this issue is complex. Consider as you study carefully these two articles what might be required to assist in making a decision as to the best way to bring about changes in racial and gender relations.

YES

bell hooks

BLACK WOMEN AND FEMINISM

Toward the end of 1987 I spoke at Tufts University at an annual dinner for black women. My topic was "Black Women in Predominantly White Institutions." I was excited by the idea of talking with so many young black women but surprised when these women suggested that sexism was not a political issue of concern to black women, that the serious issue was racism. I've heard this response many times, yet somehow I did not expect that I would need to prove over and over that sexism ensures that many black females will be exploited and victimized. Confronted by these young black women to whom sexism was not important, I felt that feminism had failed to develop a politics that addresses black women. Particularly, I felt that black women active in black liberation struggles in the 1960s and early 1970s, who had spoken and written on sexism (remember the anthology *The Black Woman,* edited by Toni Cade Bambara?) had let our younger sisters down by not making more of a sustained political effort so that black women (and black people) would have greater understanding of the impact of sexist oppression on our lives.

When I began to share my own experiences of racism and sexism, pointing to incidents (particularly in relationships with black men), a veil was lifted. Suddenly the group acknowledged what had been previously denied—the ways sexism wounds us as black women. I had talked earlier about the way many black women students in predominantly white institutions keep silent in classes, stating emphatically that our progress in such places requires us to have a voice, to not remain silent. In the ensuing discussion, women commented on black fathers who had told their daughters "nobody wants a loud-talking black woman." The group expressed ambivalent feelings about speaking, particularly on political issues in classroom settings where they were often attacked or unsupported by other black women students.

Their earlier reluctance to acknowledge sexism reminded me of previous arguments with other groups of women about both the book and the film *The Color Purple.* Our discussions focused almost solely on whether portraying brutal sexist domination of a black female by a black male had any basis in reality. I was struck by the extent to which folks will go to argue that sexism in black communities has not promoted the abuse and subjugation of black women by black men. This fierce denial has its roots in the history of black people's response to racism and white supremacy. Traditionally it has been important for black people to assert that slavery, apartheid, and continued discrimination have not undermined the humanity of black people, that not only has the race been preserved but that the survival of black families and communities are the living testimony of our victory. To acknowledge then that our families and communities have been undermined by sexism would not only require an acknowledgement that racism is not the only form of domination and oppression that affects us as a people; it would mean critically challenging the assumption that our survival as a people depends on creating a cultural climate in which black men can achieve manhood within paradigms constructed by white patriarchy.

Often the history of our struggle as black people is made synonymous with the efforts of black males to have patriarchal power and privilege. As one black woman college student put it, "In order to redeem the race we have to redeem black manhood." If such redemption means creating a society in which black men assume the stereotypical male role of provider and head of household, then sexism is seen not as destructive but as essential to the promotion and maintenance of the black family. Tragically, it has been our acceptance of this model that has prevented us from acknowledging that black male sexist domination has *not* enhanced or enriched black family life. The seemingly positive aspects of the patriarchy (caretaker and provider) have been the most difficult for masses of black men to realize, and the negative aspects (maintaining control through psychological or physical violence) are practiced daily. Until black people redefine in a nonsexist revolutionary way the terms of our liberation, black women and men will always be confronted with the issue of whether supporting feminist efforts to end sexism is inimical to our interests as a people.

In her insightful essay, "Considering Feminism as a Model for Social Change," Sheila Radford-Hill makes the useful critique that black women producing feminist theory, myself included, focus more on the racism of white women within feminist movement, and on the importance of racial difference, than on the ways feminist struggle could strengthen and help black communities. In part, the direction of our work was shaped by the nature of our experience. Not only were there very few black women writing feminist theory, but most of us were not living in or working with black communities. The aim of *Ain't I A Woman* was not to focus on the racism of white women. Its primary purpose was to establish that sexism greatly determines the social status and experience of black women. I did not try to examine the ways that struggling to end sexism would benefit black people, but this is my current concern.

Many black women insist that they do not join the feminist movement because they cannot bond with white women who are racist. If one argues that there really are some white women who are resisting and challenging racism, who are genuinely committed to ending white supremacy, one is accused of being naive, of not acknowledging history. Most black women, rich and poor, have contact with white women, usually in work settings. In such settings black women cooperate with white women despite racism. Yet black women are reluctant to express solidarity with white feminists. Black women's consciousness is shaped by internalized racism and by reactionary white women's concerns as they are expressed in popular culture, such as daytime soap operas or in the world of white fashion and cosmetic products, which masses of black women consume without rejecting this racist propaganda and devaluing of black women.

Emulating white women or bonding with them in these "apolitical" areas is not consistently questioned or challenged. Yet I do not know a single black woman advocate of feminist politics who is not bombarded by ongoing interrogations by other black people about linking with racist white women (as though we lack the political acumen to determine whether white women are racists, or when it is in our interest to act in solidarity with them).

At times, the insistence that feminism is really "a white female thing that has nothing to do with black women" masks black female rage towards white women, a rage rooted in the historical servant-served relationship where white women have used power to dominate, exploit, and oppress. Many black women share this animosity, and it is evoked again and again when white women attempt to assert control over us. This resistance to white female domination must be separated from a black female refusal to bond with white women engaged in feminist struggle. This refusal is often rooted as well in traditional sexist models: women learn to see one another as enemies, as threats, as competitors. Viewing white women as competitors for jobs, for companions, for valuation in a culture that only values select groups of women, often serves as a barrier to bonding, even

in settings where radical white women are not acting in a dominating manner. In some settings it has become a way of one-upping white women for black women to trivialize feminism.

Black women must separate feminism as a political agenda from white women or we will never be able to focus on the issue of sexism as it affects black communities. Even though there are a few black women (I am one) who assert that we empower ourselves by using the term feminism, by addressing our concerns as black women as well as our concern with the welfare of the human community globally, we have had little impact. Small groups of black feminist theorists and activists who use the term "black feminism" (the Combahee River Collective is one example) have not had much success in organizing large groups of black women, or stimulating widespread interest in feminist movement. Their statement of purpose and plans for action focus exclusively on black women acknowledging the need for forms of separatism. Here the argument that black women do not collectively advocate feminism because of an unwillingness to bond with racist white women appears most problematic. Key concerns that serve as barriers to black women advocating feminist politics are heterosexism, the fear that one will be seen as betraying black men or promoting hatred of men and as a consequence becoming less desirable to male companions; homophobia (often I am told by black people that all feminists are lesbians); and deeply ingrained misogynist attitudes toward one another, perpetuating sexist thinking and sexist competition.

Recently I spoke with a number of black women about why they are not more involved in feminist thinking and feminist movement. Many of them talked about harsh treatment by other black women, about being socially ostracized or talked about in negative and contemptuous ways at all-female gatherings or at conferences on gender issues. A few people committed to feminist politics described times when they found support from white women and resistance from black women peers. A black woman scheduled on a panel arrived late and couldn't find a seat in the room. When she entered and had been standing for a while, I greeted her warmly from the podium and encouraged her to join me as there were seats in front. Not only did she choose to stand, during the break she said to me, "How dare you embarrass me by asking me to come up front." Her tone was quite hostile. I was disturbed that she saw this gesture as an attempt to embarrass her rather than as a gesture of recognition. This is not an isolated case. There are many occasions when we witness the failure of black women to trust one another, when we approach one another with suspicion.

Years ago I attended a small conference with about 20 black women. We were to organize a national conference on black feminism. We came from various positions, politics, and sexual preferences. A well-known black woman scholar at a prestigious institution, whose feminist thinking was not deemed appropriately advanced, was treated with contempt and hostility. It was a disturbing time. A number of the black women present had white women companions and lovers. Yet concerning the issue of whether white women should be allowed to attend the conference, they were adamant that it should be for black women only, that white women all too often try to control us. There was no space for constructive critical dialogue. How could they trust white women lovers to unlearn racism, to not be dominating, and yet in this setting act as though all white women were our enemies? The conference never happened. At least one black woman went away from this experience determined never to participate in an activity organized around black feminists or any other feminists. As a group we failed to create an atmosphere of solidarity. The only bonds established were along very traditional lines among the folks who were famous, who talked the loudest and the most, who were more politically correct. And there was no attempt to enable black women with different perspectives to come together.

It is our collective responsibility as individual black women committed to feminist movement to work at making space where black women who are just beginning to explore feminist issues can do so without fear of hostile treatment, quick judgments, dismissals, etc.

I find more black women than ever before are appearing on panels that focus on gender. Yet I have observed, and other black women thinkers have shared as well, that often these women see gender as a subject for discourse or for increased professional visibility, not for political action. Often professional black women with academic degrees are quite conservative politically. Their perspectives differ greatly from our foremothers who were politically astute, assertive, and radical in their work for social change.

Feminist praxis is greatly shaped by academic women and men. Since there are not many academic black women committed to radical politics, especially with a gender focus, there is no collective base in the academy for forging a feminist politics that addresses masses of black women. There is much more work by black women on gender and sexism emerging from scholars who do literary criticism and from creative fiction and drama writers than from women in history, sociology, and political science. While it does not negate commitment to radical politics, in literature it is much easier to separate academic work and political concerns. Concurrently, if black women academics are not committed to feminist ethics, to feminist consciousness-raising, they end up organizing conferences in which social interactions mirror sexist norms, including ways black women regard one another. For the uninitiated coming to see and learn what feminism centered on black women might be like, this can be quite disillusioning.

Often in these settings the word "feminism" is evoked in negative terms, even though sexism and gender issues are discussed. I hear black women academics laying claim to the term "womanist" while rejecting "feminist." I do not think Alice Walker intended this term to deflect from feminist commitment, yet this is often how it is evoked. Walker defines womanist as black feminist or feminist of color. When I hear black women using the term womanist, it is in opposition to the term feminist; it is viewed as constituting something separate from feminist politics shaped by white women. For me, the term womanist is not sufficiently linked to a tradition of radical political commitment to struggle and change. What would a womanist politic look like? If it is a term for black feminist, then why do those who embrace it reject the other?

Radford-Hill makes the point:

Not all black feminists practice or believe in black feminism. Many see black feminism as a vulgar detraction from the goal of female solidarity. Others of us, myself included, see black feminism as a necessary step toward ending racism and sexism, given the nature of gender oppression and the magnitude of society's resistance to racial justice.

I believe that women should think less in terms of feminism as an identity and more in terms of "advocating feminism"; to move from emphasis on personal lifestyle issues toward creating political paradigms and radical models of social change that emphasize collective as well as individual change. For this reason I do not call myself a black feminist. Black women must continue to insist on our right to participate in shaping feminist theory and practice that addresses our racial concerns as well as our feminist issues. Current feminist scholarship can be useful to black women in formulating critical analyses of gender issues about black people, particularly feminist work on parenting. (When I first read Dorothy Dinnerstein, it was interesting to think about her work in terms of black mother-son relationships.)

Black women need to construct a model of feminist theorizing and scholarship that is inclusive, that widens our options, that enhances our understanding of black experience and gender. Significantly, the most basic task confronting black feminists (irrespective of the terms we use to identify ourselves) is to educate one another and black people about sexism, about the ways resisting sexism can empower black women, a process which makes sharing feminist vision more difficult. Radford-Hill identifies "the crisis of black womanhood" as a serious problem that must be considered politically, asserting that "the extent to which black feminists can articulate and solve the crisis of black womanhood is the extent to which black women will undergo feminist transformation."

Black women must identify ways feminist thought and practice can aid in our process of self-recovery and share that knowledge with our sisters. This is the base on which to build political solidarity. When that grounding exists, black women will be fully engaged in feminist movement that transforms self, community, and society.

NO
Vivian V. Gordon

BLACK WOMEN, FEMINISM AND BLACK LIBERATION: WHICH WAY?

The position presented here will no doubt be loudly condemned by some who point to a so-called common oppression of all women and thereby proclaim that this oppression is the basis for a Black/White women's coalition....

Many Black Americans are increasingly distressed by the obvious surrender of much within the Black community to a promise of a "better situation" through integration—which, for the dominant group, usually means movement from a Black culture into White conformity,—and which has often failed in its rewards to Black people even where reported to have taken place. Moreover, it would appear that the integrative process provides little hope for real changes in the immediate future, but encourages the additional losses of vital African American talent and resources.

... From this perspective, it becomes apparent that Black women and the Black community must carefully scrutinize appeals from White dominated movements with Eurocentric underpinnings. Black women who identify with the women's liberation movement will internalize the rhetoric and perspective of that movement and become alienated from themselves (self-hate), and alienated from the race, as well as from a splendid record of activities against racism. It is important, therefore, that any focus on African American women be evaluated to determine the collective benefits or losses to the African American community....

[W]e could consider it reasonable for African American women to form *time-limited, issue-specific* coalitions with White women. It is *only* within these parameters that a Black/White women's coalition, such as that required by Jesse Jackson through his "rainbow coalition" could be accomplished. Emphasis is given to the time-limited, issue-specific nature of such a White–Non-White women's coalition, for many Black women of today remember the extent to which a similar "rainbow-type" coalition in the 1960's resulted in the displacement of Black women by White women from key positions in the movement....

White women have historically and consistently *welcomed Black men* into organizational efforts while at the same time *excluding Black women....*

After a look at the life conditions of Black women and those of the general Black community; exchange with dynamic and concerned Black women from a range of socio-economic backgrounds; and exchange with Black women scholars contributing to research and the historic evaluation of the Black woman's experience, one can only conclude that there are some dynamic incompatibilities between African American women and feminism as advocated by the women's liberation movement....

CIVIL RIGHTS IN THE 1960's AND THE EMERGENCE OF WOMEN'S STUDIES

One of the newest programs within higher education is women's studies which followed the path cleared by Black college students in the 1960's when they demanded representation, participation and relevance in higher education through classes and then programs of Afro-American studies.

The primary focus of women's studies has been upon gender-specific discrimination and the inattention to, as well as the lack of analyses of women's roles in the development of the nation. The first *women*'s studies class was taught in the *late 1960*'s and was based on the model set by Afro-American Studies. Presenting themselves as "woman as nigger," predominantly White groups of women in higher education spoke of their oppression as analogous to that of the Black American....

With a few exceptions, women's studies follow in the tradition of the Eurocen-

tric perspective of higher education, only with a gender-specific theme. Most often the curriculum does not include significant numbers of courses, if any, about non-White women. Where such courses are present, the Black female experience is cast into a "traditional" course in which the Black female/Black male pathology model emerges. In those instances where this traditional literature has been abandoned, and, in particular, where there is some specific curriculum representation of Black women, the perspective which usually dominates is that of the radical feminist and the radical feminist lesbian who certainly present valid issues of oppression, but, who do not represent the primary experiences of the pluralistic majority of Black women.

Moreover, the perspective of most women's studies programs is that Black and White women have suffered a common experience of oppression which is gender-specific. There is a pervasive unwillingness to acknowledge the distinctively *different nature* of oppression for White and non-White women. Seldom is attention given the extent to which White women have benefited from the oppression of Black women and/or have been active participants in racism....

Given the fact that race and sex are ascribed characteristics and since in American society these two characteristics relegate non-Whites to a caste group with limited influence and economic opportunity, it might be argued that the African American female is born into a trilogy of oppression from which there are very limited opportunities for escape. Survival under these conditions is at best tenuous....

We are all familiar with the denigrating labels which confront the Black woman....

Such images are presented and reinforced through every means for education and communication within the society; from the all-powerful television, to movies, to radio, to award-winning books praised by culturally selective White critics. Each generation of Black women has grown up with its version of the Beulah, the Sapphire, the tragic semi-precious mulatto, the long-suffering abused survivalist, the so-called bourgeois college woman snob. The tragedy is the extent to which many Black women have internalized these stereotypes and have eventually assumed such roles—thus, participating in a self-fulfilling prophecy as well as the process of victim blaming.

In spite of a long history of the manipulation of these stigmas which enhance the control and power of the major perpetrators of racism, sexism and economic oppression, the majority of Black women have managed to maintain positive self-identities, and to experience some levels of success as mothers, wives, sisters and daughters; as leaders, activists, women working outside of the home; and as women generally contributing to the quality of life within the African American community. Traditional history, and in large measure African American studies and women's studies, have most often excluded any focus upon the experiences of these Black women....

To the extent that White female leaders and scholars refuse to acknowledge this difference in the nature of the oppressive experiences of Black and White women in America, it is certain that there can never be a viable coalition between African American and Euro-American women. As is evident from these very terms, we are speaking about two historically different cultural orientations.

Black women can not negate their Afro-centricity just as White women can not negate their Eurocentricisms....

White feminists who point to a so-called lack of involvement by Black women in women's issues reflect a lack of awareness of the historic role of Black women. Such feminists also fail to realize the extent to which they accept and continue to be influenced by the White male-dominated record of women's history and African American events....

Repeatedly, White feminists have been unwilling to acknowledge the extent to which they have participated either overtly or through complicity in the oppression and destruction of Black women. Also, such women have not been willing to admit their privileged position of control over the immediate lives of most *contemporary* Black women. For example, how many White women feminists provide security for their domestics through (1) minimum wages, (2) a retirement plan, (3) sick leave with pay, (4) maternity leave, or (5) a confrontation with their fathers, husbands, sons, brothers and lovers who are the perpetrators of sexual harassment against Black women? White women in the workforce have higher status and most often are in positions of superior power to Black women who have historically been in the workforce in greater numbers and over longer time periods.

SEXUAL POLITICS

Contemporary White feminists often attempt to impose upon Black women a definition for Black male/female relationships based upon their perspectives which identify all men as the enemy. Such women point to examples of Black male abuse of Black women and call to Black women for disassociation with Black males as if such men were in the same positions of power as White males.

Clearly, sexism and abuse of Black women by Black men can be observed and may be documented to exist as a serious problem within the Black community. However, the Black community vis-a-vis Black women, must define their own problems and the means through which those problems might best be resolved with minimal injury to all....

To combat these devastating and self-destructive situations within the African American community, the historic alliance between Black men and Black women, politically and socially as defenders, developers and lovers of each other must be strengthened, and in many instances completely reestablished. The gender divisions which the contemporary White feminist movement could promote among Black women would be counter-productive to this vital unifying effort. To be respected by others and in order to be in a workable coalition posture, an oppressed people must first and foremost seek to address their own personal/internal issues.

POSTSCRIPT

Should Black Women Join the Feminist Movement?

This issue has a complicated history. Unlike some of the other issues in this book, which deal with empirical and/or conceptual questions (disputes over facts and their interpretations, or over terms and their scientific meaning and adequacy), this issue is normative. Normative issues deal with what is perceived as "ought to be" or should be. Yet it is vital that these kinds of issues, like all social issues, be resolved by informed dialogue, carefully prepared and reasoned debate.

In part this issue may be resolving itself, at least among professionals who are females. Many are joining both Black and white liberation movements. An even larger number are joining traditional professional organizations, such as the American Bar Association (ABA), the American Criminological Society, the American Sociological Association, and so on, and are also creating and joining professional associations consisting of Blacks or Black females exclusively. This, of course, does not resolve the issue for nonprofessional Black females.

Separatism is often functional for relatively powerless groups. It provides much needed social solidarity, generates group morale, and helps clarify the issues, goals, and means to achieve the goals. Moreover, by relying almost exclusively on "insider knowledge" (see Issue 1), impasses in planning and decision-making are reduced.

Others contend, though, agreeing with bell hooks, that an important way to educate ignorant, though well-meaning, whites is to integrate and work with them. It is also argued that joining the larger feminist movement in the long run will be more helpful to both women and Blacks since the combined resources would be far greater.

Meanwhile, Black women's needs are being partially addressed in society. According to social scientists such as Thomas Sowell and Walter Williams, among all racial minorities, the incomes of Black females who graduate from college is approaching that of comparable level white males.

One of the earliest arguments against Black women joining the contemporary women's liberation movement is Linda La Rue, "Black Liberation and Women's Lib," *Transaction* (November/December 1970). A recent supportive article agreeing with bell hooks is Cleo Kocol's "Black Feminists," *The Humanist* (September/October 1989). A thorough study of the connections between feminism and the Black movement is *Feminism and Black Activism in Contemporary America*, by I. D. Solomon, (Greenwood Press, 1989). A moving account of the uniqueness of Black women in America is Patricia Morton's *Disfigured Images: The Historical Assault on Afro-American Women* (Greenwood Press, 1991). An earlier discussion is Toni Cade's *The Black Woman* (Signet, 1970). For a work that offers views on Black women as feminists and also addresses the additional oppression experienced by Black lesbians, see Barbara Smith, editor, *Home Girls: A Black Feminist Anthology* (Kitchen Table: Women of Color Press, 1983) and E. F. White's "Listening to the Voices of Black Feminism," in *Radical America* (1984). For a provocative feminist attack on Ice-T and Marky Mark types, as well as the rap group 2 Live Crew and others who put women down, see Pearl Cleage's *Deals with the Devil and Other Reasons to Riot* (Ballantine Books, 1993).

A good overview of some of the problems that Hispanic feminists face is D. A. Segurn and Beatriz M. Pesquera's "Beyond Indifference and Antipathy: The Chicana Movement and Chicana Feminist Discourse," in *Aztlan* (vol. 19, no. 2, 1992). A broader perspective is found in Elly Bulkin et al., *Yours in Struggle: 3 Feminist Perspectives on Anti-Semitism and Racism* (Firebank Books, 1988) and in E. C. Du Bois and V. Ruiz, editors, *Unequal Sisters: A Multicultural Reader in U.S. Women's History* (Routledge, 1990). On the complicated relationship between white mistresses and their slaves, see *A Northern Woman in the Plantation South: Letters of Tryphena Blanche Fox*, edited by W. King (University of South Carolina Press, 1993).

For additional discussions of the issue, see bell hooks's *Ain't I a Woman: Black Women and Feminism* (South End Press, 1981) and *Yearning: Race, Gender, and Cultural Politics* (South End Press, 1990). She has coauthored with Cornel West *Breaking Bread: Insurgent Black Intellectual Life* (South End Press, 1991). Among the many excellent women's studies references, two that pertain to this issue that are helpful and accessible are *Women's Movements of the World: An International Directory and Reference Guide*, edited by S. Shreir (Oryx Press, 1988) and *Women of Color in the United States: A Guide to the Literature*, edited by B. Redfern (Garland Press, 1990).

ISSUE 9

Are Positive Images of African Americans Increasing in the Media?

YES: J. Fred MacDonald, from *Blacks and White TV: African Americans in Television Since 1948*, 2d ed. (Nelson-Hall, 1992)

NO: Ash Corea, from "Racism and the American Way of Media," in John Downing et al., eds., *Questioning the Media: A Critical Introduction* (Sage Publications, 1990)

ISSUE SUMMARY

YES: Professor J. Fred MacDonald sees the need for improvements in images of African Americans presented on television, yet he feels that TV producers, because of their desire to reach Black consumers, have significantly altered, for the better, images of Blacks in the media.

NO: Professor Ash Corea insists that Blacks remain underrepresented as actors, directors, and executives in the television media. Some roles for Blacks continue to be demeaning, and Blacks, like other minorities, are disproportionately linked on television with crime.

Arguably, the presentation of racial and ethnic groups in the mass media and entertainment industries, especially television, may be one of the most important influences on social mores regarding prejudice and discrimination. Certainly most studies consistently document the many hours spent by Americans watching television. Although mass communications experts agree that programs are not "magic bullets" that inevitably alter attitudes, for better or worse, the importance of television programming is real.

Thus if images on television demean, distort, or even ignore minorities, then the positive effects of other institutions and social forces to reduce prejudice and discrimination may be undermined. Social scientists of the cultural production school of thought argue that cultural hegemony or dominance of one group over others is often maintained by the mass media.

What are the facts? Are positive images of Blacks increasing? As you carefully read the two articles, notice the cynicism both articles express toward the mass media. For instance, MacDonald, who feels that television programs are rapidly including Blacks, Black-related issues, and are showing Blacks more frequently in a positive light, attributes this to economic motives alone, not benevolence on the part of owners and producers. Blacks constitute an important market; therefore, to get advertisers to pay big money for advertisements, the producers have to convince them that the viewing market for such programs is large.

MacDonald also indicates that there are a growing number of Blacks behind the camera (though this is probably less true for television than for Hollywood movies). However, this is a secondary consideration as compared to the profit motives of owners and producers, according to MacDonald and Corea.

Both MacDonald and Corea paint a dismal picture of the mass media's treatment of minorities in the past. While many commentators, including a former director of the Federal Communications Commission (FCC), have characterized TV as a "giant wasteland," MacDonald and Corea present the additional charges of racism.

Corea has several complaints that you should note. In addition to her concerns that Blacks are underrepresented in most positions, she argues that Blacks are still occasionally depicted as buffoons. She is especially incensed about the linkage between crime and race. Not only are several Black actors in different television series portrayed as being former criminals (to show, Corea suggests, that Blacks have an automatic insider's knowledge of crime, even when they are going straight), but the news coverage of crime is also biased. She explores several examples of specific serious crimes and how they were covered as well as the way that Black crime is exaggerated on daily news shows.

As you review MacDonald's discussion, consider examples of ethnic and racial minority programs and/or coverage that might have been inspired by altruism rather than only a profit motive. If positive images of minorities are increasing, is it primarily, as MacDonald's thesis states, a result of the need for minority viewers?

Finally, consider both authors' treatment of minorities in the media in the past. Can the standards, values, and norms of today be imposed on the actions of people who lived in different times? Should they be?

YES   J. Fred MacDonald

AFRICAN AMERICANS AND THE
NEW VIDEO REALITIES

After decades of racial misrepresentation and damaging bias in U.S. television, the situation for blacks in white TV has been changing significantly since the early 1980s. With networks in decline and national television evolving toward a new relationship with its public, the medium is slowly evidencing a new racial attitude. This is because the infrastructure of the industry is changing. Ultimately, TV is a medium of advertising, and money is its mother's milk. Since American television has always been fueled by sponsors' dollars, it has been dedicated to attracting large audiences for the commercials of its advertisers. If material forces alter this fundamental arrangement, then those in the business must adapt or perish.

New business conditions by the 1990s have made African Americans a prized target audience, one to be respected by programmers and appreciated by advertisers. Although the secondary characterizations and stereotyping of the Age of the New Minstrelsy may endure, before the camera blacks are gradually emerging from predictable, subordinate roles. Behind the camera minority presence remains small, but here, too, there have been modest developments in which blacks have begun to exert influence over program production and content. Together, these changes constitute a breach in the racial logjam that chronically has blocked African Americans from fair and open access to the video industry. These changes also represent a move toward fulfilling the original promise of prejudice-free TV, a condition that seems more realizable in the final decade of this century than at any time in the history of the medium.

But there remains serious weakness in the new attitude of television toward black America. As director Melvin Van Peebles noted on the CNN *Showbiz Today* telecast of April 28, 1989, "Now, television has offered a substantial opportunity—not as substantial as we would like, not as equitable. But on the whole it's moving a little bit." Although created by substantial changes in the structure of television, this movement toward an honest treatment of

From J. Fred MacDonald, *Blacks and White TV: African Americans in Television Since 1948*, 2d ed. (Nelson-Hall, 1992), pp. 251–263. Copyright © 1992 by J. Fred MacDonald. Reprinted by permission of Nelson-Hall, Inc., Publishers. Notes omitted.

minorities is still recent and fragile. The improvements of the last several years do not constitute an immutable transformation. The improvements remain defenseless against pressures created by economic calamities, deteriorating international relations, and social and political tensions within the United States....

* * *

In understanding the place of blacks in contemporary TV, there is also a lesson from recent history to consider. Just as social, economic, and political developments in the early 1970s eroded the Golden Age for blacks in the industry, so too might future realities adversely affect the positive trends of the past several years. Unless their presence takes root in the infrastructure of the business, blacks will always be vulnerable.

Adding to the ambiguity of this improving situation is an apparent confusion among blacks about their own image in popular culture. With a greater potential for honest African-American representation, questions are being debated within the black community. Should blacks be shown only as middle class and assimilated, as are most whites, or is this a denial of racial authenticity? Should blacks be portrayed in terms of the urban underclass, especially when such imagery might appear as crude or unaccomplished? Should the folk images of rural blacks—often with characteristics that have fed the distorted, racist stereotypes so familiar in American pop culture—be propagated now as authentic, or should they be buried as anachronistic and self-defeating? Can African Americans dare to accept a full range of racial characters—from the dynamic chairman of the corporate board to the dimwitted buffoon—when the predominantly white audience has a persistent history of prejudice, when black socioeconomic mobility remains constricted, and when television still has not opened its doors to full and unfettered participation by minorities?

In the new television arrangement most people of color have been assimilated into the middle class where they now display the behavioral norms of bourgeois white America. Yet, this "Bill Cosby" image has received its share of criticism, attacked for being unrealistic, unrepresentative, and misleading. Certainly, there is a substantial black middle class whose housing, dress, language, education, income level, value system, and life-style are little different from its Caucasian equivalent. In 'fact, the black bourgeoisie rose from about 10 percent of the African-American population in 1960 to more than one-third of it by 1991. Moreover, many scholars have long asserted that social class is more crucial than race or ethnicity in determining social behavior. Still, as it did at the time when *Julia* was a popular series, such representation invites criticism for proposing an unauthentic model for blacks.

Importantly, there is a substantial portion of the African-American population that does not meet middle-class criteria. Blacks still earn fifty-six cents for every dollar earned by whites. Many live in substandard housing located in "black sections" of the nation's large cities. Here these disadvantaged people constitute a lower class, even an underclass. They attend devitalized schools, and are victimized by an oppressive political and economic system still unwilling to address adequately their needs. Too often, they are further hampered by broken homes, drug abuse, poverty, and insufficient job skills.

The frustrating reality of this social element is infrequently depicted in the new video order. Seldom does TV portray the indignities that blacks routinely encounter, regardless of social or economic status. Seldom, too, does the medium present life in the inner city with compassion or understanding. In a report issued in 1989, the National Commission for Working Women of Wider Opportunities for Women concluded that blacks on television were being unrealistically represented. "Real-world racism, which is pervasive, subtle, and blatant, is commonplace in America but virtually invisible on entertainment television," according to the report. It pointed out, too, that 90 percent of the minority characters on TV—and most of these were African Americans—were middle-class and rich, while the working class and the poor made up less than 10 percent of those images. Yet, according to the report, more than 40 percent of minority men and 60 percent of minority women subsist on less than $10,000 annually. The report also criticized TV entertainment for misleading viewers by suggesting that racial harmony and an egalitarian work place were everyday realities, and by offering racial injustice as a matter of individual immorality instead of the result of oppressive social structures.

Nevertheless, there is little doubt that U.S. television has begun to change. After a half-century of moral protestation, some in the industry may have been persuaded that African Americans must be treated fairly because it was the "democratic" or "right" thing to do. But the driving force behind this new video reality is more substantial than any spiritual conversion. When he appeared on

a segment of the CBS program *West 57th Street* on May 27, 1989, director Spike Lee well illustrated that the basis for the new openness in Hollywood rested in economics, not ethics. Although he spoke of the motion picture industry, his comments were applicable to TV production as well. "Hollywood only understands economics. I mean, they could hate you, I mean they could call me 'nigger this' and 'nigger that' behind my back, they probably do—you know, 'young nigger upstart,' whatever. But they look at it, when they get their reports from the office, and they see my films are making money." Lee continued, "No matter what they think of me, they're still going to continue to fund them because the films are making money. But if the time ever arises where you stop making money, 'You're outta here!'"

* * *

In essence, improved African-American representation in modern television is the result of a simple equation: first, there are many more stations and consequently greater competition for viewers and profits; second, there are sizable minority audiences, the most prominent of which is the black viewership, whose loyalty is now highly desirable; and third, each minority audience appreciates positive depiction of itself on TV. When added together, the resulting programs will attract viewers, make money, and inspire others to create respectful images of minorities.

One influential organization leading the way toward improved racial representation has been Black Entertainment Television (BET), a national cable channel that targets African-American viewers. Established in 1980 by Charles Johnson, BET has been supported by three cable corporations interested in attracting African Americans: Tele-Communications, Inc., Great American Broadcast Company, and the Time Warner subsidiary, Home Box Office (HBO). In its first years, BET programmers relied greatly on weekly football and basketball games of small black colleges, as well as on network reruns and music videos. Among the old series finding new life on BET were heralded, but short-lived offerings such as *The Lazarus Syndrome*, *Paris*, and *Frank's Place*. By the early 1990s, however, BET moved decisively into original programming. Here, shows have ranged from an evening newscast with a black perspective and a nightly entertainment-gossip program (*Screen Scene*) to a weekend music and talk show for teenagers (*Teen Summit*).

Despite the swelling popularity of BET and other cable operations, over-the-air broadcasting continued to dominate viewing patterns in the 1980s and early 1990s. Certainly, audience figures plummeted at the three networks, dropping from a cumulative 56.6 rating/90 share in the 1979–80 season to a 41.5 rating/67 share by 1988–89, to a 37.5 rating/63 share for 1990–91, but no single cable channel could match ABC, CBS, or NBC in terms of audience size. It is significant, moreover, that advertisers did not desert free TV. Convinced that the three networks still delivered the largest audiences for their sales pitches, sponsors by late 1988 still placed 81 percent of their advertising dollars in network shows.

* * *

Although cable success and network attrition delivered the message that African Americans constituted a desirable target audience, this was still no insurance against inflammatory racial representation. No character inflamed the argument over black TV imagery more than Bosco "B.A." (Bad Attitude) Barracus, the muscle-bound mechanic who with several white misfits formed the rugged and popular mercenaries of *The A-Team*. As portrayed by the highly-publicized bouncer and bodyguard, Mr. T, Barracus was a caricature of the action-adventure hero when he appeared on NBC from early 1983 to mid-1987. B.A. had his soft spots: he may have been big and black and menacing, but he drank milk, loved children, and was afraid to fly in airplanes. Such subtleties of character paled, however, before his foreboding, sometimes snarling presence. With his Mohawk haircut, several pounds of gold jewelry, and physical strength, B.A. was the scary black man no white person ever wanted to meet in an alley late at night. Still, he was a controllable angry black man, a Vietnam veteran, a growling warrior who was smart, inventive, and tame—a patriot who now waged "our" just struggle against "their" evil threat.

NBC tried to soften Mr. T's image. As the hero of his own animated children's program, *Mr. T*, seen on Saturday mornings in 1984, he was much less menacing. At Christmas time in 1984 and 1985, the network paired him with *petit* Emmanuel Lewis in *Christmas Dream*, a tender story of a sidewalk Santa Claus attempting to rekindle the Christmas spirit in a lonely little boy. Publicity stressed the actor's popularity with youngsters. *TV Guide*, for example, "unmasked" him in mid-1984, noting that "Mr. T's exterior may be rough, tough and gruff—but the kids of America know that beneath all that jewelry on the chest of *The A-Team* star beats a heart of gold." The magazine then printed the generally worshipful assessments of Mr. T written by children in the third, fourth, and fifth grades.

But it was already too late. Mr. T as B.A. Barracus had become the symbol of the industry's chronic failure to depict African Americans constructively. In testimony given in the fall of 1983 before the House Subcommittee on Telecommunications, Consumer Protection, and Finance, Mr. T and his video persona became metaphors for the distorted portrait of black Americans offered by network TV. Actor Bernie Casey railed against white industry executives who continued to produce misinformed and mendacious programs—against "those men [who] continue to give us the collective Mr. T." According to Casey, "We as people of color cannot afford the callousness exercised upon us by insensitive people making decisions that are thoughtless... decisions that continue to perpetuate the kind of imagery that warps the psyche of the viewership for generations." In a similar vein, Robert Hooks reminded the same House committee that the networks determine what black images appear on TV. "We don't own the networks, we don't own the airwaves, so we can't come back at NBC if they say Mr. T is it. Then the world embraces Mr. T, and it is unfair to blacks."...

With more consequence, two white sports personalities lost their jobs when they unguardedly expressed their antediluvian racial opinions on TV. Baseball executive Al Campanis of the Los Angeles Dodgers suggested on *ABC News Nightline* (April 6, 1987) that there were few African-American managers or front-office executives in baseball because they were intellectually inferior, because "they may not have some of the necessities.... I don't say all of them, but they certainly are short. How many quarterbacks do you have, how many pitchers do you have that are black?" He carried his comments further, asking "Why are black men, or black people, not good swimmers? Because they don't have the buoyancy."

Less than a year later, gambling expert Jimmy "The Greek" Snyder of CBS Sports offered a bizarre genetic history lesson to a reporter for WRC-TV in Washington, D.C. (January 15, 1988). According to this highly-paid odds-maker and football analyst, black athletes were physically superior to white athletes. This, he explained, was because slave owners in earlier centuries had practiced selective breeding programs, mating strong black males with strong black females to produce the most rugged workers possible.

While egregious displays of racism might be dismissed as occasional tastelessness or the personal ignorance of individuals, there was something deeply sinister when familiar racial stereotypes appeared premeditatedly as series regulars. During the first two seasons of *Miami Vice*, Charlie Barnett played a silly street informant, Noogie Lamont, whose facial grimaces and addled banter were more appropriate for a minstrel-show endman than an occasional character in this polished Florida police drama. Moreover, his juxtaposition to the other sophisticated black and white personalities in the series only accentuated the distortion inherent in "the Noogman."

... [R]ecent series television has not just resurrected vintage stereotypes, it has popularized a new negative type. Although the crime rate in African-American society remains a deplorable reality, there has been little attempt by entertainment TV to explain this social crisis in terms of its roots in poverty, ignorance, discrimination, unemployment, frustration, alienation, and anger. Instead, in television fiction black crime has taken on an exciting mystique. Outlaw behavior has become an asset, in fact, as many black characters have been created as reformed criminals now working for "the system." Even harmless Anthony on *Designing Women* is an ex-convict. From a streetwise con man turned investigative reporter on *The Insiders*, to a comical escapee from a Texas chain gang on *Stir Crazy*, to a paroled murderer now investigating cases for a white female lawyer on *Gabriel's Fire*, entertainment TV has propagated the message that no one knows crime like blacks know crime. Such imagery also has suggested that lawlessness is generic to African-American manhood, and that criminality has its rewards since it provides a useful street education to these crooks-turned-good-guys.

Compounding the linkage of racial minorities to crime, network and local newscasts constantly focus on lawlessness among African Americans. While black-on-black crime statistics are staggering, the constant stream of distressing TV pictures—a bloody corpse on the ground and a drive-by shooting investigated, robbery or rape suspects jailed, drug pushers and addicts, vandalism in the projects—present black urban communities as virtual war zones. Add to this the rash of police actuality shows such as *Cops* and *America's Most Wanted* that entered television in the 1990s, and the impression received is one of rampant inner city outlawry created by uncontrollable black marauders.

The writer Ishmael Reed has lashed out at such imagery, reminding Americans that reality communicated through network television news is a distortion. According to Reed, while TV news associates blacks with drugs 50 percent of the time, in actuality 15 percent of the drug users in the U.S. are black and 70 percent are white. Although the majority of Americans affected by homelessness, welfare, unwed parenthood, child abuse and rape are whites, again TV journalism disproportionately associates these conditions with minorities. In damning "the chief source of information that Americans receive about the world," Reed was blunt. "The networks' reasoning seems to be that if blacks weren't here, the United States would be a paradise where people would work 24 hours a day, drink milk, go to church, and be virgins until marriage." ...

* * *

Were such negative projections the most plentiful minority images on television, there would be little hope for improvement of African-American representation. But there have been developments in television that cautiously augur well for the future, indications that some industry executives understand that the new video order has made the old racial prejudices counterproductive. This is not to suggest that the response of television to African Americans has been quick or sufficient or equitable; the mentality that excluded and stereotyped the race for so long still dominates the industry. Nonetheless the pattern of black representation emerging since the late 1980s suggests that U.S. television is becoming racially more responsible.

NO

Ash Corea

RACISM AND THE AMERICAN
WAY OF MEDIA

Many writers argue that media merely reflect what is happening "out there." What is more, on television African-Americans, women, and White men seem to have the same opportunities that exist in the society. Eddie Murphy can mock Stevie Wonder and other African-American celebrities, Mr. T can be charming to little White children, Bill Cosby can make it to the top of the ratings, Geraldo Rivera can make the headlines, Connie Chung can draw top newscaster salary. So it must be true: Everyone has the same opportunities.

However, in the United States the overwhelming factor that defines the position a group will occupy is color. Education, wealth, occupation, gender, and religion are also part of the picture, but nevertheless, to be an African-American normally means occupying the bottom strata. This in turn limits access to the benefits produced within this society. As a group, African-Americans compete with other groups discriminated against, such as Hispanics and Native Americans, for the honor of being at the bottom. Gender does intervene in this matrix: Women occupy a lower position when compared to men. But in this complex array of factors four clear points emerge.

First, White men occupy the apex of the hierarchy in the United States, in terms of both power and status. Second, White women earn lower salaries (on average, two-thirds those of White men) and have much less political influence. Third, African-American men have less political influence still and are paid substantially less than White men. Finally, African-American women earn less than the other three groups, although they have greater access than African-American men to very low-paying jobs such as babysitting, fast-food restaurant work, and cleaning. They have the very least political power.

For those citizens of the United States who have difficulty believing the evidence before their own eyes, seemingly endless studies have documented this pattern in detail, from Gunnar Myrdal's *An American Dilemma* (1944) through the series of reports issued in 1989 by the Special Committee on Children, Youth and the Family of the U.S. House of Representatives.

From Ash Corea, "Racism and the American Way of Media," in John Downing et al., eds., *Questioning the Media: A Critical Introduction* (Sage Publications, 1990). Copyright © 1990 by Sage Publications, Inc. Reprinted by permission. Notes and references omitted.

So far, then, it has been suggested that there is in reality, if not in TV reality, a distinct relationship between color and access by certain groups to wealth and power. These groups are further subdivided by gender, with White men at the apex, followed by White women and then African-American men. At the very bottom are African-American women. A similar analysis would generally be valid for Latinos, Native Americans, and Asian-Americans.

As the discussion now moves to a consideration of how media, in particular television, relate to this reality, the following three questions should be kept in mind:

(1) Do African-Americans and White Americans occupy the same positions within the controlling structures of the media?

(2) Does television portray African-Americans and White Americans as being equal with each other and coexisting in a multiracial environment?

(3) What factors are there that could militate against African-Americans and White Americans receiving equal treatment on television?

AFRICAN-AMERICANS AND EMPLOYMENT IN MEDIA

Consider the following statement by an African-American TV executive who was asked about the operation of power in the television industry:

Positions of real power have been in the past, and continue to be, reserved for a network of white males who all know each other, run the industry, and occasionally allow a token number of White women to preside with them over the decision making process.

One could dismiss this TV executive's statement as sour grapes. However, in 1986 a report titled *Minority Broadcasting Facts* was released by the National Association of Broadcasters, and in it were the following figures on the numbers of general managers of commercial TV stations who were non-White: 9 African-Americans and 5 Latinos. There were also 4 African-American TV station managers. Yet in the United States there are nearly 1,300 commercial TV stations. Clearly, then, African-Americans are not overwhelmingly represented in the controlling structures of television.

The Federal Communications Commission also released an equal opportunity trend report in 1988 that outlined ethnic minority employment in television and cable over the period 1983–1987. Ethnic groups were subdivided between males and females, and also between categories of employment. During 1987 the overall number of people employed was 176,159, compared with 160,967 for 1983. The proportion of minority professionals increased a little, from 15.3% in 1983 to 16.2% in 1987, or 28,590 in all, mainly due to a few more Latino professionals. The 1987 percentages for minorities subdivided by gender were as follows: 4.2% African-American women; 4.7% African-American men; 2.2% Latinas; 3.4% Latinos. However, the figures also showed that ethnic minorities were underrepresented in the top four groups, which jointly account for about 85% of all positions: officials and managers, 10.6% (3,832); professionals, 14.7% (8,006); technicians, 19.8% (6,345); sales workers, 10.0% (2,391). According to Dr. Edward Wachtel in a report titled *Television Hiring Practices*, issued by the Office of Communication of the United Church of Christ, if we were to look more closely at these categories we would see that they serve to mask the real underrepresentation of African-Americans in the power structure of the electronic media. Wachtel suggests that a more accurate picture would be given by matching of minority employment with salary, because that would provide a more adequate picture of the real situation. Is a "sales worker," for example, an executive selling ad spots to corporations, or that executive's typist?

So in answer to the first question posed we can draw the following conclusion. Ethnic minorities such as African-Americans exhibit a minimal presence in the upper echelons of influence in television, especially in the three big networks.

TV AND AFRICAN-AMERICANS: HOSTILITY, APARTHEID, OR AVOIDANCE

Television, argues Michael Winston, from its early stages, either was directly hostile to African-Americans or ignored them: "It was to be 'white' not simply, as newspapers were, in its employment practices, but in its projection of American life, insofar as it reflected American reality at all."

In spite of the civil rights movements of the 1940s, 1950s, and 1960s, in spite of the Black power movements of the 1960s and 1970s, there still exists among many White people an underlying belief in and image of the United States as essentially a White country. African-Americans are seen as being peripheral to the growth and development of the United States. Essentially, African-Americans are stereotyped as "a problem" in an otherwise harmonious country. For example, in urban America

to be a mugger is synonymous with being African-American or Hispanic. The immediate image we accept as the norm is that of Whites being mugged by African-Americans and Hispanics.

How did this belief that all African-Americans are potential muggers originate and become so embedded in the culture? Although [Stuart Hall,] a leading Black communications scholar in Britain, has traced out the genesis of the image in British media, the full story is yet to be told for the United States.

Let us, however, refresh our memories on how television handled the incident of the jogger who was raped and viciously beaten in Central Park in 1989. By contrast, consider the media treatment of the so-called preppie murder, which occurred in the same park in 1987.

In the television news coverage of the former incident, viewers were informed that the jogger was an investment banker, which immediately set the tone that she was a worthy person. Next, they were informed that the attack occurred in the part of Central Park that borders Harlem, a predominantly poor African-American and Latino neighborhood. Viewers were bombarded with the details of how the woman was brutally beaten, raped, and left to die by these cruel African-American and Hispanic young thugs. One particular young man was singled out as being from a good family, with a bright future and doing very well at school. There was in general, however, a dearth of information about the conditions and environment of these young African-Americans, while there was an implied and shared assumption that all African-American men are liable to be violent, cruel, and vicious muggers, the kind of people who would predictably perpetrate such a crime on decent White women.

We should pause, however, to ask about the young White man who, in 1987, raped and murdered a white woman in Central Park—an incident the press labeled "the preppie murder." He was portrayed as a fine, upstanding young man who, under the influence of drugs and alcohol coupled with sexy provocation from the young woman, lost his head and accidentally strangled her. Television did not dwell with the same intense attention on the victim, or on the barbarism of this act. Instead, they presented the viewers with extenuating circumstances that would enable them to understand that this was not a premeditated crime, but just an unforeseen accident. (If only the dead girl's body could itself become an "accident.")

By contrast, the young men who raped and beat the jogger (who narrowly survived the incident) were not shown as having any circumstances that might extenuate *their* barbarous behavior. Attention was not focused on the harsh poverty of much of Harlem as an extenuating factor, justifiably or not, nor—more to the point—did the media trouble to ask the basic question of what kinds of individuals most of the young men were. The television coverage did not dwell on how some of these young men had been terrorizing the residents in their apartment buildings for months on end. It was not until the White woman jogger was mugged that these residents experienced some respite from the terror and harassment they had endured without any police protection or interest. Only White victims seemed to count.

Why were these two incidents treated so differently by television, especially given that in the preppie case the White woman was dead, while the jogger survived? Color. In the Central Park incident it was African-Americans attacking fine, respectable Whites, not a "preppie" behaving "out of character." Television viewers were presented with well-established categories that they took for granted and accepted as real.

On the other hand, the Central Park preppie murder was unreal. Young, wealthy, White men did not murder respectable White women. Therefore, the woman was at fault. She must have been a quasi-prostitute, loose, asking for it, deserving of what happened to her. Otherwise she would not have been killed by a White man in Central Park.

Viewer outrage against the attackers of the Central Park jogger was phenomenal. There were suggestions that they should be castrated, locked up and the keys thrown away, given the death sentence. The preppie murder did not evoke such an avid response. The situation was presented as being unclear as to whether the suspect actually did commit the murder. On television he was shown leaving court with his parents and lawyer. A Catholic bishop was wheeled out as a character reference. Indeed, the whole tone of the proceedings on television lacked the "hang 'em high" lynching response meted out to the attackers of the Central Park jogger.

Were these two incidents treated the same by television? No. Both crimes were hideous, and the attackers should be punished. However, one victim was dead, while the other, though badly beaten and raped, was alive and recovering. Why are the African-Americans more deserving of punishment than a White murderer? We can subscribe to that position only if we accept the established belief that African-Americans are violent, uncontrollable, and uncivilized, or if we consider it obvious that they require more punishment regardless of what crimes they have committed.

These two violent incidents are important because they illustrate that African-American and White American offenders are not portrayed as being equally deserving of punishment. The television treatment of both events was presented within a context that relied on accepted racial belief about African-Americans. That belief can be stated as follows: African-Americans have an inherent tendency to mug, rape, murder, and otherwise disrupt the normal orderly processes characteristic of White society in the United States of America (the preppie murder notwithstanding).

To move to more everyday TV, let us examine the virtual apartheid that exists in most television situation comedies. African-Americans and White Americans are not portrayed as living or interacting harmoniously. Sitcoms are either African-American or White American (rarely the former, until the success of *The Jeffersons* and then *The Cosby Show*). Also, as Gray observes, many all-Black sitcoms have not stirred from stereotyped and demeaning portrayals. He comments on the patronizing, even contemptuous, assumptions behind a series like *Diff'rent Strokes*, which was integrated in the formal sense, but centered on a White man adopting two Black boys. In fact, television has invariably followed the successful formula from radio, which presented African-Americans in a demeaning manner....

In general, as TV developed, African-Americans either were portrayed as simple, happy, uneducable buffoons, or they were ignored. A classic example of their being ignored is the fact that many Vietnam War documentaries scarcely included or mentioned them, even though African-Americans were greatly over-represented in the fighting compared to their numbers in the population.

A different but very important example is to be seen in the development of art in the United States, especially music, where African-Americans have also played a central role. Television, radio, and the music industry have managed to take over the cultural forms produced by African-Americans—such as blues, jazz, and swing—without their actual participation. The original swing bands were those of Duke Ellington and Count Basie, yet it was bands such as Glen Miller's and the Dorsey Brothers' that were dubbed the "Kings of Swing." Some readers might argue that Duke Ellington and Count Basie were recognized by TV as being talented and great musicians, but was it just coincidental that the Glenn Miller Band and the Dorsey Brothers Band received much more time on radio, television, and film?

If it was coincidental, why has there never been an African-American musical star with his or her own musical television series, with national syndication and a national advertising sponsor who would willingly buy the series? For example, in 1956–1957, the *Nat King Cole Show* premiered on NBC. In spite of the efforts of NBC and the show's popularity, the show never found a national sponsor. None of the conglomerates wanted to be closely identified with a "Negro program."...

Thus regardless of whether we are discussing the presentation of African-Americans in a barbaric situation such as the crime committed against the Central Park jogger, or in sitcoms, or in TV documentaries about the Vietnam War, or the cultural appreciation of music in this society, there is one compelling factor that we cannot ignore: the presentation of African-Americans as marginal in this society. There is no parity between African-Americans and Whites on television. Apart from some TV commercials full of instant cheerfulness around food or drink, African-Americans and White Americans are not shown as living in an integrated society, where they interact as friendly equals, respectful of each other's needs and tolerant of each other's differences.

RACIST STEREOTYPING ON TV: FROM AMOS 'N' ANDY TO COSBY

To understand the long roots of these problems in U.S. television, we have to begin with *Amos 'n' Andy*, which was initially a very popular radio show and then was transferred to television. The *Amos 'n' Andy* radio formula originated with racial stereotypes derived from White vaudeville entertainers performing in "blackface," that is, with their faces painted with caricatural African features. On radio, the characters of Amos and Andy were played by two White comedians, Freeman Gosden and Charles Correll. Gosden, who was from South Virginia, attributed his mastering of "Negro dialect" to having been raised by an African-American housekeeper. He also had from childhood a close friend called Snowball, who lived in his household as the boys grew up. According to Gosden, Snowball was the source of his humor for the show.

The stereotypes that Gosden and Correll portrayed on radio in the 1920s and 1930s served a variety of purposes in the social and political arena of the epoch. The characters of Amos and Andy were

identified as having no education and, by definition, no intelligence. African-Americans did not have the vote in 1938, when this radio program was at its zenith. The implication that White Americans derived from this program was very crude: African-Americans are grossly ignorant and uneducated. Therefore, to give them the vote, decent jobs, political power, would be tantamount to reducing American democracy to a racial injustice—to Whites.

In 1951 *Amos 'n' Andy* premiered on television with African-American actors instead of Whites in blackface. How did African-Americans respond to this presentation of themselves on White television? This episode is important, not only in the development of the racial politics of American television, but also in the acknowledgment that audiences can be active, not merely passive, in their responses to media. The National Association for the Advancement of Colored People (NAACP) sought an injunction to prevent CBS from putting the program on television. Several groups sensitive to the African-American struggle for civil rights condemned *Amos 'n' Andy* as an affront to social achievement. The Michigan Federation of Teachers called the TV series "a gross and vulgar caricature of fifteen million Negro citizens of our country." Several eminent African-Americans blasted the show, describing it as the slow and steady poison of 20 years on radio, which was now transferred to TV. The African-American *Pittsburgh Courier* led a campaign to have the show pulled.

One question that must not be ducked is why African-Americans agreed to portray themselves and their race in such a demeaning manner. The answer is simple: job opportunities. African-American actors were overwhelmingly excluded from TV and film except as infrequent guest stars on variety shows or as "walk-ons" (usually in the role of house servants); very rarely were they stars in filmed or live drama. Examples of this exclusion are legion. The great singer Lena Horne was originally allowed only as far as a film sound track, while a White actress mouthed the words on camera. Paul Robeson, the distinguished actor, thinker, and political campaigner, appeared as co-lead in a film glorifying British colonialism in Africa (*Sanders of the River*). Hattie McDaniel, attacked by some African-Americans for her role as maid to Scarlett in *Gone with the Wind*, snapped that she would rather earn $7,000 a week acting a maid than $7 being one. *Amos 'n' Andy* provided regular employment for 142 African-Americans who were paid a handsome salary and had a chance to develop their careers.

However, the purpose of this discussion is to demonstrate that the television industry quite consciously developed a program written, produced, and directed by White men that broadcast a stereotypical projection of African-American life. Has there been a radical change in the media industry since then as far as African-Americans are concerned? Quite frankly no, despite appearances that might seem to be to the contrary.

During the 1970s, African-Americans achieved increasing visibility in news coverage because of the political events of that era. Although the political upheavals in the 1960s and 1970s resulted in a few more African-Americans being able to participate in TV, the overall numbers in any part of the production process, as actors, producers, camera operators, or executives, have not risen significantly. Contributions of African-Americans to television since the 1970s should not be casually dismissed. However, the manner in which they have been treated on TV despite their contributions has been very dishonorable and disrespectful of their sensibilities.

We should acknowledge that African-Americans have gained a significant market as actors and actresses in TV commercials and also public service announcements. But major producers still continue to avoid employing the many talented African-Americans outside the advertising sphere. Some of the stereotypes that are still very active in producers minds are depicted in Robert Townsend's comic yet serious feature film, *Hollywood Shuffle*.

The issue is how to interpret greater visibility. African-Americans are more visible on television, and are not as subjected as they were in the *Amos 'n' Andy* era. In 1988 one of television's top four White House journalists was Cable News Network's Bernard Shaw, an African-American. Nevertheless, despite these individual gains, African-Americans as a group do not have the same degree of opportunity as do White people as a group in the television industry.

POSTSCRIPT

Are Positive Images of African Americans Increasing in the Media?

Historically, the mass media has reflected the biases and attitudes of the general public. A controversial issue in mass communications is how often and how much have the media not only been a reflection of social mores but a creator of negative images. Has the media cleaned up their act?

One thing to be aware of in doing social scientific research, especially on problems needing policy solutions, is the rapidity of change. In both of these selections, the facts are largely based on research carried out in the 1980s. A quick look at almost any listing of television programs today would show many new programs that feature Blacks and other minorities in relative abundance as compared to the past, and more programs being written and directed by minorities. This was less so the case when MacDonald and Corea wrote.

In sum, attempting to comprehend the impact of any mass media or other contrived cultural production, especially if presented as entertainment, is highly problematic, and facile conclusion should be avoided.

Michael Parenti's *Make-Believe Media: The Politics of Entertainment* is a short, concise overview of the problem of mass communication as deception. See especially chapter 8, "Black Images in White Media," (St. Martin's Press, 1992). For an earlier, fairly systematic study of portrayals of Blacks in films (it found three-fourths to be unfavorable), see R. Colle, "Negro Images in the Mass Media," *Journalism Quarterly* (Spring 1968). For a look at one segment of the entertainment media see *Black Musical Theatre: From Coontown to Dreamgirls*, by A. Woll (Louisiana State University Press, 1989). An excellent recent study that examines opinions of minorities is *Race, Class, and Culture: A Study in Afro-American Mass Opinion*, by R. Smith and R. Selter (SUNY Press, 1993).

A good study of Mexicans in film is A. G. Pettit's *Images of the Mexican American in Fiction and film* (Texas A & M Press, 1980). See also Carlos Cortes, "Power, Passivity, and Pluralism: Mass Media in the Development of Latino Culture and Identity," in *Latino Studies Journal* (January 1993). This is an outstanding article that provides both historical and current insights.

For an overview of Hispanic responses to films in film reviews, see "Chicano Cinema and the Horizon of Expectations: A Discursive Analysis of Film Reviews, by C. Noriega, in *Aztlan* (Fall 1988–1989). For a discussion of mass media treatment of Italians and other minorities, see M. Parenti (cited above, 1992).

PART 3

Ethnic Stratification: Power and Inequality

In addition to wanting to know about the nature of the values and norms shared by members of a society, and how society forms the individual (i.e., people learn how to be Irish, Jewish, Catholic, American, Black, female), sociologists also deal with inequality. Why is it that in all societies some are more equal than others? What are the forms of these inequalities and their consequences? For years sociologists have pointed out the importance of ethnicity and race for creating and maintaining systems of stratification (i.e., the distribution of society's power, wealth, and opportunities). Recently, however, some scholars have used a cultural production perspective to study inequality. They seek to determine the pervasiveness of oppression and exploitation within any community of people in order to help them to empower themselves with new knowledge and new awareness. But how should this knowledge be used to most effectively challenge and change the system?

- Should Minorities Continue to Demand More Rights?

- Does "Lower-Class" Culture Perpetuate Poverty Among Urban Minorities?

- Is Affirmative Action Reverse Discrimination?

- Are Hispanics Making Significant Progress?

- Is Systemic Racism in Criminal Justice a Myth?

ISSUE 10

Should Minorities Continue to Demand More Rights?

YES: David Hatchett, from "The Future of Civil Rights in the Twenty-first Century," *Crisis: The Journal of Lay Catholic Opinion* (January 1992)

NO: Glenn Loury, from "The Struggle to Return to Self-Help," *Issues and Views* (Winter 1992)

ISSUE SUMMARY

YES: Writer and social commentator David Hatchett sees greater internationalization in the future of the civil rights movement. And he completely concurs with several prominent Black leaders that the desperation of many Black communities alone justifies continued demands for more rights.

NO: Boston University professor of economics Glenn Loury traces the debate between Black leaders W. E. B. Du Bois and Booker T. Washington that rocked the Black intellectual community 80 years ago. Loury sides with Washington in recommending self-help over government favors, which he says casts Blacks into playing the role of the victim.

What can and should governments do to address discrimination? Should minorities look to government action to end discrimination and demand more rights? These questions are fiercely debated and are at the heart of the selections by David Hatchett and Glenn Loury.

Some people concur with Loury that civil rights leaders risk stagnation at best, a backlash at worse, in the rights movement by continuing to focus on the "classic interplay between the aggrieved black and the guilty white." Loury does not in any way discount the horrible abuses that Blacks and other minorities have been subjected to as their rights have been denied or abridged. However, borrowing from Booker T. Washington (1856–1915), the conservative Black leader and founder of Tuskegee Institute, Loury insists that self-help is imperative for minority groups. To Loury and other Black intellectuals such as Thomas Sowell and Shelby Steele, sufficient pump priming by the government has been done to equalize rights.

David Hatchett, based on his many years of direct observation of minority oppression, on interviews with major Black leaders, and on recent summaries of economic trends, could not disagree more. Although he does not discuss the historical roots of his argument, his thinking embraces the main ideas of W. E. B. Du Bois (1868–1963), the Harvard Ph.D. who spent many years debating Booker T. Washington's call for Black self-help. Du Bois demanded that Blacks organize and fight for equal rights, and he fought against the idea that Blacks, through hard work, thrift, and good habits, had to first demonstrate that they "deserved" the rights that whites already enjoyed as citizens.

In education, housing, public safety, and jobs—areas where segregation and discrimination have been outlawed and remedied through legal measures—Blacks and other racial minorities continue to face problems not encountered by dominant group members. For Loury and those who endorse his point of view, Black progress on the equal rights front depends "on the acknowledgment and rectification of the dysfunctional behaviors which plague Black communities."

Not so at all, counters Hatchett. First, not only is the civil rights movement neither dead nor no longer needed, but it is being revived through its internationalization. That is, Hatchett argues, more and more Asians and Latinos, and also the poor and dispossessed, are aligning with Blacks in the civil rights movement. The complexion, potency, and accomplishments of the movement in the twenty-first century will be different and stronger, he insists. He points out that the basic rights of Blacks are still not being addressed, and he looks at injustices for Blacks and for poor whites as well.

As you read these two concise and lively articles, be aware of the very different intellectual traditions they reflect. Try to identify both logical and factual strengths and weaknesses in each perspective. What segment among minorities would benefit from government action? In what ways, based on your reading of these two articles and on other minority-related materials you've read that deal with poverty, could you argue that as long as many live in abject poverty, it is cruel to accuse them of "playing the victim"?

YES

David Hatchett

THE FUTURE OF CIVIL RIGHTS IN THE TWENTY-FIRST CENTURY

The 1963 March on Washington was the culmination of the civil rights movement of the 1960's. While millions of people watched the event on television, more than 250,000 people gathered on the grassy lawn in front of the Lincoln Memorial to hear a number of black leaders call on the federal government to extend the civil liberties guaranteed by the Constitution to all United States citizens.

Whitney Young, John Lewis, A. Philip Randolph and Roy Wilkins all spoke that day, but the speech by Dr. Martin Luther King, Jr. captured the moment.

"We can never turn back," King told the nation when he took the podium. " ... We can never be satisfied as long as the Negro is victim of the unspeakable horrors of police brutality. We can never be satisfied as long as our bodies, heavy with the fatigue of travel, cannot gain lodging in the motels of the highways and the hotels of the cities.... We can never be satisfied as long as the Negro cannot vote."

King's speech and the gathering before the memorial shook the nation to its foundations.

Ten months later the Congress passed legislation prohibiting unions and employers of more than 100 workers from discriminating in hiring, apprenticeship or promotion "against any individual because of his race, color, religion, sex or national origin." The legislation also outlawed segregation in stores, offices and other institutions serving the public.

In 1965 President Johnson signed into law the Voting Rights Act, which allowed the federal government to directly intervene to overturn measures which prohibited blacks from exercising their rights to vote.

The years since the passage of the civil rights legislation that followed the March on Washington have seen blacks gain unprecedented access to mainstream institutions.

In 1940 only 2 percent of African Americans had completed college, compared with 5 and 7.5 percent of white males and females, respectively. But by

1980, blacks represented 10 percent of the college population.

In the 1980's, the term Buppie (Black Urban Professionals) came into vogue to describe the new class of black professionals who were gradually inching their way toward the top of America's professional hierarchy, as the sight of black television and radio commentators, corporate executives, and doctors and lawyers became commonplace.

Politically, blacks have gained what Dr. David A. Bositis, senior research assistant at the Joint Center for Political and Economic Studies, calls "insider status." Where there were less than 500 black elected officials in 1965, there are more than 7,400 today, including 26 members of the House of Representatives.

"I do not know of anywhere else in the world where minorities have advanced as fast as they have in this nation in such a short time," states Benjamin Hooks, Executive Director of the National Association for the Advancement of Colored People.

But a recent interview with Dorothy I. Height, President of the National Council of Negro Women, at the Council's offices on Connecticut Avenue in downtown Washington, D.C. seemed light years away from the sweltering highways King and thousands of others marched across to get the nation to confront the injustices it had heaped on the backs of blacks and other minorities.

Sitting behind a desk stacked high with papers, reports and memos with her swivel chair pulled so close to its outer edge that she seemed to have barely enough room to breathe, Height looked more like some high-powered corporate executive than the director of one of the most influential civil rights organizations in the country.

Despite her best efforts, she was interrupted time and again by phone calls or aides asking her for instructions. A full-figured woman with a direct, pointed manner, Height's attention became focused when the questioner mentioned the role of women in the civil rights movement.

The closest black women came to the podium during the speeches at the Lincoln Memorial during the 1963 March on Washington was singer Mahalia Jackson's gospel song, Height pointed out.

Black women were the majority of the people at the meetings and demonstrations during the 1960's, but most of the leadership positions in the civil rights movement were held by black men.

In black organizations black women need to be more assertive in making sure that their voices are heard and that their specific needs [are] taken into account, Height says.

"Women are now moving into significant positions of power in society," states Dr. Cornel West, chairman of the black studies department at Princeton University. "Anita Hill was just the tip of the iceberg. The ecological movement will also be a strong force," West continues.

Women's and immigrant rights, environmental protection and a host of other issues not directly addressed by the speakers at the 1963 march or the ensuing civil rights legislation are now critical to any notions of social justice. There were less than 1 million Asian Americans in 1960. Today, there are over seven (7) million of them, together with 21 million Hispanics.

How will these new players in the civil rights game change commonly accepted views on social justice and the way civil rights organizations have traditionally fought racism and discrimination?

At 2 a.m. on December 23, 1989, the Sengupta family's pick-up truck was bombed in the driveway of the family's home in old Bethpage, Vt. This was the second such bombing to which the family had been subjected. Prior to the bombing, the Senguptas had received anonymous, racially hostile notes and phone calls, and had their yard booby-trapped and destroyed on several occasions. The Senguptas were the only Asian family in the area.

The police were able to identify and apprehend a suspect only after his girlfriend turned him in to authorities.

Several years ago in Jersey City, N.J. a group known as the "Dot Busters" attacked a number of East Indians in the city.

While the image of the nightrider and vigilante assaults against blacks have been the central fixtures of racial violence in 20th century America, the fastest-growing category of hate crimes are those directed against Asians and gays.

"Despite whatever economic status they may attain, Asians are seen as perpetual outsiders," said Stan Mark, program director of the Asian-American Legal Defense and Education Fund in New York City. Thousands of Japanese Americans were put into concentration camps in World War II despite the fact that they had been citizens for generations.

"If the economy goes bad and the competition is with Japan, all Asians are seen as the enemy," said Dr. Madhulika Khandelwal, a history professor at the Asian-American Center at Queens College in New York City.

Asian-Americans faced discriminatory laws that practically eliminated all entry into the United States by these groups. Asian-Americans already living in the country were forced to endure laws in many Western states which discriminated against them in much the same manner as the Jim Crow segregation edicts reduced blacks to second-class in the south.

This had a major impact on the Asians who were living in America before the 1960's, states Charles Chin, the education director of the Chinatown History Museum in New York City. But most of the Asians living in the United States arrived after 1960.

"They did not live through the civil rights movement and they do not have a sense of U.S. history and politics," Khandelwal states. "In terms of interethnic relations, this has caused some problems with blacks, who the new Asian immigrants sometimes see through the traditional ethnic stereotypes," Khandelwal adds. "Blacks, on the other hand, often look upon their new Asian neighbors as competitors," Khandelwal says.

Mark points out, however, that all immigrant groups need time to get acquainted with American society. Twenty years is the average time it takes a person who migrates to the United States to become fully familiar with the country, Mark continues.

Frank Hernandez, executive director of the Southwest Voter Registration Project in San Antonio, is of the opinion that as the country moves toward the next century the concept of civil rights will increasingly focus on such matters as immigrant rights and cultural issues. Half of the adult Latinos in California do not have citizenship, Hernandez continues. "There is an increasing demand that this population be allowed to participate in the electoral process," Hernandez states.

People who do not speak English as their native language also need protections, Hernandez adds.

Hernandez descried Latinos and blacks as two poor powerless minorities who—despite occasional differences—work well together most of the time. He argues that opinion polls show that there are few differences between blacks and Latinos on most issues which affect their communities.

The glittering accomplishments of the civil rights movement, however, are juxtaposed with the near desperation of much of the black community. Prison, drugs, homelessness and other problems have ravaged so many African-Americans that children born into black families in the 1980s and 1990s are often referred to as members of the "lost generation."

In 1984, the black median family income was only 56 percent that of the white median family income. The black unemployment rate was 15.9 percent, against 6.5 percent for whites. And over one-third of African Americans lived in poverty—including 50 percent of black children.

Simultaneous with this, a number of analysts say, whites are increasingly less willing to sanction any substantial government assistance to blacks and the poor.

"Most whites only see signs of progress in the black community, such as the middle-class blacks presented during the Clarence Thomas hearings," said William Schneider, a political analyst at the American Enterprise Institute. "Whites do not see the problems affecting blacks, such as homelessness, being the result of racism. To whites, it looks like the civil rights organizations are pushing an out-of-date agenda."

Schneider's views are supported by a recent Wall Street Journal survey where 59 percent of blacks thought that laws protecting minorities should be strengthened, while only 14 percent of whites felt that way.

A number of authorities laid much of the blame for this on the Reagan and Bush presidencies which have cut social service budgets and opposed the extension of civil rights laws to a greater extent than any other presidential administrations in modern history.

Arriving tired and late at his Washington office for an interview with a reporter, Rep. John Lewis (D-Ga) could only wring his hands over the state of the nation. Wearing a brown business suit, the stocky 5'7" Lewis reflected all the passion and intensity which has made him a five-term Congressman and a prominent enough civil rights leader during the 1960's to join King in delivering a speech at the Lincoln Memorial during the March on Washington.

"We will have chaos like that in Northern Ireland or Lebanon," Lewis stated, emotion creeping into his eyes as he tightly clasped his hands together while sitting on a couch adjacent to a picture window that gave a picturesque early evening view of the halls of Congress. "You cannot leave millions of our young people in the inner cities without a sense of the future. You are sowing the seeds of discontent."

"There is a lack of 'leadership' in this country in the White House and Congress, where no one seems willing to confront many of the problems facing the nation," Lewis continues.

"The crime and other problems affecting urban America will either be solved by federal intervention or a veritable police state will have to be established," Lewis said.

Leaning over the couch so far that his knee touched the floor as he gestured with his hands, Lewis argued that the civil rights movement had to make sure that it kept pace with the changes in the country as the nation neared the year 2000.

"The civil rights movement (in the next century) will not be as we know it today. It will have to be more inclusive. Blacks must actively seek alliances with Latinos, Asians and progressive whites."

Dr. Manning Marable, a political science professor at the University of Colorado at Boulder, goes even further, flatly declaring that black leaders need to realize that the "civil rights movement is over. Reagan killed it," Marable continues. "(Blacks) have to look for new allies."

While agreeing that the country is changing, Benjamin Hooks takes the position that the established civil rights groups are well prepared to confront the America of the year 2000:

"Our viewpoint has to be the same. We have always advocated for the rights of minorities and we will continue in that thrust. The year 2000 will not be magic. Discrimination will still be here. Through coalitions, we have always actively fought for the rights of women and minorities. The NAACP, for instance, has supported the struggle of immigrants for better living conditions and opposed the designation of English as the country's official language."

In Height's view, blacks have taken the lead on civil rights because "they have been the most consistently subjected group in society." Height argues, however, that the National Council of Negro Women has always branched out to other women of color.

"We (the civil rights organizations) have always talked about equity for all Americans, including Asians and Hispanics," said Joseph Lowery, president of the Southern Christian Leadership Conference. "The shift for us is to full employment with good wages." Lowery says the new full employment economy will have to have a jobless rate of zero, not the 5 or 6 percent that is currently considered to be full employment.

The challenge for the civil rights movement, Lowery believes, is to change the perception of many Americans that blacks and poverty are synonymous. "There are more whites living in poverty than the entire black population of this country. Civil rights groups have got to show that poverty is not good for the country as a whole," Lowery said.

Lowery's views are echoed by the Urban League's report "Playing to Win: A Marshall Plan for America." The plan calls for the federal government to spend $50 billion over the next 10 years to improve the country's education system and repair its roads, bridges, airports and other economic fixtures. The Urban League recommendations say that the rebuilding program can be paid for by a combination of increased taxes, debt financing, spending transfers and reductions in the defense budget.

"Blacks have got to build an agenda of inclusiveness," states John E. Jacob, president of the National Urban League, Inc. "We have to make people understand that you cannot solve the education problem until you educate black people. We have got to make business understand that you cannot build a national workforce until you help minorities and women."

The key issue is that programs which help the black community must be seen as being beneficial to the entire country, Jacob continues.

Jacob believes that the country is nearing an historic crossroads, where it can either go down the lane of cultural pluralism and integration or that of segregation, inequality and reaction.

Charles Chin perhaps best sums up the role Asians and Latinos will play in the next generation of struggle when he noted that their rapidly expanding populations will "internationalize" the civil rights struggle and may finally help to settle the questions about minority rights which have been lingering since the end of the Civil War.

NO

Glenn Loury

THE STRUGGLE TO RETURN TO SELF-HELP

Tough and unrelenting, the underlying premises of Booker T. Washington's philosophy offer a sound guide to the future for American blacks.

The conflict between Clarence Thomas's black supporters and his critics recalls the epochal struggle over public ideas among blacks, which raged at the turn of the century between the followers, respectively, of Booker T. Washington and W. E. B. Du Bois. Washington was a conservative advocate of a philosophy of self-help; Du Bois was a radical exponent of a strategy of protest and agitation for reform. While he lived, Washington's view was the orthodoxy. In the end the ideas of the Du Bois camp nevertheless prevailed and is today's orthodoxy. It is an orthodoxy fiercely defended by the civil rights establishment from the criticism of radical dissidents like Thomas, just as Washington defended his, and with similar methods.

But there are signs that a new era is dawning, and that, in the contemporary struggle over the ideas which will inform efforts to improve the black condition into the 21st century, the principles laid down by Booker T. Washington will be rediscovered, and play an important role. What are those principles? They are, fundamentally, an understanding about how blacks should respond to the great philosophical and political problems created by our history of degradation, and the fact of our unequal citizenship.

Washington believed the response should be, in the main, to concentrate on the development of blacks' capacities to exploit such opportunity as already lay at hand, and to rely on the expectation that, as such development was seen to proceed, we would come into a stronger position to make a successful claim for the full rights of citizenship.

BRAINS, PROPERTY AND CHARACTER

He saw two factors preventing blacks from enjoying the status in American society which was our due: actual defects of character as manifest in patterns of behavior and ways of living to be observed among the black masses; and the racist attitudes of whites. He believed that blacks had both an opportunity and a duty to address the former difficulty; and that, in so doing, we would go a long way toward overcoming the latter. He preached a litany of self-improvement; he emphasized the Protestant virtues of thrift, industry, cleanliness, chastity, orderliness; he urged above all else that we blacks must make ourselves *useful*— to our families, our neighbors, and our fellow citizens.

All of this sounds quaint today. But this programmatic focus on self-help was actually not very controversial at the time. What stimulated opposition was Washington's rejection of mass political agitation as a strategy. He thought the active pursuit of civil rights to be premature and dangerous for blacks. "Brains, property, and character for the Negro will settle the question of civil rights," he said.... Washington preached the unapologetic embrace of responsibility for one's own freedom.

I intend here no revisionist reassessment of the historical effects of these two schools of thought on the evolution of the black condition. It is important that I not be misunderstood to suggest that history has proven Booker T. Washington to have been right, and W. E. B. Du Bois to have been wrong, in their great debate about what blacks should have done 90 years ago. My claim is more modest: *Given the way in which our history has evolved, and looking candidly at the current problems which confront our people, I claim that the animating spirit and underlying premises of Washington's philosophy now offer a sounder guide to the future for blacks than do those which are reflected in the world view of his critics.*

Herbert Storing pointed toward this conclusion, in 1963, when he made a defense of Washington's position:

> Yet when the harsh words have been said, when the blame is assigned, when many rights have been granted and are actually enjoyed, Washington's soft, tough words still speak. Opportunities are limited. How well have we used those that are open? Rights are still curtailed. Have we prepared to exercise those we have?
>
> The Negro is blamed for too much of American crime. Are we nevertheless responsible for too much of it? The Negro is less than completely free. Do we know what freedom is? The Negro is a second-class citizen. Are we fit for first-class citizenship? The Negro can find deficiencies, in these respects and countless others, in every phase of American life, but his own deficiencies are not one whit removed by pointing out those of others.
>
> The Negro can serve himself, as he can serve his country, only by learning and thereby teaching the lesson that Theodore Roosevelt said was 'more essential than any other, for this country to learn,... that the enjoyment of rights should be made conditional upon the performance of duty.'

These are harsh, unpalatable words to the modern political ear, carefully attuned as it is to the possibility of giving offense. Such words were politically incorrect, even in 1963. And I surely do not maintain by repeating them here that there is any question of blacks being "fit for first class citizenship."

ACKNOWLEDGE THE NEGATIVE BEHAVIORS AND RECTIFY THEM

But it *is* fair to ask now about opportunities unexploited, about rights unexercised, about whether we are too much responsible for what ails our urban centers, about duty and obligation. It is fair to inquire, with the many cries for "Freedom Now!" ringing out from angry, defiant protesters on behalf of racial justice across the land, whether we have a clear conception of what this "freedom thing" really is, of what being free and responsible participants in this democratic polity actually requires of us. It is, I think, necessary to question what it takes for one to stand truly equal among one's fellows; to explore the limits of a rights-oriented approach to the problem of inequality between racially distinct populations in our contemporary national life; to deal with issues of dignity, shame, personal responsibility, character and values, deservingness....

Here then is the crux of my argument: *Further progress toward the attainment of equality for black Americans, broadly and correctly understood, depends most crucially at this juncture on the acknowledgement and rectification of the dysfunctional behaviors which plague black communities, and which so offend and threaten others.* Do this, and much else will follow. It is more important to address this matter effectively, than it is to agitate for additional rights. Indeed, success in such agitation has become contingent upon effective reform efforts mounted from within the black community....

The point on which Washington was clear, and his critics I think were not, is that progress such as this must be earned, it cannot be demanded. He understood that when the effect of past oppression is to leave a people in a diminished state, the attainment of true equality cannot rely on the generosity of others, but must ultimately derive from self-elevation. It is of no moment that historic wrongs may have caused current deprivation, for justice is not the issue here. The issues are

dignity, respect, and self-respect—all of which are preconditions for true equality between any peoples.

CONTEMPT, SHAME AND RAGE

The classic interplay between the aggrieved black and the guilty white, in which the former demands and the latter conveys a recognition of the historic injustice, is not an exchange among equals. Neither, one suspects is it a stable exchange. Eventually it may shade into something else, something less noble— into patronage, into a situation where the guilty one comes to have contempt for the claimant, and the claimant comes to feel shame, and its natural accompaniment, rage, at his impotence.

Thus Booker T. Washington argued: "It is a mistake to assume that the Negro, who had been a slave for 250 years, gained his freedom by the signing, on a certain date, of a certain paper by the President of the United States. It is a mistake to assume that one man can, in any true sense, give freedom to another. Freedom, in the larger and higher sense every man must gain for himself." This, I insist, is not an "unmanly" or "acquiescent" or "race traitorous" sentiment. Quite the contrary, this is the candid exhortation of a leader who has understood a hard truth about the condition of his people: to look their emancipator squarely in the eye, they must first raise themselves from their current level.

Nor is this the rhetoric of an apologist for the crimes of others. Rather, it is the unapologetic embrace of responsibility for one's own freedom. Consider the fact that, unlike Du Bois and his followers, Washington lived out his life in the south, among the poor blacks of his time; that he built from nothing, and in the midst of white reactionaries, a permanent, lasting institution which, to this day, helps to meet the needs and expand the opportunities of his people.

Nor is Washington's sentiment anachronistic, appropriate to the second generation after slavery, but irrelevant today. For the basic thrust of today's civil rights posture looks to the "signing, on a certain date, of a certain paper by the President," or by a federal judge, to deliver freedom to blacks.

CONCEDING DIGNITY IN AN APPEAL FOR SYMPATHY

In so doing, rights advocates avoid the necessary hard work of facilitating internal reform for their people, which would help to reverse the diminishing effect of past violations of rights. They seek to lay responsibility for the hard realities of contemporary ghetto life on the shoulders of whites, citing the fact that whites have not treated blacks as justice would require. They argue as Du Bois did: "If they accuse Negro women of lewdness and Negro men of monstrous crime, what are they doing but advertising to the world the shameless lewdness of those Southern men who brought millions of mulattoes into the world? . . . Suppose today Negroes do steal; who was it that for centuries made stealing a virtue by stealing their labor?" But this argument concedes far too much *dignity* for the sake of an appeal for *sympathy*. Can we really expect whites to agree that black "lewdness" or criminality is but a derivative consequence of white's depraved condition, for which whites, not blacks, are ultimately responsible? Do we really believe it ourselves? . . .

A civil rights advocate teaches the exhortation: "I *am* somebody." True enough, but the crucial question is: "so what?" Because I am somebody, I will not accept unequal rights. Because I am somebody, I will waste no opportunity to better myself. Because I am somebody, I will respect my body by not polluting it with drugs or promiscuous sex. Because I am somebody—in my home, in my community, in my nation—I will comport myself responsibly. I will be accountable, I will be available to serve others as well as myself. It is the doing of these fine things, not the saying of any fine words, which teaches oneself, and others, that one *is* somebody. . . .

AN EXHIBITIONISM OF NON-ACHIEVEMENT

Because we are free human agents we are obligated to strive to reverse the debilitating patterns of social life which limit our progress. We are rightly judged by the extent to which we meet this responsibility. The liberal exchange, in which victimized blacks insist upon relief from guilt-ridden whites, often points away from this necessity to be engaged in our own improvement. It leads to a perverse "exhibitionism of non-achievement" by blacks (for example, the remorseful recitation of statistics showing that more black men are in prisons than in colleges). It is as if the fact of our failure to meet a certain standard or surmount a certain obstacle must of necessity constitute evidence of a social or political failing by the larger society. Even when whites accept this exchange, one harbors the disquieting suspicion that they don't really believe in it— that they suspect the non-achievement has another, less respectable but never spoken, explanation. . . .

GOVERNMENT CANNOT TRANSFORM INDIVIDUAL LIVES

What ultimately is at stake in our halting efforts to widen the national dialogue on racial matters is the determination of whether we Americans are going to fall apart, fighting with and picking at each other for the next two generations, or whether we are going to find some way to pull ourselves together and go forward into the 21st century as a strong, world competitive multi-ethnic nation. This is about whether we can develop and sustain sufficient ties across the many boundaries that separate us as to enable us to cooperate in our mutual interest....

Advocates of a new public philosophy for black Americans are drawing on an old wisdom, well suited for our times. To advocate self-help, to argue that affirmative action cannot be a long-run solution to the racial inequality problem, to suggest that some of what is transpiring in black communities reflects a spiritual malaise, to note that fundamental change will require that individual lives be transformed in ways that governments are ill-suited to do, to urge that we must look to how black men and women are relating to each other, how parents are bringing up their children, that we have to ask ourselves what values inform the behavior of our youth—to do these things is not to take a partisan position, or vent some neoconservative ideology. Rather, to take this radically dissident line of departure from today's orthodoxy is to speak what, for many blacks, is a truth inherited from our ancestors; a truth we know as a result of our awareness of our history coming out of slavery; a truth reflected in the ambiguous but great legacy of Booker T. Washington.

POSTSCRIPT

Should Minorities Continue to Demand More Rights?

This is certainly an issue in which the facts and discussion fuel a thirst for more information. Has the civil rights movement reached a plateau? What happens now? Besides mentioning education and family life as areas for concern, are there other areas of concern in the Black community?

For a recent insightful article on the continuing deprivations of Black families and the futility of present policies, see Ellis Cose, "Protecting the Children," *Newsweek* (August 30, 1993). For a summary of political activism of the past year, see Peter Lin, "More Malcolm's Year than Martin's" in *History Today* (April 1993). An interesting article that looks at strategies still used to deny minorities job opportunities is K. Necerman and J. Kirschenman, "Hiring Strategies, Racial Bias, and Inner-City Workers," in *Social Problems* (November 1991). Another indicator of economic rights deprivation is the recent *U.S. Census Bureau 1993 Report on Poverty and Income Statistics for 1992*, which shows that approximately 38 million Americans are living below the poverty line. A series of philosophical essays looking at rights and citizenship is *Citizenship and Social Theory*, edited by B. Turner (Sage, 1993). Among the many studies further documenting slow to non-existent gains of minorities is *Income and Status Differences Between White and Minority Americans: A Persistent Inequality*, edited by S. Chan (The Edwin Meilen Press, 1990)

A more conservative perspective, which challenges those that say more federal spending is the only thing that can be done help minorities in poverty is John Sibley Butler's *Entrepreneurship and Self-Help Among Black Americans: A Reconsideration of Race and Economics* (State University of New York Press, 1993). Another book describing self-help is D. J. Nonti's *Race, Development, and the New Company Town* (State University of New York Press, 1993).

In *Rayford W. Logan and the Dilemma of the African-American Intellectual* (University of Massachusetts Press, 1993), you can find a discussions of a Black historian whose work supports Loury's ideas. For two excellent discussions of early Black leaders, such as Washington and Du Bois, who debated this very issue, and from whom both Hatchett and Loury draw from, see B. Quarles and D. Sterling's *Lift Every Voice* (Doubleday, 1965) and John White, *Black Leadership in America* (Longman, 1990).

ISSUE 11

Does "Lower-Class" Culture Perpetuate Poverty Among Urban Minorities?

YES: Edward Banfield, from *The Unheavenly City* (Little, Brown, 1970)

NO: William Ryan, from *Blaming the Victim* (Pantheon Books, 1971)

ISSUE SUMMARY

YES: Political scientist Edward Banfield, in a classic debate, argues that it is the life-styles of the poor that keep them impoverished. This so-called culture of poverty thesis examines the values and behaviors of the poor and finds in them the causes of poverty.

NO: Social critic and psychologist William Ryan counters that Banfield's thesis is a corruption of science and only functions to blame the victim for society's ills. Economic discrimination, racism, and a history of maltreatment explains poverty among urban minorities, not life-styles that are often rational efforts to survive in an irrational situation.

There are three major conceptual problems that sociologists attempt to answer. The first concerns the why of social order: Why does society hang together? How, for instance, is it possible that, on the first day of class, students meeting their teacher, and often each other, for the first time nonetheless know how to interact, to play the role of students? Most people, even during times of rapid change or public disorder usually do what is expected of them. Society hangs together. It functions. Why?

The second major problem that sociology examines is the one of how does society get into you? Each generation somehow transmits its values, attitudes, language, and so on to the next. This is the problem of socialization: how do you learn to be the person you become?

The last problem is the why of social inequality. Why is it that in all societies some people are "more equal" than others? This, of course, has to do with social stratification. All societies have different bases for dividing people. Inequality based on age and gender are among the most prevalent. Wealth, power, and education all function in industrial societies as a way of dividing people and are also the results of inequality. In the United States, race has been an important source of division or stratification. As a consequence of pervasive discrimination in employment, education, housing and so on, a disproportionately high number of Blacks have lived in poverty as compared to Anglos, as have other racial minorities.

Drawing from Oscar Lewis's classic (and highly controversial) article, "Culture of Poverty," *Scientific America* (October 1967), Banfield insists that the poor are trapped in a situation of despair, hopelessness, and permanent poverty as a resultant of their life-style. He describes the poor as present-oriented and pleasure-driven; they have habits inimical to thrift, industry, and achievement.

Ryan cannot believe he is hearing this. He argues that Banfield and others who support his ideas are simply covering over bigoted and racist labels with sociological jargon. He contends that "cultural deprivation," "present orientation," and so on are merely buzz words for "them" (i.e., racial minorities whose lack of money and opportunities, not their life-style, separate them from others).

Ryan dismisses Banfield's thesis that the poor are truly different. "Yeah, they have less money," he says. Their life-style is not the problem.

In the past 25 years, sociologists of minority relations and poverty would like to think that we have advanced beyond this debate. Yet as you read Banfield and Ryan, the discussion will sound uncannily familiar, particularly if you are tuned into what currently exists in the mass media.

YES

Edward Banfield

THE FUTURE OF THE LOWER CLASS

So long as the city contains a sizable lower class, nothing basic can be done about its most serious problems. Good jobs may be offered to all, but some will remain chronically unemployed. Slums may be demolished, but if the housing that replaces them is occupied by the lower class it will shortly be turned into new slums. Welfare payments may be doubled or tripled and a negative income tax instituted, but some persons will continue to live in squalor and misery. New schools may be built, new curricula devised, and the teacher-pupil ratio cut in half, but if the children who attend these schools come from lower-class homes, they will be turned into blackboard jungles, and those who graduate or drop out from them will, in most cases, be functionally illiterate. The streets may be filled with armies of policemen, but violent crime and civil disorder will decrease very little. If, however, the lower class were to disappear—if, say, its members were overnight to acquire the attitudes, motivations, and habits of the working class—the most serious and intractable problems of the city would all disappear with it.

[The] serious problems of the city all exist in two forms—a normal-class and a lower-class form—which are fundamentally different from each other. In its normal-class form, the employment problem, for example, consists mainly of young people who are just entering the labor market and who must make a certain number of trials and errors before finding suitable jobs; in its lower-class form, it consists of people who prefer the "action" of the street to any steady job. The poverty problem in its normal-class form consists of people (especially the aged, the physically handicapped, and mothers with dependent children) whose only need in order to live decently is money; in its lower-class form it consists of people who live in squalor and misery even if their incomes were doubled or tripled. The same is true with the other problems—slum housing, schools, crime, rioting; each is really two quite different problems.

The lower-class forms of all problems are at bottom a single problem: the existence of an outlook and style of life which is radically present-oriented and which therefore attaches no value to work, sacrifice, self-improvement, or service to family, friends, or community. Social workers, teachers, and law-enforcement officials—all those whom Gans calls "caretakers"—cannot achieve their goals because they can neither change nor circumvent this cultural obstacle....

Robert Hunter described it in 1904:

> They lived in God only knows what misery. They ate when there were things to eat; they starved when there was lack of food. But, on the whole, although they swore and beat each other and got drunk, they were more contented than any other class I have happened to know. It took a long time to understand them. Our Committees were busy from morning until night in giving them opportunities to take up the fight again, and to become independent of relief. They always took what we gave them; they always promised to try; but as soon as we expected them to fulfill any promises, they gave up in despair, and either wept or looked ashamed, and took to misery and drink again,— almost, so it seemed to me at times, with a sense of relief.

In Hunter's day these were the "undeserving," "unworthy," "depraved," "debased," or "disreputable" poor; today, they are the "troubled," "culturally deprived," "hard to reach," or "multiproblem." In the opinion of anthropologist Oscar Lewis, their kind of poverty "is a way of life, remarkably stable and persistent, passed down from generation to generation among family lines." This "culture of poverty," as he calls it, exists in city slums in many parts of the world, and is, he says, an adaptation made by the poor in order to defend themselves against the harsh realities of slum life.

The view that is to be taken here [is that] there is indeed such a culture, but that poverty is its effect rather than its cause. (There are societies even poorer than the ones Lewis has described— primitive ones, for example—in which nothing remotely resembling the pattern of behavior here under discussion exists.) Extreme present-orientedness, not lack of income or wealth, is the principal cause of poverty in the sense of "the culture of poverty." Most of those caught up in this culture are unable or unwilling to plan for the future, to sacrifice immediate gratifications in favor of future ones, or to accept the disciplines that are required in order to get and to spend. Their inabilities are probably culturally given in most cases—"multi-problem" families being normal representatives of a class culture that is itself abnormal. No doubt there are also people whose present-orientedness is rationally adaptive rather than cultural, but these probably comprise only a small part of the "hard core" poor.

Outside the lower class, poverty (in the sense of hardship, want, or destitution) is today almost always the result of external circumstances—involuntary unemployment, prolonged illness, the death of a breadwinner, or some other misfortune. Even when severe, such poverty is not squalid or degrading. Moreover, it ends quickly once the (external) cause of it no longer exists. Public or private assistance can sometimes remove or alleviate the cause—for example, by job retraining or remedial surgery. Even when the cause cannot be removed, simply providing the nonlower-class poor with sufficient income is enough to enable them to live "decently."

Lower-class poverty, by contrast, is "inwardly" caused (by psychological inability to provide for the future, and all that this inability implies). Improvements in external circumstances can affect this poverty only superficially: One problem of a "multiproblem" family is no sooner solved than another arises. In principle, it is possible to eliminate the poverty (material lack) of such a family, but only at great expense, since the capacity of the radically improvident to waste money is almost unlimited. Raising such a family's income would not necessarily improve its way of life, moreover, and could conceivably even make things worse. Consider, for example, the H. family:

> Mrs. H. seemed overwhelmed with the simple mechanics of dressing her six children and washing their clothes. The younger ones were running around in their underwear; the older ones were unaccounted for, but presumably were around the neighborhood. Mrs. H. had not been out of the house for several months; evidently her husband did the shopping. The apartment was filthy and it smelled. Mrs. H. was dressed in a bathrobe, although it was mid-afternoon. She seemed to have no plan or expectations with regard to her children; she did not know the names of their teachers and she did not seem to worry about their school work, although one child had been retained one year and another two years. Mrs. H. did seem to be somewhat concerned about her husband's lack of activity over the weekend—his continuous drinking and watching baseball on television. Apparently he and she never went out socially together nor did the family ever go anywhere as a unit.

If this family had a very high income—say, $50,000 a year—it would not be considered a "culture of poverty" case. Mrs. H. would hire maids to look after the small children, send the others to boarding schools, and spend her time at fashion shows while her husband drank and watched TV at his club. But with an income of only moderate size—say 100 percent above the poverty line—they would probably be about as badly off as they are now. They might be even worse off, for

Mrs. H. would be able to go to the dog races, leaving the children alone, and Mr. H. could devote more time to his bottle and TV set....

Welfare agencies, recognizing the difference between "internally" and "externally" caused poverty, have long been trying first by one means and then another to improve the characters or, as it is now put, to "bring about personal adjustment" of the poor. In the nineteenth century, the view was widely held that what the lower class individual needed was to be brought into a right relation with God or (the secular version of the same thing) with the respectable (that is, middle- and upper-class) elements of the community. The missionary who distributed tracts door to door in the slums was the first caseworker; his—more often, her—task was to minister to what today would be called "feelings of alienation."

> The stranger, coming on a stranger's errand, becomes a friend, discharging the offices and exerting the influence of a friend....

Secularized, this approach became the "friendly visitor" system under which "certain persons, under the direction of a central board, pledge themselves to take one or more families who need counsel, if not material help, on their visiting list, and maintain personal friendly relations with them." The system did not work; middle- and upper-class people might be "friendly," but they could not sympathize, let alone communicate, with the lower class. By the beginning of the twentieth century the friendly visitor had been replaced by the "expert." The idea now was that the authority of "the facts" would bring about desired changes of attitude, motive, and habit. As it happened, however, the lower class did not recognize the authority of the facts. The expert then became a supervisor, using his (or her) power to confer or withhold material benefits in order to force the poor to do the things that were supposed to lead to "rehabilitation" (that is, to a middle-class style of life). This method did not work either; the lower class could always find ways to defeat and exploit the system. They seldom changed their ways very much and they never changed them for long. Besides, there was really no body of expertise to tell caseworkers how to produce the changes desired. As one caseworker remarked recently in a book addressed to fellow social service professionals:

> Despite years of experience in providing public aid to poor families precious little is yet known about how to help truly inadequate parents make long term improvements in child care, personal maturity, social relations, or work stability.

Some people understood that if the individual's style of life was to be changed at all, it would be necessary to change that of the group that produced, motivated, and constrained him. Thus, the settlement house. As Robert A. Woods explained:

> The settlements are able to take neighborhoods in cities, and by patience bring back to them much of the healthy village life, so that the people shall again know and care for one another....

When it became clear that settlement houses would not change the culture of slum neighborhoods, the group approach was broadened into what is called "community action." In one type of community action ("community development"), a community organizer tries to persuade a neighborhood's in-formal leaders to support measures (for instance, measures for delinquency control) that he advances. In another form of it ("community organization"), the organizer tries to promote self-confidence, self-respect, and attachment to the group (and, hopefully, to normal society) among lower-class people. He attempts to do this by encouraging them in efforts at joint action, or by showing them how to conduct meetings, carry on discussions, pass resolutions, present requests to politicians, and the like. In still another form ("community mobilization"), the organizer endeavors to arouse the anger of lower-class persons against the local "power structure," to teach them the techniques of mass action—strikes, sit-ins, picketing, and so on—and to show them how they may capture power. The theory of community organization attributes the malaise of the poor to their lack of self-confidence (which is held to derive largely from their "inexperience"); community mobilization theory, by contrast, attributes it to their feelings of "powerlessness." According to this doctrine, the best cure for poverty is to give the poor power. But since power is not "given," it must be seized.

The success of the group approach has been no greater than that of the caseworker approach. Reviewing five years of effort on the part of various community action programs, Marris and Rein conclude:

> ... the reforms had not evolved any reliable solutions to the intractable problems with which they struggled. They had not discovered how in general to override the intransigent autonomy of public and private agencies, at any level of government; nor how to use the social sciences practically to formulate and evaluate policy; nor how, under the sponsorship of

government, to raise the power of the poor. Given the talent and money they had brought to bear, they had not even reopened very many opportunities.

If the war on poverty is judged by its ability "to generate major, meaningful and lasting social and economic reforms in conformity with the expressed wishes of poor people," writes Thomas Gladwin, "... it is extremely difficult to find even scattered evidence of success." ...

Although city agencies have sent community organizers by the score into slum neighborhoods, the lower-class poor cannot be organized. In East Harlem in 1948, five social workers were assigned to organize a five-block area and to initiate a program of social action based on housing, recreation, and other neighborhood needs. After three years of effort, the organizers had failed to attract a significant number of participants, and those they did attract were upwardly mobile persons who were unrepresentative of the neighborhood. In Boston a "total community" delinquency control project was found to have had "negligible impact," an outcome strikingly like that of the Cambridge-Somerville experiment—a "total caseworker" project—a decade earlier. Even community mobilization, despite the advantages of a rhetoric of hate and an emphasis on "action," failed to involve lower-class persons to a significant extent. Gangsters and leaders of youth gangs were co-opted on occasion, but they did not suffer from feelings of powerlessness and were not representative of the class for which mobilization was to provide therapy. No matter how hard they have tried to appeal to people at the very bottom of the scale, community organizers have rarely succeeded. Where they have appeared

to succeed, as, for example, in the National Welfare Rights Organization, it has been by recruiting people who had some of the *outward* attributes of the lower class—poverty, for example—but whose outlook and values were not lower class; the lower-class person (as defined here) is incapable of being organized. Although it tried strenuously to avoid it, what the Mobilization for Youth described as the general experience proved to be its own experience as well:

Most efforts to organize lower-class people attract individuals on their way up the social-class ladder. Persons who are relatively responsible about participation, articulate and successful at managing organizational "forms" are identified as lower-class leaders, rather than individuals who actually reflect the values of the lower-class groups. Ordinarily the slum's network of informal group associations is not reached.

NO

William Ryan

BLAMING THE VICTIM

Twenty years ago, Zero Mostel used to do a sketch in which he impersonated a Dixiecrat Senator conducting an investigation of the origins of World War II. At the climax of the sketch, the Senator boomed out, in an excruciating mixture of triumph and suspicion, "What was Pearl Harbor *doing* in the Pacific?" This is an extreme example of Blaming the Victim.

Twenty years ago, we could laugh at Zero Mostel's caricature. In recent years, however, the same process has been going on every day in the arena of social problems, public health, anti-poverty programs, and social welfare. A philosopher might analyze this process and prove that, technically, it is comic. But it is hardly ever funny.

Consider some victims. One is the miseducated child in the slum school. He is blamed for his own miseducation. He is said to contain within himself the causes of his inability to read and write well. The shorthand phrase is "cultural deprivation," which, to those in the know, conveys what they allege to be inside information: that the poor child carries a scanty pack of cultural baggage as he enters school. He doesn't know about books and magazines and newspapers, they say. (No books in the home: the mother fails to subscribe to *Reader's Digest*.) They say that if he talks at all—an unlikely event since slum parents don't talk to their children—he certainly doesn't talk correctly. Lower-class dialect spoken here, or even—God forbid!—Southern Negro. *(Ici on parle nigra.)* If you can manage to get him to sit in a chair, they say, he squirms and looks out the window. (Impulse-ridden, these kids, motoric rather than verbal.) In a word he is "disadvantaged" and "socially deprived," they say, and this, of course, accounts for his failure (*his* failure, they say) to learn much in school.

Note the similarity to the logic of Zero Mostel's Dixiecrat Senator. What is the culturally deprived child *doing* in the school? What is wrong with the victim? In pursuing this logic, no one remembers to ask questions about the collapsing buildings and torn textbooks, the frightened, insensitive teachers, the six additional desks in the room, the blustering, frightened principals, the relentless segregation, the callous administrator, the irrelevant curriculum, the bigoted or cowardly members of the school board, the insulting history book, the stingy taxpayers, the fairy-tale readers, or the self-serving faculty of the local teachers' college. We are encouraged to confine our attention to the child and to dwell on all his alleged defects. Cultural deprivation becomes an omnibus explanation for the educational disaster area known as the inner-city school. This is Blaming the Victim.

Pointing to the supposedly deviant Negro family as the "fundamental weakness of the Negro community" is another way to blame the victim. Like "cultural deprivation," "Negro family" has become a shorthand phrase with stereotyped connotations of matriarchy, fatherlessness, and pervasive illegitimacy. Growing up in the "crumbling" Negro family is supposed to account for most of the racial evils in America. Insiders have the word, of course, and know that this phrase is supposed to evoke images of growing up with a long-absent or never-present father (replaced from time to time perhaps by a series of transient lovers) and with bossy women ruling the roost, so that the children are irreparably damaged. This refers particularly to the poor, bewildered male children, whose psyches are fatally wounded and who are never, alas, to learn the trick of becoming upright, downright, forthright all-American boys. Is it any wonder the Negroes cannot achieve equality? From such families! And, again, by focusing our attention on the Negro family as the apparent *cause* of racial inequality, our eye is diverted. Racism, discrimination, segregation, and the powerlessness of the ghetto are subtly, but thoroughly, downgraded in importance.

The generic process of Blaming the Victim is applied to almost every American problem. The miserable health care of the poor is explained away on the grounds that the victim has poor motivation and lacks health information. The problems of slum housing are traced to the characteristics of tenants who are labeled as "Southern rural migrants" not yet "acculturated" to life in the big city. The "multiproblem" poor, it is claimed, suffer the psychological effects of impoverishment, the "culture of poverty," and the deviant value system of the lower classes; consequently, though unwittingly, they cause their own troubles. From such a viewpoint, the obvious fact that poverty is primarily an absence of money is easily overlooked or set aside.

The growing number of families receiving welfare are fallaciously linked together with the increased number of illegitimate children as twin results of promiscuity and sexual abandon among members of the lower orders. Every important social problem—crime, mental illness, civil disorder, unemployment—has been analyzed within the framework of the victim-blaming ideology. In the following pages, I shall present in detail nine examples that relate to social problems and human services in urban areas.

It would be possible for me to venture into other areas—one finds a perfect example in literature about the underdeveloped countries of the Third World, in which the lack of prosperity and technological progress is attributed to some aspect of the national character of the people, such as lack of "achievement motivation"—but I plan to stay within the confines of my own personal and professional experience, which is, generally, with racial injustice, social welfare, and human services in the city.

I have been listening to the victim-blamers and pondering their thought processes for a number of years. That process is often very subtle. Victim-blaming is cloaked in kindness and concern, and bears all the trappings and statistical furbelows of scientism; it is obscured by a perfumed haze of humanitarianism. In observing the process of Blaming the Victim, one tends to be confused and disoriented because those who practice this art display a deep concern for the victims that is quite genuine. In this way, the new ideology is very different from the open prejudice and reactionary tactics of the old days. Its adherents include sympathetic social scientists with social consciences in good working order, and liberal politicians with a genuine commitment to reform. They are very careful to dissociate themselves from vulgar Calvinism or crude racism; they indignantly condemn any notions of innate wickedness or genetic defect. "The Negro is *not born* inferior," they shout apoplectically. "Force of circumstance," they explain in reasonable tones, "has *made* him inferior." And they dismiss with self-righteous contempt any claims that the poor man in America is plainly unworthy or shiftless or enamored of idleness. No, they say, he is "caught in the cycle of poverty." He is trained to be poor by his culture and his family life, endowed by his environment (perhaps by his ignorant mother's outdated style of toilet training) with those unfortunately unpleasant characteristics that make him ineligible for a passport into the affluent society.

Blaming the Victim is, of course, quite different from old-fashioned conservative ideologies. The latter simply dismissed victims as inferior, genetically defective, or morally unfit; the emphasis is on the intrinsic, even hereditary, defect. The former shifts its emphasis to the environmental causation. The old-fashioned conservative could hold firmly to the belief that the oppressed and the victimized were born that way—that way being defective or inadequate in character or ability. The new ideology attributes defect and inadequacy to the malignant nature of poverty, injustice, slum life, and racial difficulties. The stigma that marks the victim and accounts for his victimization is an acquired stigma, a stigma of social, rather than genetic, origin. But the stigma, the defect, the fatal difference—though derived in the past from environmental forces—is still located *within* the victim, inside his skin. With such an elegant formulation, the humanitarian can have it both ways. He can, all at the same time, concentrate his charitable interest on the defects of the victim, condemn the vague social and environmental stresses that produced the defect (some time ago), and ignore the continuing effect of victimizing social forces (right now). It is a brilliant ideology for justifying a perverse form of social action designed to change, not society, as one might expect, but rather society's victim.

As a result, there is a terrifying sameness in the programs that arise from this kind of analysis. In education, we have programs of "compensatory education" to build up the skills and attitudes of the ghetto child, rather than structural changes in the schools. In race relations, we have social engineers who think up ways of "strengthening" the Negro family, rather than methods of eradicating racism. In health care, we develop new programs to provide health information (to correct the supposed ignorance of the poor) and to reach out and discover cases of untreated illness and disability (to compensate for their supposed unwillingness to seek treatment). Meanwhile, the gross inequities of our medical care delivery systems are left completely unchanged. As we might expect, the logical outcome of analyzing social problems in terms of the deficiencies of the victim is the development of programs aimed at correcting those deficiencies. The formula for action becomes extraordinarily simple: change the victim.

All of this happens so smoothly that it seems downright rational. First, identify a social problem. Second, study those affected by the problem and discover in what ways they are different from the rest of us as a consequence of deprivation and injustice. Third, define the differences as the cause of the social problem itself. Finally, of course, assign a government bureaucrat to invent a humanitarian action program to correct the differences.

Now no one in his right mind would quarrel with the assertion that social problems are present in abundance and are readily identifiable. God knows it is true that when hundreds of thousands of poor children drop out of school—or even graduate from school—they are barely literate. After spending some ten thousand hours in the company of professional educators, these children appear to have learned very little. The fact of failure in their education is undisputed. And the racial situation in America is usually acknowledged to be a number one item on the nation's agenda. Despite years of marches, commissions, judicial decisions, and endless legislative remedies, we are confronted with unchanging or even widening racial differences in achievement. In addition, despite our assertions that Americans get the best health care in the world, the poor stubbornly remain unhealthy. They lose more work because of illness, have more carious teeth, lose more babies as a result of both miscarriage and infant death,

and die considerably younger than the well-to-do.

The problems are there, and there in great quantities. They make us uneasy. Added together, these disturbing signs reflect inequality and a puzzlingly high level of unalleviated distress in America totally inconsistent with our proclaimed ideals and our enormous wealth. This thread—this rope—of inconsistency stands out so visibly in the fabric of American life, that it is jarring to the eye. And this must be explained, to the satisfaction of our conscience as well as our patriotism. Blaming the Victim is an ideal, almost painless, evasion.

The second step in applying this explanation is to look sympathetically at those who "have" the problem in question, to separate them out and define them in some way as a special group, a group that is *different* from the population in general. This is a crucial and essential step in the process, for that difference is in itself hampering and maladaptive. The Different Ones are seen as less competent, less skilled, less knowing—in short, less human....

The ultimate effect is always to distract attention from the basic causes and to leave the primary social injustice untouched. And, most telling, the proposed remedy for the problem is, of course, to work on the victim himself. Prescriptions for cure, [are] invariably conceived to revamp and revise the victim, never to change the surrounding circumstances. They want to change his attitudes, alter his values, fill up his cultural deficits, energize his apathetic soul, cure his character defects, train him and polish him and woo him from his savage ways.

... The old, reactionary exceptionalistic formulations are replaced by new progressive, humanitarian exceptionalistic formulations. In education, the out-moded and unacceptable concept of racial or class differences in basic inherited intellectual ability simply gives way to the new notion of cultural deprivation: there is very little functional difference between these two ideas. In taking a look at the phenomenon of poverty, the old concept of unfitness or idleness or laziness is replaced by the newfangled theory of the culture of poverty. In race relations, plain Negro inferiority—which was good enough for old-fashioned conservatives—is pushed aside by fancy conceits about the crumbling Negro family. With regard to illegitimacy, we are not so crass as to concern ourselves with immorality and vice, as in the old days; we settle benignly on the explanation of the "lower-class pattern of sexual behavior," which no one condemns as evil, but which is, in fact, simply a variation of the old explanatory idea. Mental illness is no longer defined as the result of hereditary taint or congenital character flaw; now we have new causal hypotheses regarding the ego-damaging emotional experiences that are supposed to be the inevitable consequence of the deplorable child-rearing practices of the poor.

In each case, of course, we are persuaded to ignore the obvious: the continued blatant discrimination against the Negro, the gross deprivation of contraceptive and adoption services to the poor, the heavy stresses endemic in the life of the poor. And almost all our make-believe liberal programs aimed at correcting our urban problems are off target; they are designed either to change the poor man or to cool him out.…

But, in any case, are the poor really all that different from the middle class? Take a common type of study, showing that ninety-one percent of the upper class, compared to only sixty-eight percent of the poor, prefer college education for their children. What does that tell us about the difference in values between classes?

First, if almost seventy percent of the poor want their children to go to college, it doesn't make much sense to say that the poor, as a group, do not value education. Only a minority of them—somewhat less than one-third—fail to express a *wish* that their children attend college. A smaller minority—one in ten—of the middle class give similar responses. One might well wonder why this small group of the better-off citizens of our achieving society reject higher education. They have the money; many of them have the direct experience of education; and most of them are aware of the monetary value of a college degree. I would suggest that the thirty percent of the poor who are unwilling to express a wish that their children go to college are easier to understand. They know the barriers—financial, social, and for black parents, racial—that make it very difficult for the children of the poor to get a college education. That seven out of ten of them nevertheless persist in a desire to see their children in a cap and gown is, in a very real sense, remarkable. Most important, if we are concerned with cultural or subcultural differences, it seems highly illogical to emphasize the values of a small minority of one group and then to attribute these values to the whole group. I simply cannot accept the evidence. If seventy percent of a group values education, then it is completely illogical to say that the group as a whole does *not* value education.

A useful formulation is to be found in Hyman Rodman's conception of the "lower class value stretch" which, to give a highly oversimplified version, proposes that members of the lower class *share* the dominant value system but *stretch* it to include as much as possible of the variations that circumstances force upon them. Rodman says:

Lower class persons in close interaction with each other and faced with similar problems do not long remain in a state of mutual ignorance. They do not maintain a strong commitment to middle class values that they cannot attain, and they do not continue to respond to others in a rewarding or punishing way simply on the basis of whether these others are living up to the middle class values. A change takes place. They come to tolerate and eventually to evaluate favorably certain deviations from the middle class values. In this way they need not be continually frustrated by their failure to live up to unattainable values. The resultant is a stretched value system with a low degree of commitment to all the values within the range, including the dominant, middle class values.

In Rodman's terms, then, differences in range of values and commitments to specific elements within that range occur primarily as an *adaptive* rather than as a *cultural* response....

The most recent, and in many ways the best information on [the related issue of child rearing] comes to us from the Hylan Lewis child-rearing studies, which I have mentioned before. Lewis has demonstrated (finally, one hopes) that there really *is* no "lower class child-rearing pattern." There are a number of such patterns—ranging from strict and overcontrolled parenting, to permissiveness, to down-right neglect—just as in Lewis' sample there are a variety of different kinds of families—ranging from those with rigid, old-fashioned standards of hard work, thrift, morality and obsessive cleanliness, to the disorganized and disturbed families that he calls the "clinical poor." Lewis says:

... it appears as a broad spectrum of pragmatic adjustments to external and internal stresses and deprivation.... Many low income families appear here as, in fact, the frustrated victims of what are thought of as middle class values, behavior and aspirations.

We return, finally, to where we began: the concept of Deferred Need Gratification. The simple idea that lower class folk have, as a character trait, a built-in deficiency in ability to delay need gratification has been explored, analyzed and more or less blown apart by Miller, Riessman, and Seagull. They point out that the supposed commitment of the middle classes to the virtues of thrift and hard work, to the practices of planning and saving for every painfully-chosen expenditure is, at this point in time, at best a surviving myth reflecting past conditions of dubious prevalence. The middle classes of today are clearly consumption-minded and debt-addicted. So the comparison group against which the poor are judged exists largely as a theoretical category with a theoretical behavior pattern. They go on to raise critical questions, similar to those I have raised earlier in this chapter. For example, on the question of what one would do with a two thousand dollar windfall, there was a difference between class groups of only five percent—about seventy percent of the middle class said they would save most of it, compared with about sixty-five percent of the lower class. On the basis of this small difference (which was statistically, but not practically, significant), the researchers, you will remember, had concluded that working-class people had less ability to defer need gratification. This conclusion may reflect elegant research methodology, but it fails the test of common sense....

As for the idea that the poor share a culture in the sense that they subscribe to and follow a particular, deviant prescription for living—a poor man's blueprint for choosing and decision-making which accounts for the way he lives—this does not deserve much comment. Every study—with the exception of the egregious productions of Walter Miller—shows that, at the very least, overwhelming numbers of the poor give allegiance to the values and principles of the dominant American culture.

A related point—often the most overlooked point in any discussion of the culture of poverty—is that there is not, to my knowledge, *any evidence whatever* that the poor perceive their way of life as good and preferable to that of other ways of life. To make such an assertion is to talk pure nonsense....

Perhaps the most fundamental question to ask of those who are enamored of the idea that the poor have one culture and the rich another is to ask, simply, "So what?" Suppose the mythical oil millionaire behaves in an unrefined "lower class" manner, for example. What difference does that make as long as he owns the oil wells? Is the power of the Chairman of the Ways and Means Committee in the state legislature diminished or enhanced in any way by his taste in clothing or music? And suppose every single poor family in America set as its long-range goal that its sons and daughters would get a Ph.D.—who would pay the tuition?

The effect of tastes, child-rearing practices, speech patterns, reading habits, and other cultural factors is relatively small in comparison to the effect of wealth and influence. What I am trying to suggest is that the inclusion in the analytic process of the elements of social stratification that are usually omitted—particularly economic class and power—would produce more significant insights into the circumstances of the poor and the pressures and deprivations with which they live. The simplest—and at the same time, the most significant—proposition in understanding poverty is that it is caused by lack of money. The overwhelming majority of the poor are poor because they have, first: insufficient income; and second: no access to methods of increasing that income—that is, no power. They are too young, too old, too sick; they are bound to the task of caring for small children, or they are simply discriminated against. The facts are clear, and the solution seems rather obvious—raise their income and let their "culture," whatever it might be, take care of itself.

The need to avoid facing this obvious solution—which is very uncomfortable since it requires some substantial changes and redistribution of income—provides the motivation for developing the stabilizing ideology of the culture of poverty which acts to sustain the *status quo* and delay change. The function of the ideology of lower class culture, then, is plainly to maintain inequality in American life.

The millionaire, freshly risen from the lower class, whose crude tongue and appalling table manners betray the newness of his affluence, is a staple of American literature and folklore. He comes on stage over and over, and we have been taught exactly what to expect with each entrance. He will walk into the parlor in his undershirt, gulp tea from a saucer, spit into the Limoges flower pot, and, when finally invited to the society garden party, disgrace his wife by saying "bullshit" to the president of the bank. When I was growing up, we had daily lessons in this legend from Jiggs and Maggie in the comic strip.

This discrepancy between *class* and *status*, between possession of economic resources and life style, has been a source of ready humour and guaranteed fascination for generations. The centrality of this mythical strain in American thought is reflected again in the strange and perverse ideas emerging from the mouths of many professional Pauper Watchers and Victim Blamers.

In real life, of course, Jiggs' character and behavior would never remain so constant and unchanging over the decades. The strain between wealth and style is one that usually tends to be quickly resolved. Within a fairly short time, Jiggs would be coming into the parlor first with a shirt, then with a tie on, and, finally, in one of his many custom-made suits. He would soon be drinking tea from a Limoges cup, and for a time he would spit in an antique cuspidor, until he learned not to spit at all. At the garden party, he would confine his mention of animal feces to a discussion of the best fertilizer for the rhododendron. In real life, style tends to follow close on money, and money tends to be magnetized and attracted to power. Those who try to persuade us that the process can be reversed, that a change in style of life can lead backward to increased wealth and greater power, are preaching nonsense. To promise that improved table manners can produce a salary increase; that more elegant taste in clothes will lead to the acquisition of stock in IBM; that an expanded vocabulary will automatically generate an enlargement of community influence—these are pernicious as well as foolish. There is no record in history of any *group* having accomplished this wondrous task. (There may be a few clever individuals who have followed such artful routes to money and power, but they are relatively rare.) The whole idea is an illusion of fatuous social scientists and welfare bureaucrats blinded by the ideology I have painstakingly tried to dissect in the previous chapters.

POSTSCRIPT

Does "Lower-Class" Culture Perpetuate Poverty Among Urban Minorities?

The "why" of social inequality, many contend, remains at the heart of sociology. In addition to asking what functions inequality serves, sociologists also ask what are the inequality structures or forms in different societies? Traditionally, power is the most important variable. Wealth, income, and education, these, too, serve to distinguish various strata of society.

Banfield attributes the culture of poverty as "causing" and/or maintaining poverty. Ryan and many others counter that poverty causes the culture.

Both Ryan and Wilson are correct in pointing out that many poor minority members are able to achieve economic improvements. For instance, Blacks who are middle class now number approximately one-third or more compared to 20 percent in the 1960s. If this is so, then how can Banfield claim that the culture of poverty is impossible to break out of?

The initial statement of the thesis debated in this issue is "Culture of Poverty," by Oscar Lewis, in *Scientific American* (October 1966). For a very different, more traditionally sociological view of urban communities, see the classic study by Louis Wirth, *The Ghetto* (University of Chicago Press, 1928). For a recent updating of the issue and a series of analyses that generally challenge Banfield, see *The Ghetto Underclass*, edited by W. J. Wilson (Sage, 1993). For a view distinct from both Ryan and Banfield, see Cornel West's *Race Matters* (Beacon Press, 1993). Another contrasting perspective is L.E. Lynn, Jr., et al., *Inner-City Poverty in the United States* (National Academy Press, 1993).

A new category of poor not systematically considered by Ryan and Banfield is *The Visible Poor: Homelessness in the United States*, by Joel Blau (Oxford University Press, 1993). A recent study of how little help welfare programs often are and how resourceful those living in the "culture of poverty" have to be is Kathryn Edin's "Surviving the Welfare System," in *Social Problems* (November 1991). A study derived from the Black poor in Britain that also challenges Banfield's thesis and partially concurs with Ryan is J. Solomos, *Black Youth, Racism, and the State: The Politics of Ideology and Policy* (Cambridge University Press, 1988). Another contrasting study is Richard Williams's *Hierarchical Structures and Social Value: The Creation of Black and Irish Identities in the United States* (Cambridge University Press, 1990). An edited book by J. Jackson, *Life in Black America*, provides different views (Sage, 1990). For a good review of books that examine the urban experiences of racial minorities, see V. J. Williams, Jr., in the *Journal of Ethnic History* (Fall 1991).

ISSUE 12

Is Affirmative Action Reverse Discrimination?

YES: Shelby Steele, from *The Content of Our Character* (St. Martin's Press, 1990)

NO: Herman Schwartz, from "In Defense of Affirmative Action," *Dissent* (Fall 1984)

ISSUE SUMMARY

YES: Associate professor of English Shelby Steele contends that instead of solving racial inequality problems, affirmative action mandates have generated racial discrimination in reverse.

NO: Professor of law Herman Schwartz argues that we must somehow undo the cruel consequences of racism that still plague our society and its victims.

Among the many intriguing ironies, paradoxes, and contradictions of human behavior, including those social relations having to do with racial and ethnic minorities, the debate over affirmative action is one of the most intellectually fascinating and emotional.

Most Americans like to view themselves as fair. Publicly, recent polls show, most Americans favor equal opportunities for all people. However, how to accomplish fairness and equal opportunity is cause for controversy.

The civil rights movement of the 1960s and 1970s, along with passage of civil rights legislation at the state and federal level, which prohibited discrimination, made formal acts of discrimination illegal and were designed to promote equality in jobs, education, and housing.

Affirmative action programs, i.e., taking steps to ensure the hiring of minority group members according to predetermined numerical goals, had their start in the defense industries receiving federal funds during World War II. Black civil rights leaders of the time campaigned to end discrimination in employment areas where jobs were being created with federal monies. However, over time, these programs have become controversial and the debate has grown ever more complex.

Some ethnic minorities have long been opposed to affirmative action, because for them pre-set numbers for inclusion have always meant "quotas" in the sense of limitations or restrictions. Indeed, as incredible as it may seem, Harvard University, as well as many other colleges and universities, had strict quotas until the 1930s on the number of Jewish students permitted to enroll. Other major universities had unofficial quotas on Asians, Hispanics, women, Catholics, etc. Blacks were generally simply barred. There was not even a pretense at "fairness."

For many, then, including some Black scholars and traditionally liberal-minded citizens, mandated percentages of any social category has been a negative use of law and ineffective policy. And some argue that it has not been beneficial in promoting equality and fairness in schools, colleges, and neighborhoods, or in occupations and careers.

On the other hand, proponents of affirmative action, such as Professor Herman Schwartz, are likely to throw up their hands and ask in disbelief, "Are you kidding?" To begin with, this point of view argues, there are many forms of affirmative action. It does not have to be a quota system. Some variants or applications reflect rationality and correct application of the law. At other times, employers, possibly confused by the rapid changes in employment practices, execute the new hiring guidelines in an unworkable fashion. Others deliberately sabotage affirmative action guidelines to confuse their employees and/or because they strongly oppose having to hire any minority group members.

Minorities have been discriminated against, oppressed, and exploited. Do affirmative action programs level the playing field? Or are there negative consequences that promote reverse discrimination? As you read these two important articles, note all the arguments that are presented. Who makes the better case?

YES

Shelby Steele

AFFIRMATIVE ACTION:
THE PRICE OF PREFERENCE

In a few short years, when my two children will be applying to college, the affirmative action policies by which most universities offer black students some form of preferential treatment will present me with a dilemma. I am a middle-class black, a college professor, far from wealthy, but also well-removed from the kind of deprivation that would qualify my children for the label "disadvantaged." Both of them have endured racial insensitivity from whites. They have been called names, have suffered slights, and have experienced firsthand the peculiar malevolence that racism brings out in people. Yet, they have never experienced racial discrimination, have never been stopped by their race on any path they have chosen to follow. Still, their society now tells them that if they will only designate themselves as black on their college applications, they will likely do better in the college lottery than if they conceal this fact. I think there is something of a Faustian bargain [sacrificing values for material gain] in this.

Of course, many blacks and a considerable number of whites would say that I was sanctimoniously making affirmative action into a test of character. They would say that this small preference is the meagerest recompense for centuries of unrelieved oppression. And to these arguments other very obvious facts must be added. In America, many marginally competent or flatly incompetent whites are hired everyday—some because their white skin suits the conscious or unconscious racial preference of their employer. The white children of alumni are often grandfathered into elite universities in what can only be seen as a residual benefit of historic white privilege. Worse, white incompetence is always an individual matter, while for blacks it is often confirmation of ugly stereotypes. The Peter Principle [which states that in a hierarchy, every employee tends to rise to the level of his or her incompetence] was not conceived with only blacks in mind. Given that unfairness cuts both ways, doesn't it only balance the scales of history that my children now receive a slight preference over whites? Doesn't this repay, in a small way, the systematic denial under which their grandfather lived out his days?

From Shelby Steele, *The Content of Our Character* (St. Martin's Press, 1990). Copyright © 1990 by Shelby Steele. Reprinted by permission of St. Martin's Press, Inc., New York, NY.

So, in theory, affirmative action certainly has all the moral symmetry that fairness requires—the injustice of historical and even contemporary white advantage is offset with black advantage; preference replaces prejudice, inclusion answers exclusion. It is reformist and corrective, even repentant and redemptive. And I would never sneer at these good intentions. Born in the late forties in Chicago, I started my education (a charitable term in this case) in a segregated school and suffered all the indignities that come to blacks in a segregated society. My father, born in the South, only made it to the third grade before the white man's fields took permanent priority over his formal education. And though he educated himself into an advanced reader with an almost professorial authority, he could only drive a truck for a living and never earned more than ninety dollars a week in his entire life. So yes, it is crucial to my sense of citizenship, to my ability to identify with the spirit and the interests of America, to know that this country, however imperfectly, recognizes its past sins and wishes to correct them.

Yet good intentions, because of the opportunity for innocence they offer us, are very seductive and can blind us to the effects they generate when implemented. In our society, affirmative action is, among other things, a testament to white goodwill and to black power, and in the midst of these heavy investments, its effects can be hard to see. But after twenty years of implementation, I think affirmative action has shown itself to be more bad than good and that blacks—whom I will focus on in this essay—now stand to lose more from it than they gain.

In talking with affirmative action administrators and with blacks and whites in general, it is clear that supporters of affirmative action focus on its good intentions while detractors emphasize its negative effects. Proponents talk about "diversity." and "pluralism"; opponents speak of "reverse discrimination," the unfairness of quotas and set-asides. It was virtually impossible to find people outside either camp. The closest I came was a white male manager at a large computer company who said, "I think it amounts to reverse discrimination, but I'll put up with a little of that for a little more diversity." I'll live with a little of the effect to gain a little of the intention, he seemed to be saying. But this only makes him a half-hearted supporter of affirmative action. I think many people who don't really like affirmative action support it to one degree or another anyway.

I believe they do this because of what happened to white and black Americans in the crucible of the sixties when whites were confronted with their racial guilt and blacks tasted their first real power. In this stormy time white absolution and black power coalesced into virtual mandates for society. Affirmative action became a meeting ground for these mandates in the law, and in the late sixties and early seventies it underwent a remarkable escalation of its mission from simple anti-discrimination enforcement to social engineering by means of quotas, goals, timetables, set-asides and other forms of preferential treatment.

Legally, this was achieved through a series of executive orders and EEOC [Equal Employment Opportunity Commission] guidelines that allowed racial imbalances in the workplace to stand as proof of racial discrimination. Once it could be assumed that discrimination explained racial imbalances, it became easy to justify group remedies to presumed discrimination, rather than the normal case-by-case redress for proven discrimination. Preferential treatment through quotas, goals, and so on is designed to correct imbalances based on the assumption that they always indicate discrimination. This expansion of what constitutes discrimination allowed affirmative action to escalate into the business of social engineering in the name of anti-discrimination, to push society toward statistically proportionate racial representation, without any obligation of proving actual discrimination.

What accounted for this shift, I believe, was the white mandate to achieve a new racial innocence and the black mandate to gain power. Even though blacks had made great advances during the sixties without quotas, these mandates, which came to a head in the very late sixties, could no longer be satisfied by anything less than racial preferences. I don't think these mandates in themselves were wrong, since whites clearly needed to do better by blacks and blacks needed more real power in society. But, as they came together in affirmative action, their effect was to distort our understanding of racial discrimination in a way that allowed us to offer the remediation of preference on the basis of mere color rather than actual injury. By making black the color of preference, these mandates have reburdened society with the very marriage of color and preference (in reverse) that we set out to eradicate. The old sin is reaffirmed in a new guise.

But the essential problem with this form of affirmative action is the way it leaps over the hard business of developing a formerly oppressed people to the point where they can achieve proportionate representation on their own (given equal opportunity) and goes straight for the proportionate representation. This may satisfy some whites of their innocence and some blacks of their power, but it does very little to truly uplift blacks.

A white female affirmative action officer at an Ivy League university told me what many supporters of affirmative action now say: "We're after diversity. We ideally want a student body where racial and ethnic groups are represented according to their proportion in society." When affirmative action escalated into social engineering, diversity became a golden word. It grants whites an egalitarian fairness (innocence) and blacks an entitlement to proportionate representation (power). *Diversity* is a term that applies democratic principles to races and cultures rather than to citizens, despite the fact that there is nothing to indicate that real diversity is the same thing as proportionate representation. Too often the result of this on campuses (for example) has been a democracy of colors rather than of people, an artificial diversity that gives the appearance of an educational parity between black and white students that has not yet been achieved in reality. Here again, racial preferences allow society to leapfrog over the difficult problem of developing blacks to parity with whites and into a cosmetic diversity that covers the blemish of disparity—a full six years after admission, only about 26 percent of black students graduate from college.

Racial representation is not the same thing as racial development, yet affirmative action fosters a confusion of these very different needs. Representation can be manufactured; development is always hard-earned. However, it is the music of innocence and power that we hear in affirmative action that causes us to cling to it and to its distracting emphasis on representation. The fact is that after twenty years of racial preferences, the gap between white and black median income is greater than it was in the seventies. None of this is to say that blacks don't need policies that ensure our right to equal opportunity, but what we need more is the development that will let us take advantage of society's efforts to include us.

I think that one of the most troubling effects of racial preferences for blacks is a kind of demoralization, or put another way, an enlargement of self-doubt. Under affirmative action the quality that earns us preferential treatment is an implied inferiority. However this inferiority is explained—and it is easily enough explained by the myriad deprivations that grew out of our oppression—it is still inferiority. There are explanations, and then there is the fact. And the fact must be borne by the individual as a condition apart from the explanation, apart even from the fact that others like himself also bear this condition. In integrated situations where blacks must compete with whites who may be better prepared, these explanations may quickly wear thin and expose the individual to racial as well as personal self-doubt.

All of this is compounded by the cultural myth of black inferiority that blacks have always lived with. What this means in practical terms is that when blacks deliver themselves into integrated situations, they encounter a nasty little reflex in whites, a mindless, atavistic reflex that responds to the color black with alarm. Attributions may follow this alarm if the white cares to indulge them, and if they do, they will most likely be negative—one such attribution is intellectual ineptness. I think this reflex and the attributions that may follow it embarrass most whites today, therefore,

it is usually quickly repressed. Nevertheless, on an equally atavistic level, the black will be aware of the reflex his color triggers and will feel a stab of horror at seeing himself reflected in this way. He, too, will do a quick repression, but a lifetime of such stabbings is what constitutes his inner realm of racial doubt.

The effects of this may be a subject for another essay. The point here is that the implication of inferiority that racial preferences engender in both the white and black mind expands rather than contracts this doubt. Even when the black sees no implication of inferiority in racial preferences, he knows that whites do, so that—consciously or unconsciously—the result is virtually the same. The effect of preferential treatment—the lowering of normal standards to increase black representation—puts blacks at war with an expanded realm of debilitating doubt, so that the doubt itself becomes an unrecognized preoccupation that undermines their ability to perform, especially in integrated situations. On largely white campuses, blacks are five times more likely to drop out than whites. Preferential treatment, no matter how it is justified in the light of day, subjects blacks to a midnight of self-doubt, and so often transforms their advantage into a revolving door.

Another liability of affirmative action comes from the fact that it indirectly encourages blacks to exploit their own past victimization as a source of power and privilege. Victimization, like implied inferiority, is what justifies preference, so that to receive the benefits of preferential treatment one must, to some extent, become invested in the view of one's self as a victim. In this way, affirmative action nurtures a victim-focused identity in blacks. The obvious irony here is that we become inadvertently invested in the very condition we are trying to overcome. Racial preferences send us the message that there is more power in our past suffering than our present achievements— none of which could bring us a *preference* over others.

When power itself grows out of suffering, then blacks are encouraged to expand the boundaries of what qualifies as racial oppression, a situation that can lead us to paint our victimization in vivid colors, even as we receive the benefits of preference. The same corporations and institutions that give us preference are also seen as our oppressors. At Stanford University minority students—some of whom enjoy as much as $15,000 a year in financial aid—recently took over the president's office demanding, among other things, more financial aid. The power to be found in victimization, like any power, is intoxicating and can lend itself to the creation of a new class of super-victims who can feel the pea of victimization under twenty mattresses. Preferential treatment rewards us for being underdogs rather than for moving beyond that status—a misplacement of incentives that, along with its deepening of our doubt, is more a yoke than a spur.

But, I think, one of the worst prices that blacks pay for preference has to do with an illusion. I saw this illusion at work recently in the mother of a middle-class black student who was going off to his first semester of college. "They owe us this, so don't think for a minute that you don't belong there." This is the logic by which many blacks, and some whites, justify affirmative action—it is something "owed," a form of reparation. But this logic overlooks a much harder and less digestible reality, that it is impossible to repay blacks living today for the historic suffering of the race. If all blacks were given a million dollars tomorrow morning it would not amount to a dime on the dollar of three centuries of oppression, nor would it obviate the residues of that oppression that we still carry today. The concept of historic reparation grows out of man's need to impose a degree of justice on the world that simply does not exist. Suffering can be endured and overcome, it cannot be repaid. Blacks cannot be repaid for the injustice done to the race, but we can be corrupted by society's guilty gestures of repayment.

Affirmative action is such a gesture. It tells us that racial preferences can do for us what we cannot do for ourselves. The corruption here is in the hidden incentive *not* to do what we believe preferences will do. This is an incentive to be reliant on others just as we are struggling for self-reliance. And it keeps alive the illusion that we can find some deliverance in repayment. The hardest thing for any sufferer to accept is that his suffering excuses him from very little and never has enough currency to restore him. To think otherwise is to prolong the suffering....

The mandates of black power and white absolution out of which preferences emerged were not wrong in themselves. What was wrong was that both races focused more on the goals of these mandates than on the means of the goals. Blacks can have no real power without taking responsibility for their own educational and economic development. Whites can have no racial innocence without earning it by eradicating discrimination and helping the disadvantaged to develop. Because we ignored the means, the goals have not been reached, and the real work remains to be done.

NO

Herman Schwartz

IN DEFENSE OF AFFIRMATIVE ACTION

The Reagan administration's assault on the rights of minorities and women has focused on the existing policy of affirmative action. This strategy may be shrewd politics but it is mean-spirited morally and insupportable legally. . . .

Affirmative action has been defined as "a public or private program designed to equalize hiring and admission opportunities for historically disadvantaged groups by taking into consideration those very characteristics which have been used to deny them equal treatment." The controversy swirls primarily around the use of numerical goals and timetables for hiring or promotion, for university admissions, and for other benefits. It is fueled by the powerful strain of individualism that runs through American history and belief.

It is a hard issue, about which reasonable people can differ. Insofar as affirmative action is designed to compensate the disadvantaged for past racism, sexism, and other discrimination, many understandably believe that today's society should not have to pay for their ancestors' sins. But somehow we must undo the cruel consequences of the racism and sexism that still plague us, both for the sake of the victims and to end the enormous human waste that costs society so much. Civil Rights Commission Chairman Pendleton has conceded that discrimination is not only still with us but is, as he put it, "rampant." As recently as January 1984, the dean of faculty at Amherst College wrote in the *New York Times:*

> In my contacts with a considerable range of academic institutions, I have become aware of pervasive residues of racism and sexism, even among those whose intentions and conscious beliefs are entirely nondiscriminatory. Indeed, I believe most of us are afflicted with such residues. Beyond the wrongs of the past are the wrongs of the present. Most discriminatory habits in academia are nonactionable; affirmative action goals are our only instrument for focusing sustained attention.

The plight of black America not only remains grave, but in many respects, it is getting worse. The black unemployment rate—21 percent in early 1983— is double that for whites and the gap continues to increase. For black 20- to 24-year-old males, the rate—an awful 30 percent—is almost triple that for whites; for black teenagers the rate approaches 50 percent. More than half of

From Herman Schwartz, "In Defense of Affirmative Action," *Dissent* (Fall 1984). Adapted from Herman Schwartz, "In Defense of Affirmative Action," in Leslie Dunbar, ed., *Minority Report* (Pantheon Books, 1984). Copyright © 1984 by Herman Schwartz. Reprinted by permission of Pantheon Books, a division of Random House, Inc.

all black children under three years of age live in homes below the poverty line. The gap between white and black family income, which prior to the '70s had narrowed a bit, has steadily edged wider, so that black-family income is now only 55 percent of that of whites. Only 3 percent of the nation's lawyers and doctors are black and only 4 percent of its managers, but over 50 percent of its maids and garbage collectors. Black life expectancy is about six years less than that of whites; the black infant mortality rate is nearly double.

Although the situation for women, of all races, is not as bad, the average earnings of women still, at most, are only two-thirds of those of their male counterparts. And the economic condition of black women, who now head 41 percent of the 6.4 million black families, is particularly bad; a recent Wellesley study found that black women are not only suffering in the labor market, but they receive substantially less public assistance and child support than white women. The economic condition of female household heads of any race is just as deplorable: 90 percent of the 4 million single-parent homes are headed by women, and more than half are below the poverty line. Bureau of Labor Statistics data reveal that in 1983 women actually earned *less* than two-thirds of their male counterparts' salaries, and black women earned only 84 percent of the white female incomes. In his 1984 State of the Union address, President Reagan claimed dramatic gains for women during the 1983 recovery. A *Washington Post* analysis the next day charitably described his claims as "overstated," noting that the Bureau of Labor Statistics reports (on which the president relied) showed that "there was no breakthrough.

The new jobs which the president cited included many in sales and office work, where women have always found work" and are paid little.

We must close these gaps so that we do not remain two nations, divided by race and gender. Although no one strategy can overcome the results of centuries of inequity, the use of goals and timetables in hiring and other benefit distribution programs has helped to make modest improvements. Studies in 1983 show for example, that from 1974 to 1980 minority employment with employers subject to federal affirmative action requirements rose 20 percent, almost twice the increase elsewhere. Employment of women by covered contractors rose 15 percent, but only 2 percent among others. The number of black police officers nationwide rose from 24,000 in 1970 to 43,500 in 1980; that kind of increase in Detroit produced a sharp decline in citizen hostility toward the police and a concomitant increase in police efficiency. There were also large jumps in minority and female employment among firefighters, and sheet metal and electrical workers.

Few other remedies work as well or as quickly. As the New York City Corporation Counsel told the Supreme Court in the *Fullilove* case about the construction industry (before Mayor Edward Koch decided that affirmative action was an "abomination"), "less drastic means of attempting to eradicate and remedy discrimination have been attempted repeatedly and continuously over the past decade and a half. They have all failed."

What, then, is the basis for the assault on affirmative action?

Apart from the obvious political expediency and ideological reflex of this administration's unvarying conclusion that the "haves" deserve government help and the "have-nots" don't, President Reagan and his allies present two related arguments: (1) hiring and other distributional decisions should be made solely on the basis of individual merit; (2) racial preferences are always evil and will take us back to *Plessy vs. Ferguson* and worse.

Quoting Dr. Martin Luther King Jr., Thurgood Marshall, and Roy Wilkins to support the claim that anything other than total race neutrality is "discriminatory," Assistant Attorney General Reynolds warns that race consciousness will "creat[e]... a racial spoils system in America," "stifle the creative spirit," erect artificial barriers, and divide the society, It is, he says, unconstitutional, unlawful, and immoral.

Midge Decter, writing in the *Wall Street Journal* a few years ago, sympathized with black and female beneficiaries of affirmative action programs for the "self-doubts" and loss of "self-regard" that she is sure they suffer, "spiritually speaking," for their "unearned special privileges."

Whenever we take race into account to hand out benefits, declares Linda Chavez, the new executive director of the Reagan Civil Rights Commission, we "discriminate," "destroy[ing] the sense of self."

The legal position was stated by Morris Abram, in explaining why the reshaped Commission hastened to do Reagan's bidding at its very first meeting by withdrawing prior Commission approval of goals and timetables:

> I do not need any further study of a principle that comes from the basic bedrock of the Constitution, in which the words say that every person in the land shall be entitled to the equal protection of the law. Equal means equal. Equal does not mean you have separate lists of blacks and whites for promotion, any more than you have separate accommodations for blacks and whites for eating. Nothing will ultimately divide a society more than this kind of preference and this kind of reverse discrimination.

In short, any form of race preference is equivalent to racism.

All of this represents a nadir of "Newspeak," all too appropriate for this administration in Orwell's year. For it has not only persistently fought to curtail minority and women's rights in many contexts, but it has used "separate lists" based on color, sex, and ethnic origin whenever politically or otherwise useful.

For example, does anyone believe that blacks like Civil Rights Commission Chairman Clarence Pendleton or Equal Employment Opportunities Commission Chairman Clarence Thomas were picked because of the color of their eyes? Or that Linda Chavez Gersten was made the new executive director for reasons having nothing to do with the fact that her maiden and professional surname is Chavez?

Perhaps the most prominent recent example of affirmative action is President Reagan's selection of Sandra Day O'Connor for the Supreme Court. Obviously, she was on a "separate list," because on any unitary list this obscure lower-court state judge, with no federal experience and no national reputation, would never have come to mind as a plausible choice for the highest court. (Incidentally, despite Ms. Decter's, Mr. Reynolds's, and Ms. Chavez's concern about the loss of "self-regard" suffered by beneficiaries of such preferences, "spiritually speaking" Justice O'Connor seems to be bearing her loss and spiritual pain quite easily.) And, like so many other beneficiaries of affirmative action given an opportunity that would otherwise be unavailable, she may perform well.

This is not to say that Reagan should not have chosen a woman. The appointment ended decades of shameful discrimination against women lawyers, discrimination still practiced by Reagan where the lower courts are concerned, since he has appointed very few female federal judges apart from Justice O'Connor—of 123 judgeships, Reagan has appointed no women to the courts of appeals and only 10 to the district benches. Of these judgeships, 86 percent went to white males. But the choice of Sandra O'Connor can be explained and justified only by the use of affirmative action and a separate list, not by some notion of neutral "individual merit" on a single list.

But is affirmative action constitutional and legal? Is its legal status, as Mr. Abram claims, so clear by virtue of principles drawn from the "basic bedrock of the Constitution" that no "further study" is necessary?

Yes, but not in the direction that he and this administration want to go. Affirmative action is indisputably constitutional. Not once but many times the Supreme Court has upheld the legality of considering race to remedy the wrongs of prejudice and discrimination. In 1977, for example, in *United Jewish Organizations vs. Carey*, the Supreme Court upheld a New York statute that "deliberately increased the nonwhite majorities in certain districts in order to enhance the opportunity for election of nonwhite representatives from those districts," even if it disadvantaged certain white Jewish communities. Three members of the Court including Justice Rehnquist explained that "no racial slur or stigma with respect to whites or any other race" was involved. In the *Bakke* case, five members of the Court upheld the constitutionality of a state's favorable consideration of race as a factor in university admissions, four members would have sustained a fixed 16 percent quota. In *United Steelworkers of America vs. Weber*, a 5:2 majority had that private employers could set up a quota system with separate lists for selecting trainees for a newly created craft program. In *Fullilove vs. Klutznick*, six members of the Court led by Chief Justice Burger unequivocally upheld a congressional set-aside of 10 percent for minority contractors on federal public works programs.

All members of the present Court except for Justice O'Connor have passed on affirmative action in one or more of these four cases, and each has upheld it at one time or another. Although the decisions have been based on varying grounds, with many differing opinions, the legal consequence is clear: affirmative action is lawful under both the Constitution and the statutes. To nail the point home, the Court in January 1984 not once but *twice* rejected the Justice Department's effort to get it to reconsider the issue where affirmative action hiring plans are adopted by governmental bodies (the Detroit Police Department and the New York State Corrections system), an issue left open in *Weber*, which had involved a private employer.

The same result obtains on the lower-court levels. Despite the persistent efforts of Reagan's Justice Department, all the courts of appeals have unanimously and repeatedly continued to sustain hiring quotas.

Nor is this anything new. Mr. Reynolds told an audience of prelaw students in January 1984 that the Fourteenth Amendment was intended to bar taking race into account for any purpose at all, and to ensure race neutrality. "That was why we fought the Civil War," he once told the *New York Times*. If so, he knows something that the members of the 1865–66 Congress, who adopted that amendment and fought the war, did not.

Less than a month after Congress approved the Fourteenth Amendment in 1866 the very same Congress enacted eight laws exclusively for the freedman, granting preferential benefits regarding land, education, banking facilities, hospitals, and more. No comparable programs existed or were established for whites. And that Congress knew what it was doing. The racial preferences involved in those programs were vigorously debated with a vocal minority led by President Andrew Johnson, who argued that the preferences wrongly discriminated against whites.

All these governmental actions reflect the obvious point that, as Justice Harry Blackmun has said, "in order to get beyond racism, we must first take account of race. There is no other way." Warren Burger, our very conservative chief justice, had made the point even clearer in the prophetic commentary on this administration's efforts to get the courts to ignore race when trying to remedy the ravages of past discrimination. Striking down in 1971 a North Carolina statute that barred considerations of race in school assignments, the chief justice said:

> The statute exploits an apparently neutral form to control school assignments' plans by directing that they be "color blind"; *that requirement, against the background of segregation, would render illusory the promise of Brown.* Just as the race of students must be considered in determining

whether a constitutional violation has occurred so also must race be considered in formulating a remedy... *[color blindness] would deprive school authorities of the one tool [race consideration] absolutely essential to fulfillment of their constitutional obligation to eliminate existing dual school systems....* [Emphasis added.]

But what of the morality of affirmative action? Does it amount to discrimination? Is it true, as Brian Weber's lawyer argued before the Supreme Court, that "you can't avoid discrimination by discriminating"? Will racially influenced hiring take us back to *Plessy vs. Ferguson*, as Pendleton and Reynolds assert? Were Martin Luther King, Jr., Thurgood Marshall, Roy Wilkins, and other black leaders against it?

Hardly. Indeed, it is hard to contain one's outrage at this perversion of what Dr. King, Justice Marshall, and others have said, at this manipulation of their often sorrow-laden eloquence, in order to deny a handful of jobs, school admissions, and other necessities for a decent life to a few disadvantaged blacks out of the many who still suffer from discrimination and would have few opportunities otherwise.

No one can honestly equate a remedial preference for a disadvantaged (and qualified) minority member with the brutality inflicted on blacks and other minorities by Jim Crow laws and practices. The preference may take away some benefits from some white men, but none of them is being beaten, lynched, denied the right to use a bathroom, a place to sleep or eat, being forced to take the dirtiest jobs or denied any work at all, forced to attend dilapidated and mind-killing schools, subjected to brutally unequal justice, or stigmatized as an inferior being.

Setting aside, after proof of discrimination, a few places a year for qualified minorities out of hundreds and perhaps thousands of employees, as in the Kaiser plant in the *Weber* case, or 16 medical-school places out of 100 as in *Bakke*, or 10 percent of federal public work contracts as in *Fullilove*, or even 50 percent of new hires for a few years as in some employment cases—this has nothing in common with the racism that was inflicted on helpless minorities, and it is a shameful insult to the memory of the tragic victims to lump together the two.

This administration claims that it does favor "affirmative action" of a kind: "employers should seek out and train minorities," Linda Chavez told a *Washington Post* interviewer. Apart from the preference involved in setting aside money for "seeking out" and "training" minorities (would this include preference in training programs like the *Weber* plan, whose legality Mr. Reynolds said was "wrongly decided"?), the proposed remedy is ineffectual—it just doesn't work. As the "old" Civil Rights Commission had reported, "By the end of the 1960s, enforcement officials realized that discernible indicators of progress were needed." Consequently, "goals and timetables" came into use....

There are indeed problems with affirmative action, but not of the kind or magnitude that Messrs. Reynolds and Abram claim: problems about whether these programs work, whether they impose heavy burdens, how these burdens can be lightened, and the like. They are not the basis for charges that affirmative action is equivalent to racism and for perverting the words of Dr. King and others.

"Equal is equal" proclaims Morris Abram, and that's certainly true. But it is just as true that equal treatment of unequals perpetuates and aggravates inequality. And gross inequality is what we still have today. As William Coleman, secretary of transportation in the Ford administration, put it,

For black Americans, racial equality is a tradition without a past. Perhaps, one day America will be color-blind. It takes an extraordinary ignorance of actual life in America today to believe that day has come.... [For blacks], there is another American "tradition"—one of slavery, segregation, bigotry, and injustice.

POSTSCRIPT

Is Affirmative Action Reverse Discrimination?

Affirmative action, like capital punishment, the decriminalization of drugs, and abortion, generates considerable heat. "The term conjures up the vilest of connotations," says Virginia governor L. Douglas Wilder. "It has become like a four-letter word" (*Business Week*, July 8, 1991).

"Quotas," "managing diversity," "minority outreach," "preferential treatment," "reverse discrimination," are all terms frequently used for affirmative action. They indicate the confusion and emotion surrounding the concept.

Yet Schwartz writes, "The plight of black America not only remains grave, but in many respects, it is getting worse." Recent reports from the U.S. Bureau of Labor Statistics show that Blacks still constitute only 7.4 percent of administrative positions as compared to 31.6 percent of whites in those positions. One third of all laborers remain Black.

Gertrude Ezorsky's *Racism and Justice: The Case for Affirmative Action* (Cornell University Press, 1993) has been praised by some leading scholars. However, perhaps reflecting the depth of the debate, others dismiss the work for what they see as its selective misuse of legal cases and for providing no new information on the issue. See, for instance, Barry R. Gross's review of Ezorsky in *Society* (January/February 1993).

For a concise overview of the problem with the various statistics used to show "successes" and "failures" of affirmative action, see *Business Week*'s cover story of July 8, 1991. For several articles that survey the pros and cons of affirmative action and analyze the impact of ideological attacks and defenses, see *Change: The Magazine of Higher Learning* (March/April 1993). A good justification can be found in the interesting and scholarly *The Afro-American Jeremiad: Appeals for Justice in America*, by D. Howard-Pitney (Temple University Press, 1990). A discussion that is helpful for background information is Hugh Davis Graham's *The Civil Rights Era* (Oxford University Press, 1990).

A somewhat technical discussion of the philosophical principles pertaining to justice and equality is T. Negel's *Equality and Partiality* (Oxford University Press, 1992). For a broad cross-cultural comparative analysis of preferential policies and what he concludes are their invariably disastrous consequences, see Thomas Sowell, *Preferential Policies: An International Perspective* (William Morrow and Company, 1990).

ISSUE 13

Are Hispanics Making Significant Progress?

YES: Linda Chavez, from *Out of the Barrio: Toward a New Politics of Hispanic Assimilation* (Basic Books, 1991)

NO: Robert Aponte, from "Urban Hispanic Poverty: Disaggregations and Explanations," *Social Problems* (November 1991)

ISSUE SUMMARY

YES: Scholar, business consultant, and former political candidate Linda Chavez takes great pride in documenting the accomplishments of Hispanics. They are making it in America, she says.

NO: Michigan State University social scientist Robert Aponte suggests that social scientists, following an agenda driven by government policy, have concentrated on Black poverty, which has resulted in a lack of accurate data and information on the economic status of Hispanics. Researchers have also tended to treat Hispanics as a whole. Aponte argues that disaggregation of demographic data shows that Hispanics are increasingly poor.

For years, almost all minority relations scholars reflected a social psychological approach to the study of ethnic and racial minority relations. That is, they were interested in explaining attitudes and values and life-styles of minorities. Sociologists were also interested in patterns of interaction, especially stages of assimilation of immigrants.

Scholarly interest in the dominant group was concentrated on dominant group attitudes toward, stereotypes of, and prejudices and discrimination against minorities. The distinction between prejudice (an attitude) and discrimination (behavior) was developed. Looking at institutional power arrangements, including systematic racism in the marketplace, government, education, religion, and so on, was largely nonexistent until the 1960s. Most scholarly works on racial and ethnic relations concentrated on the values, beliefs, and attitudes among the white majority that were inconsistent with American ideals of equality.

But since the 1960s, the race and ethnicity has come to be seen as not just the working out of individual attitudes and life-styles but as a fundamental dimension of social stratification. Minority conflict was reconceptualized as not simply a clash of cultures and myths but as conflict that results when one group attempts to obtain greater equality, and another group acts to maintain their advantageous position.

Understanding poverty came to be seen as important to understanding the effects of inequality, and data on poverty was needed as a basis for policy formulation. Unemployment rates, degree of residential segregation, percentage on welfare assistance, percentage in managerial positions, and so on came to characterize the questions asked by sociologists, economists, and politicians about minorities. The very idea of "poverty" found its way back into mainstream sociology and public discourse. The benchmark for this shift was probably in the early 1960s with the publication of Michael Harrington's *The Other America.*

Both Chavez and Aponte acknowledge methodological and definitional problems inherent in researching poverty. And neither one assumes a zero sum model of minority-majority economic relations. That is, economic gains of ethnic minorities, including Hispanics, are not viewed as "taking something away from" the majority. As minorities obtain economic success, all of society gains.

In almost every other respect, however, Chavez and Aponte disagree. They clearly have a different definition of poverty. Which is more accurate, would you say?

Chavez sees many Hispanic leaders dishonestly inflating the extent of poverty in order to create political capital for themselves and their group. She feels that government research and programs encourage some minority groups to jockey for entitlements by exaggerating the types and extent of Hispanic poverty.

Aponte also feels that significant, nonscientific factors have structured poverty research and policies. However, his interpretation is quite different. He feels that governmental policies based on identifying, and partially correcting, Black poverty, as commendable as they may be, have sometimes functioned to neglect the equally serious problem of Hispanic poverty. He is also incensed that researchers who ought to know better have generally collapsed Hispanics into one homogeneous ethnic group. He suggests that analytically and empirically there are huge differences in life chances and quality of life among various Hispanic groups.

Note as you review both of these articles that sometimes they draw from the same data sets but reach very different conclusions. How can that be? Drawing from both Chavez and Aponte, identify an ethnic or racial group in which there are large variations among those you know personally. According to Aponte, how might thinking about and viewing every member of an ethnic group as the same be misleading?

YES

Linda Chavez

OUT OF THE BARRIO

IN THE BEGINNING

Before the affirmative action age, there were no *Hispanics*, only Mexicans, Puerto Ricans, Cubans, and so on. Indeed, few efforts were made to forge an alliance among the various Hispanic subgroups until the 1970s, when competition with blacks for college admissions, jobs, and other rewards of affirmative action made it advantageous for Hispanics to join forces in order to demand a larger share of the pie. In addition to having no common history, these groups were more or less geographically isolated from one another. Mexican Americans lived in the Southwest, Puerto Ricans in the Northeast, mostly in New York, and Cubans in Florida; . . .

The Second World War marked a turning point for Hispanic activism. Hispanics served with great distinction in the war, earning more Congressional Medals of Honor per capita than any other group. Moreover, unlike blacks, Hispanics served in integrated military units, which brought them into contact with other Americans and introduced them, for the first time, to Americans who lived outside the Southwest. More than 100,000 Puerto Ricans served in the military during the war; later, many of these men and their families decided to migrate from the island in search of greater economic opportunity in the United States. Hispanics returned from the war expecting better treatment than was the standard fare for Mexican Americans and Puerto Ricans in most places. Hispanics wanted to increase their earnings and social standing, live where they wanted, and send their children to better schools. Indeed, there was significant upward mobility for Mexican Americans in the period, especially in California and other areas outside Texas, and for the Puerto Ricans who migrated to New York City. . . .

* * *

"Each decade offered us hope, but our hopes evaporated into smoke. We became the poorest of the poor, the most segregated minority in schools, the lowest paid group in America and the least educated minority in this nation."

This view of Hispanics' progress by the president of the National Council of La Raza, one of the country's leading Hispanic civil rights groups, is the prevalent one among Hispanic leaders and is shared by many outside the Hispanic community as well. By and large, Hispanics are perceived to be a disadvantaged minority—poorly educated, concentrated in barrios, economically impoverished; with little hope of participating in the American Dream. This perception has not changed substantially in twenty-five years. And it is wrong.

Hispanics have been called the invisible minority, and indeed they were for many years, largely because most Hispanics lived in the Southwest and the Northeast, away from the most blatant discrimination of the Deep South. But the most invisible Hispanics today are those who have been absorbed into the mainstream. The success of middle-class Hispanics is an untold—and misunderstood—story perhaps least appreciated by Hispanic advocates whose interest is in promoting the view that Latinos cannot make it in this society. The Hispanic poor, who constitute only about one-fourth of the Hispanic population, are visible to all. These are the Hispanics most likely to be studied, analyzed, and reported on and certainly the ones most likely to be read about. A recent computer search of stories about Hispanics in major newspapers and magazines over a twelve-month period turned up more than eighteen hundred stories in which the word *Hispanic* or *Latino* occurred within a hundred words of the word *poverty*. In most people's minds, the expression *poor Hispanic* is almost redundant.

HAS HISPANICS' PROGRESS STALLED?

Most Hispanics, rather than being poor, lead solidly lower- middle- or middle-class lives, but finding evidence to support this thesis is sometimes difficult. Of course, Hispanic groups vary one from another, as do individuals within any group. Most analysts acknowledge, for example, that Cubans are highly successful. Within one generation, they have virtually closed the earnings and education gap with other Americans. (For a broad range of social and economic indicators for each of the major Hispanic groups, see table 1.) Although some analysts claim that the success of Cubans is due exclusively to their high socioeconomic status when they arrived, many Cuban refugees—especially those who came after the first wave in the 1960s—were in fact skilled or semiskilled workers with relatively little education. Their accomplishments in the United States are attributable in large measure to diligence and hard work. They established enclave economies, in the traditional immigrant mode, opening restaurants, stores, and other émigré-oriented services.... But Cubans are as a rule dismissed as the exception among Hispanics. What about other Hispanic groups? Why has there been no "progress" among them?

The largest and most important group is the Mexican American population.... [I]ts leaders have driven much of the policy agenda affecting all Hispanics, but the importance of Mexican Americans also stems from their having a longer history in the United States than does any other Hispanic group. If Mexican Americans whose families have lived in the United States for generations are

Table 1

Characteristics of Hispanic Subgroups and Non-Hispanics

	Mexican-Origin*	Puerto Rican	Cuban	South/Central American	Other Hispanic	Non-Hispanic
Total population (in millions)	13.3	2.2	1.0	2.8	1.4	246.2
Median age	24.1	27.0	39.1	28.0	31.1	33.5
Median years of schooling (1988)	10.8	12.0	12.4	12.4	12.7	12.7
Percentage in labor force						
Male	81.2%	69.2%	74.9%	83.7%	75.3%	74.2%
Female	52.9%	41.4%	57.8%	61.0%	57.0%	57.4%
Percentage of unemployed	9.0%	8.6%	5.8%	6.6%	6.2%	5.3%
Median earnings (1989)						
Male	$12,527	$18,222	$19,336	$15,067	$17,486	$22,081
Female	$8,874	$12,812	$12,880	$10,083	$11,564	$11,885
Percentage of married-couple families	72.5%	57.2%	77.4%	68.7%	69.8%	79.9%
Percentage of female-headed families	19.6%	38.9%	18.9%	25.0%	24.5%	16.0%
Percentage of out-of-wedlock births	28.9%	53.0%	16.1%	37.1%	34.2%	23.9%**
Percentage of families in poverty	25.7%	30.4%	12.5%	16.8%	15.8%	9.2%

Sources: Bureau of the Census, *The Hispanic Population in the United States: March 1990*, Current Population Reports, ser. P-20, no. 449; median years of schooling are from *The Hispanic Population of the United States: March 1988*, Current Population Reports, ser. P-20, no. 438; out-of-wedlock births are from National Center for Health Statistics, *Advance Report of Final Natality Statistics, 1987*.

*Mexican-origin population includes both native- and foreign-born persons.

**Includes black out-of-wedlock births, 63.1% and white births, 13.9%.

not yet making it in this society, they may have a legitimate claim to consider themselves a more or less permanently disadvantaged group, like blacks. That is precisely what Mexican American leaders suggest is happening. Their proof is that statistical measures of Mexican American achievement in education, earnings, poverty rates, and other social and economic indicators have remained largely unchanged for decades. In 1959 the median income of Mexican-origin males in the Southwest was 57 percent that of non-Hispanics. In 1989 it was still 57 percent of non-Hispanic income. If Mexican Americans had made progress, it would show up in improved education attainment and earnings and in lower poverty rates, so the argument goes. Since it doesn't, progress must be stalled.

In the post–civil rights era, the failure of a minority to close the social and economic gap with whites is assumed to be the result of persistent discrimination. Progress is perceived not in absolute but in relative terms. The poor may become less poor over time, but so long as those on the upper rungs of the economic ladder are climbing even faster, the poor are believed to have suffered some harm, even if they have made absolute gains and their lives are much improved. However, in order for Hispanics (or any group on the lower rungs) to close the gap, they must progress at an even greater rate than non-Hispanic whites; their apparent failure to do so in recent years causes Hispanic leaders and the public to conclude that Hispanics are falling behind. Is this a fair way to judge Hispanics' progress? In fact, it makes almost no sense to apply this test today (if it ever did), because the Hispanic population itself is changing so rapidly. This is most true of the Mexican-origin population.

In 1959 the overwhelming majority of persons of Mexican origin living in the United States were native-born, 85 percent. Today only about two-thirds of the people of Mexican origin were born in the United States, and among adults barely one in two was born here. Increasingly, the Hispanic population, including that of Mexican origin, is made up of new immigrants, who, like immigrants of every era, start off at the bottom of the economic ladder. This infusion of new immigrants is bound to distort our image of progress in the Hispanic population, if each time we measure the group we include people who have just arrived and have yet to make their way in this society.

... In 1980 there were about 14.6 million Hispanics living in the United States; in 1990, nearly 21 million, an increase of about 44 percent in one decade. At least one-half of this increase was the result of immigration, legal and illegal.... [T]his influx consists mostly of poorly educated persons, with minimal skills, who cannot speak English. Not surprisingly, when these Hispanics are added to the pool being measured, the achievement levels of the whole group fall. It is almost inconceivable that the addition of two or three million new immigrants to the Hispanic pool would not seriously distort evidence of Hispanics' progress during the decade. Yet no major Hispanic organization will acknowledge the validity of this reasonable assumption. Instead, Hispanic leaders complain, "Hispanics are the population that has benefitted least from the economic recovery." "The Myth of Hispanic Progress" is the title of a study by a Mexican American professor, purporting to show that "it is simply wrong to assume that Hispanics are making gradual progress toward parity with Anglos." "Hispanic poverty is now comparable to that of blacks and is expected to exceed it by the end of this decade," warns another group.

Hispanics wear disadvantage almost like a badge of distinction, as if groups were competing with each other for the title "most disadvantaged." Sadly, the most frequently heard complaint among Hispanic leaders is not that the public ignores evidence of Hispanics' achievement but that it underestimates their disadvantage. "More than any group in American political history, Hispanic Americans have turned to the national statistical system as an instrument for advancing their political and economic interests, by making visible the magnitude of social and economic problems they face," says a Rockefeller Foundation official. But gathering all Hispanics together under one umbrella obscures as much information as it illuminates, and may make Hispanics—especially the native-born—appear to suffer greater social and economic problems than they actually do.

In fact, a careful examination of the voluminous data on the Hispanic population gathered by the Census Bureau and other federal agencies shows that, as a group, Hispanics have made progress in this society and that most of them have moved into the social and economic mainstream. In most respects, Hispanics—particularly those born here—are very much like other Americans; they work hard, support their own families without outside assistance, have more education and higher earnings than their parents, and own their own home. In short, they are pursuing the American Dream—with increasing success.

WORK

Hispanic men are more likely to be members of the labor force—that is, working or looking for work—than non-Hispanic whites. Among all Mexican-origin men sixteen years old or older in 1990, for example, participation in the labor force was substantially higher than it was for non-Hispanic males overall—81 percent compared with 74 percent. This fact bodes well for the future and is in marked contrast to the experience of black men, whose labor force participation has been steadily declining for more than twenty years. Most analysts believe that low attachment to the labor force and its correlate, high dependence on welfare, are prime components of underclass behavior. As the political scientist Lawrence Mead writes in this book *Beyond Entitlement: The Social Obligations of Citizenship*, for many persons who are in the underclass, "the problem is not that jobs are *unavailable* but that they are frequently *unacceptable*, in pay or condition, given that some income is usually available from families or benefit programs." In other words, persons in the underclass frequently choose not to work rather than to take jobs they deem beneath them.... The willingness of Hispanic men to work, even at low-wage jobs if their skills qualify them for nothing better, suggests that Hispanics are in no immediate danger of forming a large underclass.

... During the 1980s, 3.3 million new Hispanic workers were added to the work force, giving Hispanics a disproportionate share of the new jobs. Hispanics benefited more than any other group in terms of employment growth in the last decade. By the year 2000, they are expected to account for 10 percent of the nation's work force.

EARNINGS

... Hispanic leaders charge that Hispanics' wages have failed to keep pace with those of non-Hispanics. Statistics on average Hispanic earnings during the decade appear to bear this out, but they should be viewed with caution. The changing composition of the Hispanic population, from a predominantly native-born to an increasingly immigrant one, makes an enormous difference in how we interpret the data on Hispanic earnings. Since nearly half of all Hispanic workers are foreign-born and since many of these have immigrated within the last ten years, we should not be surprised that the average earnings of Hispanics appear low. After all, most Hispanic immigrants are semi-skilled workers who do not speak English, and their wages reflect these deficiencies. When huge numbers of such workers are added to the pool on which we base average-earnings figures, they will lower the mean....

When earnings of native-born Mexican American men are analyzed separately from those of Mexican immigrants, a very different picture emerges. On the average, the weekly earnings of Mexican American men are about 83 percent those of non-Hispanic white men—a figure that cuts in half the apparent gap between their earnings and those of non-Hispanics. Even this gap can be explained at least in part. Schooling, experience, hours worked, and geographical region of residence are among several factors that can affect earnings. When we compensate for these variables, we find that Mexican American men earn about 93 percent of the weekly earnings of comparable non-Hispanic white men. English-language proficiency also plays an important role in the earnings of Hispanics; some economists assert that those who are proficient in English experience "no important earnings differences from native-born Anglos."...

EDUCATION

Contrary to popular opinion, most Mexican American young adults have completed high school, being nearly as likely to do so as other Americans. But the popular press, the federal government, and Hispanic organizations cite statistics that indicate otherwise. They claim that about 60 percent of all Mexican-origin persons do not complete high school. The confusion stems, as it does with earnings data, from lumping native-born Hispanics with immigrants to get statistical averages for the entire group....

Traditionally, Hispanics, like blacks, were more likely to concentrate in fields such as education and the social sciences, which are less remunerative than the physical sciences, business, engineering, and other technical and professional fields. Recently this trend has been reversed; in 1987 (the last year for which such statistics are available), Hispanics were almost as likely as non-Hispanic whites to receive baccalaureate degrees in the natural sciences and were more likely than they to major in computer sciences and engineering.

OCCUPATIONAL STATUS

Fewer Hispanic college graduates will mean fewer Hispanics in the professions and in higher-paying occupations, but this does not translate into the doomsday predictions about their achievement that advocacy organizations commonly voice. It does not mean, for example, that there will be a "a permanent Hispanic underclass" of persons "stuck in poverty because of low wages and deprived of upward mobility," as one Hispanic leader suggested in a *New York Times* article. It may mean, however, that Hispanics will be more likely to hold jobs as clerks in stores and banks, as secretaries and other office support personnel, as skilled workers, and as laborers.... Only in the managerial and professional and the service categories are there very large differences along ethnic lines: 11 percent of all Hispanic males are employed in managerial or professional jobs compared with 27 percent of all non-Hispanics; conversely, 16 percent of the Hispanic males compared with only 9 percent of the non-Hispanic males are employed in service jobs. But these figures include large numbers of immigrants in the Hispanic population, who are disproportionately represented in the service industry and among laborers.

An increasing number of Hispanics are self-employed, many in owner-operated businesses. According to the economist Timothy Bates, who has done a comprehensive study of minority small businesses, those owned by Hispanics are more successful than those owned by blacks. Yet Mexican business owners, a majority of whom are immigrants, are less well educated than any other group; one-third have completed less than twelve years of schooling. One reason why Hispanics may be more successful than blacks in operating small businesses, according to Bates, is that they cater to a nonminority clientele, whereas blacks operate businesses in black neighborhoods, catering to black clients. Hispanic-owned businesses are concentrated in the retail field; about one-quarter of both Mexican and non-Mexican Hispanic firms are retail businesses. About 10 percent of the Mexican-owned firms are in construction.

POVERTY

Despite generally encouraging economic indicators for Hispanics, poverty rates are quite high; 26 percent of all Hispanics live below the poverty line. Hispanics are more than twice as likely to be living in poverty than are persons in the general population. Two factors, however, distort the poverty data: the inclusion of Puerto Ricans, who make up about 10 percent of Hispanics, one-third of whom live in poverty; and the low earnings of new immigrants. The persistence of poverty among Puerto Ricans is one of the most troubling features of the Hispanic population....

An exhaustive study of the 1980 census by Frank Bean and Marta Tienda, however, suggests that nativity plays an important role in poverty data, as it does in earnings data generally. Bean and Tienda estimate that the poverty rate among U.S.-born Mexican Americans was nearly 20 percent lower than that among Mexican immigrants in 1980. Their analysis of data from the 1970 census, by contrast, shows almost no difference in poverty rates between Mexican Americans and Mexican immigrants, with both groups suffering significantly greater poverty in 1970 than in 1980. This implies that while poverty was declining among immigrants and the native-born alike between 1970 and 1980, the decline was greater for Mexican Americans.

THE PUBLIC POLICY IMPLICATIONS OF SUCH FINDINGS

For most Hispanics, especially those born in the United States, the last few decades have brought greater economic opportunity and social mobility. They are building solid lower-middle- and middle-class lives that include two-parent households, with a male head who works full-time and earns a wage commensurate with his education and training. Their educational level has been steadily rising, their earnings no longer reflect wide disparities with those of non-Hispanics, and their occupational distribution is coming to resemble more closely that of the general population. They are buying homes—42 percent of all Hispanics owned or were purchasing their home in 1989, including 47 percent of all Mexican Americans—and moving away from inner cities....

*　*　*

There is much reason for optimism about the progress of Hispanics in the United

States.... Mexican Americans, the oldest and largest Hispanic group, are moving steadily into the middle class, with the majority having established solid, working- and middle-class lives. Even Mexican immigrants and those from other Latin American countries, many of whom have very little formal education, appear to be largely self-sufficient. The vast majority of such immigrants—two-thirds—live above the poverty line, having achieved a standard of living far above that attainable by them in their countries of origin.

There is no indication that any of these groups is in danger of becoming a permanent underclass. If Hispanics choose to (and most *are* choosing to), they will quickly join the mainstream of this society.... [T]he evidence suggests that Hispanics, by and large, are behaving much as other ethnic groups did in the past. One group of Hispanics, however, appears not to be following this pattern. Puerto Ricans occupy the lowest rung of the social and economic ladder among Hispanics, and a disturbing number of them show little hope of climbing higher.

... Puerto Ricans are not simply the poorest of all Hispanic groups; they experience the highest degree of social dysfunction of any Hispanic group and exceed that of blacks on some indicators. Thirty-nine percent of all Puerto Rican families are headed by single women; 53 percent of all Puerto Rican children are born out of wedlock; the proportion of men in the labor force is lower among Puerto Ricans than any other group, including blacks; Puerto Ricans have the highest welfare participation rate of any group in New York, where nearly half of all Puerto Ricans in the United States live. Yet, on the average, Puerto Ricans are better educated than Mexicans and nearly as well educated as Cubans, with a median education of twelve years....

SOME HOPEFUL SIGNS

Despite the overall poor performance of Puerto Ricans, there are some bright spots in their achievement—which make their poverty seem all the more stark. While the median family earnings of Puerto Ricans are the lowest of any Hispanic groups, *individual* earnings of both male and female Puerto Ricans are actually higher than those of any other Hispanic subgroup except Cubans. In 1989 Puerto Rican men had median earnings that were 82 percent of those of non-Hispanics; Puerto Rican women's median earnings were actually higher than those of non-Hispanic women. Moreover, the occupational distribution of Puerto Ricans shows that substantial numbers work in white-collar jobs: nearly one-third of the Puerto Rican males who are employed work in managerial, professional, technical, sales, or administrative support jobs and more than two-thirds of the Puerto Rican females who work hold such jobs.

Moreover, Puerto Ricans are not doing uniformly poorly in all parts of the country. Those in Florida, Texas, and California, for example, perform far better than those in New York....

In fact, as their earnings attest, Puerto Ricans who hold jobs are not doing appreciably worse than other Hispanics, or non-Hispanics, once their lower educational attainment is taken into account. The low overall achievement of Puerto Ricans is simply not attributable to the characteristics of those who work but is a factor of the large number of those—male and female—who are neither working nor looking for work....

WHERE DO PUERTO RICANS GO FROM HERE?

Many Puerto Ricans are making it in the United States. There is a thriving middle class of well-educated professionals, managers, and white-collar workers, whose individual earnings are among the highest of all Hispanic groups' and most of whom live in married-couple families. These Puerto Ricans have done what other Hispanics and, indeed, most members of other ethnic groups have: they have moved up the economic ladder and into the social mainstream within one or two generations of their arrival in the United States....

The crisis facing the Puerto Rican community is not simply one of poverty and neglect. If anything, Puerto Ricans have been showered with too much government attention.... The fact that Puerto Ricans outside New York succeed proves there is nothing inevitable about Puerto Rican failure. Nor does the existence of prejudice and discrimination explain why so many Puerto Ricans fail when so many other Hispanics, including those from racially mixed backgrounds, are succeeding.

So long as significant numbers of young Puerto Rican men remain alienated from the work force, living by means of crime or charity, fathering children toward whom they feel no responsibility, the prospects of Puerto Ricans in the United States will dim. So long as so many Puerto Rican women allow the men who father their babies to avoid the duties of marriage and parenthood, they will deny their children the promise of a better life, which has been the patrimony of generations of poor immigrants' children. The solution to these problems will not be found in more government programs. Indeed, government has been an accomplice in enabling fathers to abandon their responsibility. Only the Puerto Rican community can save itself, but the healing cannot begin until the community recognizes that many of its deadliest wounds are self-inflicted.

... Hispanics have not always had an easy time of it in the United States. Even though discrimination against Mexican Americans and Puerto Ricans was not as severe as it was against blacks, acceptance has come only with struggle, and some prejudices still exist. Discrimination against Hispanics, or any other group, should be fought, and there are laws and a massive administrative apparatus to do so. But the way to eliminate such discrimination is not to classify all Hispanics as victims and treat them as if they could not succeed by their own efforts. Hispanics can and will prosper in the United States by following the example of the millions before them.

NO

Robert Aponte

URBAN HISPANIC POVERTY: DISAGGREGATIONS AND EXPLANATIONS

Nearly a quarter century since the passage of the Civil Rights Act and the initiation of the massive War on Poverty effort, substantial proportions of inner city minorities appear more hopelessly mired in poverty than at any time since these efforts were undertaken (Tienda 1989, Wacquant and Wilson 1989b, Wilson 1987). The poverty rate among central city blacks, for example, stood at about one person in three in 1989, having risen from a rate of one in four two decades earlier (U.S. Bureau of the Census 1980, 1990). Equally ominous is the poverty rate of central city Latinos (Hispanics), some three in ten, which exceeds that of central city whites by a factor of nearly two and one half (U.S. Bureau of the Census 1990). Associated with these indicators of deprivation among urban minorities have been other signs of potential distress. Available evidence indicates that minorities are experiencing rates of joblessness, welfare receipt, and female headship substantially in excess of the rates prevailing among whites (Tienda 1989, Tienda and Jensen 1988, Wacquant and Wilson 1989b, Wilson and Neckerman 1986).

These important issues have not escaped research attention, but until the 1980s, this research focused almost exclusively on blacks among the minority groups and how they compared to whites (Wilson and Aponte 1985). Indeed, prior to the 1980s, empirical research on the poverty of Hispanics in the United States beyond small scale studies was difficult to perform for lack of data. Hence, as we enter the 1990s, far too little is known about the complex configuration of factors underlying Latino poverty. In addition, while the various reports from the Current Population Survey began producing detailed information on "Hispanics" in the 1970s, often presenting the trends alongside those of blacks and whites, it was not until the mid 1980s that we began to consistently receive detailed, individualized data on the major ethnic groups within the hybrid category of "Hispanic." What little systematic research has been done on the topic has far too often treated the hybrid category as a single group.

From Robert Aponte, "Urban Hispanic Poverty: Disaggregations and Explanations," *Social Problems,* vol. 38, no. 4 (November 1991), pp. 516–528. Copyright © 1991 by The Society for the Study of Social Problems. Reprinted by permission. Notes and references omitted.

Any reliance on the aggregate category "Hispanic" is fraught with a high potential to mislead. For analytic purposes beyond the most superficial generalizations, it is crucial that social and economic trends among Hispanics studied be as fully disaggregated as possible if an inquiry is to reveal rather than obscure the dynamics underlying the statistical indicators.* The major current streams of research on minority poverty have produced precious few paradigms with relevance to the Latino population, in part because of the lack of research directed toward the group as a whole, but also because of the failure to consider the individual national groupings separately. Even those analyses incorporating disaggregated indicators need to be interpreted with careful attention paid to the appropriate historic and contemporary circumstances surrounding the various Hispanic groups' incorporation into the mainland United States society.

In the relatively short period that the detailed data have been available, much of significance has been revealed that is consistent with the perspective advanced here. It has been shown, for example, that poverty among Puerto Ricans, the most urban and second largest Latino group, has hovered at a rate averaging over 40 percent in the last several years—a rate second to none among the major ethnic or racial groups for which there is data, and one substantially higher than that of the other Hispanic groups (cf. U.S. Bureau of the Census 1985a, 1986, 1987b, 1988, 1989b). In addition, the rate of poverty for all Hispanics has grown far more rapidly in recent

years than that of whites or blacks, as dramatically shown in an important recent report by the Center on Budget and Policy Priorities (Greenstein et al. 1988).

The report notes that the 1987 Hispanic poverty rate of slightly greater than 28 percent is less than 5 percentage points lower than that of blacks, traditionally the poorest group, and nearly three times that of whites, despite the fact that the labor force participation rate of Hispanics is somewhat higher than that of these other groups. Moreover, the increase in Hispanic poverty over the 1980s shown in the Policy Center Report has been fueled largely by increases in poverty among two parent families. Thus, it cannot be blamed on the relatively modest rise in Hispanic single parent families over this particular period, nor can it easily be pinned on sagging work efforts, given the higher than average participation in the workforce of the group.

Importantly, the patterns outlined above appear to defy common sense interpretations. For example, the idea that discrimination can account for the patterning of such indicators falls short of explaining why Puerto Ricans are poorer than blacks even though they almost certainly experience far less discrimination (Massey and Bitterman 1985). Likewise, a human capital perspective by itself cannot explain why Mexicans, who speak poorer English than Puerto Ricans and are less educated than whites and blacks as well as Puerto Ricans, are more often employed than persons of the other three groups (U.S. Bureau of Labor Statistics 1990)....

---

* [Disaggregation is breaking down data into smaller, more meaningful parts to better understand the information.—Ed.]

DISAGGREGATIONS AND CONTEXT

To speak of Hispanic poverty in urban America at present is to speak of the two largest groups, those of Mexican and those of Puerto Rican extraction, who together account for roughly three-fourths of all U.S. Hispanics. Together these two groups accounted for over 80 percent of all 1987 Hispanic poor within metropolitan areas, their central cities taken separately, or the continental United States as a whole (U.S. Bureau of the Census 1989a). Cubans, the next largest group, have accounted for only about five to six percent of all Hispanics during the 1980s and have significantly lower rates of poverty (U.S. Bureau of the Census 1987a, 1989b; see also U.S. Bureau of the Census 1989b). Hence, this article focuses on Latinos of Mexican or Puerto Rican extraction.

While the diverse groups that comprise the remainder of the Latino population have not yet been numerous enough to have a great impact on the indicators for all Hispanics, it does not follow that their experiences have been trouble free. As noted by the Policy Center Report (Greenstein et al. 1988), available data suggests that many of these other groups are experiencing substantial poverty....

Contrasting sharply with the Cuban experience, the processes whereby Mexicans and Puerto Ricans entered the mainstream urban economy entailed a number of common features. Characteristics shared by these incoming groups include mother tongue, economic or labor migrant status, relatively low levels of skill, inadequate command of English, and little formal education. In addition to their relatively modest social status upon entry, these groups generally re-ceived no special government assistance, and each sustained a fair amount of discrimination.

Though the urban settlement of Puerto Ricans on the mainland occurred rapidly, was highly concentrated in a major northern city, and began largely after the Second World War, among Mexicans the process transpired throughout much of the 20th century, was far more gradual and diffuse, and was contained largely within the southwest section of the country. Indeed, in only a few midwestern cities—notably Chicago—where small proportions of each group have settled, do Mexicans and Puerto Ricans maintain any substantial co-residence. In addition, the Puerto Ricans entered as citizens and were thereby entitled to certain rights that were available to only some Mexicans.

From less than 100,000 at the end of the Second World War, the Puerto Rican population on the mainland grew to well over 1 million by 1970, at which time a solid majority were residents of New York City (Moore and Pachon 1985). Although by 1980 the city no longer contained a majority of the nearly two million members of the group, most of those living elsewhere still resided in large metropolitan cities, and mainly in the Northeast....

While rapid immigration by Puerto Ricans is no longer evident, Mexican immigration into both urban and rural areas has continued in recent years. The estimated population of nearly 12 million Mexican-origin Hispanics in 1988 accounted for nearly 63 percent of all mainland Latinos and was about five times the size of the estimated 2.3 million Puerto Ricans (U.S. Bureau of the Census 1989b). If present trends continue, the gap in population size separating these groups will further widen.

These settlement differences may affect social mobility in several ways. First, the economic well-being of Puerto Ricans can be expected to hinge heavily on economic conditions *inside* the major cities of the eastern end of the snowbelt, especially New York, and be particularly dependent on the opportunity structure confronting the less skilled in those areas. Such conditions have not been favorable in recent decades due to the widely documented decline in manufacturing, trade, and other forms of low skilled employment that was most evident in northern *inner cities* beginning with the 1950s and accelerating during the 1970s (Kasarda 1985, Wacquant and Wilson 1989b). Moreover, such jobs have not returned to these places, even where sagging economies have sharply rebounded (as in New York and Boston), since the newer mix of jobs in such areas still tend to require more skills or credentials than previously (Kasarda 1983, 1988).

By contrast, Mexican Hispanics are more dependent upon the opportunity structures confronting less skilled labor in southwestern cities and their suburbs but without heavy reliance on only one or two such areas or on *central city* employment. These areas are believed to have better job prospects for the less skilled than northern cities because of the continued employment growth in low skilled jobs throughout the entire postwar period (Kasarda 1985, Wacquant and Wilson 1989b).

A second important distinction concerns social welfare provisions. Specifically, Puerto Ricans have settled into the *relatively* more generous states of the North, while their counterparts populate a band of states with traditionally low levels of assistance. A notable exception to this is California—the state with the largest number of Mexican Hispanics. However, many among the group in that state are ineligible for assistance due to lack of citizenship. At the same time, many eligible recipients likely co-reside with undocumented immigrants subject to deportation if caught. No doubt many of the impoverished among both such groups will not apply for assistance for fear of triggering discovery of the undocumented in their families or households.

As of 1987, *no state* in the continental U.S. provided enough AFDC [Aid to Families with Dependent Children] benefits to bring families up to the poverty line.... Recent research by Jencks and Edin (1990) demonstrates conclusively that very few AFDC families can survive in major cities on just the legally prescribed income; most are forced to cheat, many turn to petty crimes for supplementary income, and some even slip into homelessness (cf. Ellison 1990, Rossi and Wright 1989).

However, this was not always so (Tobier 1984, National Social Science and Law Center 1987). For example, in New York city during the late 1960s, the maximum AFDC benefit package for a family of three, discounting food stamps, could raise the family's income to 97 *percent* of the poverty line (Tobier 1984). The payment levels declined gradually during the first part of the 1970s....

The statistical indicators on these groups are consistent with such expectations. For example, among men aged 20 years and over, Puerto Ricans had a labor force participation rate 10 percentage points lower than that of Mexican origin men in 1987 (U.S. Bureau of Labor Statistics 1988), representing a widening of the respective 1977 gap of only five percentage points. The employment-to-population ratios exhibited a similar gap, but they remained unchanged over the ten year period, with the Puerto Rican ratio trailing that of the Mexican origin group by 10 percentage points (Newman 1978), suggesting that the Mexican unemployment rate is catching up to the Puerto Rican rate (Greenstein et al. 1988). Although these are national level trends, they should reflect urban conditions since both groups have become highly urbanized. As expected, Puerto Ricans are also poorer than Mexicans. The central city poverty rate for Puerto Ricans in 1987 was 46 percent, with the corresponding rate for Mexicans 30 percent. The metropolitan area rates were similarly distributed. Likewise, the proportion of families headed by women among central city Puerto Ricans was 49 percent, while only about 21 percent of the Mexican origin families were so headed (U.S. Bureau of the Census 1989a).

Finally, the Current Population Survey reveals that employed Puerto Ricans, on average, earn more than employed Mexicans (U.S. Bureau of the Census 1989b). The survey also reveals that many more Mexican families in poverty have members in the work force than do poor Puerto Rican families, while a substantially higher proportion of the latter group receive government assistance. For example, in 1987, 72 percent of all Mexican origin families in poverty had at least one member in the work force compared to only 24 percent of the Puerto Rican families. Conversely, 72 percent of Puerto Rican families in poverty that year received all of their income from some form of assistance or transfer compared to 25 percent of the Mexican families (U.S. Bureau of the Census 1989a). In spite of the "assis-

tance," not one of these needy families was brought over the poverty line, and many were left with incomes well below the designated level!

It seems likely that the kind of approach urged here, one that maximizes sensitivity to the varying conditions of the individual Latino groups' plights, can help in interpreting trends among data that are largely aggregated. For example, the Policy Center Report reached a number of findings that can be pushed further. The report concluded that recent increases in Hispanic poverty are associated only weakly, if at all, with recent increases in female headship or joblessness within the group. Rather, the poverty increases were strongly associated with declining real wages. The report also noted that the increase in poverty occurred mainly among Mexicans and in the Sunbelt and Midwest. However, the report did *not* make a connection between these factors.

Attending to Latino subgroup differences provides an explanation. We would expect declining real wages to bring more Mexicans into poverty than Puerto Ricans because proportionately more Mexicans hold very low wage jobs. In turn, Mexican dominance in the three regions outside of the Northeast helps explain why those regions, but *not* the Northeast, were more affected by the rise in poverty traceable to real wage declines, even as the Puerto Rican dominated northeastern region maintained the highest level of poverty.

Finally, consideration of the continuation of Mexican immigration leads to a second hypothesis about their vulnerability to falling real wages: Mexicans are employed in regions plagued by labor market crowding resulting from continued immigration, especially since much of it consists of "undocumenteds," a group that clearly constitutes cheaper labor. This especially hurts those with lower levels of education, since they are most likely to compete directly with the latest newcomers. Indeed, the Report singles out the lesser educated Hispanics as the group sustaining the most increased hardship....

Explanations of Urban Poverty

Most current popular theories about urban poverty fall short of fully accounting for the plight of the Hispanic poor because of a narrow focus on blacks. In spite of the apparent deficit, disaggregating the Hispanic figures allows us to apply some of this work to at least one of the two major groups under study.

The culture of poverty. The idea of a "culture of poverty" generally traces back to the work of Oscar Lewis (1959, 1966) who coined the phrase, although others have advanced similar notions. Lewis developed the core ideas of the argument while studying Mexican and Puerto Rican families. The work suggests that culturally-based attitudes or predispositions such as "present mindeness" and "obsessive consumption" are the major barriers to economic mobility for many of the poor, implying that providing opportunities to the poor will not be enough: some will need "cultural uplifting" as well. The major strength of the idea for my purposes is that it can apply equally well to the poor of any of the Latino groups.

However, the theory is largely discredited within academic circles.... In fact, numerous subsequent studies of poor people's values and attitudes have found little support for the theory (Corcoran et al. 1985, Goodwin 1972, Irelan et al. 1969)....

The welfare-as-cause argument. In his book *Losing Ground*, Charles Murray (1984) argues that the liberalization of welfare during the late 1960s and early 1970s made work less beneficial than welfare and encouraged low-income people to avoid work and marriage, in order to reap the benefits of welfare, and that this is a primary source of the rise in female headship and, indirectly, poverty itself....

We might ask if welfare payments were so lucrative, why did the poor fail to escape poverty, at least while "on the dole", but Murray does not address this issue.... Moreover, studies on the effects of welfare availability to changes in family structure have produced few results supporting a connection, the overall consensus being that such effects as they exist are relatively weak (Wilson and Neckerman 1986. U.S. General Accounting Office 1987).... Thus, welfare appears unlikely to be a major cause of female headship or joblessness among Hispanics, as among blacks. However, it may properly be seen as a major cause of Latino poverty insofar as so many of the Hispanic impoverished who are legally entitled to assistance are left destitute by miserly benefit levels while many other equally needy Hispanics are denied benefits altogether.

The mismatch thesis. This explanation... focuses mainly on older, northern, industrial towns. It finds recent urban poverty rooted in the movement of manufacturing and other blue-collar employment away from snowbelt central cities where blacks and Hispanics make up increasingly larger proportions of the population. As blue-collar industry moved from the cities to the suburbs and from the Snow Belt to the Sun Belt, central city job growth occurred primarily in white-collar jobs for which the black and Hispanic central city residents often did not qualify for lack of skills or credentials.

... While studies based on data for 1970 or earlier have tended to disconfirm the hypothesis, work on more recent periods has largely produced supporting results (Holzer 1991). Hence, the argument remains a viable hypothesis about joblessness in northern central cities. Once again, however, the idea offers no explanation for the poverty of Mexicans since relatively few live in those areas....

Labor market segmentation theories (dual labor market theory). According to early versions of labor market segmentation theories, racial and ethnic minorities were intentionally relegated to the "secondary" sector of the labor market characterized by highly unstable work with low pay and little room for advancement (Cain 1976). More recent versions often suggest that disadvantaged native workers all but openly shun such jobs because of their undesirable characteristics and that immigrants are therefore "imported" to fill the positions (Piore 1979)....

Though clearly of important explanatory potential, the segmentation theory falls short of providing a complete explanation for the patterns in question.... Thus, the argument would appear to operate better in cities such as New York which have received large numbers of immigrants in recent years than in places such as Buffalo, Cleveland, Philadelphia, or Rochester with proportionately fewer such persons. (Waldinger 1989). Yet, Puerto Ricans in these cities appear as plagued by poverty and joblessness as those in New York (U.S. Bureau of the Census 1985b)....

The Underclass Hypothesis. The underclass argument, proposed by William Julius Wilson (1987, 1988), begins with the observation that declining housing discrimination and rising incomes among some blacks have enabled many to leave the older central city ghettos. Their departure from the highly segregated and traditionally underserviced areas, characterized by higher than average rates of physical deterioration, exacerbates the purely economic problems confronted by the remaining population....

Ghetto residents subjected to the described conditions constitute Wilson's underclass. The combined material and environmental deprivation confronted by the group anchors them firmly to prolonged poverty, welfare dependence, and assorted illicit enterprises.... Once again, among Hispanics, only the Puerto Rican poor are as geographically isolated as poor blacks and, therefore, appear to be the only Hispanic population for which this explanation can hold.

CONCLUSION

... The data and discussions presented here, while far from providing a definitive analysis of Hispanic poverty, provide support to a number of generalizations about the problems and potential solutions. Decreased employment opportunities for the less skilled and educated, severely depressed wages among the employed, and restricted or nonexistent welfare benefits comprise the major causes of urban Hispanic poverty. Expanding employment, increasing wages, providing a better living to those unable to work, and promoting higher levels of human capital attainment are major public policy imperatives if these problems are ever to be adequately addressed.

POSTSCRIPT

Are Hispanics Making Significant Progress?

Early in the twenty-first century Hispanic/Latino Americans will be the largest minority in the United States, according to demographers. As Aponte shows, a major problem in understanding Hispanic poverty, which for some is so intense that they are considered an underclass, is the large variations in income, education, and status among groups of Spanish-speaking Americans.

As Chavez shows, many Hispanics have paralleled other ethnic and racial minority "success stories" of "making it" in the United States. Yet her data ignore significant pockets of poverty.

Are Hispanics making significant progress? Or is it an illusion, already crumbling in the face of America's recent economic downturns? Do all racial minorities require the same government programs?

For cutting edge research and policy recommendations on the very real problem of continuing Latino poverty, see *Latinos in a Changing U.S. Economy*, edited by Rebecca Morales and F. Bonilla (Sage, 1993). An excellent article that looks at the effects of residential segregation and Hispanic poverty is Anne M. Santiago and M. G. Wilder, "Residential Segregation and Links to Minority Poverty: The Case of Latinos in the United States," in *Social Problems* (November 1991).

A helpful comparison between different minority groups and majority whites is *Income and Status Differences Between White and Minority Americans: A Persistent Inequality*, edited by S. Chan (Mellon Studies in Sociology, 1990).

Additional comparisons of Hispanics with other groups include Reynolds Farley, "Blacks, Hispanics, and White Ethnic Groups: Are Blacks Uniquely Disadvantaged?" *American Economic Review* (May 1990); "Blacks Holding Ground, Hispanics Losing in Desegregaton," *Phi Delta Kappan* (January 1987); and R. M. Jiobu, *Ethnicity and Inequality* (State University of New York Press, 1993).

A look at ethnic identity, including that of Latinos, is found in *Ethnic Identity: Formation and Transmission Among Hispanics and Other Minorities*, edited by M. Bernal and G. Knight (State University of New York Press, 1993). Ethnographic accounts of the experiences of ethnics includes: *Inside Separate Worlds: Life Stories of Young Blacks, Jews, and Latinos*, edited by D. Schoem (University of Michigan Press, 1991). A useful discussion of the uniqueness of Chicano poverty research is Irene I. Blea's *Toward a Chicano Social Science* (Praeger, 1988).

ISSUE 14

Is Systemic Racism in Criminal Justice a Myth?

YES: William Wilbanks, from "The Myth of a Racist Criminal Justice System," *Criminal Justice Research Bulletin* (vol. 3, no. 5, 1987)

NO: Coramae Richey Mann, from "The Reality of a Racist Criminal Justice System," *Criminal Justice Research Bulletin* (vol. 3, no. 5, 1987)

ISSUE SUMMARY

YES: Florida International University criminology professor William Wilbanks advances the thesis that the criminal justice system is not now racist, and he says that claims that it is are myths.

NO: Indiana University criminologist Coramae Richey Mann generously welcomes Wilbanks's ideas as part of a healthy debate. However, after careful research and thought, she dismisses them as analytically and empirically flawed and, however unintentional, permeated with elitism.

Historically, within the field of minority group research, virtually no expression of racism was more blatant, widespread, and easy to document than the mistreatment of Blacks by the criminal justice system. In most states, Blacks were more likely to be arrested, obliged to stand trial (or more likely, persuaded to plea bargain—enter a guilty plea), given longer prison sentences, or sentenced to death. The latter was especially true in the South.

Blacks were also much more likely to be intimated by the police and subject to being rounded up when a crime needed to be solved immediately. Blacks were more likely to be held incommunicado and generally harassed as well as tortured.

Lynchings of Blacks (3,446 between 1882–1968) were at least implicitly sanctioned by local police, and they were brutal and gruesome affairs. Almost nothing was ever done to prosecute the murderers. Lynching and its sanctioning by officials was symbolically the most important image of criminal justice racism.

Wilbanks, though not the first, was one of the few to challenge the perception that the system is still racist. Wilbanks does not deny that racism has existed in the system and he does not deny there are individuals in the system who are racists, from police officers to probation officers. But he insists that the criminal justice system is no longer plagued by institutional racism. To claim otherwise, he says, is to perpetuate a myth.

Coramae Richey Mann is well aware of the tradition of racism in American institutions, including the legal and criminal justice systems. And she agrees that the criminal justice system has changed. But racism, she argues, is still rooted in American institutions.

She also raises some questions about Wilbanks's exclusive use of quantitative data. Mann argues that on an issue as empirically complicated as this one, at the very least a researcher ought to triangulate data collection. That is, data (facts and information) should be collected in several ways, including the gathering of qualitative information (e.g., ethnographic observations, interviews with knowledgeable subjects, and so on). Wilbanks did little of this.

As you read this debate (which has been going on for years now but without resolution), think about the moral and policy implications of Wilbanks's thesis.

As you read Mann, pay close attention to her methodological criticisms of Wilbanks. She has been attacked venomously over this part of the debate. In what ways is Mann's conception of science and sociology similar to Professor Collins's in Issue 1? Is Mann rejecting Wilbanks as an outsider? How do you think Robert Merton (also Issue 1) might mediate the debate?

YES

William Wilbanks

THE MYTH OF A RACIST CRIMINAL JUSTICE SYSTEM

White and black Americans differ sharply over whether their criminal justice system is racist. The vast majority of blacks appear to believe that the police and courts do discriminate against blacks, whereas a majority of whites reject this charge. A sizable minority of whites even believe that the justice system actually discriminates **for** blacks in "leaning over backward" for them in reaction to charges of racism from the black community and the media.

The contrasting views of blacks and whites as to the fairness of the criminal justice system are of more than academic interest as research indicates that the higher level of offending by blacks may be due in part to the belief that "the system" is unfair. This belief produces a "justification for no obligation" or the attitude that "I don't respect a system that is racist, and so I don't feel obliged to abide by the laws of that system." This view in the collective has led to riots in Miami and other cities. Furthermore, the hostility to police generated by the belief has led to a mutual expectation of violence between police and blacks that has produced more violence as part of a self-fulfilling prophesy. Finally, the white backlash to affirmative action programs may be due in part to the perception that blacks complain about racism in a society that actually practices reverse discrimination (favoritism toward blacks).

THE THESIS

I take the position that the perception of the criminal justice system as racist is a myth. This overall thesis should not be misinterpreted. I do believe that there is racial prejudice and discrimination **within** the criminal justice system, in that there are individuals, both white and black, who make decisions, at least in part, on the basis of race. I do not believe that **the system** is characterized by racial prejudice or discrimination **against** blacks. At every point from arrest to parole there is little or no evidence of an overall racial effect, in that the percentage outcomes for blacks and whites are not very different. There is evidence, however, that some individual decision makers (e.g., police officers, judges) are more likely to give "breaks" to whites than to blacks. However,

From William Wilbanks, "The Myth of a Racist Criminal Justice System," *Criminal Justice Research Bulletin*, vol. 3, no. 5 (1987). Copyright © 1987 by William Wilbanks. Reprinted by permission.

there appears to be an **equal** tendency for other individual decision makers to favor blacks over whites. This "canceling-out effect" results in studies that find no **overall** racial effect.

The assertion that the criminal justice system is not racist does not address the reasons why blacks appear to offend at higher rates than whites before coming into contact with the criminal justice system. It may be that racial discrimination in American society has been responsible for conditions (e.g., discrimination in employment, housing and education) that lead to higher rates of offending by blacks, but that possibility does not bear on the question of whether the criminal justice system discriminates against blacks. Also, the thesis that racism is not systematic and pervasive in the criminal justice system does not deny that racial prejudice and discrimination have existed or even been the dominant force in the design and operation of the criminal justice system in the past.

DEFINING RACISM

One of the main barriers to the discussion and resolution of the issue of racism in the criminal justice system involves the multiple uses and meanings of the term "racism." Definitions of this term range from a conscious attitude by an individual to an unconscious act by an institution or even to the domination of society by white culture. I have suggested that the term "racism" be abandoned in favor of the terms "racial prejudice" (an attitude) and "racial discrimination" (an act).

Any discussion of the pervasiveness of racism in the justice system is clouded by the tendency of Accusers (e.g., those who claim the system is racist) to use a double standard in that the term is used only to apply to whites. For example, it is often pointed out that 50% of the victims of police killings are black and that this fact alone presents a prima facie case of racism. But it is seldom pointed out that 50% of the police officers who are killed are victimized by blacks. If the first fact indicates racism by white police officers why does not the second fact indicate racism by black killers of police?

At times the use of the term racism appears to constitute a "non-falsifiable thesis" in that any result is defined as racist. For example, in McCleskey v. Georgia (a case before the U.S. Supreme Court this term) the petitioner claims that he received the death penalty because he (a black) killed a white whereas those who kill blacks seldom receive the death penalty.* Thus lenient treatment given to black killers (or those who kill black victims) is defined as racism. But if black killers had been more likely to be sentenced to death that result would also be (and has been) viewed as racist. Thus the term is defined so that any result is indicative of racism (i.e., a non-falsifiable thesis). The double standard of racism is also seen in this case in that the death penalty statistics actually indicate harsher treatment of white than black killers but this result is not seen as racism (against whites).

In a similar fashion a lower percentage of blacks (than whites) being convicted has been interpreted by Accusers as racist in that this result indicates that charges against blacks were often without substance. On the other hand, if more blacks were convicted this result would also be viewed by Accusers as being in-

---

* [The U.S. Supreme Court supported Georgia, and McCleskey has since been executed.—Ed.]

dicative of racism since black defendants were treated more harshly.

THE DATA

The book [*The Myth of A Racist Criminal Justice System*, of which this article is a summary] was undertaken to explain why blacks in the U.S. are 8 times more likely, on a per capita basis, to be in prison than are whites. The major point of the book is that the approximate 8:1 per capita ratio of blacks to whites in prison is the result of an approximate 8:1 level in offending and not the result of racial selectivity by the police and the courts. In other words, the 8:1 black to white ratio at offending is not increased as offenders are brought into and processed by the criminal justice system.

Some original data are presented in an appendix to the book on the black vs. white gap from arrest to incarceration in prison for two states—California and Pennsylvania. In 1980 felony cases, blacks in California were arrested 5.1 times as often as whites. This black/white gap increased to 6.2 at incarceration. Thus the black/white "gap" increased by 20% from arrest to prison. However, the reverse occurred in Pennsylvania where the 8.1 gap at arrest decreased to 7.4 at incarceration (a decline of 9%). Overall, it would appear that the black/white gap does not increase from arrest to prison. Thus there is no evidence overall that black offenders processed by the criminal justice system fare worse than white offenders.

But perhaps the black/white gap at arrest is a product of racial bias by the police in that the police are more likely to select and arrest black than white offenders. The best evidence on this question comes from the National Crime Survey which interviews 130,000 Americans each year about crime victimization. Those who are victimized by violent crime are asked to describe the offenders (who were not necessarily caught by the police) as to age, sex and race. The percent of offenders described by victims as being black is generally consistent with the percent of offenders who are black according to arrest figures. For example, approximately 60% of (uncaught) robbers described by victims were black and approximately 60% of those arrested for robbery in the U.S. are black. This would not be the case if the police were "picking on" black robbers and ignoring white robbers.

Given the above figures, those who claim that racism is systematic and pervasive in the criminal justice system should explain why the black/white gap does not cumulatively increase from arrest to prison. Furthermore, those who claim racism is pervasive should be asked to specify the number of black offenders that are thought to receive harsher treatment (e.g., whether 10%, 50% or 100%) and the extent of that "extra" harshness in cases where "it" is given. For example, at sentencing do those mistreated black offenders receive on the average a 10%, 50% or 100% harsher sentence?

There is a large body of research on the alleged existence of racial discrimination at such points as arrest, conviction and sentencing. The bibliography of my books lists over 80 sentencing studies which examined the impact of race on outcome. A number of scholars have examined this large body of research and concluded that there is no evidence of systematic racial discrimination. James Q. Wilson, the most prominent American criminologist, asserts that the claim of discrimination is not supported by the evidence as did a three volume study of the sentencing literature by the National Academy of Sciences.

METHODOLOGICAL PROBLEMS

However, some studies do claim to have found evidence of racial discrimination. However, as Wilson and others have pointed out, most of these studies are marked by flaws in design or interpretation. One chapter of *The Myth of a Racist Criminal Justice System* is devoted to seven models of design and/or interpretation which have been utilized in studies of the possible existence of racial discrimination. Many of the studies claiming to have found racial discrimination utilized a model of analysis that ensured such a result.

But many readers will be thinking at this point that "one can prove anything with statistics" and thus that the validity of the claim for a racist criminal justice system should be determined by what one knows by personal experience or observation. However, the layperson's confidence in and reliance upon "common-sense" in rejecting the statistical approach to knowledge in favor of what one knows by personal experience and observation is misplaced. The layperson does not take into account the impact of bias (and in some cases racial prejudice) in personal experience and observation.

Let us take, for example, the question as to whether there is racial discrimination in the use of force by the police. Those who reject studies of large numbers of "use of force" incidents which do not show evidence of racial discrimination by race of victim suggest that "unbiased" observation will reveal racism. But suppose that several people see a white police officer hit a black youth. There are a multitude of explana-tions (e.g., the youth hit the officer first, the youth resisted authority, the officer was the macho type who would hit any victim who was not properly deferential, the officer was a racist) for such an act. The tendency is for those with a particular bias to select that explanation which is consistent with their bias. For example, other police officers or white citizens might select the explanation that the youth resisted authority while black citizens might select the explanation that the officer was a racist. In either case the observer simply infers the explanation that is most consistent with his/her bias and thus knowledge via observation is anything but unbiased. Large scale statistical studies allow one to control for factors (other than race) which might impact on a decision or act. Without such studies those who disagree on the impact of racism will simply be trading anecdotes ("I know a case where...") to "prove" their case.

CONCLUSION

Racial prejudice, in my view, is the process by which people assign positive traits and motives to themselves and their race and negative traits and motives to "them" (the other race). Blacks tend to see the beating of a black youth by a white police officer as being indicative of racism (an evil motive or trait attributed to the "out-group") while whites (or police officers) tend to see the beating as being the result of some improper action by the black youth. The white view is also influenced by the assigning of evil motives or traits to the out-group (to the black youth). In both cases the observers, whether black or white, have been influenced by racial prejudice in their assigning of blame or cause for the incident.

My basic position is that both the black and white views on the extent of racism in the criminal justice system are "ignorant" in that personal knowledge is gained primarily via observation and experience—methods which are heavily influenced by bias and racial prejudice. In other words, racial prejudice keeps the races polarized on this issue since each race sees the "facts" which "prove" its thesis. Statistical studies of large numbers of blacks and whites subjected to a particular decision (e.g., the use of force) are a safeguard against personal bias and are far more valid as a means to "truth" than personal observation and experience. It is my view that an examination of those studies available at various points in the criminal justice system fails to support the view that racial discrimination is pervasive. It is in this sense that the belief in a racist criminal justice system is a myth.

The Myth of a Racist Criminal Justice System examines all the available studies that have examined the possible existence of racial discrimination from arrest to parole. For example, the chapter on the police examines the evidence for and against the charge that police deployment patterns, arrest statistics, the use of force ("brutality") and the use of deadly force reflect racism. The chapter on the prosecutor examines the evidence for and against the charge that the bail decision, the charge, plea bargaining, the provision of legal counsel, and jury selection are indicative of racism. The chapter on prison looks at evidence concerning the possibility of racism as reflected through imprisonment rates for blacks vs. whites, in racial segregation, in treatment programs, in prison discipline and in the parole decision. In general, this examination of the available evidence indicates that support for the "discrimination thesis" is sparse, inconsistent, and frequently contradictory.

NO

Coramae Richey Mann

THE REALITY OF A RACIST CRIMINAL JUSTICE SYSTEM

I first heard of Bill Wilbanks' *The Myth of a Racist Criminal Justice System* at the Academy of Criminal Justice Sciences' annual meeting in Orlando during a panel discussion of urban crime in Black communities where the book rapidly became the focus of attention and outrage expressed by the panel and participants. The discussion clearly suggested that *The Myth* was the antithesis of the book I am writing, *Minorities, Crime and Public Policy*. Two subsequent readings of Wilbanks' book confirmed my original impression; therefore, when Editor Frank Williams invited me to present an alternative view to *The Myth*, I strongly agreed that another perspective was demanded.

In the two years that I have taught my undergraduate course on race and crime, the classes were fraught with anxiety and frustration in the face of the students' personal misconceptions, ignorance about American minorities, and reliance on racial stereotypes, particularly as applied to crime. There clearly was a need for a text which could present the "minority" side. With the arrival of *The Myth*, the need increased for a more balanced presentation of the topic.

As I view it, there are two major issues involved which must be definitively addressed. First, that Wilbanks is mistaken and that there *is* racial prejudice and discrimination in the criminal justice system (and throughout the United States' social system) which is *rooted* in racism. And second, the linchpin of his thesis not only relies on a simplistic and rather naive view of what takes place in the "real world" of criminal justice—out in the trenches so to speak—but also Wilbanks' complete dependence on quantitative data for his "proof" results in his dismissal of the rich qualitative data available which he erroneously describes as "anecdotal" or as reported by "lay persons." It is this latter elitism that is most problematic.

DEFINITIONS

Despite the use of the eye-catching and inflammatory term *racist* in the title of his book, Wilbanks quickly and inexplicably abandons the term *racism* and substitutes *racial prejudice* and *racial discrimination* in its stead. It is my

From Coramae Richey Mann, "The Reality of a Racist Criminal Justice System," *Criminal Justice Research Bulletin*, vol. 3, no. 5 (1987). Copyright © 1987 by Coramae Richey Mann. Reprinted by permission. References omitted.

contention that all terms are applicable when the plight of minorities in the criminal justice system is examined. Although Wilbanks limited his thesis to Blacks, in this alternative view, I refer to all racial minorities, since racial prejudice, racial discrimination, and racism are directed at non-whites in this country.

Wilbanks cited, but glossed over, the impressive, in-depth, objective national assessment of the impact of the criminal justice system on minorities by the National Minority Advisory Council on Criminal Justice (1980:1) which used five study methods (literature review, public hearings, commissioned specific issue studies, field studies, and critical analyses of criminal justice programs and policies) to reach the conclusion that "... for minorities all over the nation, the issues, above all others, are political and economic exploitation and *racism*, the basic causes of conflict and disorder in the American criminal justice system." (Emphasis added) Racism connotes power, thus, by definition, in only very few limited instances can a minority person have a quantum of power; and since they lack institutional power, it is definitionally impossible for American minorities to be identified as racist.

An Afro-American does not need to go to Brighton Beach (New York) to find out about racial prejudice and violence, an American Vietnamese need not travel to Boston or Florida to be insulted and violently attacked, nor does a Mexican American have to go to Los Angeles or a Native American (Indian) anywhere in the continental United States to experience differential treatment simply because of their color. All any of these persons have to do to face racial prejudice and discrimination is to be non-white in America today. As a minority who

for a life time has experienced prejudicial treatment because of my race (and gender) I totally disagree with Wilbanks' contention that racial prejudice against minorities "appears to be declining" (p. 146). More in accord with our urbane times, racial prejudice has not declined but has simply "gone underground" and become much more subtle. That is, it has become institutionalized—the process that "institutionalized racism" connotes.

THE REALITY: AN ALTERNATE VIEW

Aside from the observation that Wilbanks often contradicts his own thesis throughout the book and adopts a chauvinistic approach by consistently reporting research to substantiate his position and skimming over contrary views (particularly qualitative studies), such detailed critique is left to book reviewers. The focus of this alternative view is therefore best served through analyses and comments that respond to Wilbanks' challenges to the discrimination thesis, or DT as he calls it, which is contrasted with NDT or a non-discrimination thesis (pp. 144–147).

1. After repeatedly stating that the research is "sparse," Wilbanks is chagrined that with or without controls, "a sizable race effect" cannot be demonstrated at decision points throughout the criminal justice system. Aside from not defining "sizable," "substantial," or even "race effect," Wilbanks uses his aggregate study in two states (California and Pennsylvania) for one year (1980) as the exemplar. This is curious, since in his later recommendations for future research, Wilbanks states that aggregate studies of decision making should be abandoned in favor of studies concentrating on individual

decision makers (a point I strongly endorse), since research "attempting to validate the DT or the NDT has been seriously deficient" (p. 147). Thus we find that aggregate studies should not be used, yet such studies are an integral part of Wilbanks' thesis; notably his own California/Pennsylvania aggregate data (Appendix). Interestingly, in California Wilbanks' data revealed a 19 percent increase in the black/white "gap" from arrest to incarceration; whereas Pennsylvania showed a slight decrease in the black/white gap (p. 145). Nonetheless the "gaps" continued to exist which is the major concern of a DT position. Unfortunately, the value of this effort is diminished since Wilbanks did not use any controls in the study. Wilbanks comments that "no study has examined the racial gap for all the decision points from arrest to incarceration" (p. 151). However, Petersilia (1983) reports such a study and the same has been reported for women felons (Mann, 1984). Petersilia (1983:93) found that minorities were "less likely to be given probation, more likely to receive prison sentences, more likely to get longer sentences, and more likely to serve a longer time in prison than whites after controlling for offense seriousness, prior record and prison violence."

2. A perplexing tactic that Wilbanks uses throughout The Myth, in addition to the "blaming the victim" approach, is the frequent use of an "apples and oranges" argument by the constant introduction of reverse sexism and reverse racism. The theoretical debate on whether female offenders are treated more leniently or more harshly by the criminal justice system is about as divided as that on race discrimination, but it is not the issue the book purports to address. Thus, the constant reference to "sexism" and

"white discrimination" in The Myth tends to detract from the major thesis.

3. Wilbanks wonders why there is an overrepresentation of blacks in both arrests and incarcerations and the racial gap does not increase cumulatively. Again, he bases this interpretation of the black/white gap on his two state study where in one state, it did increase. It should also be noted that an examination of the Uniform Crime Reports (UCR) for the past seven years (1979–1985) indicates that there is also an overrepresentation of arrests of Hispanic Americans, Asian Americans and Native Americans disproportionate to their numbers in the population (Mann, forthcoming). Also, contrary to Wilbanks' incitive and untrue statement that according to the UCR, 50 percent of those arrested in 1984 for sex offenses were black, for the period 1979–1985, black arrests for sex offenses showed little variation from 1979 (20.2 percent) to 1985 which was also 20.2 percent (U.S. Department of Justice, 1980; Table 25; 1986; Table 38).

4. A point stressed throughout the book is that the dropping of charges against blacks by the police or prosecutor, and less convictions are interpreted as "more lenient treatment" than that received by whites, although harsher treatment is realized by blacks at the "back end" of the system. As Joan Petersilia's (1983:92) highly respected study of racial disparity in the criminal justice system clearly notes: minority suspects were more likely to be released after arrest because the police did not have strong cases! This is not more lenient treatment, but contrarily, could be viewed as discriminatory treatment since they were arrested without sufficient evidence in the first place.

5. Similar to other questionable figures cited throughout the book, Wilbanks

challenges the DT by offering 1979 figures alleging that the southern (prejudiced) states (e.g. Mississippi) have the lowest black/white incarceration gap while those less racially prejudiced states (Minnesota, Wisconsin, Iowa, New Hampshire) have higher gaps (p. 146). However, it appears that the interpretation is in error since this would be the expected finding to support a discrimination thesis. Furthermore, according to *Prisoners in State and Federal Institutions* (U.S. Department of Justice, 1980; Table 6, p. 18), totalling *all* known incarcerated minorities yields the following minority/white percentages by race: Mississippi (54.5/27.1) or 2:1, Minnesota (26.7/72.3) or 1:2.7, Iowa (19.9/80) or 1:4, Wisconsin (42.9/58.8) or 1:1.4, New Hampshire (4.9/95.1) or 1:19.4 which are not as dramatic as the figures reported by Wilbanks for these same states a year earlier.

6. As with the erroneous charges of disproportionate black sex offense arrests (see #3 above), Wilbanks asserts that blacks are more likely to choose white victims to attack, rape, and rob, than black victims. The 1983 Bureau of Justice Statistics publication (1985:5) he cites supports all other victimization findings that violent crime is predominantly *intraracial* by stating:

> Violent crime had intraracial as well as interracial aspects. On the one hand, most violent crimes against whites were committed by white offenders (78%); most violent crimes against blacks were committed by black offenders (87%); and most violent crimes committed by white offenders were against white victims (98%). On the other hand, 55% of the violent crimes committed by black offenders were against white victims.

It is the last sentence that concerns Wilbanks and leads to his charge of black racism, when he emphasizes "choice" of victim. Two possible explanations come to mind with this statistic. First, victimization surveys which report *perceived* offenders have specific limitations where blacks are concerned. With rape, for example, white rape victims tend to report black offenders more than white rape offenders (Hindelang, 1978), while conversely, black rape victims have a tendency to under-report white male rapists (Weis and Borges, 1973); rapists of Spanish heritage are often reported as black; other racial characteristics and stereotypes may influence the victims' accounts (Hindelang, 1978); false accusations based on discovery with a black lover (Baughman, 1966) or racial prejudice (see Mann, forthcoming).

Second, the issue is not necessarily "choice" of a white victim, but availability. Whites have little hesitancy to enter segregated minority communities to undertake business and/or socialize with non-whites. On the other hand, a minority, particularly a black, is not only conspicuous in an all-white community, but is rarely welcomed and more frequently subject to attack. In sum, more "integration" in minority communities yields disproportionately more potential white victims than there are available black victims in white areas.

7. In his Conclusion Wilbanks states, "My basic position is that both black and white views on the extent of racism in the criminal justice system are 'ignorant' in that personal knowledge is gained primarily via observation and experience—methods which are heavily influenced by bias and racial prejudice." Such a statement is an affront to careful researchers who use observational meth-

ods and practitioners who rely upon and report their experience in the field. The accusation that they cannot be objective demonstrates a bias as well as a paucity of knowledge about qualitative research methods.

Clearly, one method is insufficient to explore such a sensitive issue as racism in the criminal justice system. As Wilbanks suggests, future research on this question should concentrate on individual decision makers (p. 147). This cannot be fully accomplished without qualitative methods such as observation, interviews, biographical analyses, testing, card sorts, and similar techniques. It is the melding of the micro and macrolevels of data gathering and analysis where we will hopefully come together for meaningful answers to the provocative questions Wilbanks raises. *The Myth of a Racist Criminal Justice System* introduces more questions than it provides answers, which makes it a long overdue catalyst for all social scientists interested in racial injustice.

POSTSCRIPT

Is Systemic Racism in Criminal Justice a Myth?

What did you decide? Mann almost challenges you personally to get inside a police car, walk around the barrios, listen in on private snatches of conversation of police officers, judges, and prison guards; to take your camera and snap some shots of a person who is of a racial minority being arrested.

Wilbanks, with equal feeling, repeats that the numbers tell the story. Blacks are not necessarily being arrested unfairly; they are not being denied their constitutional rights; they are not more likely to receive longer sentences upon conviction for the same crime; nor are they less likely to be denied parole. The conclusion, then, Wilbanks insists, is that it is a myth to label the system as still being racist.

For outstanding current information on crime rates, criminal justice personnel, crime victims, and almost all matters related to crime including race, you may order free bulletins from the Bureau of Justice Statistics, U.S. Department of Justice, Washington, DC 20531. For a more comprehensive delineation of his thesis, see Wilbanks's *Myth of a Racist Criminal Justice System* (Brooks/Cole, 1987). For Coramae Mann's most recent work challenging Wilbanks, see her *Unequal Justice* (Indiana University Press, 1993).

Two interesting recent books that deal with the cultural backdrop that often legitimizes discrimination within American institutions, including criminal justice, see *Hate Crimes: The Rising Tide of Bigotry and Bloodshed,* by J. Levin and J. McDevitt (Plenum, 1993) and M. J. Matsuda et al., *Words That Wound: Critical Race Theory, Assaultive Speech, and the First Amendment* (Westview Press, 1993).

Carefully read the newspapers for the next several days. Are you able to identify reports on the criminal justice system that substantiate Wilbanks's thesis and/or the concerns of Coremae Richey Mann?

A study that documents racism within capital crime sentencing is A. Aguirre, Jr., and D. Baker, "Empirical Research on Racial Discrimination in the Imposition of the Death Penalty," *Criminal Justice Abstracts* (March 1990). For a discussion of young black males in the criminal justice system, see Marc Mauer's *Young Black Men and the Criminal Justice System* (The Sentencing Project, 1990). A succinct comparison of inmates in the United States and other nations can be found in Marc Mauer's "Americans Behind Bars," *Criminal Justice* (Winter 1992).

PART 4

Immigration, Demographic Changes, and Pluralism

With the single important exception of indigenous peoples, everyone on this continent, whether a minority or majority group member, is an immigrant or a descendant of an immigrant. A sociologist will tell you that once people are placed together, they predictably form patterns and mosaics, with uniformities and configurations that can be detected and explained. What patterns are formed when so many people, and so many different people, come together? How are vital myths—for example, the myth of the melting pot—formed, threatened, or altered when new demographic processes occur? How have other countries experienced massive immigration? Do culturally informed, modern minorities in the United States want to be part of the melting pot?

- Is Italy Solving Its Immigration Problem?

- Is There an Ethnic Revolt Against the Melting Pot?

ISSUE 15

Is Italy Solving Its Immigration Problem?

YES: Marco Martiniello, from "Italy: Two Perspectives—Racism in Paradise?" *Race and Class* (January/March 1991)

NO: Paul Kazim, from "Italy: Two Perspectives—Racism Is No Paradise!" *Race and Class* (January/March 1991)

ISSUE SUMMARY

YES: Marco Martiniello, a professor at the European Institute of Florence University in Italy, admits that the suddenness of Italy's immigration problem caught Italians off-guard, yet he feels that rational steps are being taken to resolve the problem.

NO: Film researcher Paul Kazim argues that Italy is far more racist than it cares to admit. To him, the government's responses to the problem of immigration as well as the growing hostility toward immigrants demonstrates this. The government's amnesty program, he feels, sometimes results in little more than "authorized starving."

Unlike the United States, in modern times, European nations (and, for that matter, most others) have been nations of emigration, that is, out-migration. Between 1820 and 1940, for example, some 60 million people left Europe, with approximately two-thirds going to the United States. Since 1861 when Italy achieved unification, 26 million Italians have emigrated, mostly to the United States. This figure is almost one-half of Italy's current total population of 56.5 million. Moreover, within many European nations, citizens were often greatly restricted in their movements around the country. Immigration was relatively rare, as was internal migration. This contrasts sharply with the United States experience, where borders were fairly permeable and travel between states virtually unrestricted.

Since World War II (1941–1945) significant demographic changes have occurred worldwide, especially in Europe. The reasons include the upheavals caused by the war itself; the need for inexpensive labor as northern and western European countries began to rebuild; the decision by people in the poorer countries of England's commonwealth to take advantage of the right to immigrate to England or other parts of the United Kingdom; the new international division of labor (NIDL); and the phenomenal expansion of populations in the underdeveloped countries (UDCs) and less developed countries (LDCs) of the Third World. There was thus both a "push" as well as a "pull" influencing these demographic changes.

But as European economic growth slowed in the late 1980s, the abundance of jobs dried up, and many countries began to realize that so-called guest workers from Turkey, Asia, and Africa were drawing unemployment and receiving other social service benefits, as were their families. As part of the human rights revolution, the United Nations and various international groups proposed that labor did not migrate, people did. Therefore, host countries ought to welcome families, not just individual workers. This was fine during economic good times, but such accommodation began to be strained when "guests" came to be perceived as a burden.

Germans, for example, were shaken to find a small but potent force attacking its immigrants. Skinheads, neo-Nazis, and other atavistic throwbacks terrorized, beat, and even burned alive foreigners living and working in Germany.

Italy, unlike other European countries, or the United States, was free of immigrant concerns until the 1980s. Then, for the first time in its recent history, immigration became a social problem. The Italian case study was selected for inclusion in this book for several reasons. It provides an opportunity to see how issues pertaining to racial and ethnic relations get played out in another country. Also, immigration is a key concept in the study of racial and ethnic relations. Lastly, immigration, the movement of vast numbers of peoples around the globe and the impact it will have on societies, is going to be a topic of continuing debate as the end of the twentieth century approaches.

In Italy in 1990 the Martelli Law was passed. This, you should notice from each discussion, has had both positive and negative effects on immigration. Also notice Italy's system of classification of foreigners. Is it a sensible solution or possibly part of the problem? In addition to the distinction between the *immigrati* (the majority of immigrants) and the *extra communitari* (political refugees), Italy separates foreigners who are part of the European Community from others, which usually implies Africans and Asians.

Note the various parts of North and Central Africa that most immigrants come from. Are they mostly men or women? Ages? Educational training?

Italy, then, represents an interesting case study since its problem is new and the stages that most countries pass through in defining and responding to the problem often take generations. Italy's response is highly condensed into less than a decade.

YES

Marco Martiniello

RACISM IN PARADISE?

The beginning of the 1970s marked a fundamental reversal in the history of migration in Italy. For more than a century before that, the transalpine peninsula had been one of the greatest supplies of labour power, first to North America and Latin America, then to other European countries, especially France, and also to Australia. There are today more than five million Italians dispersed throughout the world. But Italian emigration started to diminish even as the economic 'miracle' began to take shape, exclusively in the north and centre of the 'boot'. Now, the only Italian emigrants are those who put their mental abilities at the service of world industry.... Thus, while most European countries began to erect legal barriers at the beginning of the 1970s to prevent migration, Italy became, almost unawares, an importer of labour power, enticed by the image of paradise conjured up in the phrase 'made in Italy'. It is only recently, especially since 1986 and more spectacularly since the summer of 1989, that immigration has become an important issue in the media and in politics, in debates which cross the whole of Italian society.

SOME CHARACTERISTICS OF IMMIGRATION IN ITALY

A preliminary remark—when one speaks of immigration and immigrants in Italy, one is not referring to the rich retired Germans or English who live in the Tuscan countryside, or to American students or businessmen based in Florence, Rome or Milan. The term 'immigrant' is only applied to non-EC citizens from a Third World country who come to Italy to work. As for refugees and candidates for political asylum, they constitute a separate sub-category—the *'immigrati extracommunitari'* ["immigrant outside the community"].

How many of these immigrants are there? At the moment, no-one in Italy can say precisely, though everyone has his or her own estimate. There is a real war of numbers which is monopolising the energy of social science researchers. The National Institute of Statistics (ISTAT) recently estimated the non-EC presence in Italy as being 963,000 persons, a figure which includes Americans, Swiss and Austrians. As far as Third World 'immigrants' alone are concerned, their numbers, according to the most serious estimates, do not exceed 800,000—that is, just over 1 per cent of the population. And yet

From Marco Martiniello, "Italy: Two Perspectives—Racism in Paradise?" *Race and Class*, vol. 32, no. 3 (January/March 1991). Copyright © 1991 by The Institute of Race Relations, England. Reprinted by permission. Some notes omitted.

some people talk of an 'invasion' to characterise the migratory phenomenon in Italy!

Certainly, the impression of an invasion is created by the greater visibility of a fraction of these immigrants who live in the centre of the large towns. So, for example, the area around the Termini railway station in Rome gives to commuters—but also to tourists—a false image of the real situation, simply because of the concentration of *extra-communitari* who are easily recognised by the colour of their skin. This form of appropriation of certain parts of the urban space, nevertheless, points to a characteristic of immigration in Italy. It is primarily an urban phenomenon. Thus, the capital, Milan, Turin, Bologna, Florence and Naples are often major poles of attraction for immigrants, who move readily from one of these towns to another. There is also a transitory movement to the countryside, rural regions calling for seasonal immigrant workers for various harvests.

The origins of immigrants now living in Italy correspond to two different phases of migration: the earlier, mainly covering the period from 1970 to 1985; the recent, which began after that date. The first consisted mainly of Africans from the Italian ex-colonies and Iranian political refugees, but also included Filipino domestic workers and, in some parts of Sicily, Moroccans and Tunisians. But after 1986, Senegalese, as well as new waves of Tunisians and Ghanaians, began to arrive. There are now a number of different nationalities, mostly in the peninsula. With the exception of women domestic workers from the Philippines and Cape Verde, however, most of the new immigrants are young men, already urbanised in their countries of origin and with relatively high educational levels: 36.5 per cent have secondary school certificates or a university diploma and 23.3 per cent a professional diploma, according to a survey carried out... in December 1989. It is, however, very unusual for them to find employment in Italy commensurate with their diplomas and qualifications. They are nearly all economically active, but their entry into the Italian labour market is almost always precarious and illegal.

Immigrants gain employment in Italy in two main ways. On the one hand, some are employed in areas which have been abandoned by Italians. In other words, by accepting employment on conditions which Italians refuse, immigrants supply an unsatisfied demand in a number of sectors. In agriculture, immigrant workers are used for the various harvests, in several regions in both the north and south. They receive derisory salaries, often have no work contract and, consequently, no legal protection. In industry, small- and medium-sized enterprises in the north are increasingly seeking foreign labour already in Italy, either legally or illegally, to undertake unskilled work for wages which Italians would refuse. Furthermore, immigrant workers are sometimes recruited legally, then submitted to a special regime of flexible working. This was the case, for example, in the 1989 agreement signed between the Turin employers and trade unions over the legal engagement of immigrant workers to replace Italian workers in night shifts, on Sundays or on bank holidays. One should, therefore, treat with caution the theory about competition between Italians and foreigners on the labour market.

On the other hand, a second group seems to have created their own sphere where demand did not seem to exist before... the availability of immigrant labour seems to have created its own demand. In travelling sales, in particular, there is no explicit demand for immigrant labour, and yet this is often the point of entry into employment for many immigrants. And if one looks at the situation more closely, it appears that the more or less legal zones of the market economy which control such activities have rapidly created a demand for immigrant labour. In fact, immigrant travelling sales is largely controlled by illegal organisations which have taken maximum advantage of the most vulnerable section of immigrant labour. It is the same logic which leads organised crime to recruit immigrants into prostitution or soft drugs trafficking. Leaving part of the soft drugs trade in the hands of powerless immigrants allows its real controllers to increase profits while reducing risks.

It is clear that this type of exploitation of immigrants is only possible when there is a complete vacuum in immigration policy, which was the case until recently. In fact, most immigrants had no legal status or rights in Italian society until the adoption of the 'Martelli law', to which I shall return later. And obviously, people without protection need to deploy every means of survival, even if it is illegal.

From this brief outline of immigration certain aspects specific to Italy emerge:
• Unlike the immigration to northern Europe after the Second World War, that to Italy is not the result of explicit recruitment organised by the state and employers with trade union endorsement. It is, rather, the result of a conjuncture between an implicit appeal from Italy and 'push' factors in the countries of origin.
• Italy is still mainly at the stage of the immigration of workers, even if family reunification is already taking place for those who came in on the earlier waves of immigration.
• Immigration in Italian society is relatively modest in quantitative terms compared to the older European countries of immigration.

ITALY'S RESPONSE TO IMMIGRATION

As a new phenomenon, immigration poses questions and difficulties for society in general, as well as for politicians, since Italy is much more accustomed to exporting its poor than receiving them from other countries.

As far as society in general is concerned, immigration has delivered indirectly a strong upper-cut to the image of 'Italiani, brava gente' (Italians—a kind people) that Italians love to present and which is recognised by the world up to a certain point. After a long period of public and also political indifference to immigration and immigrants, Italian society has started to show increasing signs of unease and intolerance towards immigrants. Verbal as well as physical attacks on the 'new Italians' have become more and more frequent since the mid-1980s. Two of the most serious—and which were most discussed—were the assassination of a young black South African exile in the Naples region in August 1989 and the anti-immigrant raid during the Florence carnival in March 1990, which reached the French and British press. These two events, far from isolated, stoked up the debate on racism in Italy significantly. Italian society has come to question itself about the possibility of its own hidden racism. For some, there is no doubt that Italy is racist, just like other European countries. For others, it is not a question of racism but of the problems which arise from an inadequate sharing out of the insufficient resources produced by the Italian 'miracle'. Still others see Italy as going through a pre-racist period which, if we are not careful, could lead to racist wars in Italian cities.

Italian society today is going through a profound identity crisis as a result of the erosion of the two traditional poles of its social structure, one centred in the Catholic church and the other in the Communist party. Above and beyond the crisis of their reproduction and ideological renewal is the fact that these two groups of institutions, so central to Italian society, can no longer fulfil the functions of socialisation and identification for the younger generation as once they used to do. In a country like Italy, where the national entity is of recent origin, and somewhat fragile, the decline of the traditional poles of social identification could be the origin of a sense of insecurity and a diffuse malaise in society.

The growing economic dualism of Italian society is also bringing similar consequences. The wound, which has never healed, of modern Italian history—the economic backwardness of the southern regions of the 'boot'—seems to be getting worse. While the northern regions are at the forefront of technological progress, enjoy exceptionally high levels of productivity and are thus among the foremost areas of advanced capitalism, the south, with some exceptions, is stagnating. Unemployment there is very high, productivity weak, technological development slow. This unequal development, and the interpretations which are given to it, deepen the malaise to which I have already referred.

This malaise expresses itself most directly in two phenomena, which are also connected to displays of intolerance toward non-European immigrants and toward southerners. First, there is the violence around football, which is the action of organised groups of pseudo-supporters who target not just supporters of the opposite team but also immigrant workers. Thus, the aggressors at the 'Mardi Gras' festival in Florence belonged to the 'ultras' of Fiorentina. Or again, last May, Juventas supporters who had to change trains at Genoa on their way back from a match in the south, attacked several North Africans who were in their way. And that is not counting the anti-southern and anti-immigrant chants which one hears more and more in Italian stadiums. Second, there is the growing phenomenon of 'leagues' (Lega Lombarda, Liga Veneta, etc.); right-wing regional parties of the north whose success depends on mobilising anti-southern and anti-immigrant sentiments.

Thus, immigration and racism constitute major political issues, both domestically and on the European level in the run-up to 1991. Internally, electoral considerations seem to guide the positions taken and the proposals made by the different parties about immigration and, more precisely, migration policy. At the European level, Italy is attempting to get rid of the image prevalent in other EC countries, of having 'leaky frontiers', which are considered to pose serious difficulties over free movement of European nationals within the EC after 1992. Following direct or indirect, implicit or explicit pressure from the rest of the Community, it has set up mechanisms to control immigrants: to stop them, on the one hand, and, on the other, to 'integrate' those[1] who are already within its borders. Hence, the 'Martelli law' of 28 February 1990, which also deals with political refugees. This law (named after the vice-president of the Council), together with law 943 passed in December 1986, constitutes the framework of Italian migration policy. The basis of the 'Martelli law' was a government decree adopted in December 1989 aimed at solving the urgent problems of immigration. To control migration, it posts an annual programme for the entry of immigrant workers to be established jointly by the ministries concerned (foreign affairs, interior, planning and employment). It is important to stress that in an interview given to the daily *La Repubblica* on 9 June 1990, Martelli clearly implied that, from 1991, frontiers would be virtually closed. As for 'integration', the law confirms the regularisation of foreigners living in Italy before December 1989, which had al-ready been promised by the government. As from 29 June 1990, it is impossible for illegal immigrants to gain access to legal status. Thus, Italy is attempting to pass as rapidly as possible from having no legal conditions on immigration to aligning itself with other EC countries so as to make a unified Community policy on migration possible. In a way, Italy has to jump a number of stages and simply follow, as closely as possible, the pattern set by other European countries. This desire to line up alongside its EC partners shows itself particularly in Italy's signing of the Schengen agreements in October 1990.

NOTE

1. The concept of 'integration' poses the same sort of confusions in Italy as elsewhere.

NO

Paul Kazim

RACISM IS NO PARADISE!

To nearly 200 Bangladeshi, Indian, Pakistani and Sri Lankan immigrant work-ers on hunger strike in Milan, the giant hoarding [billboard] suspended high opposite the city's famous Duomo cathedral, advertising the 'True Colours of Bennetton', was nothing but a cruel joke. Gazing down, in an image of racial harmony, were two women, one black, one white, holding a Chinese baby. But these immigrant workers had already seen the true colours of Italian society.

Miserable, cold and hungry, they sat on cardboard sheets in a make-shift camp on Milan's Piazza Vetra, a large, grassy, crapping zone for many of the city's dogs. Highly qualified, they had come to Italy, equipped with degrees, doctorates and high hopes. But wakened to their Italian reality, they organised themselves as the Milan branch of the United Asian Workers' Association, a body set up by homeless Asian workers in Rome. Step two was to embark on a desperate hunger strike—not something they had anticipated writing home about to their families.

'We thought Italy was a civilised country where we could find jobs, good money and nice homes. But they treat dogs better than us. We were so wrong', said Mohammed Riaz. It was an understandable mistake: Milan, seen by these men from Dacca, Lahore and Delhi, was Europe's citadel of a designer capitalism that promised them jobs, money and homes.

Riaz and his colleagues resorted to the hunger strike after being unceremo-niously removed from their sit-in under the Largo Treves offices of Milan's social security chief, Roberto Bernardelli. He had promised them 300 blankets. Consistent with his past promises of accommodation for these immigrants, promises as vacant as many of Milan's buildings, Bernardelli's blankets never materialised. As the hunger strike began, Bernardelli, the Italian flag hanging behind him, gave interviews about the gradual but inevitable acceptance by Italian society of its new multi-racial reality.

There was, though, nothing gradual about the need of these workers for accommodation. Collectively huddled in nearby cloisters for warmth and security, the hunger strikers were forcibly cleared out by police in a drenching downpour. The hunger strike was over, but they were still living on Milan's

From Paul Kazim, "Italy: Two Perspectives—Racism Is No Paradise!" *Race and Class*, vol. 32, no. 3 (January/March 1991). Copyright © 1991 by The Institute of Race Relations, England. Reprinted by permission. Notes omitted.

streets. An occupation of the Santa Ambrogio church ended when police threw them back on to the streets. The hunger strikers had earlier been removed from an empty council building—on the premise that it was unfit for human habitation. Others were thrown out of a disused garage and moved to a fairground.

Arriving in Milan from Rome, they had encountered a city where unemployment is low but jobs are few. A brusque, unfriendly city where African migrants wander the streets, trying to sell leather goods and cigarettes to style-conscious Milanese, who would rather spend extravagantly on Gucci and Vacheron-Constantin designer items than buy no-style, no-label goods from a nobody African hawker.

They thought Milan must have more to offer than Rome. Italy's capital had dashed many of their hopes, offering them no work, and only hotel accommodation that quickly ate into whatever money they had brought with them. Time was passed sitting amongst the trees of the Piazza del Cinquecento or on the steps of the Piazza della Repubblica. They watched young Senegalese men laying down their blanket displays of bags, wallets, purses, cigarettes, leather straps, leather belts, sunglasses and beads, items they forlornly hoped to sell to tourists.

Near Rome's main bus terminal, they saw large groups of Filipino men and women chatting, playing cards, eating rice and chicken out of large 'cook-up' pots, as they waited to go on their night or early shifts as cleaners, au-pairs, hotel porters and kitchen staff. In Rome, only the Filipinos have any sort of job or security.

Two months or so later, tired and broke, many of those who would end up on hunger strike made their way to Rome's Stazione Centrale where they saw Somalian men and women sitting, talking at tables in the concourse cafe, much to the irritation of the Roman waiters urging them to order or move on. But the hunger strikers were most interested in checking train fares and times to the north—to Turin, Genoa, Bologna, Reggio Nell'Emilia, Florence and, of course, Milan, the 'real Italy', where they expected jobs and homes.

Italy's post-war economic growth has rested on such a migration of workers from the underdeveloped rural south to the rapaciously industrialising urban north. But Milan's economy did not need this latest set of arrivals from the south. Most of these immigrants had been in Italy since March 1989, drawn by the Martelli decree, the amnesty granted to illegal immigrants. Mistakenly, they believed the amnesty meant that socialist Italy at least would welcome them with open arms. Then, too late, they understood the true nature of the amnesty tactic—a political expedient intended to 'regularise' and take out the illegal workforce from the labour market, while at the same time stopping the entry of further 'illegals'.

The Martelli law of 28 February 1990 outlawed new Third World immigration by imposing visa requirements on people entering Italy from Morocco, Tunisia, Algeria, Turkey, Mauritania and Senegal. It provided a semblance of security for Italy's unauthorised immigrant workers—provided they beat the 28 June 1990 deadline, such workers were told they could obtain a residence permit.

Technically, a residence permit guarantees an employment card. But for those immigrant workers at the Piazza Vetra who did have low-paid, cash-only jobs as brick-layers and drivers, legality made them less attractive and more expensive to their employers. Better to be illegal and earning than be authorised and starving was how they viewed the amnesty.

Thus, to the immigrants the amnesty was scarcely worth the paper on which it was written. 'I wrote it with great sadness. The amnesty has a general principle that's very severe', Martelli said. Genuinely saddened or not, Martelli helped buy time for the government and his ruling Socialist party. The Lega Lombarda, an extreme right-wing group advocating separatism for the rich Lombardy region that includes Milan, was fanning popular resentment against immigrants. The amnesty would buy time for the government—but the Lega's call for a referendum helped it to enlarge its 20 per cent vote-catching power. Already, the Lega Lombarda had successfully whipped up local resentment against the presence of 600 homeless and mainly jobless Moroccan men, women and children at La Cascina Rosa, a shanty town erected on a derelict farm, located in a prosperous high-rise inner suburb of Milan. The Carabinieri, acting on the orders of the local magistrate, dragged the peacefully protesting Moroccans from the one haven they had from attack at night. Just weeks before, 26-year-old Foaud Ouchbani had been brutally murdered in central Milan, hit over the head by a bottle as he tried to sell cigarettes.

La Cascina Rosa, its makeshift mosque, barber's shop, surgery and restaurant, its electricity supply routed by cables from nearby street lamps, was razed to the ground by the Carabinieri. The local magistrate justified the raid on grounds that La Cascina Rosa was insanitary. True, there was a cesspool, but more smelly was the Left politics that decreed

that the only way to stop the electoral advance of the extreme Right was to destroy the self-made community of a deprived underclass.

Sending in the Carabinieri was a short-term, clumsy political expedient for Milan city council. Bernardelli's office wanted to appear to the Milanese as tough on the immigrant, and then humanitarian after the kick-in. The fear was that the Milanese were beginning to pay too much heed to the solutions offered by the extreme Right. Across Italy, unauthorised workers like these were solving employers' cheap labour problems. In Milan, where the need for cheap labour was almost zero, they were a convenient political scapegoat. Indulging anti-immigrant sentiment was seen as the only way to stop the extreme Right.

After the 'amnesty', other EC governments could no longer deride Italy as the easy way into Fortress Europe for Third World immigrants. Italy could now set up its stall in Schengenland, the unofficial title for the no-passport zone between France, Germany, the Netherlands, Belgium and Luxembourg. Once Italy had been refused entry into Schengen on account of it being Europe's weak immigration link. Now Italy has built its section of the Euro iron curtain.

Proof that the amnesty had failed to provide any real security for Italy's illegal immigrants came in a series of incidents last autumn, three months after the amnesty deadline. Italian youths set fire to an immigrant hostel in Bolzano, near Bologna. Some 120 homeless North African immigrants questioned whether the arson had been legitimated by Bolzano town councillors in their banning of any more black people from settling there.

Turin and Verona, two of the most industrial northern cities, banned immigrants from washing car windscreens at traffic lights. (From Palermo in Sicily to Naples and Milan this work has often been the only source of income for many immigrants.) African fruit-pickers were attacked in vineyards, orange groves and orchards around Naples. In the same area, along darkened roads, illuminated only by the eery fires lit by prostitutes advertising their services, African women were attacked by pimps and prostitutes angered at being under-cut by 'exotic' competition.

Italy is now a society worried by the implications of its increasing dependency on cheap, illegal foreign labour. But, to keep it cheap, it must be illegal. And to keep Italy's economy fully powered, this form of Third World development aid must succeed in getting into the country; the politics of the amnesty must remain a charade.

In a country where tomatoes are almost sacred, the Italian press reported that unauthorised African migrants in the Apulia and Puglia regions picked almost 50 per cent of the country's tomato harvest. Tomato prices, it was reported, were kept low by employing illegal African labourers at low rates of pay with no contracts.

Migrants had arrived in Italy throughout 1990 by boat via Tunis, coming to the Sicilian ports of Palermo, Trapani, Catania and Mazara del Vallo. Most were able to enter on tourist visas, even though immigration officers knew they were not tourists but potential settlers hoping to stay. Those put back on the returning ferries had been removed from Italy before, their glued passport pages slit open to reveal the removal stamps.

Yet potential immigrants were still entering Italy by clandestine and more dangerous means. Fishing boats from Tunis carried many immigrants to the southern Sicilian port of Mazara del Vallo, the closest Italian town to Tunisia, to Africa. Sleepy, blazing hot Mazara became the centre of national concern when it was revealed that almost 11 per cent of its population were non-Italian, non-EC nationals. Though more akin to Bognor Regis, Italian society came to see slumbering Mazara as Italy's Marseilles, where Europe not only meets but is swamped by Africa.

Nearly 50 per cent of Mazara's fishing boats employ cheap Tunisian or Moroccan crews. It is one of many statistics that now haunts Italian society. The biggest bogey is the projection that Italy's population will fall from its current 56 million to 45 million in 2045, of whom only one in four will be active workers. Italy, notwithstanding the Pope, has the lowest birthrate in Europe and is already paying for 19 million pensions.

Cheap Third World labour will become an even greater necessity unless Italians can heed the advice of their Labour Minister Carlo Donat Cattin who called on Italians to produce more babies 'to keep away armadas of immigrants from the southern shores of the Mediterranean'. It was a call that was echoed by Umberto Eco: 'We are not facing an immigration phenomenon. We are facing a migratory phenomenon. And like all great migrations, its final result will be an inexorable change in habits, and unstoppable interbreeding that changes the colour of skin, hair and eyes.'

But Catholic Italians are becoming more like their European Protestant counterparts: they want less children and more material gain. Nor do they want the dirty and tedious jobs in the hospitals, the fields or the domestic jobs—they want Third World workers to slop out Italian society. But the fear is growing that the Italian nation will be slopped out in the process. Either way, Third World migrant workers will face further angry and violent resentment for being, in reality, Italy's economic saviours.

POSTSCRIPT

Is Italy Solving Its Immigration Problem?

In addition to distinguishing *immigrati* and *extra communitari*, Italy formally classifies immigrants into *irregolari* (having permits no longer valid) and *clandestini* (illegally in Italy). The latter correspond to "undocumented workers" in the United States. Under the new law, those already in Italy would be able to renew or obtain resident cards and then be able to get an employment card. The *clandestini* need to find legal work. However, there is very little legal work in Italy for immigrants, Kazim points out. Thus immigrants are often better off remaining *irregolari* to get jobs. These would be low paying and without benefits, but at least they would be jobs. To many, that is better than "authorized and starving."

The countries of origin of most of Italy's known immigrants are: Morocco, approximately 12.0 percent of the immigrant population; Tunisia, 6.5 percent (41,234); the Philippines, 5.4 percent; Yugoslavia, 4.7 percent; and Senegal, 3.9 percent (Rosoli, 1993). As indicated by Martiniello, most of these immigrants are young males, and most of them are relatively highly educated. The exception are the domestic workers from the Philippines.

Italy's immigrant patterns follow a north-south axis, which is similar to the United States. As part of the 17-country Mediterranean basin, Italy receives most of its immigrants from the south. They migrate north into the more prosperous cities.

As a member of the European Community (EC), Italy's situation is especially precarious. That is, since borders are now much more permeable among EC countries, if Italy is found to be exporting many illegals (however unintentionally), this could jeopardize Italy's standing in the EC.

Martiniello mentions that a large number of immigrants engage in "traveling sales" and seems to be a little puzzled by this. This simply reflects the North African cultural patterns of trading. People are sometimes frightened by those who, even because of employment opportunities, wander from area to area. Indeed, Gypsies are among the most discriminated-against ethnic minorities in Italy and other parts of Europe.

Is Italy solving its immigration problem? Many would point out that immigration as a problem is largely a consequence of Italians simply being unprepared. Nowhere in Europe has there been official policies providing guidelines on immigration. The single exception has been France; for generations France has had working agencies to deal with foreigners.

Italy, like other European countries, rapidly went from being a nation of emigrants to one of immigrants. Yet, unlike other nations, especially Germany and England, its policies and treatment of racial and ethnic minority immigrants was seen as being based on social tolerance. In a few short years the situation has changed dramatically. A recent article that updates both Martiniello's optimism and Kazim's pessimism is Giovanna Campani's "Immigration and Racism in Southern Europe: The Italian Case," in *Ethnic and Racial Studies* (July 1993). Campanis' thoughtful discussion draws from several of the most important recent articles, including one in Italian by U. Melotti, who argues that Italy's immigration situation was initially peculiar and now is an "exemplary case." Campani feels that the shift has been from one of social tolerance to one of social crisis. He points out that, proportionately, Italy has a relatively small number of immigrants, but the problems are real.

Traditionally, among the major Mediterranean nations, Portugal was considered to be the most racially tolerant. However, according to M. Eaton's "Foreign Residents and Illegal Immigrants: Os Negros Em Portugal," *Ethnic and Racial Studies* (July 1993), that country is now showing signs of intolerance toward Black immigrants.

France, as mentioned, has also been considered a "model" nation in terms of its laws, long in place, protecting immigrants. Yet even that country is now making sharp distinctions between immigrants already in France and future immigrants. See R. Conniff's "France to Immigrants: Go Home," *The Progressive* (October 1993).

For an excellent overview of the problem, see A. Montanari and A. Cortese, "South to North Migration in a Mediterranean Perspective," and "Third World Immigrants in Italy." Both articles are in *Mass Migration in Europe*, edited by R. King (Belhaven Press, 1993). Another excellent discussion of Italian immigration policy is G. Rosoloi, "Italy: Emergent Immigration Policy," in *The Politics of Migration Policies*, edited by D. Kubat (Center for Migration Studies, 1993). Both of the above two books, by the way, have outstanding articles on immigration in other European countries.

A fascinating ethnography of immigrants in a Latin American country is *Banana Fallout: Class, Color, and Culture Among West Indians in Costa Rica*, by Trevor Purcell (UCLA Press, 1993). For an interesting comparison between Third World peoples as immigrants and poor whites, and their responses to discrimination, see *White But Poor: On the History of Poor Whites in Southern Africa 1880–1940*, edited by R. Morrell (University of South Africa, 1992).

ISSUE 16

Is There an Ethnic Revolt Against the Melting Pot?

YES: Editors of *Social Justice*, from "Five Hundred Years of Genocide, Repression, and Resistance," *Social Justice* (Summer 1992)

NO: Arthur M. Schlesinger, Jr., from *The Disuniting of America: Reflections on a Multicultural Society* (W. W. Norton, 1992)

ISSUE SUMMARY

YES: The editors of *Social Justice* reject almost all previous formulation of ethnicity and assimilation in the United States. Their aim is to "reclaim the true history" of the continent, which, they say, is one of enslavement, torture, and repression of people of color, who are now in revolt against lies and exploitation.

NO: Harvard University historian, and advisor to President Kennedy, Arthur M. Schlesinger, Jr., argues that the genius of the United States lies in its unity—the ability of its citizens to embrace basic, common values while accepting cultural diversity. He bitterly attacks "ethnic ideologues" who are bent on disuniting America, not bringing about positive changes.

> The dawn of the twentieth century found white Europe master of the world.... Never before in the history of civilization had self-worship of a people's accomplishment attained the heights that the worship of white Europe by Europeans reached.... Was there no other way for the advance of mankind? Were there no other cultural patterns, ways of action, goals of progress, which might and may lead man to something finer and higher?
>
> —W. E. B. Du Bois

"It may be too bad that dead white European males have played so large a role in shaping our culture. But that is the way it is. One cannot erase history." So Arthur M. Schlesinger, Jr., argues. "Not so," counter the editors of *Social Justice*. First, the perpetuation of the myth that only Western cultural productions are worthy of being taught is in itself a continuation of the dominance of dead white European males. Until the past few years, the editors claim, ethnic and racial minorities were treated as if they had no history, no customs, or no culture worthy of being taught.

Schlesinger counters that that is what multicultural education is: the teaching about other peoples. He says that descendants of Europeans number 80 percent in this country and that they should be able to learn about their own history. He points out that in 78 percent of all American colleges it is possible to graduate without taking a single Western history course. To him this is a consequence of the work of opponents of the United States and Western culture.

Social Justice editors contend that sexism, racism, and bigotry are so strong in the United States and that the oppressions of the past are so real and pervasive that the old culture must be torn up by its roots. A new society needs to be created.

Schlesinger and many other traditional minority relations scholars feel that this type of analysis reveals people who are locked into the insights of their own times and unfairly and inaccurately superimpose them on patterns of conduct of the past. Schlesinger also charges those who share the views of the editors of *Social Justice* with being unfair and selective in their historical analysis.

Social critics of America argue that people like Schlesinger are caught up in the iron shackles of the myths that they grew up on and simply cannot shake them off. They want to believe the myths they have taught their students and have written about for several years.

The problem, as Merton might delight in pointing out, is simply one of sharply competing frames of reference. What a new, badly needed minority theory will look like and what kind of research agenda it will contain is a question that probably many American sociologists and historians would contend remains unanswerable. As *Social Justice* editorial board member Anthony Platt puts it: "We need the kind of interdisciplinary and comparative theory that not only gives us a better grasp of the dynamics of racism and ethnicity, but also enables us to construct a political vision of equality that resonates in the public imagination. There is much to both rethink and unthink."

Schlesinger's argument is that the genius of the American experience is its ability to maintain religious, ethnic, and racial diversities in a stable fashion. The whole society is held together by the common value of *e pluribus unum*, all for one and one for all. The common goal of fitting in, working together, and assimilating enables diverse people, Schlesinger argues, to remain in the same society without civil war.

As you read these two diametrically opposed articles, try to decide what elements in both discussions provide helpful information on minority relations. Which do you feel is more historically accurate? Why? Which perspective have you been taught in American history? What might be the policy implications for the *Social Justice*'s analysis in terms of programs for minorities? Those of Schlesinger's position? Which position is more "politically correct?" Why?

YES

Editors of *Social Justice*

FIVE HUNDRED YEARS OF GENOCIDE, REPRESSION, AND RESISTANCE

With this issue of *Social Justice* the editors wish to add our voices to the millions that are reclaiming the true history of this continent over the last five centuries and celebrating its indigenous people as part of "500 years of Resistance." We do this not only out of revulsion at the crimes of genocide that began with Columbus' arrival in 1492, but also because both the genocide and native resistance to it continue today. We do this not only in tribute to the indigenous peoples, but also because their cultures and values represent a planet-saving alternative to contemporary capitalist society. We do this because understanding the global meaning of 1492 is a crucial step in making the next 500 years better than the last.

Columbus and subsequent invaders set in motion a world-historic process of European colonization, by which a nascent capitalist system expanded monumentally across the earth—in the Americas, Africa, and Asia. It was a process based on human and environmental exploitation, the legacies of which continue to this day. The merciless assault on indigenous peoples served as the bedrock upon which Western culture and the capitalist economy were built in the Americas. Indeed, Europe also semi-enslaved its own for gain, beginning with the indentured servants who came to the Americas early on.

Human society had seen racism before, but nothing could approach the forms it took on this continent as the capitalist process unfolded. The destruction of indigenous societies, the enslavement of Africans, and the theft of the mestizo homeland in today's Southwest were logical steps. All served primitive accumulation, as did the later importation of Asian labor.

We can also say that the planet had been mistreated before, but nothing could approach its post–1492 fate. Whether we think of global warming, deterioration of the ozone layer, destruction of the rain forests, or all the effects of environmental abuse on human communities, especially those of color, we know that disaster now faces life on this earth. Simply put, today's environmental crisis results from 500 years of unbridled capitalist exploitation. "Progress" has not come without a staggering price, if it can be called progress at all.

The full meaning of the European invasion of the Americas would have been unimaginable to Bartolomé de Las Casas, our best-known eyewitness. Nonetheless, he described with devastating clarity what was to become a model for such imperialist expansion. Originally a soldier with the invaders and later a priest, de Las Casas left us an account of events, *The Devastation of the Indies,* published in 1552, describing the atrocities and suffering that attended the Spanish invasion as it proceeded province by province. He apologizes repeatedly for not including every incident of horror, stating: "Were I to describe all this, no amount of time and paper could encompass this task."

What is there is enough. One hesitates to turn the page for fear of discovering another way that one human destroyed another: stabbing, dismembering, burning, beating, throwing against rocks, feeding to dogs, torturing, starving, raping, enslaving, and working to death. As described by de Las Casas, the invaders behaved like wild animals in a frenzy of blood lust—and the Spaniards were not alone among Europe's colonial assassins.

Never in history has there been such systematic destruction of an entire continent, and in so short a time. The genocide against the native peoples of Latin America was accomplished in less than 50 years. De Las Casas reports that in New Spain (Mexico), "the Spaniards have killed more Indians here in 12 years... than anywhere else in the Indies... some four million souls." Regarding the islands of San Juan (Puerto Rico) and Jamaica, he said, "I believe there were more than one million inhabitants, and now, in each of the two islands, there are no more than two hundred persons." A total of 25 million victims across the continent does not seem exaggerated and, in the opinion of some scholars, would be too low a figure.

De Las Casas' appeal to Spain's King Charles I to end the massacres produced royal edicts that went ignored by the invading soldiers and officials. Yet de Las Casas' "Brief Account" stands as an example of speaking out against injustice. It stands as a call for people today, 500 years later, to tell the truth about the history of this continent and to redress the legacy of racist violence that continues against both land and people.

Hans Koning takes up the call... by exposing the myth of Columbus as navigator, hero, discoverer. "We find ourselves in a fight," he declares, "to establish the truth about our past, *finally;* a fight about how we teach our history to our children.... It is high time *to overcome* the Columbus legacy." Ward Churchill takes on "Deconstructing the Columbus Myth" with penetrating observations about Columbus as proto-Nazi and the resemblance of "New World" settlements to Nazi rule. In another article, Bill Bigelow offers an insightful exposé of Columbus as he is presented to children, describing how an entire worldview is developed from the assumptions and historical inaccuracies of the Columbus legend.

In answering that call from de Las Casas, we must look at certain underlying issues raised by the invaders' devastation. We must ask ourselves if a profound immorality was fundamental to all Western/non-Western relations from the beginning. One answer is unavoidable: the ideological foundation of genocide is dehumanization, as the story of physical and cultural genocide in the Americas demonstrates. The native peoples were not "Christians," therefore not human. With industrialization, the denial of humanity intensified as more and more people became objects to generate profit. In their book on Brazil, *Fate of the Forest*, Susanne Hecht and Alexander Cockburn comment that because of massive destruction in the Amazon, "the extinction is not only of nature but of socialized nature."

Today we see an intensification of racism in the United States and around the world based on this same process of defining people as "the Other." African Americans, Chicanos, and other Latinos, Asian Americans, immigrants in general, and, of course, today's Native Americans—all people of color—are feeling the brunt of contemporary dehumanization. This is one reason why the fight for multiculturalism... is important. Poet-essayist Luis Rodriguez offers a vision of culture with room for both people of color and European strengths, while reminding us that we had "better be prepared to remake our continent with the full and equal participation of all." Such perspectives suggest the aggressive campaign to demand social justice that is so needed today. For both physical and cultural genocide continue; we cannot file them away as distant history, a lamentable white man's burden.

RESISTANCE ALSO CONTINUES

As Rigoberta Menchú states... "we are a people who refuse to be annihilated.... We know our struggle is just—it's the only reason we still exist." Resistance by indigenous peoples, as de Las Casas confirms, goes back 500 years and it continues today in many arenas: treaty and land rights, education, culture, language and traditional ways, repression and harassment of activists, drugs and alcohol in Native American communities, racism and exploitation.... The longstanding campaign to free Leonard Peltier, described... by Roxanne Dunbar Ortiz, offers an especially powerful symbol of the Native American resistance movement and its efforts to free political prisoners.

Native Americans are not the only people fighting the ravages of 500 post-Columbus years. Puerto Rico, whose indigenous peoples were wiped off the face of the earth within a few years, remains a full-fledged colony today.... Suzie Dod and Piri Thomas remind us of the healthy, thriving, cooperative, ecosystemic Taino people, who typify the Caribbean societies that Spain destroyed, and the very different life facing today's Puerto Rican people. There and elsewhere, respect for what we call the environment is crucial to people of color for reasons of human as well as planet survival. A movement against environmental racism has begun in the United States to combat the disproportionate presence of toxic wastes in poor and minority communities....

TOWARD A DIFFERENT 500 YEARS

No condemnation of the European invasion and colonization of the Americas can be too strong, as even the smallest study of indigenous history confirms. Yet along with righteous anger and an insistence on listening to silenced histories, the quincentennial year offers a unique chance to put forth radical alternatives to the Western expansionist model.

In her groundbreaking essay, Annette Jaimes makes a strong case for "revisioning native America," which she begins by challenging claims that indigenous peoples were "backward" in areas ranging from agriculture to medicine.

She also questions the concept of all indigenous life as unending drudgery to achieve minimum survival by pointing to societies where many have subsisted adequately or better on a few hours of work per week. What does that say about how we assess quality-of-life in relation to labor process?

Jaimes affirms that "the conceptual key to liberation of native societies is... also the key to liberating Eurocentrism from itself, unchaining it from the twin fetishes of materialism and production...." She believes that "the reemergence of a vibrant and functioning Native North America in the 21st century would offer a vital prefiguration of what humanity as a whole might accomplish." Only by recognizing the wisdom and values retained by "Stone Agers" of the modern indigenous world, she argues, "will we be able to forge a multifaceted but collectively held worldview that places materialism and spirituality in sustainable balance with one another."

With this hope of liberating modern capitalist society from itself, and thus transforming the world as shaped by European expansion 500 years ago, we can dream of a new and different 500 years to come. Nor can it be merely a dream. As María Elena Ramírez says in her "Resistance Rap" the issue is "insistence on our very existence—on our planet's existence."

NO   Arthur M. Schlesinger, Jr.

THE DISUNITING OF AMERICA

Is Europe really the root of all evil? The crimes of Europe against lesser breeds without the law (not to mention even worse crimes—Hitlerism and Stalinism—against other Europeans) are famous. But these crimes do not alter other facts of history: that Europe was the birthplace of the United States of America, that European ideas and culture formed the republic, that the United States is an extension of European civilization, and that nearly 80 percent of Americans are of European descent.

... It may be too bad that dead white European males have played so large a role in shaping our culture. But that's the way it is. One cannot erase history.

These humdrum historical facts, and not some dastardly imperialist conspiracy, explain the Eurocentric slant in American schools. Would anyone seriously argue that teachers should conceal the European origins of American civilization? or that schools should cater to the 20 percent and ignore the 80 percent? Of course the 20 percent and their contributions should be integrated into the curriculum too, which is the point of cultural pluralism.

But self-styled "multiculturalists" are very often ethnocentric separatists who see little in the Western heritage beyond Western crimes. The Western tradition, in this view, is inherently racist, sexist, "classist," hegemonic; irredeemably repressive, irredeemably oppressive. The spread of Western culture is due not to any innate quality but simply to the spread of Western power. Thus the popularity of European classical music around the world—and, one supposes, of American jazz and rock too—is evidence not of wide appeal but of "the pattern of imperialism, in which the conquered culture adopts that of the conqueror."

Such animus toward Europe lay behind the well-known crusade against the Western-civilization course at Stanford ("Hey-hey, ho-ho, Western culture's got to go!"). According to the National Endowment for the Humanities, students can graduate from 78 percent of American colleges and universities without taking a course in the history of Western civilization. A number of institutions... require courses in third-world or ethnic studies but not in Western civilization. The mood is one of divesting Americans of the sinful

European inheritance and seeking redemptive infusions from non-Western
cultures.

* * *

One of the oddities of the situation is
that the assault on the Western tradition
is conducted very largely with analytical weapons forged in the West. What
are the names invoked by the coalition
of latter-day Marxists, deconstruction-
ists, poststructuralists, radical feminists,
Afrocentrists? Marx, Nietzsche, Gramsci, Derrida, Foucault, Lacan, Sartre,
De Beauvoir, Habermas, the Frankfurt
"critical theory" school—Europeans all.
The "unmasking," "demythologizing,"
"decanonizing," "dehegemonizing" blitz
against Western culture depends on
methods of critical analysis unique to
the West—which surely testifies to the
internally redemptive potentialities of
the Western tradition.

Even Afrocentrists seem to accept sub-
liminally the very Eurocentric standards
they think they are rejecting. "Black intellectuals condemn Western civilization,"
Professor Pearce Williams says, "yet ar-
dently wish to prove it was founded by
their ancestors." ...

Radical academics denounce the
"canon" as an instrument of European
oppression enforcing the hegemony of
the white race, the male sex, and the
capitalist class....

* * *

Is the Western tradition a bar to progress
and a curse on humanity? Would it really
do America and the world good to get rid
of the European legacy?

No doubt Europe has done terrible things, not least to itself. But what
culture has not? History, said Edward
Gibbon, is little more than the register

of the crimes, follies, and misfortunes
of mankind. The sins of the West are no
worse than the sins of Asia or the Middle
East or of Africa.

There remains, however, a crucial difference between the Western tradition
and the others. The crimes of the West
have produced their own antidotes. They
have provoked great movements to end
slavery, to raise the status of women, to
abolish torture, to combat racism, to defend freedom of inquiry and expression,
to advance personal liberty and human
rights.

Whatever the particular crimes of Europe, that continent is also the source—
the *unique* source—of those liberating
ideas of individual liberty, political democracy, the rule of law, human rights,
and cultural freedom that constitute our
most precious legacy and to which most
of the world today aspires. These are
European ideas, not Asian, nor African,
nor Middle Eastern ideas, except by
adoption....

There is surely no reason for Western
civilization to have guilt trips laid on
it by champions of cultures based on
despotism, superstition, tribalism, and
fanaticism. In this regard the Afrocentrists are especially absurd. The West
needs no lectures on the superior virtue
of those "sun people" who sustained
slavery until Western imperialism abol-
ished it (and, it is reported, sustain it to
this day in Mauritania and the Sudan),
who still keep women in subjection
and cut off their clitorises, who carry
out racial persecutions not only against
Indians and other Asians but against
fellow Africans from the wrong tribes,
who show themselves either incapable of
operating a democracy or ideologically
hostile to the democratic idea, and who
in their tyrannies and massacres, their

Idi Amins and Boukasas, have stamped with utmost brutality on human rights.

... What the West would call corruption is regarded through much of Africa as no more than the prerogative of power. Competitive political parties, an independent judiciary, a free press, the rule of law are alien to African traditions.

It was the French, not the Algerians, who freed Algerian women from the veil...; as in India it was the British, not the Indians, who ended (or did their best to end) the horrible custom of *suttee*—widows burning themselves alive on their husbands' funeral pyres. And it was the West, not the non-Western cultures, that launched the crusade to abolish slavery—and in doing so encountered mighty resistance, especially in the Islamic world (where Moslems, with fine impartiality, enslaved whites as well as blacks). Those many brave and humane Africans who are struggling these days for decent societies are animated by Western, not by African, ideals. White guilt can be pushed too far.

The Western commitment to human rights has unquestionably been intermittent and imperfect. Yet the ideal remains—and movement toward it has been real, if sporadic. Today it is the *Western* democratic tradition that attracts and empowers people of all continents, creeds, and colors....

* * *

... History is littered with the wreck of states that tried to combine diverse ethnic or linguistic or religious groups within a single sovereignty. Today's headlines tell of imminent crisis or impending dissolution in one or another multi-ethnic polity—the Soviet Union, India, Yugoslavia, Czechoslovakia, Ireland, Belgium, Canada, Lebanon, Cyprus, Israel, Ceylon, Spain, Nigeria, Kenya, Angola, Trinidad, Guyana.... The list is almost endless. The luck so far of the American experiment has been due in large part to the vision of the melting pot. "No other nation," Margaret Thatcher has said, "has so successfully combined people of different races and nations within a single culture."

But even in the United States, ethnic ideologues have not been without effect. They have set themselves against the old American ideal of assimilation. They call on the republic to think in terms not of individual but of group identity and to move the polity from individual rights to group rights. They have made a certain progress in transforming the United States into a more segregated society. They have done their best to turn a college generation against Europe and the Western tradition. They have imposed ethnocentric, Afrocentric, and bilingual curricula on public schools, well designed to hold minority children out of American society. They have told young people from minority groups that the Western democratic tradition is not for them. They have encouraged minorities to see themselves as victims and to live by alibis rather than to claim the opportunities opened for them by the potent combination of black protest and white guilt. They have filled the air with recrimination and rancor and have remarkably advanced the fragmentation of American life.

... [F]or all the damage it has done, the upsurge of ethnicity is a superficial enthusiasm stirred by romantic ideologues and unscrupulous hucksters whose claim to speak for their minorities is thoughtlessly accepted by the media.... They have thus far done better in intimidating the white majority than in converting their own constituencies.

"No nation in history," writes Lawrence Fuchs, the political scientist and immigration expert in his fine book *The American Kaleidoscope*, "had proved as successful as the United States in managing ethnic diversity. No nation before had ever made diversity itself a source of national identity and unity." ...

Americanization has not lost its charms. Many sons and daughters of ethnic neighborhoods still want to shed their ethnicity and move to suburbs as fast as they can....

The ethnic identification often tends toward superficiality. The sociologist Richard Alba's study of children and grandchildren of immigrants in the Albany, New York, area shows the most popular "ethnic experience" to be sampling the ancestral cuisine.... "It is hard to avoid the conclusion," Alba writes, "that ethnic experience is shallow for the great majority of whites."

Most blacks prefer "black" to "African-Americans," fight bravely and patriotically for their country, and would move to the suburbs too if income and racism would permit.

As for Hispanic-Americans, first-generation Hispanics born in the United States speak English fluently, according to a Rand Corporation study; more than half of second-generation Hispanics give up Spanish altogether....

Nor, despite the effort of ethnic ideologues are minority groups all that hermetically sealed off from each other, except in special situations, like colleges, where ideologues are authority figures.... Around half of Asian-American marriages are with non-Orientals, and the Census Bureau estimates one million interracial—mostly black-white—marriages in 1990 as against 310,000 in 1970.

* * *

When we talk of the American democratic faith, we must understand it in its true dimensions. It is not an impervious, final, and complacent orthodoxy, intolerant of deviation and dissent, fulfilled in flag salutes, oaths of allegiance, and hands over the heart. It is an ever-evolving philosophy, fulfilling its ideals through debate, self-criticism, protest, disrespect, and irreverence; a tradition in which all have rights of heterodoxy and opportunities for self-assertion. The Creed has been the means by which Americans have haltingly but persistently narrowed the gap between performance and principle. It is what all Americans should learn, because it is what binds all Americans together.

... If we now repudiate the quite marvelous inheritance that history bestows on us, we invite the fragmentation of the national community into a quarrelsome spatter of enclaves, ghettos, tribes....

Our task is to combine due appreciation of the splendid diversity of the nation with due emphasis on the great unifying Western ideas of individual freedom, political democracy, and human rights. These are the ideas that define the American nationality—and that today empower people of all continents, races, and creeds.

"What then is the American, this new man? ... Here individuals of all nations are melted into a new race of men." Still a good answer—still the best hope.

POSTSCRIPT

Is There an Ethnic Revolt Against the Melting Pot?

This last issue, appropriately it would seem, brings together many clashing views. This debate is part of the broader "cultural war" being waged over issues regarding bilingual and multicultural education, the acceptance or rejection of traditional sociological theories of minority relations, etc.

One of the most objective and clear statements that I could find on both the issue and the stakes involved is Crawford Young's "The Dialectics of Cultural Pluralism: Concept and Reality," in *The Rising Tide of Cultural Pluralism*, edited by C. Young (University of Wisconsin Press, 1993). A critical discussion of sociology's treatment of the race problem is James B. McKee's *Sociology and the Race Problem: The Failure of a Perspective* (University of Illinois Press, 1993). This work, however, does not completely reject the system and hence is probably closer to Schlesinger in important respects.

Ronald Takaki's critical perspective parallels the editors of *Social Justice*. See his *Strangers from a Different Shore* (Little, Brown, 1989) and his *A Different Mirror: A History of Multicultural America* (Little, Brown, 1993).

Andrew Hacker's provocative and insightful *Two Nations: Black and White: Separate, Hostile, Unequal* (Charles Scribner's Sons, 1992) concurs with *Social Justice* in that he argues that Blacks have been harmed by the system and that conditions exist for a full-scale revolt against the melting pot myth. For a bitter dismissal of Hacker and others who are seen as completely misrepresenting ethnic and racial realities in the United States, see Walter E. Williams's review of *Two Nations* (*Society*, January/February, 1993). Accusing Hacker of speaking nonsensically, Williams points out that "if Black Americans were considered a nation, the sum on our yearly earnings would make us the fourteenth richest nation in the world.

For a clear presentation of the cultural production approach and its application to Great Britain, see Stuart Hall's *There Ain't No Black in the Union Jack: The Cultural Politics of Race and Nation* (Unwin Hyman, 1987).

For a novel work that attempts to combine minority resistance against social oppression and ecological destruction, see *Confronting Environmental Racism*, edited by R. Bullard and B. Chavis, Jr. (South End Press, 1993). Two interesting studies in Chicano historiography that raise important questions about scholars misunderstanding the nature and extent of oppression is Tomás Almaguer's "Ideological Distortions in Recent Chicano Historiography: The Internal Model and Chicano Historical Interpretation," and Yves-Charles Grandjeat, "Conflicts and Cohesiveness: The Elusive Quest for a Chicano History," both in *Aztlan* (Spring 1987). A similar work that looks at North American Indians is D. E. Wilkins, "Modernization, Colonialism, Dependency: How Appropriate Are These Models for Providing an Explanation of North American Indian 'Underdevelopment?' " in *Ethnic and Racial Studies* (July 1993).

CONTRIBUTORS
TO THIS VOLUME

EDITOR

RICHARD C. MONK is an associate professor of criminal justice at Coppin State College in Baltimore, Maryland. He received a Ph.D. in sociology from the University of Maryland in 1978, and he has taught sociology, criminology, and criminal justice at Morgan State University, San Diego State University, and Valdosta State College. He has received two NEH fellowships, and he coedited the May 1992 issue of the *Journal of Contemporary Criminal Justice*, which dealt with race, crime, and criminal justice. Professor Monk has done extensive work in the area of race relations. He was the chair of a session of the Missouri Valley Historical Conference in the mid-1980s that dealt with race and violence, and he chaired a session of the Southern Sociological Society Conference in Georgia in 1991, which examined issues of altruism and race. In addition to being a coeditor of *Baltimore: A Living Renaissance* (Historic Baltimore Society, 1982), a study of urban changes, he is currently revising his edited book *Structures of Knowing* (University of America Press, 1986), which partially deals with theories and research methods related to ethnic minorities. He is also working on another book entitled *A Case Study of a Lynching*, and in December 1993 he published a study on alternatives to violence in inner-city schools.

STAFF

Marguerite L. Egan   Program Manager
Brenda S. Filley   Production Manager
Whit Vye   Designer
Libra Ann Cusack   Typesetting Supervisor
Juliana Arbo   Typesetter
David Brackley   Copy Editor
David Dean   Administrative Editor
Diane Barker   Editorial Assistant
Richard Tietjen   Systems Manager

AUTHORS

ROBERT APONTE is an assistant professor of sociology in the James Madison College at Michigan State University in East Lansing, Michigan, and a research associate at the Julian Samora Research Institute. His research interests include urban poverty, the Latino population in the United States, race and ethnicity, and social demography, and he has published several essays on these issues, two of which appear in William Julius Wilson's *The Truly Disadvantaged: The Inner City, the Underclass, and Public Policy* (University of Chicago Press, 1987).

EDWARD BANFIELD is a professor emeritus of urban studies in the Department of Faculty Arts and Sciences at Harvard University and the author of a number of articles and books on urban problems, including *The Unheavenly City Revisited: A Revision of the Unheavenly City* (Scott, Foresman, 1974).

DAVID A. BELL is a former reporter and researcher for *The New Republic*.

JOHN SIBLEY BUTLER is a professor of sociology and management at the University of Texas at Austin. His research interests focus on issues of organizational behavior and entrepreneurship, on which he has published extensively. He is currently looking at the impact of entrepreneurship on future generations of Americans. His most recent book is *Entrepreneurship and Self-Help Among Black Americans: A Reconsideration of Race and Economics* (SUNY Press, 1991).

LINDA CHAVEZ, a political commentator, policy analyst, and author, is a senior fellow of the Manhattan Institute for Policy Research in Washington, D.C., and the chairperson of the National Commission on Migrant Education. She has held several positions in the U.S. government, including professional staff member of the House of Representatives' Subcommittee on Civil and Constitutional Rights (1972–1974) and staff director of the U.S. Commission on Civil Rights (1983–1985). Her articles have appeared in such publications as *Fortune*, the *Wall Street Journal*, and the *Los Angeles Times*.

PATRICIA HILL COLLINS is an associate professor in the Departments of African American Studies and Sociology at the University of Cincinnati in Cincinnati, Ohio. Her specialities in sociology include sociology of knowledge, organizational theory, social stratification, and work and occupations, but her research and scholarship have dealt primarily with issues of gender, race and class, specifically relating to African American women.

KATHLEEN NEILS CONZEN is a professor of history at the University of Chicago in Chicago, Illinois. Her publications include *Immigrant Milwaukee, 1836–1860: Accommodation and Community in a Frontier City* (Harvard University Press, 1976).

ASH COREA, a former health care worker in New York City, has produced alternative radio programs for and about women in New York City.

HERBERT J. GANS, a sociologist whose concept of *underclass* has been widely adopted by the sociological community, is the Robert S. Lynd Professor of Sociology at Columbia University in New York City. His publications include *Middle American Individualism: The Future of Liberal Democracy* (Free Press, 1988) and *People, Plans, and Policies: Essays on Poverty, Racism, and Other National Urban Problems* (Columbia University Press, 1991).

DAVID A. GERBER is a professor of history at the State University of New York at Buffalo, where he has been teaching since 1971. His research interests focus on American culture and patterns of social interaction.

VIVIAN V. GORDON is an associate professor in the Department of African American Studies at the State University of New York at Albany. She received an M.A. in sociology from the University of Pennsylvania in 1957 and a Ph.D. in sociology from the University of Virginia in 1974, and she has held academic appointments at the University of Virginia and at Wellesley College. She is a member of the Association of Black Sociologists and the Association of Black Women Historians, and she is the recipient of the 1990 Martin Luther King Service Award. Her publications include *Kemet and Other Ancient African Civilizations* (Third World Press, 1991).

DAVID HATCHETT is a freelance writer living in Brooklyn, New York.

JOSÉ HERNÁNDEZ is a professor in the Department of Black and Puerto Rican Studies at Hunter College in New York City. His research interests focus on race, minority relations, cultural sociology, and comparative sociology. He received an M.A. from Fordham University in 1961 and a Ph.D. from the University of Minnesota in 1964.

BELL HOOKS, a feminist theorist and cultural critic, is a professor of women's studies at Oberlin College in Oberlin, Ohio. She is the author or coauthor of eight books, including *Breaking Bread: Insurgent Black Intellectual Life* (South End Press, 1991), coauthored with Cornel West, and *Black Looks: Race and Representation* (South End Press, 1992).

PAUL KAZIM is a researcher with Moonlight Films, an independent, black production company in London.

SUSAN LEDLOW is a faculty associate for the University Program for Faculty Development at Arizona State University in Tempe, Arizona. During the previous eight years, she had been involved with teacher training in bilingual education progams for the University of Arizona's Mountain State Multifunctional Resource Center.

GLENN LOURY is a professor of economics at Boston University in Boston, Massachusetts. He received a B.A. in mathematics from Northwestern University and a Ph.D. in economics from the Massachusetts Institute of Technology, and he has held academic appointments at Harvard University and the University of Michigan. In addition to his work as an economic theorist, he has been actively involved in public debate and analysis of the problems of racial inequality and social policy toward the poor in the United States, which is reflected in his publication *Achieving the Dream* (The Heritage Foundation, 1990).

J. FRED MacDONALD is a professor at Northeastern Illinois University in Chicago, Illinois. He is the author of several books and articles on radio, television, and racial stereotyping, including *Don't Touch That Dial* (Nelson-Hall, 1979) and *Blacks and White TV: Afro-Americans in Television Since 1948* (Nelson-Hall, 1983).

DONALDO MACEDO is an associate professor of linguistics at the University of Massachusetts–Boston.

CORAMAE RICHEY MANN is a professor of criminal justice at Indiana University in Bloomington, Indiana. She received undergraduate and graduate degrees in clinical psychology from Roosevelt University and a Ph.D. in sociology/criminology from the University of Illinois. Her research interests focus on the juvenile and criminal justice systems, especially in their treatment of youth, women, and racial and ethnic minorities. Her publications include *Female Crime and Delinquency* (University of Alabama Press, 1984) and *Unequal Justice: A Question of Color* (Indiana University Press, 1993).

MARCO MARTINIELLO is affiliated with the European Institute at Florence University in Italy and the Catholic University of Louvain in Belgium.

ROBERT K. MERTON, an eminent sociological theorist and a well-known defender of sociology as a genuine science, is an adjunct professor at Rockefeller University, a resident scholar at the Russell Sage Foundation, and a professor emeritus at Columbia University, all located in New York City. His publications include *On the Shoulders of Giants: A Shandean Postscript* (Free Press, 1965) and *The Sociology of Science: Theoretical and Empirical Investigations* (University of Chicago Press, 1973).

EWA MORAWSKA is a professor of sociology and history at the University of Pennsylvania in Philadelphia, Pennsylvania. Her publications include *For Bread With Butter: The Life-Worlds of East-Central Europeans in Johnstown, Pennsylvania, 1890–1940* (Cambridge University Press, 1986).

GEORGE E. POZZETTA is a professor of history at the University of Florida in Gainesville, Florida, where he has been teaching since 1971. He is a member of the executive board for the American Italian Historical Association, and he has held academic appointments at Providence College and the University of Maryland, Far East Division. His publications include *Shades of the Sunbelt: Essays on Race, Ethnicity, and the Urban South* (Greenwood Press, 1988), coedited with Randall Miller.

DIANE RAVITCH, a historian of education, is an adjunct professor of history and education in the Teachers College at Columbia University in New York City. She is the author of *Troubled Crusade:*

American Education, 1945–1980 (Basic Books, 1983).

JON REYHNER is an associate professor in the Department of Curriculum and Instruction at Eastern Montana College, where he teaches education and Native American studies. He has 23 years of experience in Indian education in both public and tribally controlled schools, and he writes extensively in the field of Indian education. His publications include *Teaching American Indian Students* (University of Oklahoma, 1992).

WILLIAM RYAN is a professor in the Department of Psychology at Boston College and a consultant in the fields of mental health, community planning, and social problems. His publications include *Distress in the City* (UPB, 1969).

ARTHUR M. SCHLESINGER, JR., is the Albert Schweitzer Professor of the Humanities at the City University of New York and the well-known author of prize-winning books on Presidents Andrew Jackson, Franklin Roosevelt, and John F. Kennedy. His publications include *The Cycles of American History* (Houghton Mifflin, 1986).

HERMAN SCHWARTZ is a professor of law in the Washington College of Law at American University and the director of the William O. Douglas Inquiry into the State of Individual Freedom.

SHELBY STEELE is an associate professor of English at San Jose State University in San Jose, California.

RONALD TAKAKI is a professor of ethnic studies at the University of California, Berkeley, where he has been teaching since 1972. A member of the American Historical Association, his publications include *From Different Shores: Perspectives on Race and Ethnicity in America* (1986). He has held academic appointments at the College of San Mateo and the University of California, Los Angeles.

RUDOLPH J. VECOLI is a professor in the Department of History at the University of Minnesota at Minneapolis St. Paul and the director of the University of Minnesota Immigration and History Research Center. He is also the vice president of the executive council of the Immigration History Society and a member of the council of the American Italian Historical Association.

WILLIAM WILBANKS is a professor of criminal justice at Florida International University in Miami, Florida. He has published more than 50 book chapters and journal articles on issues of race and crime, homicide, and addiction, and he is the author of 6 books, including *The Myth of a Racist Criminal Justice System* (Brooks/Cole, 1987) and *The Make My Day Law: Colorado's Experiment in Home Protection* (University Press of America, 1990).

WALTER E. WILLIAMS is the John M. Olin Distinguished Professor of Economics at George Mason University in Fairfax, Virginia. He serves on the boards of directors for Citizens for a Sound Economy, the Hoover Institution, and the Institute for Research on the Economics of Taxation, and he serves on the advisory boards of the Landmark Legal Foundation, the Reason Foundation, and others. He writes a weekly syndicated column that is carried by approximately 100 newspapers, and he is the author of 5 books, including *America: A Minority Viewpoint* (Hoover Institution Press, 1982) and *South Africa's War Against Capitalism* (Greenwood Press, 1989).

WILLIAM JULIUS WILSON is the Lucy Flower Distinguished Service Professor of Sociology and Public Policy at the University of Chicago in Chicago, Illinois, and the director of the University of Chicago's Center for the Study of Urban Inequality, where he is currently directing a $2.8 million study on poverty, joblessness, and family structure in the inner city. His publications include *The Declining Significance of Race: Blacks and Changing American Institutions* (University of Chicago Press, 1978).

INDEX

ability grouping, in schools, 128
Abram, Morris, 217, 218, 220
admissions policies, college, affirmative action and, 215
affirmative action, 49, 224, 244; civil rights and, 181–182; controversy over, 210–220
"African American," controversy over usage of, 86–100
African immigrants, to Italy, 261, 268
Afrocentrism, 279, 280
agriculture, Italian immigrant workers in, 261
Alba, Richard, 75, 76, 281
Algerian immigrants, to Italy, 266
Alien Land Act, 51
American Dilemma, An (Myrdal), 11, 168
American Kaleidoscope, The (Fuchs), 281
Americas, European colonization of, genocide and, 274–278
"Amos 'n' Andy," as racist stereotype, 173–174
Anglocentrism, 135, 142
Aponte, Robert, on urban Hispanic poverty, 233–239
Aronowitz, Stanley, 137
Asian Americans, 305; controversy over, as "model minority," 44–61; education and, 131

Bakhtin, Mikhail, 141–142
Bakke case, affirmative action and, 218, 220
balkanization, of social science, 6
Bambara, Toni Cade, 148
Banfield, Edward, on the future of the lower class, 194–198
Barnett, Charlie, 166
Bean, Frank, 230
Bell, David A., on Asian Americans as "model minority," 44–54
Bennett, William, 135, 136
Bernardelli, Roberto, 265, 267
Beulah myth, 156
Beyond Entitlement: The Social Obligations of Citizenship (Mead), 228
biculturalism, 133
Bigelow, Bill, 275
bilingual education, 105, 111, 117, 280; controversy over, 126–144
Bill of Rights, 34
Black Power: The Politics of Liberation (Carmichael and Hamilton), 89–90
Blackmun, Harry, 219

Blacks, 305; Asians and, 53; blaming of, as victims of poverty, 199–206; and controversy over ability of nonethnic scholars to research minorities, 4–23; and controversy over affirmative action, 210–220; controversy over feminism and, 148–157; controversy over media portrayal of, 162–174; and controversy over racism in the criminal justice system, 244–253; and controversy over use of "African American," 86–100; education and, 130
Blade Runner, 44
"blaming the victims," of poverty, 199–206
Bositis, David A., 181
Brown v. Board of Education, 128
bumpy line theory, of ethnic invention and acculturation, 73–80
Bunche, Ralph, 12
Buppies, 181
Burger, Warren, 218, 219
Bush, George, 183
business, Asian Americans in, 56–57
Butler, John Sibley, on the use of the term "African American," 86–94

Cabezas, Amado, 56
campanilismo, spirit of, among Italian Americans, 68
Campanis, Al, 166
Caplow, Theodore, 7
Carmichael, Stokely, 89–90
Casey, Bernie, 166
Cattin, Carlo Donat, 268
Central Park jogger, media coverage of, 170–173
Chaves, Cesar, 34
Chavez, Linda, 217, 220; on progress made by Latinos, 224–232
Chin, Charles, 181, 185
Chin, Vincent, murder of, 46, 48, 61
Chinese Exclusion Act, 50, 51
Chung, Connie, 168
Churchill, Hans, 275
citizenship, inferior, Latinos and, 33–34
Civil Rights Act of 1964, 233
civil rights movement, 89, 130, 170; controversy over future of, 180–190; feminism and, 155–156
Clamor at the Gates (Glazer), 47, 52
class and status, discrepancy between, 206

Cockburn, Alexander, 276
Coker, Daniel, 89
Cole, Nat King, 172
Collins, Patricia Hill, on the sociological
significance of Black feminist thought, 15–23
Color Purple, The, 148
Columbus, Christopher, genocide and, 274, 275
community action groups, 197–198
community organizations: Asian American,
51–52; Black, 99; Italian Americans and, 69
compensatory education, 201
Conant, Ralph W., 7
conservative perspective: on the ghetto
underclass, increasing influence of, 30–31
Constantino, Renato, 138
Conzen, Kathleen Neil, et al., on the invention of
ethnicity, 66–72; reaction to views of, 73–80
Corea, Ash, on portrayal of Blacks in the media,
162–167
Correll, Charles, 173
Cosby, Bill, 163, 168, 172
Courts, Patrick, 139
criminal justice system, controversy over racism
in, 244–253
Crispino, James, 76
Cuban Americans: and controversy over Latino
progress, 224–239
cultural deprivation, 34
cultural differences, controversy over, as cause
of high dropout rates, 104–122
culture of poverty, controversy over, 194–206,
238
curriculum, inappropriate, for Native American
students, 108

de Las Casas, Bartolomé, 275, 276
Delany, Martin R., 89
deprivation, cycles of, and the ghetto underclass
debate, 28–31
desegregation, racial, 129, 130, 131
Devastation of the Indies, The (de Las Casas),
275
Dinnerstein, Dorothy, 152
diversity, affirmative action and, 211, 212
Dod, Suzie, 300
Donald, James, 141
Douglass, Frederick, 8
Dowd, Maureen, 75
Drake, J. G. St. Clair, 12
dropout rates, controversy over high, as caused
by cultural differences, 104–122, 202

Du Bois, W. E. B., 91; and Booker T.
Washington, 186, 187, 188, 189
dual labor market theory, of urban poverty, 239

earnings, of Latinos, 228–229, 237
Eco, Umberto, 268
economic dualism, in Italy, 263
education: Asian Americans and, 45–46, 47,
48–50, 55, 58–59; Blacks and, 97–98,
202–203; compensatory, 201; controversy over
bilingual, 126–144; and controversy over high
dropout rates as caused by cultural
differences, 104–122; influence of Western
civilization, 302–305; Latinos and, 229
Einstein, Albert, 10
elitist access, to knowledge, 5
emergent ethnicity, 67
English, as official language of the United
States, 38
English as a Second Language (ESL), 107, 131,
136
English Only movement, 135–144
entitlement and empowerment, Latinos and,
32–40
environmental issues, European colonization of
the New World and, 274–278
Equal Employment Opportunity Commission
(EEOC), 211, 217
equal protection, 217
Erikson, Erik, 105
ethnic revolt, against the melting pot, controversy
over, 274–281
ethnic studies, Latino, 39–40
ethnocentrism, 7, 105, 130, 304
Eurocentrism, 61, 154, 155, 156, 277, 278–281
European Community (EC), and controversy over
immigration and racism in Italy, 260–269
externally caused poverty, 195, 196

family: Asian Americans and, 47, 51; Blacks
and, 20–21, 98–99
fascism, 69–70
Fate of the Forest (Hecht and Cockburn), 276
federal judiciary, in school affairs, 128–129
feminism, 279; controversy over Black women
and, 15–23, 148–157
Ferlerger, Lew, 138
filiopietists, 70–71
Flexner, Abraham, 11
Forten, James, 88
Fourteenth Amendment, 219

Franklin, John Hope, 13–14
Frazier, E. Franklin, 12
"friendly visitor" system, 196–197
Fuchs, Estelle, 105
Fuchs, Lawrence, 281
Fullilove v. Klutznick, 216, 218, 220

Gans, Herbert, 67, 195; on a bumpy-line approach to ethnic invention and acculturation, 73–80
Garvey, Marcus, 89, 90
Geertz, Clifford, 67
genocide: in the New World, 274–278
Gerber, David A., et al., on the invention of ethnicity, 66–72; reaction to views of, 73–80
Ghanaian immigrants, to Italy, 261
Gibbon, Edward, 279
Giroux, Henry, 136, 141
Gladwin, Thomas, 198
"glass ceiling," for Asian American businesspeople, 56–57
Glazer, Nathan, 52, 53, 67, 75
Gompers, Samuel, 50
Goodlad, John, 105, 106
Gordon, Vivian V., on Black women, feminism and Black liberation, 154–157
Gosden, Freeman, 173
Gramsci, Antonio, 138, 279
Great Society, 34, 99

Hall, Stuart, 170
Hamilton, Charles, 89–90
Harano, Ross, 53
Harris, Abram, 88–89, 90–91
Harvard Encyclopedia of American Ethnic Groups, 53
Hatchett, David, on the future of civil rights in the twenty-first century, 180–185
Havighurst, Robert J., 105
Hecht, Suzanne, 276
Height, Dorothy I., 181, 184
Hernandez, Frank, 181–182
Hernández, José, on Latino alternatives to the underclass concept, 32–40
Herskovits, Melville, 12
Higham, John, 68
Hispanics, *see* Latinos
history, and ethnography, parallel between, 11
homeland, Blacks' identification with, 92–93
homophobia, feminism and, 150

hooks, bell, on Black women and feminism, 148–153
Hooks, Benjamin, 181, 184
Hooks, Robert, 166
Horne, Lena, 174
Horton, Willie, 137
Hughes, Langston, 89
human rights, 280
Hunter, Robert, 195
Hurston, Zora Neal, 15

identity crisis, in Italian society, 263
immersion technique, to learn English, 131, 132, 135–136
immigrants: adaptation of, ethnicity and, 66; and racism in Italy, controversy over, 260–269
Immigration Act, 45, 59
indentured servants, 274
Indian immigrants, to Italy, 265
Indian Nations at Risk (INAR) task force, 104, 108, 110
indigenous people, genocide of, and European colonization of Americas, 274–278
industry, Italian immigrant workers in, 261
infant mortality, Black, 216
insiders and outsiders, controversy over ability of, to research minorities, 4–23
institutional subordination, Latinos and, 33–34
intellectual invention, ethnicity as, 79–80
interest groups, ethnic groups as, 67, 75
internally caused poverty, 195–196
invisible minority, Hispanics as, 225
Iranian immigrants, to Italy, 261
Isaacs, Harold, 67
Italian Americans, controversy over rejection of assimilation by, 66–80
Italy, controversy over racism and immigration in, 260–269

Jackson, Jesse, 86, 89, 90, 93, 94, 95, 154
Jackson, Kenneth T., 142
Jackson, Mahalia, 181
Jacob, John E., 184–185
Jaimes, Annette, 276–277
James, William, 13
Japanese-Americans (Petersen), 51
Jewett, L. Fred, 49
Jews, Asian Americans and, 47–48, 51, 53
Jim Crow laws, 219
Johnson, Andrew, 219
Johnson, Charles, 164

Johnson, Guy B., 12
Johnson, Lyndon, 180

Kamehameha Elementary Education Project
 (KEEP), 114–115
Karenga, Maulana, 74
Kawaguchi, Gary, 56
Kazim, Paul, on racism and immigration in Italy,
 265–269
Kenney Report, 107
Khandewal, Madhulika, 182
Khoury, Nabeel A., 93
King, Martin Luther, 34, 180, 183, 217, 219, 220
Kitano, Harry, 52, 53
Klineberg, Otto, 12
knowledge, sociology of, 4–14
Koch, Edward, 216
Koning, Hans, 275
Krieck, Ernest, 5
Kuhn, Thomas S., 16–17

labor market segmentation theory, of urban
 poverty, 239
Latinos, 281; civil rights and, 181–183;
 controversy over progress of, 224–239
Lau v. Nichols, 131
Ledlow, Susan, on high dropout rates of Native
 Americans, 113–122
Lee, Alfred M., 16
Lee, Spike, 164
Lévi-Strauss, Claude, 11
Lewis, Emmanuel, 165
Lewis, Hylan, 204
Lewis, John, 180, 183–184
Lewis, Oscar, 30–31, 195
liberals: declining influence of, on ghetto
 underclass issue, 29–30; Latinos and, 34–35
life expectancy, Black, 216
Light, Ivan, 47, 52
Lippmann, Walter, 50
Literacy for Empowerment (Courts), 139
Lobby, The (Tivnan), 93
Losing Ground (Murray), 239
Loury, Glenn, on Booker T. Washington and the
 concept of self-help, 186–190
lower class value stretch, 203–204
Lowery, Joseph, 184
Lukas, J. Anthony, 136

MacDonald, J. Fred, on portrayal of Blacks and
 in the media, 162–167
Macedo, Donald, on bilingual education,
 135–144
Maitre, Joachim, 143
Mammy myth, 20
Mandle, Jay, 138
manifest destiny, Latinos and, 33, 35–36, 37
Mann, Coramae Richey, on the reality of a racist
 criminal justice system, 249–253
Mann, Horace, 127
Mannheim, Karl, 12, 16
Marable, Manning, 184
March on Washington, 180, 181, 183
Mark, Stan, 182
Marshall, Thurgood, 217, 219
Martelli law, 262, 263–264, 266, 267
Martiniello, Marco, on racism and immigration in
 Italy, 260–264
matriarchy thesis, Black, 20
Matthews, Linda, 50
Mauritanian immigrants, to Italy, 266
McCleskey v. Georgia, 245
McDaniel, Hattie, 174
McLaren, Peter, 137
Mead, Lawrence, 228
media: Asian Americans in, 60; controversy over
 portrayal of Blacks in, 162–174
melting pot, 66; controversy over revolt against,
 274–281
Menchú, Rigoberta, 276
Merton, Robert K., 17, 18; on the sociology of
 knowledge, 4–14
Mexican Americans: controversy over Latino
 progress, 224–239
Miller, Walter, 205
mismatch thesis, of urban poverty, 238–239
"model minority," controversy over Asians as,
 44–61
monolingualism, 135
monopolistic access, to knowledge, 5
Morawska, Ewa, et al., on the invention of
 ethnicity, 66–72; reaction to views of, 73–80
Moroccan immigrants, to Italy, 261, 266, 267,
 268
Mostel, Zero, 199
Moynihan, Daniel Patrick, 28–29, 67, 75
Mulkay, Michael, 17
multicultural education, 107, 135, 142, 276, 278
multiproblem poor, 195–196, 200
Murphy, Eddie, 168
Murray, Charles, 58, 238
music industry, Blacks and, 172

Mussolini, Benito, 69–70
Myrdal, Gunnar, 11–12, 168

Nation at Risk, A, 108
National Crime Survey, 246
National Educational Longitudinal Study of 1988
   (NEL:88), 108–109
National Study of American Indian Education,
   105
Native Americans, controversy over high dropout
   rates of, as caused by cultural differences,
   104–122
Natividad, Irene, 48
Navajo Student at Risk study, 105, 106, 108
New Deal, 34
New Frontier, 35
Nixon, Richard, 75
nonethnic scholars, controversy over ability of, to
   research minorities, 4–23
Novak, Michael, 67

occupational status, of Latinos, 229–230
O'Connor, Sandra Day, 217–218
Ogbu, John, 119–122
Ortiz, Roxanne Dunbar, 276
outsiders and insiders, controversy over ability
   of, to research minorities, 4–23

Pachucho violence, 34
Pakistani immigrants, to Italy, 265
paradigms, sociological, 16–17
parent involvement, lack of, for Native American
   students, 109–111
Peltier, Leonard, 276
Pendleton, Clarence, 217, 219
Peter Principle, 210
Petersen, William, 51, 53
Petersilia, Joan, 251
Philippine immigrants, to Italy, 261, 266
Philips, Susan, 114, 116
Plessy v. Ferguson, 217, 219
pluralism, affirmative action and, 211
police, racial bias by, 246
political refugees, in Italy, 260, 261
politics: Asian Americans and, 54; Blacks and,
   151–152, 181; and the schools, 126–134
Polk, James, 35

poverty: controversy over Hispanic, 224–239;
   culture of, controversy over, 30–31, 194–206;
   Latinos and, 230, 237, 238–239
Pozzetta, George E., et al., on the invention of
   ethnicity, 66–72; reaction to views of, 73–80
preferential treatment, affirmative action as,
   210–214
preppie murder, media coverage of, 170–173
present-oriented, lower class as, 194, 195, 204,
   238
primordial ethnicity, 67
Prisoners in State and Federal Institutions (U.S.
   Dept. of Justice), 252
privileged access, to knowledge, 5
Puerto Ricans, and controversy over Latino
   progress, 224–239

quotas, affirmative action and, 211, 212, 218

Race and Economics (Sowell), 48
Race, Radicalism, and Reform (Harris), 88–89
racism: affirmative action and, 210, 215, 219;
   controversy over, in the criminal justice
   system, 244–253; and immigration in Italy,
   controversy over, 260–269
Radford-Hill, Sheila, 149, 152–153
Ramirez, Maria Elena, 277
Randolph, A. Philip, 180
Ravitch, Diane, on bilingual education, 126–134
Reagan, Ronald, 46, 55, 56, 183, 184;
   affirmative action and, 215, 216, 218
Reconstruction, 34
Redding, J. S., 11
Reed, Ishmael, 167
Rehnquist, William, 218
resistance, of American indigenous people to
   European invasion, 274–278
retention, of Native American students, 108–109
reverse discrimination, affirmative action as, 211
Reyhner, John, on high dropout rates of Native
   Americans, 104–112
Riaz, Mohammed, 265
Rivera, Geraldo, 168
Robeson, Paul, 174
Rodman, Hyman, 203–204
Rodriguez, Luis, 276
Roosevelt, Franklin, D., 51
Rose, Arnold, 12
Rosen, Steve, 60
Ryan, William, on blaming the victims of poverty,
   199–206

Sampson, Milton, 89
Sapphire myth, 20, 156
Schengen agreement, 264
Schlesinger, Arthur M., Jr., on the disuniting of America, 278–281
Schneider, William, 183
Schutz, Alfred, 17, 18
Schuyler, George, 89
Schwartz, Herman, on affirmative action, 215–220
Scott, Patricia B., 19
Scott, Ridley, 44
self-employment, Latinos and, 229–230
self-help, Booker T. Washington's philosophy of, 186–190
self-sufficiency, Asian Americans and, 51
Senegalese immigrants, to Italy, 261, 266
sentencing, racial bias in, 246–247, 251
settlement houses, 197
sexual politics, Black feminism and, 156–157
Shaw, Bernard, 174
Simmel, Georg, 10, 11, 16, 18
Simpson, Alan K., 59
Snyder, Jimmy, 166
Social Justice, editors of, on genocide, repression, and resistance in the New World, 274–277
Social Systems of American Ethnic Groups, The (Warner and Srole), 74–75
Sollors, Werner, 67, 73
Sowell, Thomas, 48, 51
Sri Lankan immigrants, to Italy, 265
Srole, Leo, 74–75
standardized testing, Native American students and, 108–109
Stark, Johannes, 5
status and class, discrepancy between, 206
status anxieties, among Italian Americans, 70–71
Steele, Shelby, on affirmative action, 210–214
Storing, Herbert, 187
student protest movement, 127–128
Summer, William Graham, 7
Supreme Court, 245; affirmative action and, 216, 217, 218
symbolic ethnicity, 75

T, Mr., 165–166, 168
Takaki, Ronald: 53; on Asian Americans as "model minority," 55–61
Tannenbaum, Frank, 11–12
teachers, Native American students and, 106–108, 110–111, 114, 116

Television Hiring Practices (Wachtel), 169–170
Thatcher, Margaret, 280
Their Eyes Were Watching God (Hurston), 15
Thomas, Clarence, 183, 186, 217
Thomas, Piri, 276
Thompson, Mark R., 46
Tienda, Marta, 230
Tivnan, Edward, 93
Townsend, Robert, 174
tracking, educational, of Native American students, 109
traveling sales, Italian immigrant workers in, 261
Tunisian immigrants, to Italy, 261, 266, 268

underclass: controversy over usefulness of concept of, 28–40; Latino, 228, 229, 239
Uniform Crime Report, 251
United Jewish Organizations v. Carey, 218
United Steelworkers of America v. Weber, 218
urban phenomenon, immigration to Italy as, 261

Van Peebles, Melvin, 162
Vecoli, Rudoloph J., et al., on the invention of ethnicity, 66–72; reaction to views of, 73–80
victim-focused identity, of Blacks, affirmative action and, 213–214
violence, racial, 136–137, 182; against Asian Americans, 46, 48, 59–59, 60–61; in Italy, 262–263, 267
Voting Rights Act, 180, 217, 219

Wachtel, Edward, 169–170
Walker, Alice, 152
Wallace, Mike, 55
War on Poverty, 198, 233
Warner, W. Lloyd, 74–75
Washington, Booker T., self-help philosophy of, 186–190
Waters, Mary, 75
Weatherford, Jack, 110
Weber, Max, 10
West, Cornel, 181
Western culture, influence of, 278–281
White, E. Frances, 15–16
white male insiderism, in American sociology, 5–9, 18, 22
Wilbanks, William, on the myth of a racist criminal justice system, 244–248; reaction to views of, 249–253

Wilkerson, Doxie A., 12
Wilkins, Roy, 180, 217, 219
Williams, Frank, 249
Williams, Pearce, 279
Williams, Walter E., on the use of the term "African American," 95–100
Wilson, James Q., 246–247
Wilson, William Julius, 239; on cycles of deprivation and the underclass debate, 28–31
Winston, Michael, 170

women, *see* feminism
women's studies, civil rights movement and, 155–156
Wonder, Stevie, 168
Woods, Robert A., 197
work: in Black culture, 20–21; immigrants and, 280; in Latino culture, 228

Young, Whitney, 180